PENGUIN BOOKS

SHAKESPEARE'S KINGS

John Julius Norwich was born in 1929. He was educated at Upper Canada College, Toronto, at Eton, at the University of Strasbourg and, after a spell of National Service in the Navy, at New College, Oxford, where he took a degree in French and Russian. In 1952 he joined the Foreign Service, where he remained for twelve years, serving at the embassies in Belgrade and Beirut and with the British delegation to the Disarmament Conference at Geneva. In 1964 he resigned from the service in order to write.

His many and varied publications include two books on the medieval Norman Kingdom in Sicily, The Normans in the South and The Kingdom in the Sun, which are published by Penguin in one volume entitled *The Normans in Sicily*; two travel books, *Mount Athos* (with Reresby Sitwell) and *Sahara*; *The Architecture of Southern England*; *Glyndebourne*; two anthologies of poetry and prose, *Christmas Crackers* and *More Christmas Crackers*; *A History of Venice*, originally published in two volumes; his three-volume history of the Byzantine Empire, *Byzantium: The Early Centuries*, *Byzantium: The Apogee*, and *Byzantium: The Decline and Fall*. *A Short History of Byzantium* was published in 1997. Many of his books are published in Penguin. In addition he has written and presented some thirty historical documentaries for television, and is a regular lecturer on Venice and numerous other subjects.

For nearly thirty years Lord Norwich was chairman of the Venice in Peril Fund. He is now chairman of the World Monuments Fund in Britain. He is a Fellow of the Royal Society of Literature, the Royal Geographical Society and the Society of Antiquaries, a Companion of the Royal Victorian Order and a Commendatore of the Ordine al Merito della Repubblica Italiana.

Shakespeare's Kings

JOHN JULIUS NORWICH

PENGUIN BOOKS

PENGUIN BOOKS

Published by the Penguin Group
Penguin Books Ltd, 27 Wrights Lane, London w8 5tz, England
Penguin Putnam Inc., 375 Hudson Street, New York, New York 10014, USA
Penguin Books Australia Ltd, Ringwood, Victoria, Australia
Penguin Books Canada Ltd, 10 Alcorn Avenue, Toronto, Ontario, Canada m4v 3b2
Penguin Books (NZ) Ltd, Private Bag 102902, NSMC, Auckland, New Zealand

Penguin Books Ltd, Registered Offices: Harmondsworth, Middlesex, England

First published by Viking 1999
Published in Penguin Books 2000

5

Set in Monotype Bembo
Printed in England by Clays Ltd, St Ives plc

To
Peter Carson,
who for thirty years guided my hand
and who gave me, with so much else,
the idea for this book

Shakespeare was the theatre's greatest craftsman: he wasted no tortured ratiocination on his plays. Instead he filled them with the gaudy heroes that all of us see ourselves becoming on some bright morrow, and the lowly frauds and clowns we are today.

H. L. Mencken

Table of Contents

16. *King Henry VI Part III* [1455–1475]

17. King Edward V [1471–1483]

18. The Final Reckoning [1483–1485]

List of Illustrations

ENDPAPERS

TABLE I: THE HOUSES OF LANCASTER, TUDOR AND BEAUFORT

EDWARD III

Edward, the Black Prince — Lionel, D. of Clarence (d.1368)(see Table II) — John of Gaunt, D. of Lancaster (d. 1399) — Edmund of Langley (D. of York 1385) — Thomas of Woodstock

Blanche of Lancaster (1) = (3rd son) John of Gaunt, D. of Lancaster (d. 1399) = (3) Catherine Swynford

Richard II

John Beaufort, E. of Somerset (d. 1400) — Henry Beaufort, Bishop of Winchester — Joan Beaufort (see Table II) = Ralph Nevill, E. of Westmorland

HENRY IV (d. 1413)

John, D. of Somerset (d.1444) — Edmund Beaufort, D. of Somerset († 1455)

HENRY V (d.1422) = Katherine of Valois = (2) Owen Tudor

Edmund Tudor, E. of Richmond (d. 1456) (i) — Jasper Tudor, E. of Pembroke (d. 1495) (ii)

Margaret Beaufort = Henry, D. of Somerset († 1464) — Edmund, D. of Somerset († 1471)

HENRY VI († 1471) = Margaret of Anjou

HENRY VII (d. 1509) = Elizabeth of York (see Table II)

Edward, Prince of Wales († 1471)

TABLE II: THE HOUSES OF MORTIMER, YORK AND NEVILL

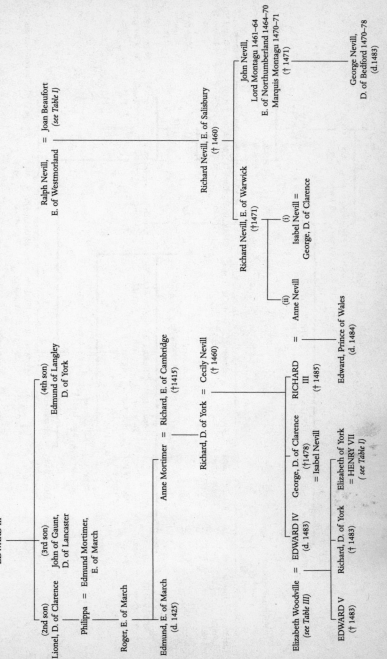

TABLE III: THE ROYAL HOUSES OF ENGLAND AND FRANCE

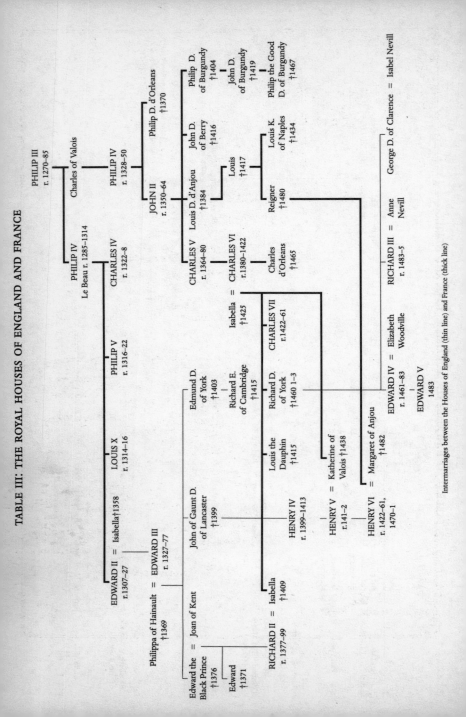

Intermarriages between the Houses of England (thin line) and France (thick line)

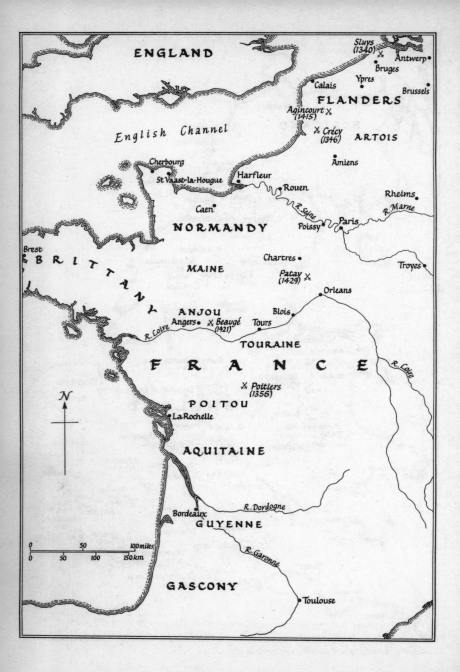

Royal Emblems

Edward III
Gold Griffin

Richard II
White Hart

Henry IV
White Swan

Henry V
Chained Swan

Henry VI
Chained Antelope

Edward IV and V
Falcon and Fetterlock

Richard III
White Boar

White Rose

Red Rose

Tudor Rose

The White Rose had long existed as a Yorkist badge; the Red Rose as the emblem of Lancaster seems to have been an invention of Henry VII. Shakespeare's garden scene is therefore not only imaginary but also an anachronism.

Introduction

My own introduction to Shakespeare's history plays took place when
I was fifteen, and was taken by my parents to see the two parts of *King
Henry IV*, in consecutive matinée and evening performances, at the
New Theatre in London. We all loved Ralph Richardson's Falstaff and
Laurence Olivier's blazing Hotspur, his hint of a stammer on every
initial 'w' giving a memorable impact to his last line; but my own
chief delight, as I remember, was the feeling – for the first time in my
life – of being transported in a time capsule back into the Middle Ages.
These, I kept reminding myself, were real people – people of flesh and
blood, people who had really lived, who were something more than
figments of an author's imagination. But the question was already there
in my mind: just how real were they? Where did history stop and drama
begin? Twenty years later at the Aldwych, the miracle occurred again
– with John Barton's and Peter Hall's superb *The Wars of the Roses*,
spread now over two whole days. This time the feeling of transportation
was even greater; this time too there was a magnificent programme,
which included a full historical résumé and, wonder of wonders, an
immense Plantagenet family tree. Would that I still had it today; alas,
it has vanished like so many other treasures, and it is, I suppose, in an
attempt to replace it as much as anything else that I have written the
book that you now hold in your hands.

Perhaps, if I were to be perfectly accurate I should have called it
Some of Shakespeare's Kings, for it is nothing if not selective. It has no
business with mythical monarchs like Lear, nor with pseudo-historical
ones like Cymbeline. It does not even consider *King John* – a play
which, for all its faults, is all, or almost all, the work of Shakespeare –
or *Henry VIII*, the major part of which is probably by John Fletcher.
Its subject is that unhappy line of Plantagenet rulers who inspired the
nine greatest of the history plays, that tremendous series that begins
with *Edward III*, continues through the two parts of *Henry IV*, *Henry*

V and the three parts of *Henry VI*, and ends with *Richard III*. Two Kings, although part of the Plantagenet line, remain unmentioned. Edward IV, under whom the English people enjoyed a dozen of the happiest and most peaceful years they had known for a century, appears in the second and third parts of *Henry VI* and again in *Richard III*; but has no play of his own. Nor (less surprisingly, since he occupied the throne for only a few weeks) does his son, the fragile little Edward V – although, as the most pitiable monarch in English history, he plays an important part in illustrating his uncle's villainy.

The mention of *Edward III* may occasion some surprise; and I readily confess that if I had written this book a year earlier than in fact I did, it would never have occurred to me to include it. I had, I think, vaguely heard of it as an apocryphal play for which one or two nineteenth-century German scholars had tentatively suggested Shakespearean authorship, but I had certainly never read it; since it did not appear in the First Folio, nor indeed in any other multi-volume edition of Shakespeare's works, there seemed no particular reason to do so. But then, suddenly, it acquired a new respectability. In 1998 it found a place in the New Cambridge edition of the plays, and as I write these words I understand that a similar volume is now in preparation for the Arden edition. Readers must turn to these works to find the various arguments for and against its authenticity; suffice it to say that its acceptance into the two series which together represent the cutting edge of Shakespearean scholarship is good enough for me. *Edward III* may not be exclusively Shakespeare's work – how many of the plays are? – but the major part of it seems to be his, and there are a number of dazzling speeches which could surely have been written by no one else:

> And never shall our bonny riders rest,
> Nor rusting canker have the time to eat
> Their light-borne snaffles nor their nimble spurs;
> Nor lay aside their jacks of gimmaled mail;
> Nor hang their staves of grained Scottish ash
> In peaceful wise upon their city walls;
> Nor from their button'd tawny leathern belts
> Dismiss their biting whinyards, till your king
> Cry out: 'Enough; spare England now for pity!'

The authentification of *Edward III* – a complete early version of which will be found as an appendix to this book – came to me as a godsend. For Edward was the royal patriarch, from whose loins all the subsequent rulers in our story directly or indirectly sprang. Virtually nothing in Shakespeare's mighty epic – not the Hundred Years War nor the Wars of the Roses, not the deposition of Edward's grandson Richard II nor the murderous ambition of his great-great-grandson Richard III – can be properly understood without going back to him. His story had somehow to be told; now, through Shakespeare, I could tell it.

But although a discussion of what we may now consider the dramatist's thirty-ninth play[1] enables us to set the scene for much of what is to follow, we are still left with an awkward gap to be filled – a gap of nearly half a century. *Edward III* stops effectively in September 1356, with the appearance of the Black Prince and his prisoner John II of France after the battle of Poitiers. The next play, *Richard II*, opens in April 1398 with the quarrel between Thomas Mowbray and Henry Bolingbroke, and covers only the last year and a half of Richard's unhappy reign. This creates what has always seemed to me a major problem: watching the play, we never quite understand what the King has done to deserve his dethronement. He has admittedly been unjust to his cousin in confiscating his estates – though another ruler might easily have executed him – but this hardly explains how Bolingbroke was able to rally virtually the whole country to his banner and seize the crown, while scarcely a voice was raised in opposition. Why was Richard already so dangerously unpopular? Why, in his last years, could he never look to his subjects for their support? Only when we follow the progress of his reign from its outset do the answers to these questions begin, all too clearly, to emerge.

To those readers, therefore, who are looking exclusively for a historical commentary on the plays, Chapters 2 to 4 must be considered as an extended exercise in scene-setting by which the unfolding drama is – I hope – made more comprehensible than it might otherwise have been. Only with Chapter 5 do we rejoin Shakespeare and continue with the second purpose of the book. For *Shakespeare's Kings* is not

---

1. If we include *Pericles, Prince of Tyre* and *Two Noble Kinsmen*, which generally figure in the most recent collected editions, though neither appear in the First Folio.

concerned simply to tell a story; it is also an attempt to hold up the plays, scene by scene, to the light of history, in order to establish where that light shines through unclouded, where it is shaded or refracted, and where – as only occasionally occurs – it is blocked out altogether. This is not always an easy task. Before we can accuse Shakespeare of departing from the historical truth, we must ourselves know precisely where that truth lies – and this is not easy either. Like him, we must rely very largely on the contemporary evidence, collected and collated in the early chronicles. True, in the four hundred years since the plays were written much new material has come to light whose existence he can never even have suspected; none the less these chronicles remain, for us as for him, our fundamental authorities.

The scholarly editions list some half a dozen or more sources for each play, but by far the most important are the chronicles of Jean Froissart (for *Edward III* and possibly *Richard II*), of Edward Hall and of Raphael Holinshed, whose names recur again and again in the following pages. Froissart was born at Valenciennes around 1333. In 1361 he came to England, where he remained for the next eight years, travelling extensively round the country under the protection of Queen Philippa, who was herself from Hainault. Returning to France in 1369, he set to work on the first of the four volumes of his *Chroniques*, a vivid and racy account of the Hundred Years War of which the English translation, made in 1523–5 by John Bourchier, Lord Berners, was certainly well known to Shakespeare. A born writer, Froissart is I fear the only one of the three chroniclers who can be read with real pleasure today.

The two Englishmen are plodders by comparison. Edward Hall, a government official under Henry VIII, began *The Vnion of the Two Noble and Illustre Famelies of Lancastre and York* around 1530; it was first published in 1548, the year after his death. Raphael Holinshed, whose birth date is unknown but who died around 1580, was initially given by his employer, the publisher Reginald Wolfe, the formidable task of writing a history of the world from the Flood to the time of Queen Elizabeth. Not surprisingly, he never completed it; but a small portion of the work appeared in 1577 as *The firste volume of the chronicles of England, Scotlande and Irelande . . . conteyning the description and chronicles of England from first inhabiting unto the Conquest*. In fact, it continues to the writer's own day. It is not always easy reading, but it constitutes the first authoritative account in English of the whole of the country's history. Shakespeare used the second, enlarged but mildly censored edition of 1587, not only for his major history plays but also for *Macbeth*, *King Lear* and *Cymbeline*.

The other, less important sources are listed and described at length in the Arden and New Cambridge editions. The only one, I think, worth mentioning here is the work of Shakespeare's fellow poet Samuel Daniel, whose *First Fowre Bookes of the ciuile warres between the two houses of Lancaster and Yorke* were published in 1595. This was to be part of a still longer epic poem which was to carry the story down to the reign of Henry VII, but after he got as far as the wedding of Edward IV Daniel decided to write a prose history of England instead. At his best, he was a superb poet – some of his sonnets are among the loveliest in the language – and in 1604 he was appointed Licenser of the Queen's Revels. There can be no doubt, therefore, that he and his work would have been well known to Shakespeare, and his influence can certainly be traced in the later plays of the canon: *Richard II*, both parts of *Henry IV*, and *Henry V*.

Although Shakespeare remains faithful to his sources for much of the time, there are – predictably enough – a good number of divergencies. From time to time he may have had to·cope with an objection from the censor; a shortage of actors may sometimes have made it necessary to eliminate some minor character and attribute his actions to another. There are even moments when the root of the trouble seems to have been nothing more than plain carelessness. But in the vast majority of instances when Shakespeare departed from historic truth he did so for the best of all reasons: to make a better play. He was, after all, a playwright – first, last and always. To him the cause of the drama was of infinitely greater importance than the slavish observance of historical truth. He was young and inexperienced – the three parts of *Henry VI* and *Richard III* are among the first plays he ever wrote, while the entire canon was finished before his thirty-sixth birthday – and the challenge of moulding what is still today one of the most turbulent periods of English history into a coherent series was a formidable one indeed. No wonder he took liberties; no wonder he frequently combined two or three different events, which in fact occurred months or even years apart, into a single scene. The miracle is that he was able to stick as closely to the truth as he did, weaving together all the various strands to create a single epic masterpiece which, for all its minor inaccuracies, is almost always right when it really matters. A would-be student of the period with only the plays to help him might draw a number of false conclusions; but the overall picture received – including that of the reign of Richard III – would not, I believe, be very far wrong.

After *Richard II* the action, though inevitably episodic, is fairly continuous; continuous enough, indeed, for it to come as something of a surprise to learn that the nine plays were written in so haphazard an order. Dating is always a problem with Shakespeare, but it is now generally agreed that he began with the three parts of *Henry VI*. These seem to have been written consecutively, with Part I begun probably in 1589, Part II in 1590 and Part III completed in 1591, which also saw the writing of *Richard III*. Next in time came *Edward III*, which dates from 1592–3, after which there is a short break, during which appear *The Taming of the Shrew*, *Two Gentlemen of Verona* and *King John*; only in 1595 does Shakespeare return to his series with *Richard II*. Another break gives us *Romeo and Juliet*, *A Midsummer Night's Dream* and *The Merchant of Venice*; then, in 1596 and 1597 respectively, the two parts of *Henry IV*. These gave rise to the third – but very different – Falstaff play, *The Merry Wives of Windsor*, so it was not until 1599 that the canon was completed with *Henry V*.

And *Henry V* is unlike all the others. Though by no means the greatest of Shakespeare's histories, it is the only one which ranks as a true epic: a patriotic paean celebrating England's only royal hero, the triumphant conclusion of a nine-part work that had taken the author the first decade of his active life. How the Queen would have loved it – knowing, as she must have known, that such a play could never have been written before her own day. When she had ascended the throne – in 1558, at the age of twenty-five – England had been a poor country, both its army and navy small and ill-equipped. Just thirty years later and thanks largely to her, it had become a great nation: one that had defeated, in the Spanish Armada, the most formidable armed expedition ever launched against its shores without losing a single vessel in the process. America, discovered less than a century before, had proved a source of riches beyond her subjects' wildest dreams. The English felt themselves reborn, and filled with an unfamiliar confidence and pride: pride in their Queen of course, but pride also in their strength, their courage, their seamanship – and their language, which had suddenly and dramatically burst into the fullness of its flower.

From this new and unexpected standpoint, it was surely only natural that they should ask themselves just what had happened. England was, after all, an ancient nation: saving only the Papacy, the oldest political entity in Europe. Already more than 500 years had passed since the Norman Conquest, and the land had been ruled by kings for more than five centuries before that. Since Edward III's day, however, it had been increasingly disunited. The rot had started under his grandson Richard, had increased dangerously with Richard's dethronement, and after a brief period of remission under Henry V had finally spread out of control under Henry's idiot son. The Wars of the Roses had continued, though intermittently, till Richard III's death at Bosworth. And then, with Henry Tudor, had come deliverance. After a century of chaos, the Tudors had forged a modern state which, by the time William Shakespeare was born on St George's Day 1564,[1] was both peaceful and prosperous. But precisely what sort of transformation had been achieved, and how? How could a monarch transform a nation? And what *was* a monarch, anyway?

These were important questions, and in the sixteenth century they could be answered most effectively through the drama. Books were still expensive luxuries, largely the preserve of scholars and wealthy intellectuals; the theatre on the other hand appealed to every class of society and could be afforded by all but the very poorest – the majority of whom would have taken little interest in it anyway. And besides, what a story there was to be told: a dazzling opportunity, even if also a formidable challenge, to any ambitious young playwright. No wonder, as the sixteenth century drew to its close, that history plays became so popular. Before, let us say, 1585 there had been only one worthy of the name: *King John*, written not by Shakespeare but by John Bale, a Suffolk man who became Bishop of Ossory in Ireland, shortly before 1536; but that was an isolated instance. It was only in the last decade of the century – when, after the defeat of the Spanish Armada in 1588, the feeling of national exhilaration was at its height – that such plays began to appear in any quantity. They included (to name but a few) an

---

1. 23 April is at least the traditional date. The parish register records his baptism on 26 April, and in those times of high infant mortality baptism normally followed only a day or two after birth. But he certainly died on St George's Day 1616, and there is a pleasant symmetry in the idea that he both entered the world and left it on the feast of England's patron saint.

anonymous drama based on Bale, *The Troublesome Raigne of King John*, which was almost certainly the inspiration for Shakespeare's own version; *The Famous Victories of Henry the Fifth*, also anonymous; *Sir Thomas More* and *The Downfall of Robert, Earle of Huntingdon* (whom the principal author, Anthony Munday, chose to identify with Robin Hood); and *Edward I*, by George Peele. Some, obviously, are better than others; but only one, it can safely be said, can be mentioned in the same breath as Shakespeare's, and could be – indeed has been – successfully staged in our own day: Christopher Marlowe's dark and majestic tragedy of *Edward II*.

In the four centuries since it was written, the Shakespearean canon has enjoyed varying fortunes. Of *Edward III* we know practically nothing. Printed in 1596, its title page describes it only as having been 'sundrie times plaied about the Citie of London'. Since then its only recorded stage productions have been one in 1986 at the Globe Playhouse in Los Angeles and one in the following year by the Welsh Theatr Clwyd, which, having opened in the little town of Mold, went on to Cambridge and then, rather surprisingly, to Taormina in Sicily. We can only hope that after 400 years of obscurity the play's new promotion to Shakespearean rank will encourage other theatre companies to try it out, and give audiences the chance to judge it for themselves.

Richard II, too, has had a curious history. After its opening on 7 February 1601 – the eve of the Earl of Essex's abortive rising – it was not apparently performed again until 30 September 1607, when it was put on by members of the ship's company of HMS *Dragon* off Sierra Leone – a safer if less probable venue, as it turned out, than the Theatre Royal, Drury Lane, where a version by Nahum Tate was suppressed in 1681 after only two performances, despite Tate's tactfully having changed the names of all the characters and retitled the play *The Sicilian Usurper*. But the deposition of a king was always a delicate subject, and Charles II can hardly be blamed, in the circumstances, for his sensitivity. Only in the nineteenth century did *Richard II* finally achieve the popularity it deserved, with Edmund Kean and his son Charles; Charles Kean's production of 1857, with its tremendous set piece of Richard's woeful entry into London in Bolingbroke's victorious train was, we are told, never forgotten by any who saw it.

Thanks to the sheer irresistibility of Falstaff, the *Henry IV* plays were a success from the start. (Only the Victorians were to find him shocking, as they did almost everything else.) For the same reason, however, producers of later centuries tended to cut most of the political and historical sections and focus the entire play on the lovable old reprobate. Not until 1913 – and then not in London but in Birmingham – did Barry Jackson give audiences the opportunity to hear the full text as Shakespeare wrote it.[1]

Surprisingly, perhaps, in view of the opportunities it offers to a great actor, as well as for its pageantry and stage effects, *Henry V* was ignored between January 1605, when it was performed at court during the Christmas revels, and November 1735, when it was revived by the Irish actor Henry Giffard at his new theatre of Goodman's Fields. The warrior king then became a favourite role for such actors as Kemble, Macready and Charles Kean; David Garrick had played only the Chorus. Less to be wondered at is the play's increased popularity in time of war. Londoners at Christmas 1914 perhaps deserved something a little more thrilling than the fifty-six-year-old Frank Benson as Henry; even this, however, must have been preferable to the production two years later by Marie Slade and her all-woman company, with Miss Slade herself in the title role. *Henry V* shares with *Richard III*[2] the distinction of having been twice made the subject of a feature film. Laurence Olivier's of 1944 – a triumph, considering the difficulties of film production in wartime and a ridiculously small budget – understandably emphasized the patriotic aspect; Kenneth Branagh's, made forty-five years later, went a good deal deeper, removing the glamour and reminding us instead of the mud and the blood and the misery of war.

The three parts of *Henry VI* have always been, as it were, the runts of the litter. We know of no early stage history of any of them, unless the 'Harey the vj', mentioned in the diary of the theatre manager Philip Henslowe as having been performed by Lord Strange's Men on 3 March 1592, can be identified with Part I. In London, apart from a single performance of Part I at Drury Lane in 1738 for some 'Ladies of Quality', and a week's run of Part II in 1864, none of the three was seen in its original form until 1923, when they were all staged on two consecutive

---

1. I remember my father – a passionate Shakespearean – telling me that the greatest Falstaff he ever saw was the sixty-five-year-old music-hall comedian George Robey, at His Majesty's Theatre in 1935.

2. There have actually been three films made of *Richard III*, if we count the two-reeler of Frank Benson's Stratford production of 1911.

nights by Robert Atkins at the Old Vic.[1] Shakespeare-lovers then had to wait another twelve years, until in the summer of 1935 Gilmor Browne, Director of the Pasadena Community Playhouse, presented a festival season of all the history plays. Over the past half-century, productions of the trilogy have still been few and far between. (I have already mentioned the Barton–Hall *Wars of the Roses* at the Aldwych theatre, where on Saturday 11 January 1964 I saw, for the first and I fear the last time in my life, an edited version of the three parts of *Henry VI* as well as *Richard III*, all performed in a single day.)

We are left with the greatest play of them all. It seems hard nowadays to believe that *Richard III* was ignored through most of the seventeenth century, and that for 150 years after that it survived only in an extraordinary version by the actor-playwright Colley Cibber, which included bits from *Richard II*, *Henry IV Part II*, *Henry V* and *Henry VI Part III*, plus several lines of his own invention. For the play as Shakespeare wrote it audiences had to wait till 1845, when it was produced by Samuel Phelps; even then, however, they preferred the Cibber version – and when Phelps restaged the play in 1861, this was the one they got. Not till the end of the nineteenth century did *Richard III* really come into its own, when Frank Benson offered productions regularly between 1886 and 1915. There can be no real doubt that the first truly definitive Richard was that of Olivier in 1944 – a vision of evil which he preserved eleven years later in his famous film version; though even this, despite his own electrifying performance and those of Ralph Richardson as Buckingham and John Gielgud as Clarence, now seems to me pedestrian when compared with the film of 1995, shot largely in Battersea Power Station, with Sir Ian McKellen in the title role.

But now I am becoming critical, and this is not a work of criticism. Anyone wanting to know more about texts, dates and sources is recommended once again to acquire the relevant volumes of the Arden or the New Cambridge editions, the most authoritative and scholarly in existence.[2] My own object has been far more modest: simply to provide lovers of Shakespeare, enthusiastic but cheerfully non-expert, with the

1. It must be said in fairness that Frank Benson had staged Part II at Stratford in 1899, 1901 and 1909, and the complete trilogy in a cycle of seven histories in 1906.

2. All references in this book are to the Arden, except of course those relating to *Edward III*, for which I have used the New Cambridge.

sort of single volume that I myself should like to have had, when my eyes were first opened to the splendour of these Histories, more than half a century ago.

John Julius Norwich
Castle Combe, November 1998

I

Edward III and the Black Prince

[1337–1377]

KING EDWARD. Lorraine, return this answer to thy lord:
I mean to visit him, as he requests;
But how? not servilely dispos'd to bend,
But like a conqueror, to make him bow.
His lame unpolish'd shifts are come to light,
And truth has pull'd the vizard from his face
That set a gloss upon his arrogance.
Dare he command a fealty in me?
Tell him, the crown, that he usurps, is mine,
And where he sets his foot, he ought to kneel:
'Tis not a petty dukedom that I claim,
But all the whole dominions of the realm;
Which if with grudging he refuse to yield,
I'll take away those borrow'd plumes of his
And send him naked to the wilderness.

                                        EDWARD III

On Monday 21 September 1327 Edward Plantagenet, the former King Edward II of England, was murdered at Berkeley Castle in Gloucester-shire. He had been deposed eight months earlier, but not before he and his infamous lover Piers Gaveston, Earl of Cornwall, had reduced the prestige of the English Crown to the lowest point in all its history. Edward was weak and impressionable, totally unable to assert himself against the ambition and greed of his favourite, who shamelessly used his hold over the King to advance his own fortunes. Had he shown the faintest degree of moderation, had he treated the great barons of the land with even a suggestion of deference and respect, they would probably have accepted the situation philosophically; instead, he rode roughshod over them all, infuriating them with his greed, ostentation and arrogance. Only two months after his coronation in 1308, they made their first demand for Gaveston's banishment; the King's reply was to appoint him Lieutenant of Ireland, and little more than a year later the odious young man was back at his side, insufferable as ever.

The barons kept up their pressure, and in 1311 Gaveston was sentenced to permanent exile from the kingdom. Even then he and Edward fought back, and early the following year the King formally announced the Earl's return and reinstatement; in doing so, however, he effectively signed his death warrant. On 19 May 1312 Gaveston surrendered at Scarborough, and a month later to the day he was publicly executed on Blacklow Hill, just outside Warwick. Somehow Edward managed to maintain a tenuous hold on the throne for another fifteen years; but his weakness and indecision, his now habitual drunkenness and his utter inability to control an unending stream of catamites – above all a certain Hugh le Despenser, a would-be successor to Gaveston – made his downfall inevitable. Eventually his own Queen, Isabella of France, together with her lover Roger Mortimer, took up arms against him and he was obliged to capitulate. On 20 January 1327 he was formally deposed, and eight months later, on 21 September, was put hideously to death.[1]

His son and successor, called Edward like his father, was a little over fourteen years old when he found himself the richest and most powerful ruler in Europe. To Scotland he could lay no claim: it had its own line of kings, the reigning monarch at that time being Robert I (the Bruce), who had trounced his father at Bannockburn thirteen years before. Both Ireland and Wales, however – although they continued to give trouble – were theoretically part of Edward's dominions: as was Gascony, which was more important than either, comprising as it did the larger part of south-west France. True, English possessions beyond the Channel were no longer what they once had been. Two centuries before, Edward's great-great-great-grandfather Henry II had claimed,

---

1. John Trevisa, who was born at Berkeley in 1326, writes in his translation (with interpolations) of Higden's *Polychronicon* that Edward was killed 'with a hoote broche putte thro the secret place posterialle' – this particularly ghastly method having been chosen principally in order that there should be no marks on the body when it was prepared for state burial in Gloucester Cathedral, but also, perhaps, as being appropriate for a suspected sodomite.

either as fiefs by inheritance or through his marriage with Eleanor of Aquitaine, almost half the area of the country we know today, including – as well as Gascony – Normandy, Brittany, Maine, Touraine, Anjou, Poitou, Guyenne and Toulouse. Since Henry's time, however, much of this had fallen away; now only Gascony was left.

In 1328, little more than a year after Edward was crowned, the French King Charles IV died in Paris, leaving – like his two brothers who had preceded him on the throne – no male issue; and suddenly not only the lost provinces but the whole of France seemed to Edward to be just possibly within his reach. He now claimed simply that his own mother, Isabella, the late King's sister, was the rightful heir; the French objected that according to the old Salic Law the crown could not pass to a woman, and that it should therefore go to the son of Charles's uncle, Philip of Valois; whereupon Edward pointed out that even if the Salic Law were to be upheld he himself, as the late King's nephew, was a closer relation than Philip, who was merely a cousin.

It is interesting to speculate how European history would have been changed had Edward's view prevailed, with England and France united under a single crown. But to the French such an outcome was clearly out of the question. Philip, after all, was already Regent; Edward, now sixteen, lived across the sea, was the senior representative of that same house of Plantagenet that in Gascony had caused nothing but trouble, and was in any case still a minor. Philip duly received his coronation as Philip VI at Rheims in May 1328, and Edward was obliged, albeit reluctantly, to recognize him as King. But this presented another problem – one of the oldest and most intractable of all those inherent in the feudal system, one which had been poisoning Anglo-French relations ever since the days of William the Conqueror: how could a sovereign of one state hold land as the vassal of a sovereign of another? The duties imposed by such vassalage were as difficult for one of them to insist upon as they were distasteful to the other to perform. Edward's title to his French lands was not in dispute; but how were those lands held – in full sovereignty or as fiefs?

The French had no doubts on the matter: so far as they were concerned the King of France retained his suzerainty under the formula *superioritas et resortum*, which allowed the people of Gascony the ultimate right of appeal to Paris. The English, however, refused to accept any such limitation of their authority. Lawyers on both sides of the Channel had been arguing for a century and more, but had succeeded only in smothering the issue under layer after layer of obfuscation, until the only point which was perfectly clear (though neither side could admit it) was that the problem was insoluble. In 1329 Edward did in fact travel to Amiens, where he did simple homage to Philip; but eight years later, on 24 May 1337, the French King declared Gascony confiscate to himself 'on account of the many excesses, rebellions and acts of disobedience committed against us and our royal majesty by the King of England, Duke of Aquitaine'. By now tension had been further increased by Edward's invasion of France's old ally, Scotland; and Philip's unilateral action came as the last straw. On 7 October Edward challenged his claim not only to Gascony but to France as well, declaring himself 'King of France and England'. The Hundred Years War had begun.

It is with this declaration that Shakespeare's *Edward III*[1] effectively opens. There is a brief preliminary exchange during which, for the sake of the audience, Edward's claim to the French throne is explained – and its justice confirmed – by Robert, Count of Artois;[2] there then enters the French Ambassador, the Duke of Lorraine, who peremptorily demands that Edward appear within forty days before the King of France to do homage for his dukedom of Guyenne – a summons which is answered in the words that form the epigraph to this chapter. We are thus given a rousing and intensely dramatic opening scene – although two small points must be made in the interests of historical accuracy. First, Edward had actually performed the required homage eight years before (though not in satisfactory form, since he had refused to appear before the French King bare-headed and with ungirt sword); second, despite the fact that both Artois and Lorraine refer to their master as John of Valois, the King of France in 1337 was in fact Philip

1. As pointed out in the Introduction, it has never been suggested that every word of the play is by Shakespeare. His name is used loosely throughout this chapter, simply because we cannot get involved here with questions of the authenticity of individual passages.

2. In fact Robert was not Count of Artois at all, that county on the death of his grandfather having been assigned to a cousin. In 1334 he had sought refuge in England, where Edward, realizing the value of a renegade French nobleman to his cause, had granted him the earldom of Richmond.

VI; John II succeeded him only in 1350.[1] Neither of these points, however, need concern us overmuch; suffice it to say that the Duke of Lorraine is sent packing and his place at centre-stage taken over by the captain of the castle of Roxborough (now Roxburgh), Sir William Montague.[2]

With Montague comes the introduction of two more strands of the story: affairs in Scotland and the King's love for the Countess of Salisbury. Montague reports that the 'league' between the English and the Scots has been 'cracked and dissevered':

> Berwick is won; Newcastle spoil'd and lost;
> And now the tyrant hath begirt with siege
> The castle of Roxborough, where enclos'd
> The Countess Salisbury is like to perish.

Edward had in fact no league with Scotland. On the contrary, fighting had continued sporadically along the border from soon after Bannockburn until in 1328, with the marriage of Bruce's four-year-old son David – soon to be King David II of Scotland – to Edward's sister Joanna, a truce had been declared – only to be broken by the Scots when they captured Berwick in 1332. Newcastle, on the other hand, did not fall to them until 1341 – the date when, according to Froissart,[3] Sir William Montague appealed to the King for help. But to attach any serious importance to these inaccuracies is to miss the point. The dramatist is not interested in historical exactitude; he is concerned only to set the general scene of almost continuous warfare along the Scottish

1. The editor of the New Cambridge edition charitably maintains that 'the existence of Philip VI is deliberately ignored in order to present a single royal French counterpart to Edward in the campaign that lasted from 1337 to 1356.'

2. There seems also to have been some confusion in the identity of Montague, but it need not concern us here.

3. Jean Froissart, the greatest prose writer of his day, was born at Valenciennes in the county of Hainault around 1337 and was brought to England by Queen Philippa in 1361 as one of her household clerks, remaining there until her death eight years later, though making frequent trips to the continent. He was at the Black Prince's court at Bordeaux when Richard was born there in 1367. His chronicle – which includes long extracts from that of an earlier compatriot, Jean Le Bel – covers the period from 1322 to the end of the century.

border, and of the consequent danger to Edward's subjects throughout the north, rich and poor alike.

Edward thus finds that he has two enemies to fight; of the two, however, he has no doubt that the King of France is by far the more formidable. Against him he orders his eldest son, Edward – whom he calls 'Ned'[1] – to raise a mighty army from every shire in the land, simultaneously arranging for appeals to be made to his father-in-law the Count of Hainault and even to the Holy Roman Emperor, Lewis IV. While such preparations are in train, 'with these forces that I have at hand', he proposes to march against King David, liberating Lady Salisbury from the castle in which she is besieged – and on the battlements of which we find her at the opening of scene ii.

The identity of this lady is not so much a mystery as the result of a chaotic confusion on the part of Froissart and other less trustworthy sources.[2] She is probably based on Alice Montague, whose husband Edward was governor of the Earl of Salisbury's castle of Wark and whom the King is known to have tried, unsuccessfully, to seduce; but once again it hardly matters. Her eavesdropping on King David and the Duke of Lorraine, as they walk the ramparts below discussing the devastation that they will wreak on England, enables her to taunt them when they flee at the news of Edward's advance; her real purpose, however, is to provide the play with a love interest and to show us the King as a lover as well as a man of action. This theme is continued throughout the long first scene of Act II. It includes much fine poetry and introduces an interesting moral dilemma when the Countess's father, the Earl of Warwick – who is no more a historical character than she is herself – is commanded by the King to persuade his daughter to yield:

> I'll say, she must forget her husband Salisbury,
> If she remember to embrace the king;
> I'll say, an oath can easily be broken,
> But not so easily pardoned, being broken;
> I'll say, it is true charity to love,
> But not true love to be so charitable;

1. Edward, the Black Prince, was seven years old in 1337.
2. It is discussed at length in the New Cambridge edition, p. 186.

I'll say, his greatness may bear out the shame,
But not his kingdom can buy out the sin;
I'll say, it is my duty to persuade,
But not her honesty to give consent.

But these two scenes – together with that which follows, in which the Countess finally brings Edward to his senses by agreeing to surrender to him only if he first kills his wife and her husband – are in a sense little more than an extended parenthesis; not until the last dozen lines of Act II do we return to the main business of the play – the war with France.

Although at an early stage Edward had established himself with his family at Antwerp as a forward base, he did not invade French territory until the autumn of 1339. Invading armies seldom comport themselves well towards local populations, but the English army seems to have behaved worse than most. The countryside was ravaged, villages laid waste. At Origny the local convent was burnt to the ground, the nuns subjected to wholesale rape. Such conduct may have been deliberately intended to provoke the King of France to battle; if so, it very nearly succeeded. When the French army finally caught up with the English near Saint-Quentin, Philip proposed a formal encounter in single combat – the old chivalric tradition was dying hard – at a site to be chosen by Edward; he stipulated only that the field should have neither trees, ditches nor marsh. Edward asked nothing better. He was twenty-five years old, at the peak of his health and vigour, with a passion for war in all its aspects. He was a regular participant at tournaments; and what, after all, was his cousin proposing but a glorified joust? No sooner had the challenge been accepted, however, than Philip had second thoughts. Froissart suggests that he listened to the advice of his uncle Robert of Anjou, King of Naples and a noted astrologer; more probably his scouts simply reported that the English King was a good deal stronger, and the English host far better organized, than he had expected. At all events he returned to Paris. The English, grumbling loudly about French cowardice, retired to Brussels for the winter.

Edward's temper was considerably improved when, in January 1340, the people of Flanders – natural allies of England because of the mutually profitable wool trade – recognized his claim to the French crown. He immediately quartered the arms of France with his own, ordered a new seal complete with *fleurs-de-lys* and adopted a surcoat of scarlet and blue, embroidered with the leopards and lilies that remain to this day on the royal escutcheon. But the Flemings, happy as they were to be an English rather than a French dependency, were merchants first and foremost, with a clear understanding of the value of money. When the King returned to England soon afterwards to hasten the delivery of the provisions and supplies he needed, they politely insisted that his wife and children should be left behind as security for the payment of his debts, Queen Philippa's own crown being put in pawn to the merchants of Cologne.

Meanwhile the French were giving increasing trouble in the Channel. Already in 1338 their privateers had raided Portsmouth and South-ampton; that October, Edward had ordered a line of stakes to be driven across the Thames to prevent similar assaults on London. The following year Dover and Folkestone had been attacked. Finally, by midsummer 1340, the King was ready to sail from the Thames estuary with the navy that he had long been preparing: some 200 vessels, carrying perhaps 5,000 archers and men-at-arms, together with horses and stores. Also accompanying him were what a contemporary described as 'a large number of English ladies, countesses, baronesses, knights' ladies and wives of London burgesses, who were on their way to visit the Queen of England at Ghent'. But just before Edward gave the order to weigh anchor there came ominous news: scouts who had been patrolling the Channel reported that a French fleet at least twice the size of his own was awaiting him at the mouth of the river Zwin near the little town of Sluys – in those days the port of nearby Bruges. His Chancellor, the Archbishop of Canterbury John Stratford, urged him even at this late stage to cancel the expedition: in such conditions, he argued, to continue would be suicide. But the King remained firm – whereupon Stratford resigned his seal of office on the spot, handing it over to his brother Robert, Bishop of Chichester – and, shortly after midnight on 22 June, gave the order to sail.

On the afternoon of the day following, as his fleet approached the Flemish coast, Edward saw for himself the strength of the huge armada that Philip had drawn up against him: 400 sail or more – 'so many', writes Froissart, 'that their masts resembled a forest'. Nineteen of them were larger than any that the English had ever seen. Characteristically, however, the King decided to attack at once. Pausing only to ensure the protection of the ladies, he spent what remained of the day deploying his ships, one carrying men-at-arms between every two with archers. Then, early in the morning of Midsummer Day,[1] he led his fleet straight into the harbour mouth.

What followed was a massacre. The French fought valiantly, but were so tightly crowded together in the narrow inlet that they could barely move. Edward bore down upon them with the wind behind him, his archers – operating from platforms or 'castles' mounted high above the decks – loosing volleys of arrows high into the air to rain down a moment later over the enemy ships, while the sharp English prows shattered the motionless French hulls like matchwood. Only when sufficient damage had been done did the longbowmen pause in their work, to allow the men-at-arms to grapple, board and fight to the death. For nine hours the battle continued; when it was finished, 230 French ships, including the flagship, had been captured and the rest destroyed, the two admirals dead among the wreckage. The fish in the harbour drank so much French blood, it was said afterwards, that had God given them the power of speech they would have spoken in French.

The last three acts of *Edward III* are devoted to the King's victories in France, and are based principally on the accounts by Froissart and Holinshed of the battles of Sluys and Crécy, respectively in 1340 and 1346; of the siege and conquest of Calais in 1346–7; and of the battle of Poitiers in 1356. We would expect Act III to begin with Sluys, and so in a way it does; but although its first scene is clearly set somewhere on the Flemish coast within sight and earshot of the battle, lines 33–61 are more suggestive of the preparations for Crécy six years later. The entire action is represented from the French point of view – presumably in order to introduce us to Edward's chief antagonists, now appearing for the first time. They are identified in the stage directions as 'King John of France, his two sons Charles [Duke] of Normandy and Philip'. We have already noted the dramatist's refusal to recognize King Philip VI, whom he confuses with John II, his son and successor.[2] This

---

1. Although the title is nowadays given to the longest day of the year, 21 June, the Feast of St John the Baptist on the 24th was then generally accepted as Midsummer Day.

2. See pp. 18–19 and note.

now leads him into still greater confusion. The Duke of Normandy in 1340 was not Charles but that same John, the future King: while the 'Philip' cannot possibly be John's son – the future Philip the Bold, Duke of Burgundy, who was born only in 1341 or 1342 – and can be identified only with his brother, Philip Duke of Orleans.

In his reference to 'our navy of a thousand sail', the King appears somewhat prone to exaggeration: Holinshed puts the number at 400, while Froissart speaks of 'mo than sixscore great vessels, besyde other'. But we are given no further information about the French fleet: the conversation shifts to the character of the English, 'Bloodthirsty and seditious Catilines', and their allies, the 'frothy Dutchmen, puff'd with double beer' – no match, clearly, for the allies of the French: 'The stern Polonian, and the warlike Dane,/The King of Bohemia, and of Sicily'. Obediently on cue, John of Luxemburg, King of Bohemia, enters with a Polish captain; they are, however, jumping the gun. As we shall shortly see, the blind King John was to fight – and die – at Crécy, in which both Poles and Danes fought as mercenaries; but that was still six years in the future.[1]

Suddenly, the mood changes. A 'mariner' arrives to describe the splendour of the English fleet:

> Majestical the order of their course,
> Figuring the horned circle of the moon:
> And on the top-gallant of the admiral,
> And likewise all the handmaids of his train,
> The arms of England and of France unite
> Are quarter'd equally by herald's art.

A few moments later, the battle has begun. The King and Philip hear it in the distance, and the mariner returns with a description that borders on the macabre:

> Purple the sea; whose channel fill'd as fast
> With streaming gore that from the maimèd fell

---

1. King Robert the Wise, of Naples and Sicily, is briefly mentioned by Froissart as having warned the French King not to fight the English; but he was not present at Sluys, and died three years before Crécy.

> As did her gushing moisture break into
> The crannied cleftures of the through-shot planks.
> Here flew a head, dissever'd from the trunk;
> There mangled arms and legs were toss'd aloft,
> As when a whirlwind takes the summer dust
> And scatters it in middle of the air.

Five years at the most separate the writing of *Edward III* and the defeat of the Spanish Armada; and it is hardly surprising that echoes of the recent victory can be heard in the mariner's two speeches. In the first – an unmistakable warning of what is to come – he describes 'The proud Armado of King Edward's ships'; the reference to 'the horned circle of the moon' would also have struck a chord with contemporary audiences, the Armada having sailed in crescent-shaped formation up the Channel before being engaged by the English fleet.[1] In the second speech, immediately after the battle, he gives the King the grim news in the clearest possible terms:

> Much did the Nonpareille, that brave ship:
> So did the Black-snake of Bullen [Boulogne], than which
> A bonnier vessel never yet spread sail:
> But all in vain; both sun, the wind and tide
> Revolted all unto our foemen's side,
> That we perforce were fain to give them way,
> And they are landed: thus my tale is done;
> We have untimely lost, and they have won.

The battle of Sluys – the first great naval victory in English history – gave Edward command of the Channel and ensured a moderately satisfactory bridgehead for his expeditionary armies for several years to come. The French army, however – in marked contrast to its navy – remained unscathed, still refusing to join battle; the Flemish allies, bored with the war, were growing ever more obstreperous; and when, at the approach of autumn, the elderly Countess of Hainault – Edward's mother-in-law and Philip's sister – emerged from the convent to which she had retired and proposed a truce, the two monarchs agreed. It was

---

1. cf. Sonnet cvii: 'The mortal moon hath her eclipse endured.'

signed on 25 September 1340 at Espléchin near Tournai, extending until midsummer of the following year. Thus, for the King of England, the first phase of the war had been only moderately successful. He had, it was true, destroyed the French fleet and acquired new allies in Flanders. On the other hand he suffered from the inherent disadvantage of all invaders of foreign territory: dangerously extended lines of communication and supply, not only inconvenient in themselves but a constant brake on progress and all too easily cut by an enemy fighting on home ground. Quick and decisive victories like that of Sluys were what he needed; he could not afford a war of slow attrition or of protracted sieges. Thus he had proved powerless against Philip's defensive strategy, and his ultimate victory over the French King seemed as far away as ever it had been.

The five years after the treaty of Espléchin saw a good deal of inconclusive fighting in Brittany and Gascony, where two of the ablest of the younger English commanders, Sir Walter Manny and the King's cousin, Henry Earl of Derby, recovered a good many important towns and castles before losing them again to Philip's eldest son, John Duke of Normandy. In the early summer of 1346, however, Edward prepared an army of some 4,000 men-at-arms and 10,000 archers, with a navy of about 700 sail which he assembled at Portsmouth. The destination of this expeditionary force – by far the greatest ever raised in England – was deliberately not revealed, obliging the French to keep their own ships widely dispersed; even the English captains were given their orders under seal, to be opened only after they had left harbour. But there seems little reason to doubt Froissart when he tells us that it was intended for Gascony, where Derby was putting up a stout resistance at Aiguillon.[1] At any rate the fleet set sail and headed westward down the Channel; but after three days the wind changed and drove the ships north against the Cornish coast. There they lay nearly a week at anchor, and it seems to have been only then that Sir Godfrey d'Harcourt, a French knight banished from his native land who had spent the past two years at the English court, persuaded the King to change his entire plan. 'Sir', he is quoted as saying,

1. Michael Packe, however (*King Edward III*, p. 149), suggests that the King had his eye on Normandy from the beginning, and that the journey as far as Cornwall was a deliberate feint to put the French off the track.

the country of Normandy is one of the richest in the world. I promise you on my life that, if you land there, none shall resist you; for its people have no experience of arms and the greatest of its knights are all at Aiguillon with the Duke. Thus will you find great towns and fortresses completely undefended, wherein your men shall have such gain as to make them rich for twenty years to come. Moreover your fleet will be able to follow you almost as far as Caen. If you therefore see fit to heed my advice, you and we shall all profit thereby.

Sir Godfrey spoke the truth, and Edward knew it. He saw too that such a landing in Normandy might well divert French troops from Gascony, thereby helping the hard-pressed Derby almost as much as if he had sailed directly to his relief. The principal danger would be that of interception by King Philip – whose army was far larger than his own – before he could link up with his Flemish allies; but his past experience of Philip's cautiousness suggested that the risk was well worth taking, and he gave the order to turn about. The fleet sailed back the way it had come, and landed at the little port of St Vaast-la-Hougue, on the eastern side of the Cotentin peninsula,[1] on 12 July.

For reasons not entirely clear,[2] the army encamped for thirty-six hours on the beach before setting off to the north-east, burning and plundering as it advanced. The unwalled towns of Barfleur and Carentan and the city of Caen were taken and sacked, and Rouen would have suffered the same fate – leaving the English in uncontested control of the lower Seine – had not the French army arrived just in time to save it. Edward had neither the time nor the money for a long siege; instead he wheeled to his right – allowing Philip to think he might be making for Gascony after all – and crossed the Seine at Poissy, birthplace of Saint Louis and site of one of the French King's favourite country palaces, in which Edward celebrated the Feast of the Assumption,

1. It is some ten miles to the north of Utah Beach, where the American 4th Division landed on 6 June 1944.
2. Possibly because the King had injured himself on landing. Froissart reports that 'he stumbled, and fell so heavily that the blood gushed from his nose. The knights who surrounded him took this for a bad omen and begged him to go back on board for that day. "Why?" retorted the King without hesitation. "It is a very good sign: it shows that the land is thirsty to receive me."' The story would be more credible if it were not also told of William the Conqueror – and, I seem to remember, Julius Caesar.

making free of his cousin's best wines. Then he reverted to his original course towards Picardy and the Low Countries. He had a stroke of luck when he reached the Somme: the bridges were down, but it was low tide and his army was able to cross at a shallow ford just before the waters rose to block off the pursuing French. This twelve-hour respite was a godsend, giving him time to find a suitable defensive position and to rest his men before the confrontation he had long been awaiting. He found it at Crécy, some twelve miles north of Abbeville on the little river Maye, with a valley – known as the Vallée des Clères – in front of him and thick woods behind. He himself took command of the centre, with the Earl of Northampton commanding his left wing and, on his right, in the care of Sir Godfrey d'Harcourt and Sir John Chandos, the sixteen-year-old Prince of Wales.[1]

The French cavalry numbering some 8,000, supplemented by 4,000 hired Genoese crossbowmen and other mercenaries from Poland and Denmark, arrived late in the afternoon of Saturday 26 August, following a heavy shower of rain. The infantry was still some way behind. For that reason alone an immediate engagement was not to be thought of, and after a brief personal reconnaissance King Philip ordered the attack deferred until the following day; but the knights in his vanguard ignored him, continuing to press forward up the hill until the English archers, no longer able to resist the temptation, loosed their first volley. By then it was too late to retire; the whole army was committed and the battle had begun. The Genoese advanced with their crossbows, the strings of which were soaking wet after the rain; but the evening sun was full in their eyes, and the English longbowmen – who had protected their own bowstrings by removing them and putting them inside their helmets – could shoot six arrows in the time it took the Italians to deliver a single bolt. The latter turned tail and fled – straight into the charging French cavalry, who mowed them down by the hundred before themselves going down under the relentless hail from the archers. Pressed hard from behind, the French attacked again and again, but – at least where the English centre and left flank were concerned – with no greater success.

---

1. There is no reason to think that his sobriquet, 'the Black Prince', probably occasioned by his black armour, was ever attached to him during his lifetime. Its earliest recorded appearance dates only from the sixteenth century.

The principal threat was to the right wing commanded by the young Prince of Wales, where a number of French knights, together with a group of Germans and Savoyards, had braved the arrows and were now fighting hand-to-hand with the English men-at-arms. At one point, Froissart tells us, the Prince was down on his knees, protected only by his standard-bearer Richard de Beaumont, who sheltered him with the banner of Wales until he once again struggled to his feet; and the Earls of Warwick and Oxford who were fighting beside him dispatched one of their knights, Sir Thomas of Norwich, to the King with an urgent appeal for help. Edward, informed of the situation, asked only whether his son was dead or wounded. On hearing that he was so far unharmed, though fighting desperately for his life, he sent Sir Thomas back to his superiors. 'Give them my command,' he said, 'to let the boy win his spurs; for if God has so ordained it I wish the day to be his, and the honour to go to him and to those in whose charge I have placed him.'

The Prince and his companions finally routed their assailants, who were forced to retire. Meanwhile, in the gathering twilight, King Philip lost all control of the battle and his army lapsed into confusion. The fighting continued until long after dark; by morning, more than a third of the French army lay dead on the field. Among them – together with the King's brother the Duke of Alençon, his nephew Guy of Blois, the Duke of Lorraine and the Count of Flanders, nine French counts and over fifteen hundred knights – was the blind John of Luxemburg, King of Bohemia, who had insisted on being led into the fray to strike at least one blow with his sword. His entourage, in order not to lose him, had tied his horse's bridle to their own; they had then 'advanced so far forward that they all remained on the field, not one of them escaping alive. They were found the next day, the knights lying round their leader, with their horses still fastened together.' The King's body was washed in warm water and wrapped in a clean linen shroud, and a solemn mass was celebrated by the Bishop of Durham for the repose of his soul; the Prince of Wales, however, appropriated his badge of the three ostrich feathers and the motto *Ich Dien* – 'I Serve' – which his distant successor still bears to this day.

Dawn brought a heavy fog – not unusual in Picardy in late August – and the Earls of Arundel, Northampton and Suffolk set off with a considerable force of mounted knights to look for the King and for any other important Frenchmen who might be trying to escape. They did not find Philip, but came instead upon the bulk of the French infantry, together with a number of high church dignitaries including the Archbishop of Rouen and the Grand Prior of the Order of St John of Jerusalem. None of these had heard anything of the battle, and at first assumed that they had come upon a group of their own compatriots. They were soon disillusioned; the English were in no mood for mercy. All the churchmen were killed in cold blood, as were the majority of the infantry – four times as many, according to one report, as lost their lives in the main encounter.

King Edward – again according to Froissart – had remained at the windmill that he had chosen for his command post and had not once donned his helmet throughout the battle. Yet it was to him, rather than to his son, that the victory truly belonged. His alone was the strategy that had made it possible, while his coolness under fire and his shrewd tactical sense stood out in marked contrast to the impetuousness and lack of control shown by his adversary.[1] It was clear, too, that he better than anyone else understood the way in which warfare was evolving. The development of the longbow, capable in skilled hands of penetrating chain mail – or even a steel breastplate – from a range of a hundred yards or more, meant that henceforth any cavalry charge could be stopped in its tracks. As for artillery, such primitive devices as existed were used exclusively for siege warfare; it would be well over a century before cannon and musketry proved their supremacy over the drawn bowstring, and the balance swung once again in favour of the aggressor rather than the defence.

And what, finally, of King Philip? Twice unhorsed and twice wounded, he had seen his standard-bearer killed in front of him and had fought as valiantly as any of his men. With the help of John, Count of Hainault, he managed to escape from the battlefield and rode under cover of darkness to the castle of Labroye, whose seneschal, roused in the small hours, demanded to know who it was who so insistently sought admittance. 'Open quickly,' answered Philip, 'for I am the

---

1. The chronicler of the Abbey of Saint-Denis suggests another reason for the French defeat: 'The common soldiers wore tight shirts, so short that they exposed their private parts every time they bent over. The noblemen, on the other hand, wore hauberks extravagantly decorated and surmounted by vainglorious feathery crests. The Lord God, offended by so much obscenity and vanity, decided to use the King of England as His flail, to beat the French host into the ground.'

fortune of France.' He was indeed. As his son was to prove ten years later at Poitiers, France could ill afford the cost of a captured king.

From Sluys the play wings us forward six years to the preliminaries to the battle of Crécy. A short introductory scene (III.ii), based on a passage in Froissart, shows the local population taking flight at the coming of the English host, after which (III,iii) Edward enters, followed shortly afterwards by his son the Black Prince. The Prince proudly lists to his father the cities he has taken since his arrival in France – in fact, father and son had made the conquests together – and tells him that the French army, 'With full a hundred thousand fighting men', is already being drawn up on the field. No sooner have the words left his lips than 'King John'[1] himself appears with his train. This is another imaginary scene, in which the two kings hurl insults at each other: Edward gives 'John' one last opportunity to give up the French throne

> Before the sickle's thrust into the corn
> Or that enkindled fury turn to flame?

but his offer is rejected with contempt:

> Edward, I know what right thou hast in France,
> And ere I basely will resign my crown
> This champion field shall be a pool of blood
> And all our prospect as a slaughter-house.

Historically there was no meeting of the two kings before the battle; nor do the chroniclers report any rousing speeches made to their respective armies of the kind made by the French King in the play. Imagined too is the ceremonial arming of the Black Prince by Edward and his nobles. Dramatically, on the other hand, the two incidents are more than justified; the arming of the Prince in particular is a brilliant touch. Battles, by their very nature, cannot be satisfactorily presented on a stage (though Shakespeare was to make the attempt on several occasions in the future). It is all the more important for the playwright to provide an adequate build-up, to leave his audience in no doubt as

1. See pp. 18–19 and note, and 23–4.

to the importance of the coming confrontation. Here we are given first a war of words, and then a series of short ceremonies which reflect all the panoply and pageantry of battle – reminding us, too, of the military qualities of the Black Prince, whose youthful vigour is such that his father names the hardened old warrior Lord Audley to fight at his side.[1]

The encounter itself is encapsulated in two brief incidents, both in III,iii and both derived from Froissart through Holinshed. The first, only a dozen lines long, shows us the breathless 'King John' with the Duke of Lorraine (who, historically, lost his life on the field, though there is no suggestion of this in the play) watching the flight of the French army – for which they rightly blame the Genoese mercenaries although, if Holinshed is to be believed, the latter certainly had a lot to bear:

The third time againe the Genowaies leapt, and yelled, and went foorth till they came within shot, and fiercelie therwith discharged their crossbowes. Then the English archers stept foorth one pase, and let flie their arrowes so wholie and so thicke togither, that it seemed to snowe. When the Genowaies felt the arrowes persing their heads, armes and breasts, manie of them cast downe their crossbowes, and cut the strings, and returned discomfited . . .

Then ye might haue seene the men of armes haue dasht in amongst them, and killed a great number of them, and euer the Englishmen shot where they saw the thickest prease: the sharpe arrowes ran into the men of armes, and into their horsses, and manie fell horsse and man amongst the Genowaies, and still the Englishmen shot . . . The throng was such that one ouerthrew another; & also among the Englishmen, there were certeine of the footmen with great kniues, that went in among the men of armes, and killed manie of them as they laie on the ground, both earles, barons, knights, and esquires.

Then, represented at considerably greater length, comes the famous occasion in which King Edward refuses to send help to his beleaguered son, despite an appeal from Audley himself:

1. Lord Audley – in fact Sir James Audley – is repeatedly presented in the play as an old man: in line 124, Prince Charles of France goes so far as to address him as 'agèd impotent'. At the time of Crécy he was in fact in his early thirties.

> Audley, content: I will not have a man,
> On pain of death, sent forth to succour him:
> This is the day ordain'd by destiny
> To season his courage with those grievous thoughts,
> That, if he break out, Nestor's years on earth,
> Will make him savour still of this exploit.

The Prince, as we know, never lived Nestor's 'three generations of men'; nor indeed did he fight in the same part of the battle as the old King of Bohemia, whose body he now brings triumphantly to his father as 'this firstfruit of my sword,/Cropp'd and cut down even at the gate of death'. There is no doubt, however, that he fought magnificently, amply deserving the knighthood that, in the play, his father now bestows upon him. He had in fact been knighted the previous July, shortly after the landing in Normandy; but once again Shakespeare is thinking dramatically rather than historically, and the brief ceremony adds immeasurably to the battle's aftermath.[1]

As soon as he had buried his dead, Edward advanced to Calais. He had no legal claim to the city: it had never been English. Even the French had long been put off by its marshy approaches and general difficulty of access; it was only in the past century or so that the Counts of Boulogne had recognized its strategic importance and developed it into the prosperous and strongly fortified city that it had now become. But to the King of England, too, its advantages were clear. Standing at the point where the Channel was at its narrowest, only twenty-two miles from the English coast, Calais promised him not only a far more convenient bridgehead than the ports of Flanders, being a good deal nearer to Gascony, but the all-important control of the eastern approach to the straits. It would not, however, be easy in the taking. Behind its formidable walls, protected by a double ditch fed by the sea itself, there waited a strong and determined garrison under an outstandingly able commander (even though he was a martyr to gout) named Jean de

---

1. It is plain that this scene (III.iv) is meant to end without the last six lines – which make no sense in the present context – and belong somewhere else. A possible explanation is suggested in the New Cambridge edition (p. 133) but need not concern us here.

Vienne. A direct assault was obviously out of the question; the only hope lay in a blockade. And so, early in September, the English encamped on the flat and windy marshes and built what was in effect a small wooden village, named by Edward Villeneuve-le-Hardi. (French was still the language of the English court.) The siege threatened to be long, so it was only sensible to make themselves as comfortable as possible.

Winter came, and spring, and summer – and still Calais held out. The blockade proved in the main successful; but the English fleet, constantly patrolling the roadstead, suffered much harassment from Norman privateers and lost no fewer than fifteen vessels during the siege. Already in October 1346 news had reached the camp that the Scots, traditional allies of France, had attempted a diversion by crossing the Tweed and laying waste the County Palatine of Durham. Edward, however, had made no move against them. He had foreseen the danger and when raising troops for his new offensive had deliberately refrained from calling out the northern border levies, whom he had left under the command of the Nevills, the Percys, the Archbishop of York William Zouche and other local magnates, so that they should be ready to deal with just such an emergency. Soon afterwards came a report that these levies had fallen on the Scots at Neville's Cross just outside Durham, cut them to pieces and taken prisoner their King, David II.[1] More good news followed: Charles of Blois, the French claimant to the duchy of Brittany, had been captured by Sir Thomas Dagworth at La Roche-Darrien, while in Gascony the French army had given up the siege of Aiguillon and retired across the Loire. Edward, however, had refused to be deflected from Calais. The city was now completely blockaded by land and sea; its only hope, as he well knew, lay in the possibility of a relief expedition – of which, after eleven months, there was still no sign.

Finally, at the end of July 1347, King Philip appeared with his army on the cliff at Sangatte, a mile or two to the west of Calais. He was horrified by what he saw. Villeneuve-le-Hardi had become a veritable town. A network of well laid-out streets surrounded a market place,

1. Another casualty of the battle was the famous Black Rood of Scotland, a piece of the True Cross set in an ebony crucifix which St Margaret, wife of King Malcolm Canmore, had left to the Scottish nation on her death in 1093. The English captured it and deposited it in the shrine of St Cuthbert in Durham Cathedral. There it remained till the Reformation, when it was lost and almost certainly destroyed.

where regular markets were held on Wednesdays and Saturdays. There were, writes Froissart, 'haberdashers' and butchers' shops, stalls selling cloth and bread and other necessities, so that almost anything could be bought there. All these things were brought over daily by sea from England, and goods and foodstuffs were also supplied from Flanders.' This prosperous little community could of course have been easily destroyed, had Philip been able to reach it; but Edward, forewarned, had made the necessary dispensations. Loading his ships with archers, catapults and bombards, he had drawn them up in the shallow water along the whole length of coast between Sangatte and Calais, making any advance along the shore impossible. The only other route, through the marshy, swampy ground behind the dunes, depended on a bridge at Nieulay where he had posted his cousin the Earl of Derby (recently arrived from Gascony) with the remaining archers and men-at-arms. The most cursory reconnaissance – effected with the full cooperation of the English – was enough to convince the King of France that the situation was hopeless. He made the usual formal request for a pitched battle at some mutually acceptable spot, but cannot have been surprised when Edward refused it. The next morning he and his army were gone.

The departure of his sovereign told Jean de Vienne all he needed to know. The citizens of Calais were by now near starvation; if Froissart is to be believed, the commander had already expelled 'all poore and meane peple' – those who could not contribute to the defence of the town and simply constituted extra mouths to feed – to the number of 1,700. Further resistance was pointless. He now signalled his readiness to surrender, provided only that the King would promise safe conduct for all the citizens. Edward first refused point-blank: Calais had cost him vast quantities of money and the lives of countless soldiers and sailors, together with almost a year of his own. But when his two envoys, Lord Basset and Sir Walter Manny, returned to report that in that event the city would continue to resist, he relented. Manny – according once again to Froissart – was sent back to Jean de Vienne with new conditions: six of the principal citizens must present themselves before the King, barefoot and bare-headed, with halters round their necks and the keys of the city and of the castle in their hands. With them he would do as he pleased; the rest of the population would be spared.

The English terms were proclaimed in the market place, and immediately the richest of all the burghers, Master Eustache de Saint-Pierre, stepped forward. Before long five others had joined him. There and then the six stripped to their shirts and breeches, donned the halters, took the keys and made their way to the gates, led by Jean de Vienne himself mounted on a pony, his sword reversed in token of submission. On their arrival before the King they knelt before him, presented him with the keys and begged for mercy. Edward refused to listen, and ordered their immediate execution; Sir Walter pleaded with him in vain. Only when Queen Philippa, then heavily pregnant, threw herself on her knees before her husband and begged him to spare them did he finally relent.

The Queen thanked him from the bottom of her heart, then rose to her feet and told the six burghers to rise also. She had the halters taken from their necks and led them into her apartment. They were given new clothes and an ample dinner. Then each was presented with six nobles and they were escorted safely through the English army and went to live in various towns in Picardy.[1]

On Saturday 4 August 1347 King Edward III entered Calais in triumph and gave orders that the entire city be evacuated. The miserable citizens were permitted to take nothing with them: houses and estates, furniture and possessions, all were left behind for the use of the English colonists whom the King brought in to take their places. The descendants of those colonists were to remain there for over two centuries until, on 7 January 1558, Calais was recaptured at last.

For nine years after the fall of Calais, the war was largely forgotten. The Black Death struck France in January 1348, and England the following July; within ten years it had killed an estimated one-third of the population living between India and Iceland. Of those who survived, the majority had other, more pressing anxieties. There were a few minor skirmishes in Gascony and Brittany, and towards the end of 1355 Edward even landed with another army at Calais; but he seems to have thought better of the operation, since he and his men were back in

---

1. There is no reason to doubt the story of the burghers of Calais; nor is there any excuse for Londoners to forget it, since a bronze cast of Rodin's famous group was acquired for the nation in 1915 by the National Art Collections Fund and now stands in Westminster Palace Gardens.

England little more than a month later. Meanwhile successive popes did their best to bring about a lasting peace; if they failed, it was because neither of the protagonists really wanted it. Edward would be satisfied with nothing less than the throne of France; Philip's son John II, who had succeeded his father in 1350, was an incorrigible and impetuous romantic whose dreams of chivalric derring-do were to betray him again and again. For the time being, both monarchs had other business on their minds; when the moment came, however, both would show themselves only too keen to continue the struggle.

In the same year as Edward's abortive Calais expedition the Black Prince, now twenty-five and his father's lieutenant in Gascony, took an army to south-west France, failing to capture Narbonne and Carcassonne but causing appalling devastation and destruction in the surrounding countryside. In 1356 he was more ambitious still, launching raids up and down the Loire to the point where King John determined to teach him a lesson, summoning all the noblemen and knights of the realm to assemble at Chartres in the first week of September with their retinues. The response was almost universal; by the time the army was ready it included the King's four sons, none of them yet out of their teens; the Constable of France, Gauthier de Brienne; two marshals; twenty-six dukes and counts; 334 bannerets; and lesser lords and knights without number, all bringing their own troops. Holinshed refers to three 'battles' (battalions) of 16,000 men each, making a total of 48,000, though he is almost certainly exaggerating. Whatever the precise figure, it was by any account a very considerable force that crossed the Loire at various points and then pressed south with all speed in pursuit of the English, catching up with them on the morning of Sunday 18 September, some seven miles south-east of Poitiers, in the valley of the little river Miosson.[1]

The French were in confident mood. For one thing, they comfortably outnumbered the English, who were probably no more than ten or twelve thousand at most; they also had reason to believe that the invaders were seriously short of food. For the rest of that day the two sides reconnoitred each other's positions and prepared for battle, while the

1. The site of the battle of Poitiers is occupied today by the farm known as La Cardinerie, formerly Maupertuis, a mile or so to the north of the former Benedictine Abbey of Nouaillé.

Cardinal Talleyrand de Périgord, who had been sent by the Pope to attempt to negotiate a peace, shuttled fruitlessly backwards and forwards between the two sides. The Black Prince, who would certainly have avoided the battle if he could, offered to restore all his prisoners without ransom and to return all the castles that he had occupied; but John would accept nothing less than his own personal surrender, with a hundred of his knights – a demand that the Prince not unnaturally refused outright. Consequently, soon after sunrise on the following day, the battle began.

It seems extraordinary that since their defeat at Crécy the French had taken no steps to raise and train enough regiments of longbowmen to pay back the English in their own coin, particularly since John was fully conscious of the danger presented by the English archers. His plan seems to have been first to send a small force of some three hundred mounted knights to charge into their midst and scatter them, before following with the main body of his army – on foot, because the marshy ground and the numerous hedges and ditches were impossible for cavalry to negotiate. The tactic proved disastrous. The knights – who represented the flower of his army and who included the Constable of France and both marshals – succumbed to the usual deluge of arrows, and after this initial massacre the battle was as good as won. The French fought valiantly, but were overwhelmed; and when the fighting was over John himself was among the prisoners. The Prince treated him with elaborate courtesy. Froissart tells of how, the evening after the battle, he gave a supper in his honour, to which he also invited the other noble captives, including thirteen counts, an archbishop and sixty-six barons. 'He himself served in all humility both at the King's table and at the others . . . insisting that he was not worthy to sit himself at the table of so mighty a prince and so brave a soldier.' Seven months later he escorted John personally to London.

The capture of John II, leaving France as it did in the hands of a nineteen-year-old Dauphin, might well have signalled the end of the war; King Edward, however, saw it differently. To him it seemed the perfect opportunity for the final decisive thrust that would win him the French crown. For the next four years he fought hard and often brilliantly; but contrary to his expectations he made no real headway, and early in 1360 he consented to peace negotiations. On 8 May, in the little village of Brétigny near Chartres, the Black Prince and the

Dauphin agreed to the terms of a treaty, subject to confirmation by their respective fathers. The French would recognize Edward's claim to Gascony and Poitou, together with various counties and towns in northern France, including Calais. They would also surrender the city of La Rochelle, of vital importance to England as the centre of the salt trade. John's ransom was fixed at three million gold crowns: he was to be released on payment of the first instalment of one-fifth of the total. No less than forty noble hostages would be given as security for the remainder, which would be paid in six more annual instalments. The King of England, for his part, would agree to renounce his claim to the throne of France and to all other regions of the country.

When the two Kings met at Calais in October, however, Edward insisted that he would make his renunciations only after the transfer to him of all the lands ceded at Brétigny, with a proviso that this should be complete by 1 November 1361. It was a deeply disingenuous stipulation, and both sides knew it. Such transfers were long and complicated; they could not possibly be completed in a single year. The fact of the matter was that Edward was determined to leave his options open. He willingly agreed to easier terms for the payment of the ransom but, as things turned out, it would have been better had the money not been paid at all. In the summer of 1363 one of the hostages, John's second son, the Duke of Anjou, broke his parole and fled. His father, horrified, declared his intention of returning immediately to London. His advisers did everything they could to dissuade him, but he remained firm. 'If good faith and honour are to be banished from the rest of the world,' he is quoted as saying, 'they should still be found in the hearts and words of princes.' He left Paris the week after Christmas, crossed the Channel in midwinter, and arrived in January 1364. Four months later he was dead, 'of an unknown illness'. Edward ordered him a magnificent funeral service at St Paul's before returning the body to France, where it was buried at Saint-Denis.

Let us return now to our play. The first scene of Act IV of *Edward III* introduces Lord Mountford, in conversation with the Earl of Salisbury. Mountford is, more properly, that Jean IV de Montfort who in 1341 claimed the dukedom of Brittany – which had been assigned to the nephew of Philip VI – and did homage for it to Edward III. Unfortunately he was captured in the same year and ended his life as a prisoner in the Louvre; but in the play he has been restored to the dukedom, and his presence therefore suggests that this short scene is set in Brittany. The incident which follows, on the other hand, in which Salisbury persuades one of his French prisoners to obtain for him a letter of safe conduct so that he may join the King at Calais, is inspired by a similar story in Froissart involving not Salisbury but another of Edward's knights, Sir Walter Manny, who had been at the siege of Aiguillon, ridden across France and, as we have seen, had arrived at Calais in time for its submission. Thus, to include it in his play, the dramatist has changed both the location of the incident and its subject. He has also given the prisoner – unidentified in Froissart – the invented name of Villiers.

Scene ii brings us to the walls of besieged Calais, immediately after King Philip's departure. It seems a little odd that Edward in his opening speech should order the siege to begin, since in fact it had already been in progress for almost a year – as is immediately indicated by the appearance of six poor men – representatives, presumably, of Froissart's 1,700 – who, having explained the reasons for their distress, are given money by Edward. There follows a brief interruption by Lord Percy, who enters with two pieces of good news: the first that King David of Scotland has been captured; the second that Queen Philippa, though heavily pregnant, is on her way. Edward then announces – personally, rather than through Sir Walter Manny – his conditions for sparing the people of Calais, giving them two days in which to comply.

Since the story of the six burghers can clearly not be completed without the presence of Philippa, we might have expected some minor telescoping of time to allow for her immediate arrival in the following scene; scene iii, however, comes as a considerable surprise, involving as it does by far the greatest chronological liberty taken in the entire play. It divides naturally into two parts: the first, which must follow shortly after scene i with Salisbury and Mountford, continues the story of Salisbury's letter of safe conduct, with Villiers requesting it from Charles of Normandy.[1] Charles at first objects; their conversation develops into a moral discussion about conflicting oaths and the laws of chivalry and has little bearing on what follows: at last, however, the Duke sees the force of Villiers's argument and Salisbury gets his letter.

---

1. At this point the Duke of Normandy was in fact the future John II. See pp. 18–19 and 23–4.

Then, in line 57, although Charles remains on stage, we suddenly leap forward a whole decade to the field of Poitiers. King John (and by now he really is King John, his father Philip VI having died six years earlier) tells Charles (who is now transmuted into John's eldest son, born in 1350 and Duke of Normandy since his father's accession) that the Black Prince is surrounded and outnumbered. The first of these statements is unhistorical – the Prince's troops were never in such difficulties – the second is true, though John's estimate of the French strength as 'threescore thousand at the least' is obviously an exaggeration.[1] Charles replies by telling his father of a threefold prophecy, the first part of which, 'When feather'd fowl shall make thine army tremble', is reported in both Froissart and Holinshed – in connection, however, not with Poitiers but with Crécy, ten years before.

There follows an extremely unhistorical account of the battle itself. It begins with a conversation between the Prince and his friend Lord Audley, who had fought beside him at Crécy, confirming King John's view of the situation:

> At Cressy field our clouds of warlike smoke
> Chok'd up those French mouths and dissever'd them:
> But now their multitudes of millions hide,
> Masking as 'twere, the beauteous-burning sun;
> Leaving no hope to us but sullen dark
> And eyeless terror of all-ending night.

Audley describes the disposition of the enemy, much as the Mariner did before the battle of Sluys,[2] and the Prince replies with words of encouragement vaguely reminiscent – though they are a good deal less polished – of the St Crispin's Day speech in *Henry V*. Next three French heralds arrive to taunt the Prince – an incident that recalls the scene of the tennis balls in the same play. He dismisses them with contempt, after which he and Audley prepare themselves for imminent death.

Then, suddenly, the sky darkens and a strange silence falls, shortly to be broken by a flight of ravens croaking over the French army. The prophecy is fulfilled and panic ensues, as more and more Frenchmen

1. See p. 37.
2. See p. 24.

take to their heels. At this point Lord Salisbury is brought before the French King, having tried unsuccessfully to make his way through the enemy ranks.[1] John orders his execution, but Salisbury shows his letter of safe conduct, signed by Charles of Normandy, who is fortunately present. An argument ensues between Charles and his father on the same lines as that between Villiers and Charles in IV.iii; the King finally capitulates and allows his prisoner to proceed on his way to Calais, but not before he has delivered a parting shot:

> Some two leagues hence there is a lofty hill . . .
> And thence behold the wretched Prince of Wales,
> Hoop'd with a band of iron round about.
> After which sight to Calice [Calais] spur amain,
> And say, the prince was smother'd and not slain:
> And tell the king, this is not all his ill,
> For I will greet him ere he thinks I will.

Meanwhile, thanks to the ravens, the tide of battle has turned and the entire French army is in flight. King John himself is taken prisoner and brought before the Black Prince; but the Prince appears far more concerned with his friend Audley, who has been seriously – though, as we later learn, not fatally – wounded.

With Act V, scene i – the last scene in the play – we are back in Calais for the conclusion of the story of the burghers. 'The two days' respite is not yet expir'd', and they duly present themselves before King Edward 'in their shirts, bare foot, with halters about their necks'. He at first condemns them, but Queen Philippa intercedes and he yields to her entreaty. Next comes a brief interlude with a certain John Copland, who has been fortunate enough to capture King David of Scotland at Neville's Cross a short time before. Despite Philippa's commission from her husband to govern in his name during his absence, Copland has refused to deliver his prisoner to anyone but the King himself and has accordingly brought him to Calais. The Queen is

---

1. Salisbury's letter was issued nine or ten years before, and Calais had already been nearly a decade in English hands. Several obvious questions arise: did he take all that time to ride through France? Is Poitiers really on the way between Brittany and Calais? But to ask such questions is to miss the point. For the purposes of the play, the siege of Calais and the battle of Poitiers were virtually contemporaneous.

understandably irritated, but Edward is pleased by Copland's flattering explanation of his motives and rewards him with a knighthood.

The scene continues with the arrival of Lord Salisbury, who brings tragic news:

> Here stood a battle of ten thousand horse:
> There twice as many pikes, in quadrant-wise . . .
> And in the midst, like to a slender point
> Within the compass of the horizon . . .
> Or as a bear fast chain'd unto a stake, –
> Stood famous Edward [the Black Prince], still expecting when
> Those dogs of France would fasten on his flesh . . .
> The battles join: and, when we could no more
> Discern the difference 'twixt the friend and foe . . .
> Away we turn'd our wat'ry eyes, with sighs
> As black as powder fuming into smoke.

Consternation follows; but a moment later, while the distraught Queen is mourning her son and the furious King is swearing vengeance, a herald enters to announce the arrival of the Prince in splendid health, accompanied by Audley – now apparently recovered – and his prisoners, King John of France and his son Philip. Edward is quick to taunt the captive King:

> So, John of France, I see you keep your word.
> You promis'd to be sooner with ourself
> Than we did think for, and 'tis so indeed:

The Prince then delivers a fine patriotic speech, leaving, however, the play's last words to his father:

> A day or two within this haven-town,
> God willing, then for England we'll be shipp'd,
> Where, in a happy hour, I trust, we shall
> Arrive, three kings, two princes, and a queen.

Once again, Shakespeare – if Shakespeare it is – has taken his usual liberties with historic truth. Edward and Philippa were not in France after Poitiers, though they were as we know present at Calais. King David of Scotland was never taken to Calais, but remained in London and Odiham in Hampshire between his capture in 1346 and his eventual ransom in 1357. But in the context of the play such details are insignificant enough. Perhaps because of its suspected multiple authorship, *Edward III* probably contains more inaccuracies than the other plays in the canon. The fact remains – and cannot be too often repeated or too strongly emphasized – that to a dramatist, accuracy is at most of secondary importance. The main events of Edward's life are all there; and the average playgoer, whether of the sixteenth or the twenty-first century, having no previous knowledge of the period, will have come away with a mental picture which, for all its bold lines and high colour, will not be so very far wrong.

The story of the last sad years of Edward's reign can be briefly told. In 1362 he made over Gascony and Poitou to his eldest son, to be held of himself as sovereign. At Bordeaux the Black Prince established a luxurious and sophisticated court where, wrote the Chandos Herald,[1] 'since God was born, never was open house kept so handsomely and honourably.' He fed 'more than fourscore knights and full four times as many squires' at his table, and maintained a vast retinue of his own: pages, valets, cooks, stewards, butlers, grooms, huntsmen and falconers, insisting that he himself be served only by a knight wearing golden spurs. His lovely wife Joan was arrayed as no Queen of England had ever been, in furs, velvets and brocades, all ablaze with jewels. At his court 'there abode all nobleness, all joy and jollity, largesse, gentleness and honour, and all his subjects and all his men loved him right dearly.'

The Herald may well have been right as far as the Prince's English followers were concerned; but the Gascons and Poitevins did not share their enthusiasm. For one thing, they were perfectly well aware that all this luxury was maintained at their expense, being made possible only by a savage taxation that increased year by year. For another, they themselves were treated as second-class citizens, and given few if any important or lucrative posts in the administration. The grumbling grew louder still when, early in 1367, the Prince involved himself in the

1. The Herald of Sir John Chandos – whose own name is unknown – wrote a fulsomely admiring biography of the Black Prince in French verse: see Bibliography.

continuing struggle between Pedro the Cruel, King of Castile[1] – whose subjects had risen in revolt – and his bastard half-brother Don Enrique of Trastamara. Pedro was strongly supported by Edward of England, two of whose sons were to marry Spanish Infantas before many more years had passed; on the other hand he had incurred the hatred of King John's son and successor Charles V, whose sister-in-law he had married, then abandoned and quite possibly murdered. Seeing his throne now seriously threatened, he had appealed to the Black Prince who, never able to resist the lure of battle, led his army across the Pyrenees, where he was joined by another force under his brother, John of Gaunt. On 3 April 1367, at Najera, the Prince won the third great victory of his career: a victory that ranked with those of Crécy and Poitiers, put Don Enrique to flight and re-established Pedro firmly on the throne of Castile.

But Najera, glorious as it was, failed to impress the Gascons. It was anyway no business of theirs, and when Pedro predictably defaulted on his promise to defray all the expenses of the expedition and the Prince in his turn announced new annual hearth taxes on the people of Guyenne, they decided that they had had enough and lodged a formal appeal to the King of France. Charles V was an intelligent, capable young man who had no delusions about the dangers ahead. Before taking any action he consulted a number of distinguished jurists from as far afield as Bologna; then, after carefully considering their opinions, he wrote to Edward in December 1368, informing him that he was legally entitled to uphold the appeal and was in fact doing so. Edward, furious at what he considered an unwarrantable incursion on his own prerogatives, laid claim once again to the title of King of France; Charles replied by declaring all his French lands confiscate. It was an almost exact repetition of what had occurred with the French King's grandfather, Philip VI, thirty-two years before. In those days, however, Edward had been just twenty-five, in full possession of his youth and vigour; now, at fifty-seven, he was failing fast and no match for his shrewd young adversary.

Thanks to the outstanding military ability of his eldest son, this should not have constituted a serious problem; but the Black Prince's health

1. Castile and Aragon were separate kingdoms until shortly after the marriage of Ferdinand of Aragon and Isabella of Castile in 1469.

was also causing concern. Soon after Najera he suffered an attack of dysentery, which soon gave way to dropsy. By the end of 1367 all his once-formidable energy seemed to be draining away. He grew fat and bloated, and two years later was 'weighed down by so great infirmity of body that he could scarcely sit upon his horse'. At the siege of Limoges in 1370 he had commanded from a litter, the brutality of his subsequent order for the massacre of some 3,000 of its citizens, regardless of age or sex, being at least partly attributable to the acute pain from which he was by now never free. He returned to England in January 1371 and retired at the age of only forty to his manor at Berkhamsted, where – apart from a brief expedition with his father in 1372 – he survived for the next five years, dying on Trinity Sunday, 8 June 1376. By now Gascony was as good as lost. John of Gaunt and others did what they could, but the French remained ensconced in their walled towns and castles, refusing to fight and frustrating all efforts to dislodge them. Brittany, left undefended, was quickly recaptured; and by the time a two-year truce was concluded at Bruges in 1375 the English possessions in France had been reduced to the city of Calais and a narrow strip of coast between Bordeaux and Bayonne – a poor enough inheritance for the Prince's son Richard when, just two years later, the crown was laid upon his head.

King Edward survived his eldest son for little over a year. On the Sunday before the Feast of John the Baptist, 21 June 1377, he died in his palace at Richmond. He had reigned for just over half a century – rather too long in fact, since although he was still only sixty-four, the last fifteen years of his life had been increasingly clouded by a premature senility. It had attacked both his mind and his body, rendering him powerless to control either the ambitious, self-seeking courtiers by whom he was surrounded or the intrigues of his mistress, Alice Perrers. After the death of Queen Philippa in 1369, his decline had accelerated rapidly. Philippa had tolerated his affair with Alice, even going so far as to install her as a Maid of the Bedchamber; she had also advised him, encouraged him, constantly reminded him of his duties as a King and prevented him from drinking too much. Bereft of her, he had slipped gradually into his long dotage.

For most of his reign he had been a good king, though not a great one. With his father Edward II, the prestige of the English Crown had sunk to its nadir; Edward III, succeeding at the age of fourteen, had restored its reputation and given back to his people their self-respect. Tall and vigorous, with thick, long, golden hair and beard, he looked every inch a King and acted like one, indefatigable on the battlefield, the hunting field and, it was said, the bedchamber. Though never outstandingly intelligent, he possessed plenty of good sound common sense and a degree of self-confidence that frequently made him seem cleverer than he was. At Crécy, Poitiers and countless lesser engagements, his armies earned for themselves – and for him – a reputation for valour and military skill unequalled by any English monarch before or since. Thus, even though his private life was known to be far from blameless, he had earned the respect, admiration and even the love of his subjects, and had maintained them till the end. At his death he was genuinely mourned, and not only by the English: his old enemy Charles V of France ordered a requiem mass at the Sainte-Chapelle in Paris, 'with as much pomp and ceremony', writes Jean Froissart, 'as if King Edward had been his own cousin'. It was to be a very long time before England was to look upon his like again.

2

The Young Richard

[1377–1381]

'In what way are those whom we call lords greater masters than ourselves? How have they deserved it? Why do they hold us in bondage? . . . Let us go to the King — he is young — and show him how we are oppressed, and tell him that we want things to be changed, else we will change them ourselves. If we go in good earnest and all together, many of those who are called serfs and are held in subjection will follow us to get their freedom. And when the King sees and hears us, he will remedy the evil, either willingly or otherwise.'

JOHN BALL, QUOTED BY FROISSART

Queen Philippa had borne her husband twelve children, of whom seven had been sons. Of the five of those sons who survived to manhood, the first had been the Black Prince; the second, Lionel Duke of Clarence, had died as early as 1368, at the age of thirty; the third consequently plays a part in this story far more important than any of his brothers. Having been born in 1340 at Ghent in the Low Countries, he was universally known as John of Ghent, or Gaunt. In 1359 he had married his cousin, Blanche of Lancaster, by whom he had had a son, Henry; and soon after the death of his father-in-law he was created Duke of Lancaster in his own right. The duchy brought with it vast estates in the north, and with it John — who also possessed the three earldoms of Leicester, Lincoln and Derby — became, after the King himself, the richest and most powerful man in England. Blanche died young, in 1369 — Geoffrey Chaucer, who was on her husband's payroll, wrote his enchanting *Book of the Duchess* in her memory — and in 1371 John married Constance, elder daughter and co-heiress of Pedro the Cruel of Castile and Leon, to whose titles — and later to whose crown — he also laid claim, although he never succeeded in making them his own.

Of the two remaining sons, Edmund of Langley was born at the royal manor of King's Langley in 1341, created Earl of Cambridge in 1362 and Duke of York in 1385. For him his father arranged a marriage to the younger of Pedro's two daughters, Constance's sister Isabella. Though he was twice to act as Keeper of the Realm, Edmund was, as we shall see, a man of little intelligence or ability. The youngest son, Thomas of Woodstock – born in 1355 after three more girls – seems to have been something of an intellectual, possessing as he did one of the finest private libraries in the country. He was greatly aided in its acquisition by the considerable wealth of his wife Eleanor, one of the joint heiresses of Humphrey Bohun, Earl of Hereford, Essex and Northampton.

The five royal princesses were a good deal less fortunate than their brothers. Two died in childhood and two more – Mary and Margaret, respectively wives of John IV, Duke of Brittany and of John Hastings, Earl of Pembroke – found married life too much for them and did not long survive their weddings. The eldest, Isabella, became the wife of Enguerrand de Coucy,[1] one of the richest and most distinguished of the forty French knights who were being kept as hostages in England as security for the as yet unpaid ransom of the King of France.[2] In the hopes that he might settle permanently in England, Edward had made him Earl of Bedford and admitted him to the recently formed Order of the Garter;[3] but de Coucy was to return to France as soon as he decently could after the death of his father-in-law, subsequently sending his unwanted wife back again to England with their younger daughter Philippa.

The laws of the royal succession were less clear in the fourteenth century than they are today, and after the death of the Black Prince there were no less than three potential aspirants to the throne. John of

1. He is also the central figure in Barbara Tuchman's brilliant portrait of the fourteenth century, *A Distant Mirror*.

2. See p. 38.

3. Recent research has done much to confirm the old story, told by both Selden and Polydore Vergil, of the young Countess of Salisbury – with whom the King was at that time in love – dropping her garter at a ball held in Calais in 1347 to celebrate the fall of the town, and of Edward picking it up and binding it round his own leg, rebuking his tittering courtiers with the words *Honi soit qui mal y pense*, 'Evil be to him who evil thinks'. If the story is indeed true, was the Countess his own future daughter-in-law? (see below, p. 55).

Gaunt could well have claimed it for himself, as the oldest surviving son of the dead King. So too – though with rather less justification – could Edmund Mortimer, Earl of March, son-in-law of John's elder brother Lionel, Duke of Clarence, who had walked with Edward's three sons immediately behind the coffin at his funeral. But Edward, doddering as he may have been, had taken all possible precautions to ensure a smooth transfer of power. 'On Christmas Day 1376,' writes Froissart,

he held a great and solemn feast in his palace of Westminster, which all the prelates, earls, barons and knights of England were commanded to attend. And there Richard, the Prince's son, was raised up and carried before the King, who invested him in the presence of the lords just mentioned with the succession to the throne of England, to hold it after his death; and he seated him at his own side. He then required an oath from all prelates, barons, knights, officers of the cities and towns, of the ports and frontier-posts of England, that they would recognize him as their King.

There must have been many people present at that feast who questioned the wisdom of entrusting the throne to a boy of ten. Royal minorities were dangerous things; John of Gaunt, who for some time already had been regent in all but name, might certainly have seemed a more sensible choice. But he was dangerously unpopular, particularly in the city of London, and Edward – who had himself succeeded at the age of only fourteen – doubtless thought it better that John should govern through his nephew rather than in his own name. And so it was that on Thursday 16 July 1377 young Richard, son of Edward the Black Prince and his wife Joan – 'the Fair Maid of Kent' – and himself 'fair among men as another Absalom',[1] was crowned at Westminster by the Archbishop of Canterbury, Simon Sudbury. The coronation service was appallingly long, and was followed by a state banquet which continued even longer; it was hardly surprising that by the end of the day its principal participant was so exhausted that he had to be carried back to his palace by his tutor Sir Simon Burley, losing one of his slippers on the way.

*

1. Adam of Usk, *Chronicle*.

Joan of Kent had been delivered of her second son at the stroke of ten on the morning of the Feast of the Epiphany, Wednesday 6 January 1367, in the Abbey of St Andrew at Bordeaux. For the first four years of his life Richard had an elder brother, called Edward after his father and grandfather and born at Angoulême two years before him; but Edward of Angoulême had died in 1371 at the age of six and Richard, small and sickly as he was, was thenceforth their only child. Many years later his cousin Henry Bolingbroke was to claim that he was not the son of the Black Prince at all, but of a Bordeaux priest; such an accusation, however, was only to be expected in the circumstances, and was almost certainly baseless. All that we know of Joan suggests that she was faithful to her husband, and he for his part loved her much.

Richard returned to England with his family in the year of his brother's death, and for the six years up to his coronation – years which were spent, presumably, with his parents at Berkhamsted – we hear little of him. There can be no doubt that the principal influence on him during that most formative period of his life was his mother; and since she was to maintain that influence until her death in 1385, it may be worthwhile saying a little more about her before this story continues. Born in 1328, she was the daughter of Edmund of Woodstock, Earl of Kent, sixth son of King Edward I. Only two years after her birth, her father was beheaded for his opposition to Edward II's widow, Isabella of France, and her lover Roger Mortimer;[1] and Joan was brought up by Queen Philippa at the court of her cousin, Edward III. Her nick-name, 'the Fair Maid of Kent', was richly deserved: she was, according to Froissart, *en son temps la plus belle de tout la roiaulme d'Engleterre et la plus amoureuse*. Not surprisingly she had many suitors, including William de Montacute, Earl of Salisbury; but at an early stage she fell in love with his steward, Sir Thomas Holland, and entered into a pre-contract of matrimony with him. Unfortunately, however, before their marriage could be solemnized Holland was called away to the wars; and Salisbury took advantage of his absence to marry Joan himself. Whether she gave her willing consent to this second commitment seems unlikely; at all events, when Holland on his return in 1349 successfully petitioned the Pope for the restitution of his conjugal rights she went back to him at

1. See p. 16.

once, and the two lived – so far as we know – happily together for the next eleven years, until his death in 1360.

Joan – since the death of her brother eight years before Countess of Kent in her own right – was, at thirty-two, still relatively young and devastatingly attractive; and it was not long before she caught the eye of the Black Prince. There were initial obstacles to their marriage. Not only was the Prince her cousin at a single remove, he was also godfather to her elder son Thomas Holland, a spiritual relationship which in the eyes of the Church created every bit as much of a problem as the physical one. Eventually, however, the King – himself not altogether immune to the Countess's charms – was persuaded to intercede with the Pope, and the two were married at Lambeth in October 1361. For the rest of her life, in England and in Aquitaine, as wife and as widow, Joan seems to have been universally loved and respected, and by no one more than by Richard her son.

Inevitably, the influence of Richard's father was less strong than that of his mother. For most of the first four years of the boy's life the Black Prince was away on campaign; after the family's return to England in 1371 he was ill and largely incapacitated, as well as being deeply distressed by the death of his elder son, whom he had always preferred to the younger. Though not ill-disposed towards Richard, he seems never to have altogether forgiven him for his slight stature and unimpressive physique. He certainly made no allowances for such defects: he was determined that the boy should be brought up as a knight and a warrior just as he himself had been, and Richard's tutors were given instructions to build up his strength and endurance and to give him a thorough training in the arts of war. The result was a feeling of inadequacy which he never managed entirely to overcome, and which was made the more intolerable by his exaggerated conception of kingship, his acute consciousness of his own royal blood and his determination to be not only a good king but a great one. An additional irritation may well have been the brilliance of his two half-brothers Thomas and John Holland, both of whom, though much older than he was – Thomas by seventeen years and John by probably fourteen or fifteen – excelled at all military and chivalric pursuits; Thomas had actually been knighted by the Black Prince on a Castilian battlefield in the year of Richard's birth.

Although the young King was still only ten and a half at the time of his coronation, there was no official regency. His mother continued to act as his guardian, while day-to-day government was entrusted to a council of twelve members, from which Richard's royal uncles were perhaps rather surprisingly excluded. There was no doubt, on the other hand, as to where the real power lay. John of Gaunt, Duke of Lancaster, occupied a unique position in the kingdom. His lands were said to extend over one-third of the entire country, while for many years he maintained at his own expense a personal retinue of no fewer than 125 knights and 132 esquires, effectively a sizeable private army. His palace of the Savoy[1] on the Thames was more magnificent than anything his nephew could boast. Such a man, it need hardly be said, might well have constituted a serious danger to the peace of the realm. He was, after all, Edward III's eldest surviving son, already thirty-seven years old at the time of Richard's coronation and possessed of all the wisdom, maturity and experience that his young nephew so obviously lacked. At a time when, after England's recent reverses in the French wars, such qualities were desperately needed, it would have been easy for him to have claimed the crown for himself. Even after the coronation had taken place he could have attacked Richard's legitimacy by challenging either the papal decision of 1349 that upheld his mother's contract with Sir Thomas Holland or the dispensation of 1361 permitting her to marry the Black Prince; similar attempts had been made before, and with Gaunt's money and influence he might well have succeeded. It is to his credit that he did none of these things, but remained a loyal subject throughout his life.

This is not to say that relations between the two were invariably easy, still less that Gaunt was ever popular among his countrymen. Just as he was the most powerful figure in the kingdom, he was also the most hated. With his father and elder brother both dead, it was inevitable that he should be regarded as the man most responsible for the decline in English fortunes over the past decade. Nor could his immense wealth and the ostentation of his court fail to arouse envy and mistrust in the hearts of those less fortunate than himself, nobles and commoners alike. It was well known, too, that despite the time he spent furthering his

---

1. The palace had been built in the thirteenth century by Peter, the future Count of Savoy and uncle of Henry III's Queen, Eleanor. Some idea of its size can be gained from the fact that it covered the area now occupied by the Savoy Hotel, Theatre and Chapel, the Victoria Embankment, Embankment Gardens and the west wing of Somerset House.

claim through his second wife to the throne of Castile, he in fact paid her little attention, preferring to spend his time with his daughters' governess, Katherine Swynford. Various other rumours, less well founded but a good deal more unsavoury, were also in circulation by the year preceding his nephew's accession: that Gaunt was not Edward's son at all, having been smuggled into Ghent Abbey to replace a daughter born to Queen Philippa; that he had poisoned his first wife's sister and was only awaiting his opportunity to do the same to Richard; and that he was secretly plotting with the Pope against the King.

Matters had come to a head early in 1377, when his protégé John Wycliffe, the radical Oxford scholar who had already become famous as a preacher against ecclesiastical abuses, was summoned to appear before the bench of bishops on charges of heresy. Seeing this – rightly – as a challenge to himself, Gaunt had engaged four doctors of divinity to speak in Wycliffe's defence; but when he attended the inquiry in person, attended by an armed retinue, in the Lady Chapel of St Paul's, it soon became clear that he had no intention of allowing the trial to continue. After a furious shouting match between himself and the Bishop of London, William Courtenay, the proceedings broke up in confusion, though not before he had announced his intention of imposing martial law throughout the city. This, however, proved a grave mistake. Courtenay and his fellow bishops had no difficulty in stirring up the London mob at this threat to their civil liberties, and a crowd of several thousand besieged the palace of the Savoy, hung the arms of the Duchy of Lancaster, reversed as a sign of treason, in Cheapside and pursued everyone they found wearing the ducal livery all the way to Westminster. Gaunt himself was obliged to seek refuge with his sister-in-law, the widowed Princess Joan, across the river in Kennington.

Peace was restored at last, thanks largely to Bishop Courtenay. The mayor, who had played a major part in the rioting, was deposed and a marble pillar was erected in Cheapside bearing the arms of Lancaster – now right way up – on a gilded shield. But it was only after Richard's accession a few months later that the quarrel was finally settled. In the presence of a delegation of Londoners, come to request that the new King should pay a formal visit to the city and compose the unfortunate differences between themselves and the Duke of Lancaster, Gaunt fell somewhat dramatically at the King's feet and begged him to pardon them. Richard of course did so, thereby acquiring an instant reputation as a peacemaker and ensuring an enthusiastic reception for his coronation a few days later.

All those concerned had good reason to congratulate themselves on the surprisingly happy conclusion to what had at one moment appeared a dangerous crisis; both sides, it seemed, had been taught a salutary lesson that they would not quickly forget. All too soon, however, both were to realize that the storming of the Savoy was but a pale rehearsal of the infinitely more serious confrontation which was already on its way.

The first four years of Richard's reign have been described by one of the leading historians of the period as 'dreary in the extreme'[1] – which, where domestic affairs were concerned, they were. On the international scene, however, the situation was eventful enough, the death in March 1378 of Pope Gregory XI having resulted in a schism in which two rival candidates, both elected by the same body of cardinals within a few weeks of each other, were desperately struggling for recognition by the princes of Europe. The real issue at stake was whether the Papacy should move back to Rome – as Gregory had attempted to move it eighteen months before his death – or whether it should respect the wishes of the French cardinals and remain at Avignon, where it had been since 1307. Of the two candidates the first to have been elected, Urban VI, had against all expectations opted for Rome; and it was this decision, combined with the Pope's overbearing and dictatorial behaviour towards the cardinals, which had resulted in their attempt to replace him and their consequent uncanonical election of the unmistakably pro-French Clement VII. The very fact that France and Scotland supported Clement was enough to persuade England to side with Urban: by doing so it also gained a powerful new ally in the French war. At home, on the other hand, the years were marked only by inconclusive manoeuvrings on the part of the several factions circling around the throne, all jockeying for position and rendering executive decisions virtually impossible.

Then, in the summer of 1381, something occurred which shook English society to its foundations: almost simultaneously, in Kent, Essex

1. Anthony Steel, *Richard II*, p. 44.

and East Anglia, in Hampshire and Somerset, in Northamptonshire, Yorkshire and the Wirral, the peasantry rose in revolt. To find the reasons we have to go back some thirty-five years to the Black Death, which had resulted in an acute shortage of labour. In former times the average villein or serf had remained on the land where he had been born, working the holding which had been allowed him and frequently suffering cruel, even inhuman exploitation. Not only was he bound to give service to his lord; he was also subject to a number of crippling extortions whose very names are today almost forgotten: merchet, on the marriage or pregnancy of his daughter; lairwite, as a penalty for adultery; heriot, on any form of inheritance. On his death the lord took his best animal and best garment; when his wife died he forfeited her best dress and their best bed, the second best going to the Church. With the outbreak of the plague, the situation was changed entirely. Instead of living at the mercy of his master he found himself a marketable commodity, potentially mobile and able to sell his labour to the highest bidder.

At least in theory: in practice things were not so easy. Wages and prices began, inevitably, to spiral; and in a desperate attempt to hold them down and to prevent a complete breakdown of the accepted social order, successive parliaments had introduced increasingly strict legislation to ensure that the peasantry remained, in both senses of the word, in its place. This legislation had begun as early as 1351 with the Statute of Labourers, which effectively made it illegal to travel from one town or district to another in search of increased pay. Subsequent laws strengthened these provisions still further: after 1360–61 such offences were even punishable by branding.

Not surprisingly, the peasants found these new measures intolerable: having for the first time come to some understanding of their true worth, they were now forbidden to turn it to their own advantage. In protest, many of them began to form leagues – precursors of our modern trades unions – and to withhold their traditional service. The landlords, faced with what was essentially a series of strikes, had little alternative but to meet their demands. The new laws proved impossible to enforce; and there consequently grew up in the 1360s and 70s a whole new class of wandering labourers able to fix their own pay and conditions of work and, after a few years, to buy leases on their own account. The yeoman farmer was born – independent, conscious of his rights, no longer prepared to be victimized. In the words of the already popular saw:

> When Adam delved and Eve span,
> Who was then the gentleman?[1]

It was an interesting question, but not one which greatly exercised the English parliament when in 1379, to defray the continuing expense of the war, it authorized a poll tax, to be collected from every lay member of the adult population. Such a measure was bound to raise an outcry; but the tax was at least graduated in such a way that the burden fell less heavily upon the poor, and in the end it was grudgingly accepted. The difficulty was that the collectors found it almost impossible to apply the necessary means test; there was large-scale evasion and the money was slow in coming in. The parliament of the following year, therefore, still more desperate for funds, trebled the basic amount of the tax from one groat per head to three – and demanded it indiscriminately from rich and poor alike.

It was a disastrous mistake. By the spring of 1381 there was evidence of widespread discontent in many parts of the country, particularly in the south-east; and on 1 June the storm broke. At Brentwood in Essex a commission of inquiry into non-payment of taxes headed by Sir Robert Belknap, Chief Justice of the King's Bench, was spontaneously set upon. In the ensuing struggle three jurors were killed; Sir Robert himself was seized, and was lucky to escape with his life. He was eventually released only after he had promised never to preside over another session. Meanwhile the revolt spread quickly throughout the county and across the river into Kent, where on 6 June insurgents from Gravesend stormed Rochester Castle and freed all its prisoners. Much the same occurred at Maidstone, where among the liberated was a fire-breathing priest named John Ball, who had been imprisoned by the Archbishop of Canterbury, Simon Sudbury, for his inflammatory preaching. At Maidstone too there appeared for the first time the man who was to assume the direction of the entire revolt, Wat Tyler – 'a

---

1. This couplet was long attributed to John Ball, one of the leaders of the revolt; it is in fact a good deal older, being commonly found in sermons of the early fourteenth century.

tiler of roofs', Froissart is careful to specify, 'and a wicked and nasty fellow.' Under Tyler's leadership – he seems to have had some military background – and with John Ball as a sort of spiritual adviser, the rebels marched on the capital, looting the Archbishop's Palace at Canterbury on the way. Covering seventy miles in two days, they reached Blackheath, on the eastern outskirts of London, on Wednesday 12 June.

The fourteen-year-old King, meanwhile, had hurried from Windsor to London, where he had prudently settled in the Tower;[1] but although fully aware of the gravity of the situation he does not seem to have been unduly alarmed. As the rebels had made clear from the outset, their quarrel was not with him but with his ministers: with officers of state such as Archbishop Sudbury (who was also Chancellor of England), the Treasurer Sir Robert Hales and John Legge, a royal serjeant-at-arms and administrator of the poll tax in Kent. By extension they also resented the entire body of churchmen, lawyers and the rich – above all men like John of Gaunt, who could have paid the poll tax for half a dozen counties without noticing it but who preferred to make an arrogant exhibition of his wealth, which they found not only unjust but insulting. Right, they had no doubt, was on their side. Even their looting had been done in the name of equality: like the already legendary Robin Hood, they had robbed the rich only to help the poor. Their consciences were clear. Their slogan was 'King Richard and the Communes', their purpose to petition their sovereign to right their wrongs – something which could be achieved, they thought, with a stroke of his pen. Once this was done, they would happily disperse to their homes.

In the circumstances, therefore, there was nothing very surprising in the King's decision on the morning of 13 June to cross the river to Greenwich, where Tyler and his friends were waiting, and to enter into direct negotiations; but neither can we wonder that, as the royal party approached the further bank and Sudbury, Hales and their colleagues saw the size and temper of the crowd gathered to receive them, they lost their nerve and refused to allow their master to land. It would have been better had they never set out. The sudden about-turn of the state barge and its hasty return to the Tower both infuriated the rebels and encouraged them; nothing could now stop them launching a major

1. The Tower of London was in those days a fortified palace as well as a prison.

assault on London. At first, still unable to cross the river, they sacked St Mary's, Southwark – now the Cathedral – and unlocked the gates of the Marshalsea prison before going on to Lambeth, where they burnt the Chancery records. Only then did they swing round once more and head for London Bridge – which, possibly through treachery on the part of those to whom it was entrusted but more probably because it was impossible to defend against such numbers, was opened to them.

The capital now lay at their mercy. The Fleet prison was stormed, and its prisoners released; the New Temple, property of the Knights of St John of Jerusalem, was sacked, together with Hales's house nearby. The rebels then moved on along Fleet Street to the Savoy, where the people of London had seen the opportunity they had long been awaiting and were already getting to work. In a veritable orgy of destruction, the contents of the greatest private house in the kingdom were destroyed, trampled under foot or flung into the Thames; the building itself was burnt to ashes. This time, we are told, there was no looting, on Tyler's specific orders: one man who tried it was himself thrown into the flames. Gaunt himself was fortunately away in the north, negotiating with the Scots; had he been found in the palace it is unlikely that he would have survived.

The rebels then turned north again to the headquarters of the Knights at Clerkenwell and destroyed it – palace, church and hospital;[1] it burnt, we are told, for seven days. Meanwhile a separate band of insurgents under a man calling himself Jack Straw had arrived from Essex, and somewhere on the outskirts of London had been reinforced by a further detachment from Hertfordshire. This combined force had then marched independently along the north bank of the Thames, taking possession of Highbury and Mile End, where Straw had finally ordered a halt. It was for the King to make the next move. Accordingly on the evening of the 13th Richard himself, speaking from the walls of the Tower, addressed the crowd on the Green below and summoned all those concerned to meet him at Mile End on the following day. In view of

1. Of the church, part of the twelfth-century chancel and crypt still survive. The existing gatehouse, which forms a bridge over St John's Lane, dates from 1504. After the dissolution of the English Order of the Knights of St John by Henry VIII it fulfilled various functions, and at one point during the reign of Elizabeth I provided offices for the Master of the Revels, who was also licenser of plays. Shakespeare himself must have visited it on innumerable occasions.

the panic which had overtaken his ministers only a few hours before, the probability is that this decision was made on his own initiative; even if it were not, it argues considerable courage on the part of a delicate and inexperienced boy of fourteen.

Thus it was that on the morning of Friday 14 June the young King, having advised Sudbury and his friends to try to escape by water, rode out of London with the mayor, William Walworth, to confront the insurgents. As he approached, several of his followers drew back; but he himself rode confidently forward to the rebels' camp. He found them reasonable, but determined. Their leaders knelt and bade him welcome, assuring him that they sought no other sovereign but himself; they demanded, however, that 'the traitors' should be surrendered to them at once. Richard replied that no man was a traitor until he was tried by due process of law; but if anyone were found guilty after such process, they were welcome to do with him as they liked. They then presented the King with a petition for the abolition of villeinage, and another for the right to sell their labour instead by free and open contract and to rent land at an annual cost of fourpence an acre. These requests he instantly granted, promising to confirm them with letters bearing his Great Seal, and to send a royal banner, as an additional token of his good faith, to each of their towns of origin. Soon afterwards he bid them a friendly farewell. He had capitulated on almost every point; but he had at least established friendly relations with them and there seemed no reason why, having obtained all that they demanded, they should not now disperse.

Thus, as Richard rode homeward, he was in all probability well satisfied with what he had achieved. He was not to remain so for long. He returned to find that the mob had forced its way into the Tower. How it managed to do so we shall never know. The garrison, we are told, numbered 600 men-at-arms and the same number of archers, all tried and trusted men; had they resisted, there can be little doubt that they would have been more than a match for the largely unarmed and untrained rabble outside. Yet for some reason they seem to have made no effort to protect those who were in their care. Sudbury, Hales, Legge and John of Gaunt's doctor, a friar named William Appleton, had been seized in the chapel where they were at their devotions, dragged out to Tower Hill and executed on the spot, after which their heads were paraded through the city and set up on pikes at London

Bridge. The mob had then burst into the chamber of the King's mother, leaving her in a state of nervous collapse. Her bed had been smashed to pieces and one or two of the intruders, she claimed, had even attempted familiarities with her, although she had not been seriously harmed. After their departure she had been taken by boat to Baynard's Castle on the riverside at Blackfriars,[1] where her son subsequently joined her.

The rebels from Essex and Hertfordshire now seem to have been satisfied; at any rate they were to give no further trouble. Wat Tyler and the men of Kent, on the other hand, remained to be reckoned with; and on the following day, Saturday 15 June, after attending mass at Westminster Abbey, the King decided on a further confrontation – this time at Smithfield, then as now the principal cattle market of the capital. It was plain from the outset, however, that the meeting would not be as easy as that at Mile End. For a week now Tyler had enjoyed a position of undisputed authority over his men. Success – and bloodshed – had gone to his head. He approached the King arrogantly, not on foot in the manner of a subject, but on horseback, determined to pick a quarrel. His demands, too, went a good deal further than those made by the men of Essex; they included the confiscation of all Church estates, the abolition of all lordships save that of the King himself and of all bishoprics but one. Conciliatory as always, Richard pretended not to notice his insolence and assured him that all his demands would be met; but this time, perhaps, he gave in a little too readily, arousing Tyler's suspicions and making him more overbearing than ever. As the conversation continued, tempers among the King's followers began to run high; and at last the Mayor of London, Walworth, able to bear it no longer, barked out an order. Immediately a group of his men set upon Tyler and dragged him from his horse; no sooner was he on the ground than one of the attendant squires, Standish by name, cut him down with his broadsword.

Here was a moment of supreme danger. Seeing the fate of their leader, the rebels surged forward. The royal party was outnumbered many times over, and could easily have been massacred. Many of those

---

1. Baynard's Castle was destroyed by the Great Fire in 1666, except for a single turret which survived until 1720. It was thoroughly excavated in 1972–4, but the findings were of little interest to any but archaeologists.

facing them had longbows, and according to one chronicler the arrows had already started to fly. It was the King once again who saved the situation. Holding up his hand for silence, he addressed the mob in a measured, reasonable tone. What more, he asked, did they want? He was their King – they had no other – and he had granted all their requests. Why did they not now hold their peace? Gradually the tumult died down; in a short time, too, Walworth – who had hurried back to the city for armed assistance – returned with a volunteer force which quickly surrounded the insurgents. Richard, however, was determined to avoid any punitive measures. Tyler's head was substituted for Sudbury's on London Bridge, but all his followers were pardoned.

There was little doubt among the King's men that they owed their lives to his courage and presence of mind. He himself, however, was anxious to reward the leaders for their loyalty. There and then in Clerkenwell Fields, he drew his sword and knighted Walworth and two other faithful Londoners who had remained firmly at his side. Only then did he return to Baynard's Castle, where his anguished mother awaited him.

The Peasants' Revolt had lasted less than a week. It had put an end to the hated poll tax, but apart from that it had achieved nothing – at least so far as those who took part in it were concerned. As peace was restored, so gradually was the King's confidence; he began to regret the readiness with which he had granted the insurgents' demands. When in Essex on 23 June a delegation asked for confirmation of his promises, he is said to have replied cuttingly: 'Villeins ye are and villeins ye shall remain.' On 2 July in Chelmsford he went further still, announcing his formal revocation of the pardons 'lately granted in haste'; and a day or two later he rode in state to St Albans, where he presided over a tribunal at which fifteen of the local ringleaders, including John Ball, were condemned to death.

The treatment of the offenders was not, by the standards of the time, unduly savage. There were no tortures, no forced confessions, no mass reprisals on innocent populations, no condemnations without honest attempts at a fair trial. A surprising number of those implicated received light sentences or were acquitted altogether. On 30 August the King declared an end to all arrests and executions. One fact, however, could not be concealed: he had broken his word. Nowadays we accept that promises made under duress are not legally binding, and it is difficult to see what Richard could have done, at Mile End or at Smithfield, other than he in fact did. In the fourteenth century, however, such arguments had little effect. If the King were to be properly respected and revered by his subjects, it was essential that he should be seen to be a man of good faith. In this Richard had failed, and it was a failure that would not be forgotten. Nor was it mitigated by the support of Parliament which, while confirming the general amnesty the following November, formally ratified the revocation. By the end of the year none the less, it was as if the most serious crisis to be faced by an English King since the Norman Conquest had never occurred at all.

Or almost. Although they may have been only half conscious of it themselves, both sides had been taught a lesson. The landlords, from the high aristocracy down to the humblest of country squires, had been forcibly reminded of how much they relied on those who tilled their soil and tended their livestock. No longer, it was clear, could these men be taken for granted. The peasantry, too, had learnt much. Villeins they might be, and villeins they might technically remain for the better part of another century; but their lot was steadily improving, and as it did so they gradually came to understand the nature of their dissatisfaction and how it might be allayed. United, they possessed formidable power. Their first attempt to exercise that power had been unsuccessful, but only because they had been foolish enough to trust in the good faith of their King. It was a mistake they would not make again.

3

Favourites and Appellants

[1381–1388]

GAUNT. A thousand flatterers sit within thy crown,
         Whose compass is no bigger than thy head . . .
         O, had thy grandsire with a prophet's eye
         Seen how his son's son should destroy his sons,
         From forth thy reach he would have laid thy shame,
         Deposing thee before thou wert possess'd,
         Which art possess'd now to depose thyself . . .

                              KING RICHARD II

The events of the summer of 1381 had brought Richard a long way
towards manhood; and the process was completed six months later –
on 14 January 1382, a week after his fifteenth birthday – by his marriage
to an imperial Princess, Anne of Bohemia. Dynastic marriages had long
been one of the principal tools of diplomacy, and this particular one
had been strongly encouraged by Pope Urban, who saw in it the first
step towards a great European league against his rival Clement; in
England, on the other hand, it had met with considerable opposition.
Daughter of Charles IV, King of Bohemia and Holy Roman Emperor,[1]
by his fourth wife Elizabeth of Pomerania, and granddaughter of the
blind John of Luxemburg who had fought so courageously if quixotically
at Crécy,[2] Anne did not immediately find a place in English hearts. If
the tomb that she shares with her husband in Westminster Abbey is

1. The line of Holy Roman Emperors – chief defenders of Christendom in the
West – had come down in almost unbroken line since Charlemagne, the first of their
number, was crowned on Christmas Day 800. The Emperor was elected by a panel
drawn from the princes of Europe, but could not assume the imperial title until he
was formally crowned by the Pope in Rome.
2. See pp. 24 and 29.

anything to go by – and tomb effigies normally tend to flatter their subjects rather than the reverse – she was a plain, rather pudding-faced girl whose family, despite its nobility, was by no means as rich as might have been expected and who brought her husband no dowry at all; indeed, before the contract could be signed he had been obliged to offer her brother a loan of £15,000. She was certainly a far cry from her principal rival, the beautiful and dashing Caterina, one of the thirty-eight children of Bernabò Visconti, ruler of Milan, who had offered Richard 'an inestimable quantity of gold' to take his daughter as queen. True, the Bohemian marriage effectively detached the House of Luxemburg from its old alliance with the Valois of France, while simultaneously bringing Richard, by virtue of his new position as the Emperor's son-in-law, a welcome measure of international prestige; but such considerations cut little ice with Anne's prospective subjects.

Fortunately, Richard loved her: not perhaps at the start – when they were both little more than children and he was dominated by his infinitely stronger mother – but increasingly after Joan's death in 1385; and as time went on Anne herself gained a measure of popularity. Meanwhile her numerous and highly cosmopolitan following revolutionized life at court. The households of Edward III and the Black Prince had been of a pronounced military character, with little formality or protocol; women were expected to know their place. With Richard, all this was changed. The military element disappeared altogether; in its place came a new atmosphere of culture and sophistication, such as had never before been seen in England – an atmosphere of which, we may be sure, both the King's father and grandfather would have mightily disapproved. There was also a strong feminine element – with ladies not only from Austria and Bohemia but from France and Germany, and even occasionally from Hungary and Poland, no longer content with their embroidery but playing on instruments, singing, and dancing to the most fashionable steps imported from the Continent.

With these developments came a fresh interest in two other aspects of the new *douceur de vivre*: cooking and dress. 'The best and royallest viander of all Christian Kings', Richard presided over what was generally agreed to be the most sumptuous table in Europe. Among the 196 recipes in his court cookery book, *The Forme of Cury*, which has fortunately come down to us,[1] we search in vain for references to the roasted oxen, haunches of venison and shoulders of mutton which represent, in the public imagination, so large and daunting a part of the royal menus. Instead, the meat seems almost invariably to have been reduced to mince or pâté, its natural taste obscured by vast quantities of sugar and exotic spices. For the first time, too, much store was set by male sartorial elegance. Previously, except on high ceremonial occasions, dress in England for the King as well as for his subjects had been essentially practical; it is in Richard's reign that we see the birth of fashion, with tailoring developed into an art. Shoulders padded, waists tightly constricted, hose skin-tight, shoes absurdly elongated with pointed toes, hats like turbans: all these were *de rigueur* for the young men about the court, with the addition in cold weather of the *houpelande* – a full-length gown with huge sleeves that also fell almost to the ground. Jewellery was everywhere – on belts and collars, sleeves and tunics, worn as badges on the breast or in chains about the neck. In comparison, the women seemed almost drab. As for the King himself, he did not follow the latest fashions; he set them. He is credited, too, with one invention that has survived uninterruptedly to our own day, the handkerchief – 'made', according to his wardrobe account, 'for carrying in his hand to wipe and cleanse his nose.' Another contemporary innovation has also been attributed to him, though whether anyone would nowadays wish to take credit for the invention of the codpiece must remain a matter for speculation.

But Richard was not only a gourmet and a dandy; he was also an intellectual, with a passion for literature. Already by the age of thirteen he was enthusiastically buying books; at the time of his death he is believed to have possessed several dozen volumes of his own – a rare thing in those days, a century before the invention of printing. And he was an active patron of the arts. At his royal banquets, in place of the old minstrels, a new race of court poets – foremost among whom was Geoffrey Chaucer – would declaim their own poems, both in French and English, to the bilingual company; for Richard was almost certainly

1. Presented by Edmund Stafford to Queen Elizabeth I, it later formed part of the Harleian Collection. It was printed for the Society of Antiquaries in 1780. For examples of the recipes – they included minced pheasant, with Greek wine, cinnamon, cloves and ginger – see Gervase Mathew, *The Court of Richard II*, pp. 23–5.

the first King of England since the Norman Conquest to speak fluent English.

Where he differed most radically from his father and grandfather was in his conception of kingship. For Edward III and the Black Prince a King was above all a warrior, a leader of his armies in battle. When not in the field, his primary duties were those of a statesman and a lawgiver. His crown, and the oil with which he had been anointed, might confer on him a special grace and the right to his subjects' loyalty; but he remained a man like any other, his feet firmly on the ground, approachable to one and all. For Richard, from his earliest years, kings were not as other men. The ceremonial of his coronation – which he never forgot – had convinced him that he was set apart from the rest. He probably knew nothing of the theories prevailing in the Byzantine Empire, where the Emperor was considered the Vice-Gerent of God on earth, standing half-way to heaven, Equal of the Apostles; but he would have wholeheartedly endorsed them. For him, too, the basis of kingship was religious rather than military. Three times, when the need arose, he was to lead his army into battle; yet kings, as he saw them, did not properly belong on the battlefield. Their place was on the throne. He presided from his royal gallery over many a tournament; but he always refused to participate himself, as his father and grandfather had loved to do. The sovereign of England could never risk being publicly unhorsed.

It is perhaps a measure of Richard's vanity that he is the first English King whose true likeness has come down to us – and not with one contemporary portrait, but with two. (Three, if we include the effigy on his tomb.) The earliest is the large panel portrait just inside the west door of Westminster Abbey. Since he is portrayed in what is obviously his early youth, wearing a high gold crown and in full regalia, it may be a coronation portrait, though it is more likely to have been painted some years later. The boy king stares out towards us from the golden ground behind him, his sad and solemn face clean-shaven and framed in thick brown hair, his long, delicate fingers seeming to caress, rather than actually to hold, the orb and sceptre in his hands. His eyes, beneath the high arched eyebrows, are heavy-lidded and tired-looking; but they are also blank and pitiless.

The second picture – the so-called Wilton Diptych, in the National Gallery in London – is itself something very like a jewel. Of its two panels, Richard appears in the one on the left, kneeling in adoration before the Virgin, who stands in the right-hand panel surrounded by a host of blue-robed angels, her child in her arms. His cloak of scarlet is richly embroidered in gold with his emblem of the white hart, which we see again in a badge on his own breast and on those of the angels. Behind him stand two royal saints, Edward the Confessor and Edmund the Martyr, with St John the Baptist. Here, in contrast to the Westminster Abbey portrait, the King's young face is full of animation as he gazes ecstatically at the heavenly pair, his hands – those long, tapering fingers again – extended before him; but the symbolism remains clear. Richard, the King, ranks with the holiest of his predecessors and is vouchsafed a vision of the heavenly glory. Even the angels are proud to bear his badge.

The one virtue immediately noticeable by its absence from both works is that of humility. We should not expect to find it in the Westminster Abbey panel, for this is a state portrait – the earliest, indeed, in the history of English painting – and state portraits are a genre, almost by definition, in which such qualities are rare. In the Wilton Diptych, on the other hand, some suggestion of self-abasement, or at least submissiveness, might not have come amiss; but once again there is no trace. True, Richard is kneeling, but this seems to be little more than a *politesse*: while the three figures behind him wear expressions of solemnity and awe he looks the Virgin dead in the eye, the suggestion of a smile on his lips, for all the world as if he were about to engage her in conversation.

Up until Richard's marriage in January 1382 it had seemed that he might eventually make a more than passable king; from that time forward it rapidly became clear that he would be nothing of the kind. Already he was showing signs of a quite alarming arrogance, self-indulgence and irresponsibility; any attempt to remonstrate with him threw him into a towering rage, provoking streams of insults and abuse that did little to increase the dignity which he was always so anxious to preserve. Thus on the death in December 1381 of Edmund Mortimer, Earl of March, who left as his heir a seven-year-old child, the King ordered his immense estates made over to members of his own household; and this was no isolated instance. Such was his insensate generosity to his favourites that he was obliged to borrow vast sums from all who would lend. Some of the crown jewels were transferred to Sir Robert Knollys as security for a loan of £2,779; soon afterwards, the crown itself was pledged to the City of London for a further £2,000. When Richard Scrope, the Chancellor, attempted to put a brake on these borrowings, Richard dismissed him from office – summarily and quite unconstitutionally, the Chancellorship being a parliamentary appointment rather than a royal one. When Archbishop William Courtenay – who had been raised in 1381 to the see of Canterbury – was bold enough to question the King's choice of counsellors, Richard drew his sword and threatened to pierce him through the heart.

Both these incidents clearly indicate the King's greatest weakness of all: his blind devotion to his favourites. Whether or not we are to believe the chronicler Thomas Walsingham's assertions that they were knights 'of Venus rather than Bellona' and that they taught the King effeminate habits, discouraging him from hunting, hawking and other manly sports, there can be no question that they were frivolous, rapacious and empty-headed, leading lives exclusively devoted to pleasure and their own gain. Chief among them at first was Thomas Mowbray, who in 1383 had inherited the earldom of Nottingham. A year older than his master, he seems to have been a pleasant enough young man, though without any particular ability. Richard soon tired of him, and the bonds between them were finally broken in 1385 when Mowbray married the daughter of the King's detested guardian, Richard, Earl of Arundel. He certainly possessed little of the charm of his successor in Richard's affections, Robert de Vere, ninth Earl of Oxford. De Vere was a distant relative of the King, several years his senior, and married to Richard's first cousin Philippa de Coucy, granddaughter of Edward III – a fact which did not prevent him from carrying on a flagrant affair with one of the Queen's Bohemian ladies, Agnes Landskron. This alone should have done much to discredit the allegations of homosexuality between himself and the King that are made by more than one contemporary chronicler; it was plain to all who knew the two men that their tastes did not lie in this particular direction. Nevertheless, Richard's effusive displays of affection and the readiness with which Oxford accepted his presents of money, land and titles would certainly have awoken Gavestonian memories if any of the King's subjects had been old enough to harbour them.

It should be emphasized that neither Mowbray, de Vere – despite his post as hereditary Chamberlain of England – nor any other of the King's favourites wielded any real authority. This, at the time of which we are speaking, was principally in the hands of the Chancellor, Michael de la Pole, Earl of Suffolk; but there was another very real power behind the throne in the person of the Vice-Chamberlain, Richard's old guardian and tutor Sir Simon Burley, now one of the richest men in the kingdom. Burley's influence on the King was exercised not only directly but also through Joan of Kent and, after her death, through the young Queen, whom he had personally brought from Bohemia; both these ladies trusted him absolutely, and Richard himself treated him with a respect that he showed towards no other member of his government.

And what, it may be asked, of John of Gaunt himself? The Duke of Lancaster remained a powerful figure – in the nature of things he could hardly have been anything else. His diplomatic mission to Scotland had kept him out of the way during the Peasants' Revolt, and its notable if modest success[1] had served in some degree at least to diminish his chronic unpopularity; the attacks on his property during the insurrection had also gained him a certain amount of sympathy among the people. He was, however, once again looking towards Spain, where the recent death of Don Enrique of Trastamara – who in 1368 had succeeded John's father-in-law Pedro the Cruel on the throne of Castile[2] – had revived all his old hopes of claiming the crown for himself. Accordingly, when Parliament reassembled in the spring of 1382, he appeared before the Commons to seek a guarantee for a loan of £60,000 to equip the necessary army. When this proposal was rejected he put forward another: that the King himself should lead an expeditionary force to France to teach young Charles VI a lesson. Once such a force was in Gascony, as he well knew, there would be little difficulty in taking it across the frontier into Castile. Again, Parliament was unenthusiastic. One more opportunity arose the following October, when the Bishop of Hereford suggested two alternative ways of dealing with England's enemies abroad: either the proposed Spanish expedition – which could now be dignified with the title of crusade, the new Castilian King, Juan I, having given his support to Clement VII as Pope – or another crusade

1. He had succeeded in negotiating a form of truce with Scotland, lasting to 2 February 1383.

2. See pp. 44–5.

against the Clementists in France and Flanders, to be led by Henry Despenser, Bishop of Norwich.

For a moment it looked as though Gaunt was to have his way after all; unfortunately for him, it was at this very moment that a French army invaded Flanders, invested Ypres and Bruges – where it impounded all the goods of the local English merchants – and brought the wool trade, one of the principal sources of royal revenue, to a virtual standstill. Once again a French invasion of England seemed a strong possibility. John of Gaunt and the Castilian schismatics were forgotten; all eyes turned to the Bishop of Norwich. From the outset, Despenser had determined that his would be a real crusade, fighting under the auspices of the Church and financed by contributions from the faithful. It was launched in an atmosphere of almost hysterical enthusiasm: Pope Urban had declared a plenary indulgence for everyone who contributed, and it seemed that all the ladies in the land were flinging their gold, silver and jewels into the Bishop's coffers.

Henry Despenser was a brave man and, having served in Italy under the papal banner, was not without military experience; he had, however, never commanded an army in the field and was totally unfit for the task with which he had been entrusted. Ignoring a last-minute attempt by the King to recall him, he embarked at Sandwich on 16 May 1383, landed at Calais and pressed forward into Flanders, where he joined up with the Flemish forces early in June. At this point his most sensible course would have been to march on Bruges, a relatively easy target; instead, he decided to besiege Ypres – a project which, since his army possessed virtually no siege equipment, was doomed from the start. Many of his more recent recruits, untrained and interested only in plunder, quickly tired of the siege and deserted; and when at the beginning of August word reached him that Philip of Burgundy was on the march with a large army, he gave the signal to retreat. His crusade had achieved precisely nothing except the discredit of the Church, in whose name vast numbers of marauding thugs had pillaged and plundered their way through a friendly country. No one was surprised when, that same autumn, Chancellor de la Pole announced the impeachment of the Bishop and his captains. Despenser was deprived of his temporal possessions, though they were returned to him two years later; the captains – several of whom had accepted bribes from the French, but who had actually fought a courageous rearguard action to cover his precipitate retreat – were sentenced to unexpectedly short terms of imprisonment. All, perhaps, were luckier than they deserved.

To John of Gaunt, the failure of the Bishop of Norwich's crusade and the consequent humiliation of all those involved must have caused more than a touch of *Schadenfreude*. He had never given up his plans for an expedition to Castile; indeed, the death of King Ferdinand of Portugal in October 1383 – which had resulted in Portugal's abandoning the Clementist cause – had left the hated King Juan more isolated than ever. But after the recent débâcle there was clearly no chance of a further grant from Parliament and Gaunt was obliged to bide his time, occupying himself with the quiet diplomacy at which he excelled, first in Flanders where he concluded a truce with Charles VI, and later once again in Scotland.

It was just as well that he absented himself from London, for his relations with his nephew were now rapidly deteriorating. The principal cause of the trouble seems to have been Richard's favourite Robert de Vere, who lost no opportunity of reminding the King that he was now seventeen, an age at which many sovereigns had shaken off their tutelage, and that it was time to rule on his own account. There was a particularly unfortunate incident at Salisbury, where Parliament met in April 1384 and a Carmelite friar named John Latimer, after saying mass for the King, informed him that Gaunt was plotting to have him murdered. Richard believed him and accused his uncle to his face, but after hearing Gaunt's dignified and convincing denial finally agreed to put Latimer under arrest pending a full inquiry. All would probably have been forgotten had not a group of knights – which included the King's half-brother John Holland – decided to take the law into their own hands. Falling upon Latimer and his escort on their way to his place of imprisonment, they seized him and, in the course of interrogating him, tortured him to death.

Such, at least, is the accepted version of the story. It may well be, however, that Latimer was killed not that the truth should be discovered, but that it should be concealed: that the unfounded charge – for such it unquestionably was – against Gaunt had been fabricated by de Vere and his cronies in a deliberate attempt to get rid of him. If so, and if the luckless friar had revealed from whom he had heard the story, its originators would have been in serious trouble. Even with Latimer out of the way, the incident was long remembered. Richard did not readily forgive his quick-tempered uncle Thomas of Woodstock, Gaunt's youngest brother, with whom his relations had heretofore been cordial, for having burst into the royal chamber in a fury when he heard the news, swearing that he would kill anyone – the King himself not excepted – who dared to impute treason to the Duke of Lancaster.

By the time Parliament met again in the autumn of 1384, its members were growing seriously concerned. With every day that passed Richard seemed more headstrong, less inclined to listen to the advice of anyone but his own closed circle of friends and sycophants. After the Peasants' Revolt and the catastrophe of the Norwich crusade, England's reputation abroad was lower than it had ever been; but he was blind to public opinion, domestic and foreign alike. While enjoying to the full the privileges of kingship he appeared utterly oblivious of its responsibilities, continuing to spend money like water and resorting to tantrums at the first breath of criticism. Clearly, he must be given something to do; would it not be best, after all, to yield to the continual pressure of John of Gaunt and to send the King, at the head of an army, to France? After some discussion a subsidy was granted and, although Richard himself remained unenthusiastic, preparations were begun. Before they had progressed very far, however, the situation in Scotland caused a rapid change of plan.

If England's relations with her wild and unruly neighbour were better than they had been for many years, credit must go above all to the efforts of John of Gaunt. These were not entirely altruistic – the more settled the situation on the border, the easier it would be for him to launch his long-delayed Spanish expedition – but they had demanded considerable diplomatic skill and had involved him in several acrimonious disputes with the Percys, the Nevills and other powerful magnates of the region. On the expiry of the most recent truce in February 1383[1] he had travelled north yet again and had actually concluded an agreement with Henry Percy, Earl of Northumberland, by the terms of which the latter assumed responsibility for the safety of the northern shires in return for a generous subsidy from the King. For Gaunt, this was a remarkable achievement; unfortunately it failed to recommend itself to the French, whose traditional friendship with Scotland – 'the auld

1. See p. 75 n.

alliance' – had long been a vital element in their struggle with England. Early in 1384 Charles VI had already sent a small detachment of troops to strengthen Scottish resolve, and in the spring of the following year these were followed by a much larger company under the command of France's foremost admiral, Jean de Vienne. For some time, too, reports had been reaching London of a third French force – a full-scale army this time – which was gathering at Sluys. If, as seemed likely, Charles VI was preparing a two-pronged pincer attack, with England being invaded simultaneously from north and south, decisive action could no longer be delayed.

And so, in the summer of 1385, the great expedition that was being prepared for France was suddenly redirected against the Scots. It would have done better to have stayed at home. The fiasco – almost on a par with that of the Norwich crusade – was not entirely the King's fault. He could not, for example, be held responsible for the drunken brawl near York, in which his half-brother John Holland – who had been heavily implicated in the Latimer affair the year before – killed the heir of the Earl of Stafford; indeed he swore to deal with Holland as a common murderer, and the bitterness between the two is said to have caused the death of their mother Joan of Kent a few weeks later. Nor, having advanced as far as Edinburgh, could he be blamed for his failure to engage the French army; Jean de Vienne, learning of his approach, had moved his men back across the border to the neighbourhood of Carlisle whence, after amusing themselves for a week or two by laying waste the few and primitive villages of Cumberland, they returned to France. But by this time the King too had had enough of Scotland and the Scots; having no desire to sample a Scottish winter, he wanted to go home. He delayed his departure long enough to confer on his two youngest uncles, Edmund of Langley and Thomas of Woodstock, the dukedoms[1] respectively of York and Gloucester, and on his faithful Chancellor Michael de la Pole the earldom of Suffolk; then, without

---

1. Until the reign of Edward III the only Duke in England was the King himself, one of whose titles was Duke of Aquitaine. In 1337, however, Edward conferred the Duchy of Cornwall on his eldest son, the Black Prince, and in 1351 he granted that of Lancaster to his second cousin Henry of Grosmont, Earl of Derby, the most faithful (and successful) of his captains, whose daughter Blanche was to be the wife of John of Gaunt. Gaunt was himself to be made a Duke, with his brother Lionel, in 1362. There were no others.

its having loosed a single arrow, he marched the great army back to London, where it was disbanded.

For John of Gaunt, who had accompanied his nephew on the campaign – indeed, his own Lancastrian army had accounted for as much as two-thirds of the entire force – but to whose advice the King had pointedly refused to listen, the Scottish expedition only confirmed what he had long suspected: that there was no longer any place for him in England. If he had a future at all it was in the Iberian peninsula where, from his point of view, the situation had continued to improve. With the help of a small English party of volunteers – mainly archers – the Portuguese had succeeded in freeing themselves once and for all from Castilian domination. They asked nothing better than the overthrow of the Clementist King Juan, and had assured Gaunt that they would do everything in their power to achieve it; if he came to claim his rightful crown he would find them brave and faithful allies. Once again Gaunt appeared before Parliament, accompanied now by envoys from Portugal; and this time he found the assembly sympathetic. True, there were other enemies closer at hand: the French were continuing to mass at the Channel ports, and at the present rate it looked as though invasion could not be long delayed. On the other hand a swift and successful campaign beyond the Pyrenees would radically alter the balance of power in western Europe; Charles VI would be obliged to give up his invasion plans and come quickly to terms. On 8 March 1386 Richard in full council recognized his uncle as King of Castile, and on 9 July Gaunt sailed with his army from Plymouth. It need hardly be said that his mistress Katherine Swynford and their four illegitimate children remained behind, as did his eldest son Henry Bolingbroke, Earl of Derby, whom he had charged to watch over his personal interests while he was away; with him, on the other hand, went his Spanish wife Constance and their three daughters, Philippa, Elizabeth and Catherine. Elizabeth had recently married Sir John Holland, constable of the army and the King's half-brother, now back in favour after the fracas at York; as for Philippa and Catherine, if anyone questioned the wisdom of taking two young unmarried girls on a distant campaign, their father's reasons were soon made clear enough.

It seems extraordinary, in retrospect, that the Duke of Lancaster should have been allowed to leave the country with a sizeable army at precisely the moment that a huge French army was gathering at Sluys for an invasion from across the Channel. As the summer took its course all the coastal towns of the south-east were put on the alert, with orders to repair their walls as necessary and to keep a close watch for anything untoward at sea. But September came and went without any attempt at a landing, and by the time Parliament met at Westminster on 1 October it was clear that none could be expected that year and that, in the words of one recent historian, 'the luxury of a domestic crisis might safely be enjoyed'.[1] Tension, nevertheless, was running high, and tempers were correspondingly short – particularly after the Chancellor Michael de la Pole, now Earl of Suffolk, had demanded yet another huge subsidy for the defence of the realm. High taxation is always unpopular; a scapegoat had to be found somewhere, and Suffolk was held responsible for all England's misfortunes. Lords and Commons together sent a delegation to the King in his Palace of Eltham[2] calling for the Chancellor's dismissal, together with that of the Treasurer, John Fordham, Bishop of Durham. The message may have been a trifle peremptory, but the delegates were certainly not prepared for the King's reply. At Parliament's request, he told them, he would not remove a scullion from his kitchen.

It was a characteristically foolish reaction: Richard had antagonized the estates unnecessarily, while in no way deflecting them from their purpose. They could hardly have expected him to obey their subsequent summons to appear before them in person, but eventually a compromise was reached, the King agreeing to receive a deputation of forty knights at Eltham to hear their complaints. He would certainly have found the forty easier to deal with than the two who finally came in their stead: his uncle the Duke of Gloucester, and the latter's close friend and associate Thomas Arundel, Bishop of Ely, brother of the hated Earl Richard. Such men were not to be intimidated; and Gloucester in particular – now thirty-one and twelve years older than the King – had no intention of allowing himself to be pushed aside by the arrogant and

1. A. Steel, *Richard II*, p. 120.

2. The old moated palace of Eltham still stands, a mile or two south-east of Greenwich. Although a royal residence since the days of Edward III, it was largely rebuilt by Edward IV in the 1470s; from this period dates the Great Hall with its tremendous hammerbeam roof. Of the building Richard knew, little or nothing now remains.

effeminate young striplings with whom his nephew chose to surround himself. His anger had been further increased a day or two previously when Richard had, in his eyes, cheapened his own recently acquired title by making Robert de Vere Duke of Ireland – dukedoms, as the King very well knew, being normally reserved for princes of the blood. Making it clear from the outset that he spoke not just for himself but on behalf of Lords and Commons alike, Gloucester reminded the King that he was legally obliged to summon Parliament once a year and to be present himself at its deliberations; if he were not, it would be invalid and its members could disperse after forty days. Richard at first tried to bluster. Accusing his uncle of plotting a rebellion, he threatened to call his kinsman, the King of France, to his aid – to which Gloucester merely pointed out that if he were to do so, Charles would seize the opportunity to destroy not the King's enemies, but the King himself. If Richard wished to keep his crown, he must mend his ways. Not only must he dismiss Suffolk and Fordham; he must drastically reduce taxation, rid his court of his vain, vapid and insanely extravagant henchmen and govern as a responsible monarch should. If he did not, Parliament had a remedy in its own hands, sanctified 'by ancient statute and recent precedent'.

Gloucester was bluffing: there was in fact no statute authorizing the deposition of a King, and Edward II's dethronement had been unconstitutional. But the precedent, legal or not, was plain enough, and those last two words had their effect. It was only sixty years since the King's great-grandfather Edward II, having been found manifestly unfit to rule, had been forcibly removed from his throne. He too had been brought low by his favourites, and Richard had no desire to follow in the same path. Sullenly he returned to Westminster, attended Parliament on 23 October and dismissed Suffolk and Fordham, replacing them with the Bishops of Ely and Hereford respectively. Suffolk was impeached, but the seven charges against him were so trivial as to be almost derisory, four of them being dismissed and the other three upheld only on technicalities. His nominal prison sentence was served at Windsor Castle, and was soon forgotten altogether.

So far the King had escaped comparatively lightly; but worse was to follow. On 20 November 1386 Parliament appointed 'a Great and Continual Council', with the declared object of getting rid of the favourites once and for all, reforming the administration and taking whatever measures might be thought necessary against the enemy. Its composition was in fact moderate enough. Of its fourteen commissioners only three – Gloucester and the two Arundels – were implacably opposed to the King; the Archbishop of York, Alexander Nevill, was a committed royalist, and the other ten were reasonable men with whom accommodation should not have been difficult. Far more worrying was the extent of its powers. It had full control over the great and privy seals and everything relating to finance; the King, moreover, was forced to swear that he would abide by all its ordinances, even if voted by a bare majority, and that he would immediately denounce anyone who advised him to move against it. There was one small consolation: the Council had been empowered to act for twelve months only. If Richard had agreed to accept it with a good grace, there is every likelihood that it would have dissolved itself when its term was completed.

But he did not accept it. Instead, he made a formal protest, insisting that neither he nor his Crown should be in any way prejudiced by Parliament or Council, nominating his friend Sir John Beauchamp as Steward of his Household – thereby breaking his promise that this appointment should be made only with the Council's advice and consent – and spending Christmas with the theoretically disgraced Suffolk at Windsor. In February 1387 he left Westminster for an extended tour of the Midlands and the North, there to rally supporters and to establish a strong royalist army based on Cheshire and North Wales. Ostensibly this recruiting was in connection with de Vere's new Duchy of Ireland, which Richard had every intention of exploiting in any way he could; in fact, however, it gave rise to that invaluable army of Cheshire archers and Welsh pikemen that was to constitute his principal support in the years ahead. And it was during this tour, in August 1387, first at Shrewsbury and a week later at Nottingham, that he sought – and obtained – legal advice against the Council.

The judges who gave this advice – and they included some of the highest in the land, including Sir Robert Tresilian, Chief Justice of the King's Bench, Sir Robert Belknap, Chief Justice of the Common Bench, and three of the latter's colleagues, Sir William Burgh, Sir John Holt and Sir Roger Fulthorp – were to claim in the following year that they had been coerced into giving the judgement they did; but since in 1386 they risked virtually nothing (whereas in 1387 their lives were in grave danger) we do not need to take their evidence too seriously. Besides, that judgement was perfectly reasonable. It could certainly have been argued that the Council was injurious to the royal prerogative, while the impeachment of the King's servants had been declared illegal as recently as 1377. The judges accordingly pronounced that the King had indeed been impeded in the exercise of his prerogative, and that those responsible for such impediments as had 'accroached the royal power' should be punished as traitors.

The decision was exactly what Richard had hoped for; but he was not yet ready to use it. Judges and witnesses alike were sworn to secrecy until such moment, after his return to London, as he could publish it to most startling effect. That return took place on 10 November 1387. Even the King was surprised by the warmth of his reception by the Londoners, who escorted him in procession, like a triumphant hero, first to St Paul's and then to Westminster. The reasons for their enthusiasm are unclear. The English fleet under the Earls of Arundel and Nottingham had indeed gained a splendid victory against the French and Spanish off Margate, had gone on to destroy the fortifications of Brest and had returned with huge quantities of wine, which had been sold off cheaply at home; but that had been almost a year ago, and it is unlikely that the euphoria – far less the wine – would have lasted quite so long. More significant, perhaps, was the fact that the King had been away for nearly ten months. He always tended to be more popular during his absence; and the Londoners had perhaps begun to despair of ever seeing him again.

The general excitement at the King's return was not shared by his two chief antagonists, the Duke of Gloucester and the Earl of Arundel. Despite the secrecy on which he had insisted, it was not long before they heard of the recent judgement against them; and they resolved to strike first. Refusing to obey the royal summons on the grounds that the King had surrounded himself with their enemies, they withdrew first to Haringey, a few miles to the north of the capital – where they were joined by Thomas Beauchamp, Earl of Warwick – and thence to Waltham Cross in Hertfordshire, where they began to rally their forces in earnest, issuing proclamations and circulating letters to the leading citizens of London and the principal religious houses, setting out the case against the King and calling for support. The response, coming as it did so soon after his enthusiastic reception only a few days before, was enough to cause Richard serious alarm. His favourites, including the Archbishop of York, urged him to fight; but there were all too many others, like old Sir Ralph Basset of Drayton, who maintained that though they would be happy to die for the King, they were rather less keen to do so for the Duke of Ireland and his friends. Fortunately, eight of the fourteen members of the hated Council were also in favour of a settlement: and it was they who rode on 14 November to Waltham, where they invited Gloucester, Arundel and Warwick to lay down their arms. The three responded with a formal Appeal (*accusatio*) against five of Richard's closest associates – Suffolk, de Vere, Tresilian, the Archbishop of York and Sir Nicholas Brembre, a former Mayor of London from whom the King had borrowed over £1,300; and the eight Councillors thereupon invited them to return with them to Westminster, where the King was waiting to receive them.

In the circumstances, such an invitation could hardly be refused; and three days later, on 17 November, the three Appellants presented themselves before the King in Westminster Hall. Their troops, however, were not disbanded. They were negotiating from strength, and they made their demands clear: the five favourites against whom they were appealing must be arrested and held until the next Parliament, when they must stand trial for offences under common law. A little to their surprise, perhaps, Richard accepted at once, even going so far as to appoint 3 February 1388 for the opening of the sitting; but he had no intention of seeing the five brought to trial. Whatever his other faults, he was loyal to his friends, for whom the next eleven weeks would allow him plenty of time to make the appropriate arrangements. As for the Appellants, he had plans for them also; but for the moment he gave no sign. Instead, he bore all three of them off to his chamber to celebrate the reconciliation.

Within days, his bad faith became evident. The writs of summons to Parliament issued in his name specifically provided that all those elected must be 'indifferent to the recent disputes'. As to the five accused, it is doubtful whether they were even arrested. They were certainly not held for long, and only Brembre remained to face his judges. Tresilian went into hiding in London; the Archbishop of York fled to the north, dressed as a simple parish priest; while Suffolk crossed the Channel to Calais disguised as a pedlar, hoping to find refuge with his brother, who was in command of the castle. He suffered a brief setback when he fell into the hands of the Governor, Warwick's brother Sir William Beauchamp, who put him on to a ship bound for Hull; but he was soon back on the Continent, and never returned to England. That left only de Vere, who headed for Chester with letters from the King instructing the Constable, Sir Thomas Molyneux, to muster all available reservists. As soon as they heard of his departure, Gloucester and his friends set about raising troops of their own, under the command of John of Gaunt's son, the twenty-year-old Henry Bolingbroke,[1] Earl of Derby, and Arundel's son-in-law Thomas Mowbray, Earl of Nottingham – two young noblemen of whom we shall be hearing a good deal more in due course.

The ensuing campaign was over in a matter of days. When de Vere, attempting to return to London, learned that the Appellants had blocked the main road near Northampton, he decided to make his way from the valley of the Severn to that of the upper Thames, following the Fosseway to Stow-on-the Wold. From there he could either take the road to Cirencester, which would be relatively safe but would distance him still further from London, or alternatively make a dash through Burford for Radcot Bridge. He chose the latter – and fell straight into the trap that had been set for him. Bolingbroke was lying in wait at the river, and before de Vere had recovered from his surprise Gloucester appeared in his rear. Abandoning his men to save themselves as best they might, he fled downstream and was soon lost in the gathering December dark. A day or two later he too was safely across the Channel. He was to live another five years, but he never saw England again.

After Radcot Bridge there could no longer be any question of accommodation between the two sides, nor – the twelve months' authority granted to the Council having expired the previous November – of any legal justification for the actions of Gloucester and his friends. The army that marched through Oxford to London just after Christmas 1387 to pitch its camp in Clerkenwell Fields was now in open rebellion against the King. Richard, badly frightened, shut himself up in the Tower; and on 28 or 29 December, after careful negotiations mediated by the Archbishop of Canterbury – for by now neither side trusted the

1. Like so many princes at this period, Henry Bolingbroke derived his name from the place in which he was born – his father's castle of Bolingbroke in Lincolnshire.

other an inch – the Appellant lords issued their ultimatum, while 500 of their armed supporters waited within the gates. They had hinted before at the possibility of deposition; now, for the first time, the suggestion became a threat.[1]

Richard no longer had any fight left in him. Thinking only of keeping his throne, he issued new writs of summons to the forthcoming Parliament omitting the offending proviso, ordered his sheriffs to round up the five accused and ensure their appearance, and made no objection when the commissioners, disempowered as they were, instituted a thorough purge of his entire household – where, in the buttery alone, they found a hundred superfluous servants. Nor were the warrants for arrest confined to the original five. Others were issued in the names of Sir Simon Burley, who lost not only the office of Vice-Chamberlain but also that of Warden of the Cinque Ports (and Dover Castle which went with it); of the King's Steward, Sir John Beauchamp; and of six of the judges who had subscribed to the Nottingham declaration, all of whom were removed from the bench. Vast numbers of courtiers, male and female, of all ranks and conditions, were summarily dismissed.

Few parliamentary sessions can have been more dramatic than that which opened in the White Hall of the Palace of Westminster[2] on 3 February 1388. The King seated himself on his throne at the far end, with the prelates on his right, the secular lords on his left, and the Bishop of Ely on the woolsack.[3] Then, at his signal, the great doors were flung open and the five Appellants – Gloucester, Arundel, Warwick, Derby and Nottingham – in surcoats of gold, marched arm in arm into the Hall. At the very outset, they sounded a note of warning. Gloucester, stepping forward,

---

1. M. V. Clarke (*Fourteenth Century Studies*, pp. 91–5) suggests that Richard was actually deposed, but that Gloucester and Bolingbroke, unable to agree on his successor, finally reinstated him and pretended that the deposition had never occurred.

2. The name survives in London's Whitehall, which runs from Trafalgar Square in the north to Parliament Square in the south. The Hall itself, however, was to be largely rebuilt, on Richard's orders, between 1394 and 1401 (see p. 102).

3. The large square bag filled with wool which had been in existence since the reign of Edward III as a symbol of the country's staple trade and as the official seat of certain high dignitaries, such as the Lords of the Exchequer and the Masters in Chancery. Today only one remains: the seat of the Lord Chancellor when he presides in the House of Lords.

disclaimed any intention of personally deposing the King and usurping his throne; in such matters, he announced – and here was the sting – he would abide by the judgement of his peers. Deposition, in other words, remained a possibility. The long preamble of the appeal was then read, in French, followed by no less than thirty-nine separate accusations – the whole reading took two hours – after which the defendants were summoned by proclamation and, when four of the five failed to appear, the Appellants demanded judgement by default. At this point the King's spokesmen struck back: before there could be any question, they claimed, of the guilt or innocence of the accused, there was the legality of the appeal to be considered. The Appellants had spoken of treason; there was, however, a perfectly good statute of 1352 on this subject, and it was clear that none of its provisions applied to any of the present charges. Moreover, though an appeal of the kind now being made was a recognized process in common law, no precedent existed for its being heard in Parliament. In these circumstances the King's advisers had thought it their duty to consult a number of judges, serjeants and other experts in both civil and common law – including several justices recently appointed by the Appellants themselves. Every single expert consulted had declared the appeal invalid.

Richard's grim satisfaction as he heard these words can well be imagined; but his enemies were ready for him. Neither civil nor common law, they retorted, had any relevance, for these were merely the creations of Parliament, which remained supreme. Thus crimes which affected the person of the sovereign, committed by persons many of whom were themselves peers, could be tried only by the Lords of Parliament themselves, with the King's assent. Whether this was, as some historians have suggested, the first great declaration of the ultimate sovereignty of Parliament over the law of the land or whether the Appellants were merely working on the Lords' natural vanity to further their own interests is beyond the scope of this narrative; but the appeal was upheld.

Now at last the charges could be considered. The defendants, it was averred, had taken advantage of the King's youth and inexperience to usurp his power. They had prevented him from attending Parliament. They had enriched themselves and their associates. They had suborned judges and perverted the law. They had conspired against the Duke of Lancaster and other nobles, including the Appellants themselves. They had induced the King to negotiate with the King of France. They had adversely influenced the loyalty of the people of London. They had led the King to pack the Commons with his followers. They had neglected, and caused the King to neglect, the defence of the realm. They had been responsible for the quasi-regal status conferred upon Robert de Vere in Ireland, without English or Irish consent, while de Vere himself had been guilty of perverting justice in Chester and had finally incited civil war.

The four fugitives were sentenced first. The life of the Archbishop of York was saved by his cloth. He was outlawed, with all his possessions declared confiscate; then, at the Appellants' insistence, his case was referred to Pope Urban, who decreed that he should be sent off *in partes infidelium* and soon afterwards, somewhat surprisingly, appointed him to the see of St Andrews.[1] The other three were condemned to death *in absentia*. Next came Brembre. When he pleaded not guilty on all charges and offered to undergo trial by battle, over three hundred of those present, including the five Appellants, flung down their gloves in challenge – 'like a fall of snow', according to one eyewitness; but this procedure was disallowed. A committee of twelve peers was then appointed to investigate the charges further, and – to the fury of the Appellants – reported that the former mayor had done nothing deserving of death; and tempers on both sides were running high when the news was brought that Sir Robert Tresilian had been captured. On being discovered, he had first taken refuge in Westminster Abbey; but Gloucester had personally given orders for the traditional right of sanctuary to be ignored. He was brought to the White Hall to hear his sentence which, despite his emphatic protestations of innocence, was immediately carried out. The former Chief Justice of England was lashed to a hurdle and dragged to Tyburn, where he was hanged on the spot. Attention now turned back to the luckless Brembre. Determined to destroy him, the Appellants summoned the mayor, recorder, guild members and aldermen of London to give further evidence of his crimes.[2] Once again the answers they received were unsatisfactory – no witness was prepared

---

1. In fact, Pope Urban was not recognized by the Scots, so the Archbishop never took up his appointment. He ended his days as a humble parish priest in Louvain, where he died in 1392. Five years later he was declared innocent of all the charges preferred against him.

2. One of them was that he had plotted to change the name of London to Troynovant.

to state categorically that Sir Nicholas deserved to die – but by now they had lost patience and condemned him anyway. On 20 February he followed Sir Robert to the scaffold.

Now it was the turn of the lesser victims. Sir John Salisbury, one of the knights of the chamber who was believed to have been the chief intermediary in negotiations with the King of France, was hanged as a traitor; other knights, including Sir James Berners, Sir John Beauchamp and Sir Simon Burley – for whose life the Queen went down on her knees before Gloucester – were accorded only the privilege of being beheaded rather than hanged. Most of the remaining offenders were released under surety, and Parliament then settled down to the more mundane tasks of keeping the royal household under strict control, turning away any further undesirable adherents and sending most of the Queen's compatriots back to Bohemia. Finally, at a ceremony held on 3 June in Westminster Abbey, Lords and Commons together renewed their oaths of allegiance and the King gave a solemn promise: in the future, he would be good.

Richard had been brought to heel, as he deserved to be; but the cost had been great indeed. In all but name, his power and authority had been usurped by a group of ambitious noblemen, able and willing to manipulate a weak parliament in their own interests. That parliament has gone down in history as the 'Merciless' Parliament; in fact, as the story of Sir Nicholas Brembre makes all too clear, it was the Appellants who were merciless. The parliament simply did as it was told. Nor was the fate of Brembre the only stain on its reputation. Of those executed, or sentenced to execution in their absence, some – though not all – may well have been greedy, self-seeking or irresponsible; but none were traitors, none were criminals, none deserved death. Nor did any of them stand a proper trial. Legal statutes were distorted or ignored altogether, opinions were deliberately misinterpreted as facts, proper judicial procedures were sidestepped.

These were dangerous precedents; and those who set them must surely bear more than a little of the responsibility for the dark deeds and civil strife which cast a steadily lengthening shadow over the next hundred years of English history. On the other hand, they were not themselves revolutionaries; they might terrify Richard with threats of dethronement, but they never forgot that he was the lawful King, and they knew only too well that any attempt to replace him would create infinitely more problems than it would solve. That is why, however brutal their treatment of his friends, they were careful to spare, so far as they could, the reputation of the King himself. Never did they publicly humiliate him, as they could so easily have done; on the contrary, they were at pains to stress his youth and inexperience. He was not himself guilty of wrong-doing; he had simply been led astray. Now that those who had tried so hard to corrupt him had been removed from the scene, there was no reason why he should not make a fresh start.

4

The King's Revenge

[1388–1398]

DUCH. But Thomas, my dear lord, my life, my Gloucester,
One vial full of Edward's sacred blood,
One flourishing branch of his most royal root,
Is crack'd, and all the precious liquor spilt,
Is hack'd down, and his summer leaves all faded,
By envy's hand, and murder's bloody axe.

KING RICHARD II

It was not altogether surprising that, for well over a year after the dissolution of the Merciless Parliament, Richard should have maintained an uncharacteristically low profile. His innocence had been proclaimed; but he had been badly frightened and had been taught, it was hoped, a sharp lesson. He conscientiously performed the duties expected of him; presided over another parliament held at Cambridge in the autumn; made no protest when Gloucester, Arundel and their friends took over the direction of the government; and allowed himself only one furious and understandable outburst, when it was reported to him that the Scots under James, Earl of Douglas, had once again crossed the border and on 5 August 1388 at Otterburn – or Chevy Chase – between Jedburgh and Newcastle, had virtually destroyed an English army, taking prisoner Henry Percy (Shakespeare's Harry Hotspur), its commander. Of personal initiative he showed no sign – until, on 3 May 1389, he quietly and unprovocatively informed the Council that, since he was now fully of age with the mistakes of his youth far behind him, he intended henceforth to rule as a monarch should, and as his grandfather had ruled before him.

It says much for the improvement in the domestic situation during the previous year that this announcement occasioned little concern to those who heard it. Richard was by now four months past his twenty-second birthday; he could not be kept on a leading-rein for ever. No objections were raised. Arundel made preparations to go crusading in Palestine, while Derby and Gloucester preferred the company of the Teutonic Knights in Prussia. Warwick retired to his estates. Meanwhile the sheriffs throughout the land were instructed to make public proclamations to the effect that the King had now personally assumed responsibility for government, while emphasizing that this would be administered as before through his Council, the leading members of which were now William of Wykeham, Bishop of Winchester, as Chancellor; Thomas Brantingham, Bishop of Exeter, as Treasurer; and Edmund Stafford, Chancellor of Oxford University and Dean of York, who was now appointed Keeper of the Privy Seal.

But Richard had not altogether regained his self-confidence; he needed further support of the kind which could come only from his own family, and his thoughts inevitably turned towards his uncle, John of Gaunt. Gaunt's Spanish campaign had been only a modified success. He had succeeded in marrying off his elder daughter Philippa to King John I of Portugal and his younger, Catherine – now Catalina – to the future King Henry III of Castile, from whom he had received an indemnity of £100,000 and an annual pension of £6,000 in token of his renunciation of his claims to that kingdom; but he had achieved no throne for himself, and no permanent peace between Castile and Aragon on the one hand and England on the other. In 1387 he had left Spain for Gascony, where he was doubtless kept fully informed of the disturbing developments at home; but his eldest son's identification with the Appellants had persuaded him – probably rightly – to remain abroad until the crisis was over. Even then he might well have elected to stay in France, had he not received an urgent appeal from his nephew to return. He landed in England in November 1389, and was welcomed with open arms. All past differences were forgotten: henceforth John stood at the King's right hand.

Richard was now steadily strengthening his own position; one fear, however, continued to disturb him. He could not forget the veiled threat made to him by his uncle three years before, the reminder of the deposition of his great-grandfather Edward II and the warning that he himself might suffer a similar fate. In the autumn of 1390 we find him at Gloucester, where Edward was buried, arranging for perpetual devotions at his shrine and seeking confirmation of the miracles that were said to have taken place there – a necessary preliminary before submitting to the Pope a request for his canonization. A year later he extracted from Parliament a guarantee that he would be 'as free in his regality, liberty and royal dignity as any of his noble progenitors . . . notwithstanding any former statute or ordinance to the contrary, notably in the time of King Edward the Second who lies at Gloucester . . . and that if any statute was made in the time of the said King Edward, in derogation of the liberty and franchise of the Crown, it should be annulled.'

The ghost of his great-grandfather had been laid at last. Perhaps, in retrospect, it might have been better had it continued to haunt him.

In this penultimate chapter of Richard's reign, England was generally considered by most of its inhabitants to be at peace. True, the war in France rumbled on; but it made little impact across the Channel, and John of Gaunt had crossed over to Calais for yet another round of negotiations to bring it to an end. The Scots were quiet. But peace, in the fourteenth century, was relative. In 1392 there were ugly scenes in London, the city having refused to grant the King one of its periodic loans. If, as the chroniclers claim, it had simultaneously granted a large one to a Lombard merchant, Richard would have had good reason to be angry; at all events he reacted with all his old impulsiveness, forcibly removing the mayor and sheriffs from office and transferring the courts and administration to York. Finally the Londoners were obliged to give in, making the King a free gift of £10,000 as the price of reconciliation. This they celebrated with a grand procession through the city; but they never entirely forgave him. When, a few years later, he would stand in need of their support, that support would not be forthcoming.

There were other disturbances in the north, beginning in 1393 in Cheshire. These seem to have been primarily directed against the Duke of Gloucester, who had thought better of his crusade in Prussia and had now rejoined Richard's Council. Gloucester's erstwhile colleague Arundel, in his nearby castle of Holt on the river Dee, was well placed to restore order but made no attempt to do so; nor did he lift a finger when another rising took place a few weeks later in Yorkshire. John of Gaunt, the principal object of the insurgents' wrath, went so far as to accuse Arundel of actively encouraging them and ultimately extracted a grudging apology; but Arundel had grown bitter and cantankerous, and was rapidly losing the goodwill of all his former friends.

Matters came to a head at the beginning of June 1394, with the sudden and unexpected death of the Queen at the age of twenty-seven. The heartbroken King, having ordered the immediate demolition of that part of the Palace of Sheen in which she had died, made plans for an impressive funeral at Westminster Abbey at which Arundel, having failed altogether to take part in the procession from the lying-in-state, appeared late and simultaneously requested permission to leave early. Richard, furious at what he believed, probably rightly, to be a deliberate insult, seized a rod from one of the vergers and struck him to the ground. After some weeks in the Tower, Arundel was arraigned before his sovereign at Lambeth Palace and obliged to take an oath for his subsequent good behaviour on a surety of £40,000.

Most of the summer of 1394 Richard spent in mourning for his wife; then, towards the end of September, he left for Ireland. The visit was, he knew, long overdue. In 1368 and again in 1380, all those English lords possessing estates in Ireland had been ordered either to return to them or to make proper provision for their defence; but the order had proved unenforceable and with every year that passed the administration had become more chaotic, with the local Irish kings and chieftains penetrating deeper and deeper into the lands of the English absentees. In 1379 Edmund Mortimer, third Earl of March, had been appointed Lieutenant and had done much to retrieve the situation in Ulster; but in 1381 he was drowned crossing a ford in County Cork, and his immense estates had passed to his seven-year-old son Roger. In the following year, with the situation growing increasingly desperate, Richard had appointed his uncle Gloucester as Lieutenant, but had subsequently changed his mind for reasons unexplained; and it was by now clear not only that he must go himself, but that he must do so at once. If his visit were to be any longer postponed, all Ireland – and its revenues – would be lost. Gloucester accompanied him, together with the young Earl of March, now twenty, the Earls of Rutland, Huntingdon and Nottingham – now completely reconciled – and a number of lesser lords. His uncle Edmund, Duke of York – Rutland's father – remained behind as Keeper of the Realm; John of Gaunt returned to Gascony and Aquitaine.

The English army landed at Waterford on 2 October 1394; but apart from the occasional small skirmish with Irish tribesmen, neither then nor later was there any serious fighting. That, as everybody knew by now, was not Richard's way. He marched by easy stages to Dublin Castle, where he settled down with his counsellors to restore law and order and re-establish his rule – essentially by confirming the chieftains in their lands in return for oaths of allegiance, granting them where necessary full legal recognition. All four Irish kings came to Dublin, where they were received with honour and granted English knighthoods, and where they cheerfully performed the acts of homage required of them. They may have been somewhat less pleased when the King insisted that they should be taught English table manners and should abandon their traditional kilts in favour of more seemly linen drawers; but they doubtless consoled themselves with the reflection that he would not be in Ireland long and that they would soon be able to revert to their old habits.

Richard in fact delayed his departure till 1 May 1395, when he and his army sailed from Waterford, leaving the Earl of March to maintain control. His Irish visit had been more successful than he or any of his advisers could have hoped, and had immeasurably increased his prestige. Not only was he popular with the people; among the nobility too, opposition had melted away. Such was his new-found confidence that he decided, typically, to risk an extraordinary gesture of defiance that would, he must have known, arouse the intense indignation of all those around him. His bosom friend Robert de Vere, in exile since the end of 1387, had been killed five years later, boar-hunting near Louvain; Richard now ordered his body brought back to England for reburial in the de Vere family vault at Earls Colne in Essex. In the course of the ceremony of reconsecration he suddenly ordered the coffin opened and gazed down on the embalmed body, clasping the dead man's hands, the fingers still heavy with jewels, and adding a further ring of his own.

Few if any of the great nobles were present at this embarrassing ceremony; most of them – one suspects rather to the King's irritation – chose to ignore it altogether. John of Gaunt, however, although he had always detested de Vere, remained rocklike in his nephew's support, his recent disappointments in Spain forgotten in the satisfaction of having finally concluded, in May 1394, a four-year truce with France. He was also much exhilarated by the demise, two months before, of his Spanish wife Constance of Castile. The two had never been close, and her death freed him to marry – with the King's willing permission – his long-time mistress Katherine Swynford, as well as to legitimize their four children.[1] These last arrangements were predictably unwelcome to John's heir Henry Bolingbroke, now Earl of Derby; but the death of Henry's own wife, Mary Bohun, in July prevented him from making any active protest.

Before long, too, plans for a still more important marriage were in the air: that of Richard himself to Isabelle, daughter of Charles VI of France.

The advantages of a French marriage were clear. The war had now continued for almost sixty years; something must be done to bring it to an end. A permanent peace was out of the question while the English remained in Calais, the surrender of which neither Richard nor his advisers were prepared to contemplate for a moment; but a royal marriage could be expected to hold the situation for a long time to come, and the French needed little persuasion to extend the earlier four-year truce to a period of no less than twenty-eight years from the signature of the final agreement on 9 March 1396. On that occasion Richard himself travelled to Paris, where Charles VI entertained him to a ceremonial banquet and he was married by proxy to Isabelle. There was, to be sure, one drawback to the match – a drawback of which Shakespeare may have been ignorant or, more probably, which he chose to overlook: while the groom was now twenty-nine, his bride was just seven. But Richard was still deeply affected by the death of his beloved Anne, and he may well have been grateful that the Princess's youth allowed him a few more years to mend his broken heart. Meanwhile he grew genuinely fond of the little girl, who received a magnificent welcome when she arrived at Calais in October; and there is no reason to suppose that the marriage would not have turned out an extremely happy one – and probably solved the problem of the succession into the bargain – had it been given the chance to do so.

Politically, however, there were disadvantages. One was that the French were not only England's traditional enemies; they were also schismatics. It was now nearly twenty years since Pope Gregory XI had

---

1. John Beaufort, the eldest, became Earl of Somerset; Henry, Dean of Wells and then Cardinal Bishop of Winchester; Thomas, Duke of Exeter. Joan married Ralph Nevill, Earl of Westmorland. Tradition – but, alas, only tradition – holds that Katherine's elder sister Philippa was the wife of the poet Geoffrey Chaucer.

ended the seventy-year exile of the papacy and returned to Rome; but a succession of antipopes continued, with the full support of the French King, to contest the title from Avignon, and any alliance with France would be sure to have unpleasant consequences on Richard's relations with Gregory's second successor, Boniface IX. An even graver cause for concern from the parliamentary point of view was a clause in the treaty in which the French royal house promised 'to aid and sustain [Richard] against all manner of persons who owe him any obedience, and also to aid and sustain him with all their power against any of his subjects'. There was nothing necessarily sinister in this; it could easily have been prompted by the ever-present danger of another peasants' revolt. On the other hand, Richard could equally well have had Gloucester and Arundel in mind, and the very idea of an English King summoning a French army to champion him against his own subjects was enough to make the marriage a good deal more unpopular than it might otherwise have been. It was scarcely surprising, in the circumstances, that those two noblemen in particular – and especially Gloucester, who had always detested the French – were loud in its condemnation; only the enthusiastic endorsement of John of Gaunt enabled Richard to ride out the storm and, in January 1397, to have Isabelle crowned Queen.

In the same month Parliament met at Westminster, the first that had sat for two years. While not actively hostile to the King, it had no intention of being intimidated. At its very first session it firmly refused any financial backing for Richard's plan – the result of a rash promise to his father-in-law Charles VI – to send an army in support of the Duke of Burgundy against Gian Galeazzo Visconti of Milan. Next, on 1 February, a petition was presented in the name of one Thomas Haxey – a formerly mysterious figure whom we now know not to have been a Member of Parliament at all, but a clerk to the Court of Common Pleas and proctor to the Abbot of Selby. Its first three clauses were unexceptionable; the fourth and last, however, was an outspoken protest against the excessive cost of the royal court owing to the presence of so many bishops, fashionable ladies and their retinues. Richard would have done well to ignore it; instead he flew into one of his ever more frequent furies and appealed to the Lords, who obediently declared it to be treason for anyone to excite the Commons to reform anything affecting the person, government or regality of a King, and on 7 February condemned Haxey, by a shameless piece of retroactive legislation, to a traitor's death. The unfortunate man was in fact reprieved only three months later and received a full pardon, but the damage was done: all the doubts and uncertainties of the previous decade had been reopened, while the readiness of the Lords to oblige the King had dangerously increased his self-confidence.

It certainly had no effect on his expenditure. Apart from his normal extravagances, Richard was now spending vast sums on the remodelling of Westminster Hall, first built as a banqueting hall by the Conqueror's son William Rufus almost exactly three centuries before. With a length of 240 feet and 70 feet across, it was already by far the largest Norman hall in England, and probably in Europe; but it had been badly damaged by fire in 1291, and though restored under Edward II it had never regained its former splendour till Richard took it in hand in 1394. Architecturally speaking, the moment could hardly have been more propitious. The King had as his master mason one of the greatest of medieval architects, Henry Yevele, who had recently completed the nave of Westminster Abbey; with Yevele was a carpenter of genius, Hugh Herland. Together, over a period of seven years, these two men produced a new Hall which, though no longer or broader than William's, was higher and infinitely more magnificent. Its chief glory was – and is – Herland's timber roof, 92 feet above the floor, the earliest large hammerbeam roof in England with the widest unsupported span; surely the finest anywhere. The Hall soon became the centre of administrative life, the setting for council meetings and often for parliaments them-selves; it was to house the law courts until 1882. Here, without any question, was Richard's greatest gift to his country: for Westminster Hall alone he deserves our lasting gratitude.

When the parliament rose, Gloucester and Arundel – who may well have been behind Haxey's petition – made little effort to conceal their disgust. They were concerned, too, at the rapid rise to power and influence of the King's new favourite, Edward Earl of Rutland; and they were irritated, to say the least, both by Richard's continued efforts to secure the canonization of Edward II and by his shameless intriguing for the crown of the Holy Roman Empire. In February they provoked a fresh outburst of royal wrath by deliberately ignoring his summons to a Council; soon afterwards, at a royal banquet held at Westminster in early July, Gloucester complained of the concessions being made to the French, including the surrender to them of Brest and Cherbourg three months before.[1] Whether he and Arundel, and perhaps Warwick – of whose doings over the past decade we know comparatively little, but who now returns to a position of some prominence – were actively plotting against the King, we shall never know. It seems unlikely; but rumours of a conspiracy soon spread, and Richard was not prepared to take any chances. He had had enough of his uncle and his friends; he would suffer them no more.

It was somehow typical of Richard's character that he should have invited his enemies to a banquet – which Thomas Walsingham was to compare with the one given by Herod at which Salome danced for the head of John the Baptist. Gloucester pleaded ill-health; Arundel also declined. Of the three, only Warwick accepted, and was initially given a warm welcome by the King; only when the feasting was over was he seized and led away to the Tower. A few weeks later Arundel was also captured – once again by trickery, Richard having sworn a solemn oath to his brother the Archbishop that he should suffer no bodily harm. He was confined to Carisbrooke Castle until such time as his fate should be decided. There remained only Gloucester. This time the King was resolved on a show of strength. With a numerous retinue which included his half-brothers Thomas and John Holland – now Earls of Kent and Huntingdon respectively – the Earls of Rutland and Nottingham and a sizeable contingent of his own household troops, he rode down by night to his uncle's castle at Pleshey in Essex; since Gloucester had refused his earlier invitation, he explained, he had no alternative but to come himself to fetch him. Taken totally by surprise, the Duke could only beg for mercy; Richard replied that he should have all the mercy that he had shown to Sir Simon Burley, for whose life the Queen had knelt in vain before him nine years before. Gloucester was dispatched in close custody to Calais to await his fate – which was not to be long in coming.

Judgement was passed at the next parliament – the last of the reign – which met on 17 September 1397. The charges were essentially those

---

1. The two ports had in fact been pledged to the English in April 1378 for the duration of the war, in return for some £20,000. With the war's end and the conclusion of the twenty-eight-year truce there was no justification for retaining them.

of treason – committed nine years before, at the time of the Merciless Parliament, when the three accused had been themselves the accusers; and the procedure followed was much the same. This time the appeal was laid by eight lords, including Richard's half-brothers Kent and Huntingdon and his cousins the Earls of Rutland and Somerset.[1] Westminster Hall being under restoration, a temporary pavilion had been erected in the palace yard, open at the sides and with an immense throne on a high platform. A somewhat more sinister note was struck at the opening session by the presence of the King's personal bodyguard of some four hundred Cheshire archers, specially recruited for the occasion.

The first surprise after the proceedings had begun was the appearance of a fourth defendant: Arundel's brother Thomas, who had been promoted from the Archbishopric of York to that of Canterbury in the previous year. In such circumstances it was surprising that he should now have been impeached on the grounds of his complicity in the events of 1386–8; the reason was almost certainly that he had refused the King's command to appoint a lay proctor to speak for the clergy – an important preliminary, since churchmen were barred by their cloth from all legal processes which might result in bloodshed. He was given no opportunity to defend himself against the charges, and on 25 September was sentenced to the confiscation of his possessions and perpetual banishment.

The eight Appellants then appeared, wearing robes of red silk bordered in white and embroidered with gold. Bowing low before the King, they requested that the three accused should now be summoned before the assembly one by one, to answer the charges laid against them. First came the Earl of Arundel, whose indictment was read out to him by John of Gaunt in his capacity as High Steward of England. Indignantly, the Earl pleaded that he had already received two pardons from the King; Gaunt pointed out that these had both been formally revoked, and the two were still arguing over their validity when the Speaker, Sir John Bushey,[2] interrupted and demanded Arundel's

1. Thomas Holland had been created Earl of Kent in 1380, his brother John, Earl of Huntingdon in 1388; Rutland was the son of the King's uncle Edmund, Duke of York, Somerset the recently legitimized son of John of Gaunt.

2. He is sometimes known as Sir John Bussy. I prefer Shakespeare's version of the name.

immediate condemnation, at which the Appellants all flung down their gloves. The trial was over. Gaunt pronounced the customary sentence of the gallows, for which the King immediately substituted the more honourable one of the block. Arundel was led off to Tower Hill where, in the presence of Kent, Somerset and his own son-in-law Nottingham, his head was severed from his shoulders.

Parliament now turned its attention to Gloucester, but was informed that the Duke was already dead. Significantly, the precise circumstances of his death were not discussed; few of those present can have been in any doubt that he had been murdered at Calais by the King's command. It remained important, however, that he should be formally branded a traitor, to allow the confiscation of his property; so he too was found guilty of treason – had he not appeared fully armed at Haringey in 1387? – his estates being forfeited to the Crown. There remained only Warwick. 'Like a wretched old woman,' writes Adam of Usk scornfully, 'he made confession of all, wailing and weeping and whining, traitor that he was, and submitting himself in all things to the King's grace.' He too was condemned to the scaffold; but – possibly because he gave useful incriminating evidence against Gloucester – Richard commuted his sentence to one of perpetual banishment on the Isle of Man.[1]

With his enemies now safely eliminated, the King could properly reward those who had remained loyal. No less than five received dukedoms: to Bolingbroke – despite his previous record – went that of Hereford; to Mowbray, Norfolk; to John Holland, Exeter; to Thomas Holland, Surrey; to Rutland, Albemarle – or, as Shakespeare calls him, Aumerle. For the Crown Richard annexed the county of Cheshire,[2] together with some of the former Arundel property next to it in the Welsh marches. All this was approved by the Parliament, which on 30 September took a solemn oath to uphold all its acts in perpetuity. It was then adjourned till 27 January 1398, when, the King announced,

---

1. He was in fact soon afterwards brought back to England and imprisoned in the Tower, where he remained until he was freed by Henry IV.

2. The special position of Cheshire goes back to Domesday, when the county seems first to have acquired palatine status together with certain special privileges. It was there that the Black Prince had been accustomed to raise the majority of his troops; and Richard, as we have seen, had already attempted to do the same in 1387 as well as on the present occasion.

it would meet at Shrewsbury, a city conveniently close to the Cheshire border.

He would have been better advised to dissolve it altogether. He had achieved his primary object where his enemies were concerned, at the cost of far less bloodshed than had been seen in 1388; and although his treatment of Arundel had caused something of an outcry, there had been curiously little reaction to the death of Gloucester. Had he been content to leave the matter there, he might yet have succeeded in holding the kingdom together. But his revenge was not yet complete, and it was his determination to carry it through to the end that was to prove his undoing. We can discount Walsingham's stories of his being tormented by the ghost of Arundel, whose body he is said to have had exhumed lest the Earl be venerated as a martyr; in such a case he is hardly likely to have agreed to a four-month adjournment. Richard was not afraid; he was, on the contrary, over-confident – and dangerously vindictive.

The Shrewsbury session did not take long. It began with a formal request, by seven of the former eight Appellants, for the repeal of all the acts and judgements of the Merciless Parliament, 'done without authority and against the will and liberty of the King and the right of his Crown'. The earldom of Suffolk was then restored to the de la Pole family, and fresh oaths were sworn on the lines of those taken at Westminster the previous September to maintain the acts of the present Parliament, with any future attempts to reverse them being considered acts of treason. Trouble came only on the third day of the session. It had already been noted that one of the Appellants, Thomas Mowbray, now Duke of Norfolk, was absent; and on 30 January Henry Boling-broke, Duke of Hereford, reported to the full assembly, at the King's command, a recent conversation with him during which, as Holinshed puts it, he had uttered 'certaine words . . . sounding highlie to the King's dishonor'. Since Mowbray left no account of the affair we are forced to rely on the parliamentary record of Henry's version, according to which, as the two were riding together from Brentford to London the month before, Mowbray remarked that they were both about to be undone because of what had happened at Radcot Bridge; and when Bolingbroke pointed out that they had both been pardoned, he assured him that, pardon or no pardon, the King intended to deal with the two of them just as he had dealt with the others. He went on to tell Henry that there was a plot, hatched by a group of lords close to the King, to kill them both at Windsor after the Parliament, together with Henry's father, John of Gaunt, the Dukes of Exeter and Albemarle and the Marquess of Dorset. They must consequently either concoct a counter-plot or flee the country while there was still time.

Richard's vindictiveness was well known, and apart from the inclusion in the list of the King's half-brother Exeter, there is nothing inherently improbable in the idea of such a plot. Whether it was true or not, however, the story was clearly damaging to Mowbray, particularly since he was not present to defend himself; and still more was it harmful to Richard, who seems to have ordered Bolingbroke to speak out only to put an end to the rumours which had been circulating for some time. He certainly had no desire to have the scandal investigated on the spot; instead, he proposed the appointment of a special committee of eighteen to look into the whole affair. Then, on 31 January, the day after Bolingbroke's testimony, he dissolved the Parliament.

5

The Triumph of Bolingbroke

[1398–1400]

RICH.   You may my glories and my state depose,
        But not my griefs; still am I King of those.
                                    KING RICHARD II

After two preliminary meetings at Oswestry and Bristol, the special
committee reassembled on 29 April 1398 at Windsor Castle. Now, for
the first time, the two Dukes appeared face to face before the King;
and it is at this point that Shakespeare raises the curtain on *The Tragedie
of King Richard the Second*, which was entered in the Stationers' Register
on 29 August 1597, though he seems to have finished it late in 1595.
His version of the confrontation is derived in all its essentials from
Holinshed's *Chronicles*,[1] though he understandably takes a few small
liberties. 'Old John of Gaunt, time-honoured Lancaster' – he was at
the time fifty-eight – is unlikely to have been present; had he been,
Holinshed would certainly have mentioned him. According to Holinshed, too, both Bolingbroke and Mowbray had unnamed knights to
speak for them – though Mowbray soon took over his own defence,
during which he freely admitted a past attempt on the life of Gaunt,
long since confessed and pardoned. It is fascinating to compare the bald
statements in Holinshed with what Shakespeare makes of them – giving
them colour, life and vigour. A single example must suffice; the *Chronicles*
report the knight who speaks for Bolingbroke:

Here is Henry of Lancaster . . . who saith, and I for him likewise say, that

1. Raphael Holinshed's *Historie of England*, which forms part of his *Chronicles of
England, Scotland and Ireland*, constitutes the first authoritative continuous account in
English of the whole of English history to date. The *Chronicles* were first published in
1577; Shakespeare, however, used John Hooker's revised and updated edition of 1587.

Thomas Mowbraie duke of Norfolke is a false and disloiall traitor to you and your roiall maiestie, and to your whole realme . . . and likewise that [he] hath received eight thousand nobles to pay the souldiers that keepe your towne of Calis, which he hath not doone as he ought: and furthermore [he] hath beene the occasion of all the treason that hath been contrived in your realme for the space of these eighteene yeares, and by his false suggestions and malicious counsell, he hath caused to die and to be murdered your right deere uncle, the duke of Glocester, sonne to king Edward. Moreover the duke of Hereford saith, and I for him, that he will prove this with his bodie against the bodie of the said duke of Norfolke within lists.

Here now is Shakespeare's translation:

> Look what I speak, my life shall prove it true:
> That Mowbray hath receiv'd eight thousand nobles
> In name of lendings for your Highness' soldiers,
> The which he hath detain'd for lewd imployments,
> Like a false traitor, and injurious villain;
> Besides I say, and will in battle prove,
> Or here, or elsewhere to the furthest verge
> That ever was survey'd by English eye,
> That all the treasons for these eighteen years
> Complotted and contrived in this land
> Fetch from false Mowbray their first head and spring;
> Further I say, and further will maintain
> Upon his bad life to make all this good,
> That he did plot the Duke of Gloucester's death,
> Suggest his soon-believing adversaries,
> And consequently, like a traitor coward,
> Sluic'd out his innocent soul through streams of blood,[1]
> Which blood, like sacrificing Abel's, cries
> Even from the tongueless caverns of the earth

1. According to Holinshed, Gloucester was smothered with towels in a feather bed. Beheading was the normal form of execution for those of exalted rank, but Gloucester, who had been neither tried nor condemned, was murdered rather than executed. The murder, whatever the method, took place at Calais in September 1397, almost certainly with the King's full knowledge and – despite his denial in I.i.133 – under Mowbray's supervision.

> To me for justice and rough chastisement;
> And, by the glorious worth of my descent,
> This arm shall do it, or this life be spent.[1]

Since the two disputants maintained their hostility and refused all the King's attempts at reconciliation, it was agreed that the quarrel should be settled in the traditional manner, by armed contest; and the encounter was fixed for St Lambert's Day,[2] 17 September, at Coventry. Word spread quickly; the public imagination was caught by the prospect of two dukes – one of them the King's own cousin – meeting each other in single combat and fighting quite possibly to the death, and noblemen and knights from all over England arrived at the little town with their ladies for what was clearly to be the social event of the year. When the great day came, one great magnate only was noticeable by his absence: John of Gaunt. After the Shrewsbury Parliament he had retired from public life, probably because the activities of his son were causing him increasing concern. (Though Froissart suggests that he fell ill only around Christmas, he may also have been already stricken by the disease that was to kill him five months later.) At any rate he never saw his son ride out to Gosford Green 'mounted on a white courser, barded with green and blue velvet, embroidered sumptuously with swans and antelopes'; nor did he hear the deafening cheers that greeted his appearance – considerably louder, we are told, than those accorded to Mowbray shortly afterwards.

To Richard, however, these cheers carried a note of menace. He had never liked his cousin or trusted him; if he were to win the coming contest, he would be the most popular man in the kingdom. On the other hand – since the outcome of all such contests was generally believed to be divinely ordained – a victory for the Duke of Norfolk would be taken by many as a sign that his charges were justified. It followed that neither should be allowed to win; besides, why should he, the King, who possessed neither the physique nor the temperament necessary to wield a lance, preside over what promised to be a dazzling exhibition of military skill? Without warning, he suddenly flung down his staff – a sign that the contest must stop before it had begun. There

---

1. I.i.87–108.
2. According at least to Shakespeare. Holinshed is less certain of the date.

would be no trial of strength; neither of the contestants would be seen to have God on their side:

> Let them lay by their helmets and their spears,
> And both return back to their chairs again . . .
> For that our kingdom's earth should not be soil'd
> With that dear blood which it hath fostered;
> And for our eyes do hate the dire aspect
> Of civil wounds plough'd up with neighbours' sword,
> And for we think the eagle-wingèd pride
> Of sky-aspiring and ambitious thoughts,
> With rival-hating envy, set on you
> To wake our peace, which in our country's cradle
> Draws the sweet infant breath of gentle sleep . . .
> Therefore we banish you our territories.

Bolingbroke was exiled for ten years; Mowbray for life.

For all those present, the sense of anticlimax must have been almost unbearable; the King's popularity, such as it was, had sustained another devastating blow. From Richard's own point of view, however, his decision was by then the only possible one. As to the discrepancy between the two sentences, the most probable explanation is that he would have sentenced both men to perpetual banishment if he dared to do so, but that Bolingbroke was too popular and too powerful. He may also have spared a thought for John of Gaunt, to whom he owed much. It is worth remembering that only six months later, with Gaunt safely in his grave, the King sentenced his son to banishment yet again – this time for life.

Richard's actions at Coventry suggest, on the whole, a considerable degree of wisdom and moderation; by the beginning of 1399, however, both these qualities seem to have deserted him. In his progresses through the country he was now invariably accompanied by his 400 Cheshire archers, together with considerable numbers of knights and squires retained in specific locations; his taste for pomp and ostentation was becoming ever more uncontrolled, as was his expenditure on buildings, clothes, furniture and luxuries of every kind. Such things could legitimately be paid for only by a successful war; since England had long been at peace, there was but one alternative – to bleed the country white. All those who had been in any way implicated in the events of ten years before were ordered to seek individual pardons before mid-summer; and these pardons did not come cheaply. Moreover the seventeen counties – they included London and more than half the entire population – which were said to have supported the original Appellants were obliged to pay up to £1,000 each to regain the King's favour. At worst it was blackmail; at best, protection money. Meanwhile Richard maintained his old habit of demanding forced loans, both from communities and from individuals. By the time he left on his second expedition to Ireland in May 1399 he owed £6,570 to the people of London, £5,550 to seventy-one other cities and towns, £3,180 to the Church and £1,220 to thirty-six individual commoners. Hostility to him was no longer confined to a few discontented nobles and their followers; the whole country was now ripe for revolution.

On 3 February 1399 John of Gaunt died at the Bishop of Ely's palace in Holborn, in his sixtieth year. He had made, so far as we can tell, no protest at the murder of his brother Gloucester – a fact which Shakespeare considers important enough to warrant a scene to itself (I.ii) – nor at the banishment of his son. There is certainly no documentary justification for his robust yet moving farewell to Bolingbroke (I.iii) after the King had pronounced sentence; as we have seen, he was not even present at the lists. But then Shakespeare's Gaunt – the grand old man of his time, full of years and wisdom, the father of his country whose dying speech on England (II.i.40ff.) figured until half a century ago in every school anthology – bears little enough resemblance to the picture we are given by Holinshed, who sees him as just another turbulent and ambitious troublemaker; more powerful, perhaps, because he is the King's senior uncle, but otherwise no better than his fellow nobles. Alternative sources for Shakespeare's character have been suggested: Froissart is one, and an anonymous play, *Woodstock*, built around Thomas of Woodstock, Duke of Gloucester, is another. But the arguments are unconvincing. By far the likeliest possibility is that he is the playwright's own creation, the ideal – and dramatically necessary – counterpart to the vapid, feckless King.

For Richard, Gaunt's death spelt the beginning of the end. Despite their many differences, the Duke of Lancaster had done everything in his power to hold the kingdom together and maintain the prestige of the crown; his loss was a bitter blow, not least because it instantly polarized the situation – the King on the one side, Henry Bolingbroke on the other. Not that a reconciliation between them was even now impossible. Had Richard recalled Henry from exile, as many believed he would; had he permitted him to attend the funeral of the father he loved; had he ensured his proper inheritance of the immense estates that were his birthright, then war might yet have been avoided and England spared the second deposition of a monarch in less than a century. Alas, he did none of these things. Far from recalling Henry, he increased his period of banishment to life; and while he allowed several of the minor bequests and provisions of Gaunt's will, he ordered the vast majority of the Lancastrian estates – those which should rightly have devolved upon his cousin – to be divided among his own chief supporters, the Dukes of Exeter, Albemarle and Surrey. To every landowner in the kingdom, the lesson was plain: in Richard's England that most fundamental law, the law of inheritance, could no longer be relied on.

By this time there could no longer be any doubt that the King's mental balance was seriously disturbed. He surrounded himself with soothsayers and charlatans who flattered him shamelessly and prophesied extraordinary achievements. On feast days, we are told, he would sit on a high throne for hours at a time, watching all who passed below him; any man who caught his eye was expected to fall to his knees. When he left the palace, only his Cheshire archers protected him from violence at the hands of his subjects. Then, some time in the spring of 1399, there came grave news from Ireland. Some nine months previously the King's Lieutenant there, the Earl of March, had been ambushed and killed; now it was reported that two of the Irish kings, O'Neill and MacMurrough, heedless of their oaths of 1394, had risen in open rebellion, which was spreading rapidly. Immediate action was called for if the country were not to be abandoned altogether. Inevitably, it would be expensive; but a sale of John of Gaunt's movable possessions – his gold, jewels and works of art, to say nothing of the furniture from his many palaces and castles – would pay for it many times over.

So Richard did not hesitate. His first Irish expedition had been a triumph; why should not his second be even more so? His advisers tried to point out that his departure from England at such a time would be an open invitation to his enemies – perhaps to the furious Bolingbroke himself; but he refused to listen. Surrey was appointed Lieutenant in place of March and sent off at once. The hopelessly incompetent Edmund, Duke of York, was once again appointed Keeper of the Realm, supported by the three chief ministers of state – the Chancellor Edmund Stafford, Bishop of Exeter; the Treasurer the Earl of Wiltshire; and Richard Clifford, Bishop of Worcester, Keeper of the Privy Seal – together with the three prominent royalists Sir John Bushey, Sir William Bagot and Sir Henry Green. In the last week in May the King made a hurried pilgrimage to Canterbury and held his last Garter feast at Windsor. Then, accompanied by the Dukes of Exeter and Albemarle, the Earls of Worcester and Salisbury and – prudently – the sons of both Bolingbroke and the murdered Gloucester, he himself set sail for Ireland.

It was to prove the greatest mistake of his life.

Henry Bolingbroke, now Duke of Lancaster, had spent the previous nine months in Paris, where he had been joined by the young Earl of Arundel – still mourning his executed father – and the latter's uncle, the Archbishop. All three were in close touch with developments across the Channel. Froissart's story that Archbishop Arundel was a secret emissary of the malcontents is palpably untrue – he had been in exile for two years already – but his nephew may well have been entrusted with a message that Bolingbroke should lose no more time. The Duke, in any case, needed little persuading: his resentment now intensified by Richard's disposal of his inheritance and recent intervention to prevent his marriage to a cousin of the French King, he was even more firmly resolved to overthrow him. He was also aware that once he were to raise his standard on English soil he would find no shortage of allies. Towards the end of June, therefore, knowing that Richard was safely in Ireland, he and the Arundels embarked at Boulogne in three small ships and with what Adam of Usk estimates as 'scarce three hundred followers'. After a brief halt at Pevensey, they sailed north and eventually landed at Ravenscar, between Whitby and Scarborough. Here in the Lancastrian heartland he could be certain of a warm welcome; when he reached Doncaster, on or about Sunday 13 July, he was joined by Henry Percy, Earl of Northumberland, his son Harry Hotspur and their cousin and rival magnate along the Scottish borders, Ralph Nevill, Earl of Westmorland, each of them with a numerous following. From that moment on the Duke of Lancaster was no longer just a nobleman with a grievance; he was the leader of a rebellion. Nevertheless, according to a story later spread by the Percys and nowhere else confirmed, he there and then swore a solemn oath that he had come only to claim his rightful inheritance; he had no designs on the throne, which Richard would continue to occupy for the rest of his life.

Meanwhile the common people, too, flocked to his banner, as well they might – for his easy charm was a far cry from Richard's cold and haughty majesty.

> . . . How he did seem to dive into their hearts
> With humble and familiar courtesy;
> What reverence he did throw away on slaves,
> Wooing poor craftsmen with the craft of smiles . . .
> Off goes his bonnet to an oyster-wench;
> A brace of draymen bid God speed him well,
> And had the tribute of his supple knee,
> With 'Thanks, my countrymen, my loving friends' –
> As were our England in reversion his,
> And he our subjects' next degree in hope.[1]

Such were their numbers, indeed, and so rapidly did they increase as Bolingbroke continued his march through Derby, Leicester, Kenilworth, Evesham and Gloucester to Berkeley Castle,[2] that they proved impossible to feed: the vast majority were sent back to their homes.

The Duke of York, as Keeper of the Realm, was his usual indecisive and ineffectual self. Now fifty-eight, a mild, gentle figure who, according to Holinshed, 'wished that the state of the commonwealth might have been redressed without losse of any man's life', he had certainly given Richard less trouble than either Gaunt or Gloucester, if only because he was incapable of any kind of initiative. The least able of all Edward III's sons, at this moment of crisis he seems to have limited his activity to transferring the government from London – the loyalty of whose citizens could never be trusted – to St Albans, mobilizing what troops he could and sending urgent messages to the King to return at once. He and his council then headed westward to meet him, only to find

---

1. I.iv.25–28, 31–36.
2. He did not cross the Cotswolds ('Cotshall') as Shakespeare suggests.

the rebel army bearing down upon them. The Earl of Wiltshire, with Bushey and Green – Sir William Bagot had already fled to Cheshire – made for Bristol to organize resistance there; but York and the rest of his colleagues sought refuge at Berkeley – an inauspicious choice, perhaps, since it was the scene of Edward II's murder in 1327 – where, when the Duke of Lancaster arrived on 27 July, they instantly submitted. (The conversation between Lancaster and York in II.iii is of course invented.) The two then hurried on together to Bristol, where York was obliged to order the surrender of the castle. Wiltshire – who, somewhat surprisingly, appears nowhere in Shakespeare's play – Bushey and Green were arrested and summarily executed, their heads being sent to adorn the gates of London, York and Bristol respectively.[1]

Two days before, on the 27th, the King had left Ireland. Despite – or perhaps partly because of – an enormous retinue, he had achieved nothing; the 'rough rug-headed kerns', whose guerrilla tactics had caused havoc among his troops on their march from Waterford through Wicklow to Dublin, had refused either to submit or to meet the army in pitched battle. At Dublin Richard had offered a reward for the capture of MacMurrough; but there were no takers, and he soon retraced his steps to Waterford, where the news of Lancaster's invasion awaited him. At once he gave orders for departure; unfortunately he listened to the treacherous advice of Albemarle, who had seen clearly enough how things were going and had secretly cast in his lot with Lancaster. Realizing that the longer Richard could be kept out of England the better, he cleverly persuaded the King to split his army, sending Salisbury ahead with an advance guard to raise more troops in North Wales while he himself with the rest of his men took the direct route across the Irish Sea.

It was a disastrous decision. The King landed at Haverfordwest and lost several days in an unsuccessful attempt to find reinforcements in Glamorgan, before jettisoning his by now totally demoralized army with most of his baggage and hastening north towards Chester, which he believed as always to be loyal. But he had wasted too much time. Bolingbroke had preceded him; and when Richard met Salisbury at Conway Castle on 11 August it was to learn that the Duke of Lancaster

---

1. There is no evidence to support Bolingbroke's castigation of Bushey and Green in III.i, with its mysterious suggestion that the latter had 'made a divorce' between Richard and Queen Isabelle.

was already in possession of the city, where he had just executed the royal representative. And there was worse news to come: Salisbury's northern army, believing widespread rumours that the King was already dead, had melted away. Gone too were Richard's erstwhile friends Worcester and – though in the play he remains loyal – Albemarle. Even now the situation was not entirely hopeless. There were friendly ships in the harbour, in any one of which he could have slipped away – to Ireland, to his native Bordeaux or even to the court of his father-in-law in Paris. But he no longer knew whom to trust; and when Northumberland and Archbishop Arundel appeared at the gates and requested an audience, he granted it at once.

The terms offered by Henry Bolingbroke seemed reasonable enough. The Lancastrian inheritance was to be restored; Bolingbroke's claim to the hereditary Stewardship of England was to be submitted to a full Parliament, free of royal control; and five unnamed counsellors were to be surrendered for trial. Northumberland – although, significantly, not Arundel – swore on the host that the King should retain his royal dignity and power, and that the Duke of Lancaster would observe the terms as agreed; and Richard voluntarily left Conway with about twenty of his men to meet his cousin before returning, as he thought, by easy stages to London. Alas, he had given his enemies more credit than they deserved. Some six miles from the mouth of the river Conway the coastal path passes over a precipitous headland named Penmaenrhos. Here he fell into an ambush – almost certainly set by Northumberland himself, though the faithless Earl subsequently denied all knowledge of it – and was carried off to Flint Castle, where Henry was waiting. Though still King, he was now a prisoner of the Duke of Lancaster, with no alternative but to do his bidding:

> What must the king do now? Must he submit?
> The king shall do it. Must he be depos'd?
> The king shall be contented. Must he lose
> The name of king? A God's name, let it go.[1]

On Henry's orders he signed writs for the summoning of Parliament, to meet at Westminster on 30 September. He was then taken through

1. III.iii.143–6.

Lichfield, Coventry and St Albans to London, where he was put in the Tower to await his conqueror's pleasure.

In the scene at Flint Castle, Shakespeare has Bolingbroke kneel before Richard and protest that he seeks only his inheritance – 'My gracious lord, I come but for mine own.' This was certainly true at the time of his landing in Yorkshire; since then, however, he had come to see that Richard could no longer continue as King. Not only, if he regained his authority, would he unquestionably take his revenge; but in the past two years his rule had been that of a tyrant, showing a degree of cruelty and faithlessness more characteristic of an oriental despot than of a King of England. The country desperately needed a strong, enlightened ruler who would govern responsibly with the advice of the old nobility rather than a bunch of self-seeking favourites. Legally, the heir apparent was Edmund Mortimer, Earl of March, great-great-grandson of Edward III through his son Lionel, Duke of Clarence and Lionel's daughter Philippa; he was, however, just eight years old. The Duke of Lancaster's claim was admittedly only through Lionel's younger brother, John of Gaunt; but his descent from the old King was entirely in the male line, he was a generation older, and his reception as he had made his way across England from Ravenscar to Gloucester had left him in no doubt of the strength of his support. Whenever he may have taken his final decision – and whether or not he had sworn an oath at Doncaster – there seems little doubt that by the time Richard was delivered into his hands his mind was made up.

Thenceforth, two steps remained to be taken. First, Richard must be legally deposed; second, he – Henry – must prove himself the rightful successor to the throne. Both steps, however, must be taken quickly, since a power vacuum might easily lead to a change of heart among the great lords of the north, or even to a move by the French King in support of his son-in-law. For the deposition there was at least the precedent of Edward II, only seventy-two years before. On Monday 29 September in the Tower, Richard signed an instrument of abdication before a group of commissioners representing the lords spiritual and temporal, the landed gentry and the law; then, laying his crown on the ground before him, he resigned it, not to the Duke of Lancaster but to God.

The problem came with the legitimization of Lancaster as his successor. Edward II had abdicated in favour of his son and undoubted heir; Henry's claim was a good deal more tenuous. Some time before, moreover, Parliament had declared the Mortimers heirs to the kingdom in the event of Richard's remaining childless. In vain did Henry now order all the records and chronicles of all the leading religious houses to be diligently scanned for useful precedents, or evidence that could be used in support of his case; there seemed little doubt that, however great his own personal popularity, the claim of the young Edmund of March was legally superior. He first tried to resurrect a curious old legend, according to which his maternal great-great-grandfather, Edmund Crouchback, had in fact been born before his brother King Edward I; but this was found (to no one's surprise) to be without foundation – fortunately, since had it been true it would have meant that not only Richard but his three predecessors had all reigned illegitimately. Next he considered claiming the crown by right of conquest; but that, it was pointed out to him, would be riding roughshod over the law of England. A third possibility lay in a special act of parliament; but this he wished to avoid at all costs, knowing as he did that what parliament had given it could also take away.

The solution, such as it was, that Henry eventually found was more subtle than any of these. It was to have himself acclaimed by an assembly which, though summoned as a parliament, was technically not a parliament at all. For a true parliament the presence of the King was essential; at this particular moment there was no King. It was thus only a great representative assembly that met, according to the summons issued by Richard at Flint, on 30 September 1399, in the still uncompleted Westminster Hall; the throne on its high dais stood empty, covered with a cloth of gold. Richard's abdication was read out by the Archbishop of York in both Latin and English, together with a schedule of thirty-three articles listing the crimes and misdeeds of which he was accused. His demands to appear in person to plead his case were simply ignored, as were the courageous representations made on his behalf by the Bishop of Carlisle and various other supporters. The assembly then agreed unanimously to accept his abdication and declared him deposed.

Now it was Henry's turn to speak:

In the name of the Father, and of the Son, and of the Holy Ghost, I, Henry of Lancaster, challenge this Realm of England, and the Crown, with all its members and appurtenances, in that I am descended by right line of the blood, coming from the good lord Henry Third, and through that right that God of His grace hath sent me, with help of my kin and of my friends to recover it; the which Realm was in point to be undone for default of governance and undoing of the good laws.

The words were deliberately vague, but they served their purpose. The entire assembly – bishops, lords and citizens – acclaimed Henry as the nation's lawful King, and he held up the signet ring which, he declared, Richard had given him on the previous day. Archbishop Arundel then led him up to the throne, from which he made another short speech of thanks, most notable, perhaps, for the following words:

It is not my will that any man think that by way of conquest I would disinherit any man of his heritage, franchise, or other rights that he ought to have, nor put him out of that that he has and has had by the good laws and customs of the Realm, except those persons that have been against the good purpose and the common profit of the Realm.

Thus, while the precise nature of his claim remained undefined, he had been careful to remind his hearers both of his descent from Henry III and of his status as conqueror; and nowhere had he referred to the authority of Parliament.

Henry's coronation followed less than a fortnight later, on St Edward's Day, Monday 13 October – the anniversary of his departure from London into exile. He was anointed with oil from a miraculous phial said to have been presented to St Thomas à Becket by the Virgin Mary and afterwards hidden at Poitiers, where it had been found by the then Duke of Lancaster, the King's grandfather. The Duke had given it to the Black Prince; and he had left it in the Tower of London, where Richard II had found it in his turn, though unfortunately too late for his own coronation. Clearly it was hoped that the use of this oil would somehow lend additional sanctity to the ceremony, emphasizing still further Henry's right to the throne.

There were recriminations, but not many. The Dukes of Albemarle, Surrey and Exeter, accused of complicity in the murder of Gloucester, pleaded *force majeure* and were merely deprived of their dukedoms, reverting to their former titles as Earls of Rutland, Kent and Huntingdon; the Bishop of Carlisle, similarly charged (though he pleaded innocent), lost his bishopric. For the rest, the new King proved surprisingly merciful: both Rutland and Huntingdon were members of the council again before the end of the year.

For impeccable dramatic reasons Shakespeare runs together various separate incidents – including the ceremonies of both the abdication and the accession – in the single scene of Act IV, set in Westminster Hall. The scene begins with Sir William Bagot and others accusing Albemarle (Aumerle) of the murder of the Duke of Gloucester, and the angry challenges by which he rejects the charges. (All this in fact occurred over two weeks later, in parliament on 16 and 18 October.) It continues with the report by the Bishop of Carlisle – in nine lines which are among the most beautiful in all Shakespeare[1] – of the death in Venice of Thomas Mowbray, Duke of Norfolk:[2]

> Many a time hath banished Norfolk fought
> For Jesu Christ in glorious Christian field,
> Streaming the ensign of the Christian cross
> Against black pagans, Turks, and Saracens;
> And, toil'd with works of war, retir'd himself
> To Italy; and there at Venice gave
> His body to that pleasant country's earth,
> And his pure soul unto his captain Christ,
> Under whose colours he had fought so long.

The Bishop then launches into the furious diatribe against Bolingbroke's actions[3] which results in his own arrest. Only then does Richard enter, to hand the crown to his cousin and to make his great abdication speech:

> I give this heavy weight from off my head,
> And this unwieldy sceptre from my hand,

---

1. IV.i.92–100.

2. He died there of the plague on 22 September 1399, on his way back from Jerusalem, and was buried in St Mark's. All that remains of his tomb – an armorial plate – can now be seen in the Hall of Corby Castle, Cumbria.

3. According to Holinshed his speech, made only on 22 October, was directed primarily against the proposal that Richard should be put on trial.

> The pride of kingly sway from out my heart;
> With mine own tears I wash away my balm,
> With mine own hands I give away my crown,
> With mine own tongue deny my sacred state,
> With mine own breath release all duteous oaths;
> All pomp and majesty I do forswear . . .

Inevitably, the legal aspects involved over both this and the accession are simplified or ignored altogether: Shakespeare is far more interested in Richard's character, and in his reactions to his deposition. All the anger has left him, all the arrogance and bombast. There remains only his own majestic self-pity: an unedifying emotion, but never – surely – more heartbreakingly expressed. The scene ends with the Abbot of Westminster giving Albemarle and the Bishop of Carlisle the first intimation of a plot – prematurely as it happens, since the first meeting of the conspirators did not take place until 17 December.

Mention of the plot leads us into Act V, where another of Shakespeare's sources assumes importance for the first time: Samuel Daniel, whose *First Fowre Bookes of the ciuile warres between the two houses of Lancaster and Yorke* bears the date 1595 on its title page. There are echoes of this long epic poem earlier in the play, but they are for the most part insignificant; only in this final act does the connection between the two become unmistakable. Daniel – who was born in 1562 and is, at his best, one of the most dazzling of all Elizabethan poets – was no more pledged to historical accuracy than was Shakespeare himself; and it may well have been he who originated the idea both of making Richard's Queen Isabelle a mature young woman rather than the girl of eleven that she in fact was, and of giving her an emotional farewell scene with her husband. The first scene of Act V is in any case sheer invention, as is York's moving comparison of Henry's and Richard's processional entries into London in the scene that follows. Henry – who, as Adam of Usk puts it, had 'within fifty days, conquered both king and kingdom' – certainly made such an entry: Holinshed describes the vast crowds that lined the streets, and the rapturousness of their welcome. But Froissart, unreliable as he may be,[1] specifically emphasizes

---

1. At this time over sixty years old, he had not visited England for thirty years, apart from a brief visit to the court at Eltham in 1395.

that Richard was not forced into any such procession; indeed, the new King's primary concern seems to have been to deal with him as quickly and discreetly as possible.

He did, however, take careful and considered advice from many of his counsellors before deciding the ex-King's fate. On 23 October, through the Earl of Northumberland, he consulted a full assembly of the House of Lords; fifty-eight of those present recommended that Richard should be removed to some secret place from which no mob could attempt a rescue. Four days later parliament was officially informed that he had been sentenced to imprisonment for life; the place of his captivity was not revealed. On 28 October he was taken in disguise from the Tower, and carried first to Gravesend and then to Leeds Castle in Kent. A few days later he was transferred from Leeds to 'Pomfret' – the Lancastrian castle of Pontefract in Yorkshire. He never saw the outside world again.

Pontefract may have been safe from mob violence; but Richard's incarceration did not prevent the former Bishop of Carlisle – now removed from his see – and a number of his friends, including Huntingdon, Kent, Rutland and Salisbury, from plotting the assassination of Henry IV and his sons during the Epiphany celebrations at Windsor on 6 January 1400. The plan might actually have succeeded had not Rutland unaccountably revealed the details to his father the Duke of York – Shakespeare, with Holinshed, has York catching sight of an incriminating letter and demanding to read it[1] – who naturally informed the King. Henry left Windsor immediately with his family for London but was unable to halt the rebels, who seized the castle – simultaneously spreading the rumour that Richard had escaped and was even then gathering an army in the valley of the upper Thames. The Londoners, however, refused to be intimidated, and within two days the King had a force of some 20,000 men. An encounter near Maidenhead was inconclusive but the insurgents were finally caught at Cirencester, where Kent and Salisbury were beheaded on 8 January. Huntingdon escaped to Shoeburyness in Essex, but was soon captured and executed in his turn; the ever-slippery Rutland turned his coat just in time. The triumphant King returned to Westminster on the 15th, preceded by a forest of long poles bearing the heads of his enemies.

1. V.ii.56ff.

By this time Richard had already been for some two months at Pontefract. Exactly how he died, and when, will always remain a mystery. Shakespeare, following Holinshed, represents him as being struck down by a certain Sir Piers Exton, who had heard an exasperated King Henry ask if there was no friend who would rid him of 'this living fear' – much as his namesake Henry II had cried out against Thomas à Becket more than two centuries before. Such a fate is certainly possible, though in view of the traditional reluctance to shed the blood of an anointed king, it has been suggested that – if there was any violence at all – smothering was more likely. Another story relates that, on hearing that the attempt to reinstate him had failed, Richard had simply turned his face to the wall, refusing all food, and died of starvation. All we can say with certainty is that on 29 January 1400 the French King and Council referred to him as being dead; and that a few days later, in the face of continuing rumours that he was alive, his body was brought to London and displayed at various stopping-places along the way. It then lay for two days in St Paul's, where the new King attended a requiem mass as pall-bearer, before being taken to King's Langley in Hertfordshire for burial. In 1413 Henry V had the body disinterred and removed to Westminster Abbey, where it was consigned to the tomb which Richard himself had built for his first wife, Anne. The effigy above, by the London coppersmiths Nicholas Broker and Godfrey Prest, was created during his lifetime and is clearly a portrait. It shows a face at once sensitive and indecisive, with a pointed nose and short forked beard, crowned with waving curls.

Shakespeare makes King Henry – once again like his distant predecessor – disown the crime, if crime there was. At the same time he cannot absolve himself of indirect responsibility, and in the last speech of the play he vows a pilgrimage, or perhaps a crusade:

> Though I did wish him dead,
> I hate the murtherer, love him murthered . . .
> I'll make a voyage to the Holy Land,
> To wash this blood off from my guilty hand.

This, too, seems to be invention. According to Holinshed, the King did indeed make such a vow; but it was in the last years of his reign rather than the first, and there was never any suggestion that it was prompted by a desire for atonement. He certainly went through all the normal formalities of mourning, and ordered a thousand masses said for the repose of Richard's soul; he was, after all, a genuinely religious man. But he would not have been human if, after hearing the news of Richard's death, his strongest emotion had been not sorrow or remorse, but relief.

6

King Henry IV Part I

[1400–1403]

PRINCE.   . . . think not, Percy,
To share with me in glory any more:
Two stars keep not their motion in one sphere,
Nor can one England brook a double reign
Of Harry Percy and the Prince of Wales.

HENRY IV PART I

At the time of his accession, King Henry IV was thirty-two years old.
He had been born on 3 April 1367, at his father's castle of Bolingbroke,
near Spilsby in Lincolnshire, just three months after his cousin Richard,
the day of the great victory won at Najera by his father John of Gaunt
and his uncle the Black Prince. When he was only ten, his grandfather
Edward III had made him a Knight of the Garter, and less than three
months afterwards, in July 1377, he had borne the principal sword at
Richard's coronation. In that year he was already styled Earl of Derby;
later he acquired the additional earldoms of Leicester, Lincoln and
Northampton; in 1397 he became Duke of Hereford and in 1399, on
the death of his father, Duke of Lancaster. According to the sixteenth-
century chronicler Edward Hall, he was 'of mean stature' but well
proportioned and compact, with fine, regular teeth and a thick, dark
red beard: Froissart describes him as *beau chevalier*. Moreover, though
he possessed none of his cousin's taste and sophistication, he certainly
did not lack intelligence. Unlike Richard, too, he had seen the world.
Between 1391 and 1393 he had travelled first to Lithuania, on a crusade
with the Teutonic Knights, and then to Jerusalem on a pilgrimage to
the Holy Sepulchre, visiting Prague and Vienna, Rhodes and Cyprus,
and on his return journey, Venice, Milan, Pavia and Paris, to say nothing
of all the principal shrines along the way. Both journeys were undertaken
in a spirit of genuine piety, for he was naturally devout. He also seems

to have been totally faithful to his wife Mary Bohun, daughter of the Earl of Hereford and Essex, who had died in 1394 while bearing him his sixth child.

At the time of Henry's accession, there was no doubt of his popularity throughout the country, the vast majority of his subjects rightly believing that he had seized the throne only because his predecessor had shown himself incapable of government. His position, however, was still dangerously weak. Under Richard, the prestige of the monarchy might have sunk lower than at any time since Edward II – perhaps since the Norman Conquest – but Richard remained the rightful King. Henry was a usurper, who had broken not only his vows of fealty but very probably another more recent oath as well. In recent years, too, Parliament had had a chance to flex its muscles, and had developed something of a taste for power. It held the purse-strings, and was determined that the King should not be allowed to forget it.

Parliament apart, the worst troubles of the first years of Henry's reign came from beyond his borders. The problem of France he had already foreseen. Charles VI could not be expected to countenance the deposition, and quite possibly the murder, of his own son-in-law; and his temper could hardly have been improved when Henry sent emissaries to him only a month after his coronation suggesting that Queen Isabelle might now make an excellent wife for the young Prince of Wales. Hardly had this ill-fated mission returned when the Scots, taking advantage of the absence in London of the Percys and the Earl of Westmorland, crossed the border and captured Wark Castle in Northumberland, doing extensive damage and holding to ransom its keeper, his family and his household. In August 1400 a vengeful Henry led a small force into Scotland, deliberately ignoring all Scottish attempts at a peaceful settlement and calling upon the King, Robert III, to do homage to him at Edinburgh on the 23rd. Robert refused, and when Henry reached Edinburgh it was to find the city gates closed against him. The Duke of Rothesay, commander of the garrison, offered battle with a limited number of knights on each side, to avoid the unnecessary shedding of Christian blood; but this the King rejected out of hand. Before the end of the month he and his men were back in England, having achieved nothing but a vague promise that his claim to overlordship would be considered. Not only did he himself never invade Scotland again; it was the last time in history that an English king crossed the border at the head of an army.

Henry had got no further than Northampton when he heard of a rising in Wales. It stemmed from a long-standing quarrel between Lord Grey of Ruthyn, one of the King's most stalwart supporters, and Owen Glendower, a rich and influential Welsh landowner whose diligent legal studies at Westminster had not prevented him from ravaging the border lands along the Wye, sacking several large towns and terrorizing the inhabitants. As the word spread, many Welshmen resident in England, including virtually all those studying at Oxford and Cambridge, returned to their homeland – a clear indication that additional forces were being recruited. On 19 September the King summoned the levies of ten shires and marched by way of Coventry and Lichfield into Shropshire, but the invaders took to the woods and forests and escaped him. The Welsh expedition ended after less than a month, as ingloriously as the Scottish had done. In the following year a Statute for Wales laid down – among several other provisions – that all lords with castles there would forfeit them if they were not properly kept, and that certain offices in North Wales were to be held by Englishmen only; but on Good Friday 1401 a party of Welshmen seized Conway Castle. Glendower's rising had begun in earnest.

If the operations in Scotland and Wales had been intended to increase the royal prestige, they had failed – though they may have taught Henry a lesson. He was back in London to receive, four days before Christmas, an outstandingly distinguished visitor: Manuel Palaeologus, Emperor of Byzantium, who had spent the past two months at Calais awaiting the King's return from the north. Henry met him at Blackheath, rode beside him into the capital, and entertained him on Christmas Day to a splendid banquet at Eltham. Though he was powerless to grant the Emperor's appeal for military aid against the encroaching Turks, he somehow contrived to find 3,000 marks to contribute to the Christian cause before bidding his guest farewell.

This represented something of an achievement, because Parliament was still keeping him on a strict financial rein. Almost continuously since his accession, Henry had been obliged to rely on loans from the wealthier of his subjects (among them the future Mayor of London Richard Whittington who, with his cat, has somewhat surprisingly passed into legend); he had already made dramatic reductions in the expenses of the court, and was forever on the lookout for further economies. One of the steady drains on his exchequer was the continued presence in England of Richard's widow, Queen Isabelle. Though she was still only eleven, her household had cost him nearly £3,000 during the first year of his reign, and once it was clear that she was not to become his daughter-in-law he was anxious to return her as soon as possible to her family. There were, however, problems. One was that her dowry – which Charles VI expected her to bring back to France – had already been completely spent; another, that a Queen of England and a Princess of France could not simply be shipped back home. She must travel in the full panoply of state – and that would itself be an expensive business. Negotiations, which began in early 1401, continued for nearly five months; a final agreement was not reached until 27 May. On 28 June Isabelle called on the King to take her leave – an embarrassing occasion for both of them, since she had been genuinely attached to her husband and doubtless believed Henry to be his murderer – and then set off for Dover.

In the circumstances, the long procession that wound its way through the London streets was muted and solemn; but it cannot have failed to impress. The Queen's immediate entourage consisted of the Duchess of Ireland – widow of Robert de Vere – Henry's mother-in-law the Countess of Hereford, the Bishops of Hereford and Durham, the Earls of Worcester and Somerset, four other lords, six knights and Isabelle's chamberlain, confessor and secretary. With them went a vast number of ladies, damsels and squires, many of whom were attended by their personal troops of yeomen, maids and grooms. The majority doubtless rode their own horses; the court nevertheless provided another ninety-four. The mourning clothes worn by Isabelle and her attendants had been made specially for the occasion; a full service of silver accompanied them, together with several suites of fine furniture. Further loans, amounting to a total of £8,000, had been raised to cover all this expenditure, and to provide the Queen herself with enough money to bestow appropriate presents on all those who had served her. The journey from London to Calais took a full month: not till 31 July was she formally handed over to a reception committee headed by Waleran of Luxemburg, Count of Saint-Pol.[1] In 1406 she was married again,

---

1. Married to a half-sister of Richard II, the Count of St Pol later declared a personal war – which was consequently not covered by the existing truce – with Henry IV, to avenge his half-brother-in-law. He took a fleet to the mouth of the Garonne in an attempt to seize the ships carrying wine to England, and in 1403 made several raids on the English coast and the Isle of Wight.

this time to her cousin, the fourteen-year-old Count of Angoulême, who in the following year succeeded his murdered father – the King's brother – as Duke of Orleans. Two years after that, in 1409, she died in childbirth. She was just nineteen.

At the time of Isabelle's departure Henry IV had been seven years a widower. With four sons by Mary Bohun, he had assured the succession; but he was still only thirty-four, and for some time he had been considering remarriage. His opportunity had come with the death in November 1399 of the elderly Duke of Brittany, John IV, who left his young wife Joan – the daughter of Charles II, King of Navarre[1] – as regent for his young son. Henry had met her, if at all, only briefly; but discreet negotiations began as soon as the fixed period of mourning for the Duke was over, and on 3 April 1402, in the absence of both parties, a proxy wedding took place at Eltham. It was almost another year before the two were able to meet as husband and wife: after a five-day crossing in the teeth of a heavy gale, Joan's ship failed to reach Southampton and landed instead at Falmouth on 19 January 1403, Henry riding the ninety-odd miles to Exeter to meet his bride. A second ceremony was held at Winchester on 7 February, and on the 26th Joan was crowned at Westminster. Five months later the Duke of Burgundy compelled her to resign the regency and to surrender her sons to his custody, so if Henry had had designs on Brittany, he was disappointed; but the marriage, though it remained childless and produced, in the number of Joan's foreign attendants, something else for Parliament to grumble about, seems on the basis of the meagre evidence available to have been a happy one, with Henry a faithful, generous and considerate husband.

Shakespeare's *History of Henry the Fourth* – there was, at the time of its first publication in 1597,[2] no suggestion of its being a First Part only – opens between the two weddings, some time during the summer of 1402. We cannot put an exact date on it, since in the very first scene

1. A small independent country between France and Spain, at the western end of the Pyrenees.
2. According to the Old Style, whereby the year began on 25 March. By the New Style, which was not officially adopted in England till 1752, the year would have been 1598.

the King simultaneously receives the news of two military encounters which were in fact separated by nearly three months. The first was a skirmish at Pilleth in Radnorshire on 22 June, during which Glendower's men had captured Edmund Mortimer, uncle of the young Earl of March. On hearing the news, Henry had decided on a major campaign to put down the Welsh once and for all; and he now summoned three separate armies – a total, it was said, of 100,000 men – respectively to Chester, Shrewsbury and Hereford, to be ready to march on 27 August. He himself would command the Shrewsbury contingent. Alas, the expedition was no more successful than its predecessors. As always, the Welsh refused to be drawn into battle. The weather, moreover, was atrocious, so bad that it was popularly attributed to magic spells cast by the Franciscan friars, who had never forgiven Henry his usurpation of the throne. On 8 September the King's tent was blown down during a hail storm: his lance fell on him, and he was saved only by the armour which – we may be surprised to read – he was wearing as he slept. Three weeks later he was back in England; once again, he had achieved nothing.

The second encounter was the battle which Shakespeare calls 'Holmedon' – better known to us as Homildon Hill. It was fought on 14 September, against a Scottish army under Archibald, fourth Earl of Douglas, which had crossed the English border some weeks before and had penetrated as far south as Durham, plundering and burning crops. On its return journey it had been intercepted by the Percy militia under Northumberland and his son Harry Hotspur and had suffered heavy losses, 500 fugitives from the field being drowned in the river Tweed. Douglas, with a number of other noble Scots, was taken prisoner. England was in sore need of a victory; yet when the news was brought to the King at Daventry, he was rather less jubilant than might have been expected. He was beginning to see the Percys, if not yet as a danger, at least as an increasing irritation. Their successes against the Scots stood out in embarrassing contrast with his own continued failures in Wales; besides, no one could fail to compare the valour of Hotspur with the dissolute life of his own son Henry:

O that it could be prov'd
That some night-tripping fairy had exchang'd
In cradle-clothes our children where they lay,
And call'd mine Percy, his Plantagenet![1]

Peremptorily, he demanded that all the prisoners should be sent at once to London; Hotspur replied that he would send all but one: the Earl of Douglas would remain in the north. Just fourteen years before, in 1388, he himself had been captured by the Scots at Otterburn (Chevy Chase) and held to ransom; revenge to him must have been particularly sweet, and Douglas was too great a prize to let out of his hands. For Henry this was the last straw. He had, as he well knew, no legal right to his claim: by the law of arms only princes of the blood royal needed to be surrendered to the King.[2] But Hotspur's refusal continued to rankle, and led indirectly to an unpleasant scene during the Parliament which met the following October.

It was on the 20th of the month that the Earl of Northumberland and his son presented themselves before the King and Parliament in the White Hall at Westminster, accompanied by the Earl of Fife and a number of other prisoners taken at Homildon Hill. Henry treated the captive Scots with every courtesy, complimenting the Earl on his gallantry and entertaining them all at his own table in the Painted Chamber; but he could not forget (or forgive) the absence of Douglas, and a furious argument ensued – it was further embittered by his refusal to allow the Percys to ransom their kinsman Mortimer[3] – ending with

1. I.i.85–88. Shakespeare, following Samuel Daniel, suggests that the two men were of similar age; and in III.ii.103 the King emphasizes the point yet again. In fact they were separated by twenty-three years. Hotspur, born in 1364, was already thirty-eight at the battle of Homildon Hill. The young Prince of Wales was fifteen – a little young even for roistering.

2. Only one of Hotspur's prisoners fell into this category: Murdoch Stewart, Earl of Fife, son of Robert, Duke of Albany and Regent of Scotland. Shakespeare (I.i.71) calls him 'Mordake' and – led astray by a misprint in Holinshed – makes him the son of Douglas.

3. Hotspur had married Mortimer's sister Elizabeth. (Not Kate, as Shakespeare calls her.) By this time it was being widely rumoured that Mortimer had deliberately sought captivity at Pilleth; Henry must also have been well aware that – as a great-grandson of Edward III – Mortimer might be held to have a stronger claim to the throne than he did himself.

his calling Hotspur a traitor and drawing his dagger. 'Not here,' cried Hotspur, 'but in the field!' and strode out of the assembly. The die had been cast.

Shakespeare, in I.iii, is once again obliged to conflate several scenes into one, in which he is guilty of a number of minor inaccuracies. Apart from those already mentioned, he confuses the Edmund Mortimer who was Glendower's prisoner and later his son-in-law with his nephew and namesake who was technically heir to the throne; he identifies the English Earls of March (who were Mortimers) with the Scottish ones (who were not); and he suggests that Hotspur had tried to keep back all his prisoners, rather than Douglas alone – even though, with the extraordinary 'popinjay' speech (I.iii.28–68), he gives him an admirable excuse for doing so. The discussion then turns from the prisoners to Mortimer, whom the King accuses of having

> wilfully betray'd
> The lives of those that he did lead to fight
> Against that great magician, damn'd Glendower

while Hotspur furiously denies the charges. After Henry's departure, the action continues with the return of Northumberland's brother Thomas, Earl of Worcester, and the decision of all three Percys to join Richard Scrope, Archbishop of York, in his intended rebellion.[1]

The entire scene, which runs to nearly three hundred lines, is dominated by Hotspur. To Holinshed – who seems first to have given him his nickname – he is simply the 'capteine of high courage' that his name suggests; in Samuel Daniel's *Ciuile Warres* we see him certainly as youthful, but also as 'rash' and 'furious'; only with Shakespeare does he emerge as a knight *sans peur et sans reproche*, a young man of dazzling brilliance, unfailing courage and volcanic energy, for whom war is not so much a political instrument as the path to glory:

> By heaven, methinks it were an easy leap
> To pluck bright honour from the pale-fac'd moon,

---

1. Shakespeare suggests that the reason for the Archbishop's disaffection is Henry's execution of his 'brother' William, Earl of Wiltshire, with Bushey and Green at Bristol three years before. The two were in fact cousins.

Or dive into the bottom of the deep,
Where fathom-line could never touch the ground,
And pluck up drowned honour by the locks,
So he that doth redeem her thence might wear
Without corrival all her dignities . . .[1]

Unstable he may have been, impatient and intolerant as well; but for Shakespeare he was a star. Far more than Prince Hal, he is the true hero of the play and its most memorable character – excepting only Sir John Falstaff himself.

And what of Falstaff? He certainly gave his creator a great deal of trouble. One of Shakespeare's minor sources for these histories was an anonymous play of little if any merit, entitled *The Famous Victories of Henry V* and published some three years before *Henry IV Part I*. In it he found a character named Sir John Oldcastle who figured as one of the young prince's drinking companions, and innocently introduced him into his own play. On its first production, both the play as a whole and the character of Oldcastle in particular caught the public imagination; but after the staging of *Henry IV Part II*[2] there was a furious protest from Oldcastle's descendant, Lord Cobham, and his family. Far from being a drunkard and a coward, they pointed out, Oldcastle had been High Sheriff of Herefordshire, had fought with courage in the Welsh wars, and in 1411 had distinguished himself in Arundel's expedition to St Cloud. Two years later he had been accused of being a Lollard – a follower of John Wycliffe[3] – and arrested; subsequently he had escaped from prison, but in 1417 he had been recaptured and burnt at the stake as a heretic. In 1563 he had gained a place in John Foxe's celebrated *Book of Martyrs*. Not surprisingly therefore, the Cobhams were outraged at this defamation of their ancestor and demanded changes.

1. I.iii.199–205.
2. Obviously not before, since the abbreviation 'Old', instead of 'Fal', occurs at I.ii.138 in the Quarto edition of 1600. We do not know why the Cobham family waited so long before complaining; perhaps they were prepared to overlook *Part I* just as they had overlooked *The Famous Victories*, but could not accept the grosser travesty of *Part II*.
3. See pp. 57, 153.

The family was too powerful to be ignored, and Shakespeare saw that something must be done. Rather than create a new character altogether, however, he turned to the first of his early *King Henry VI* plays and resurrected another historical figure, Sir John Fastolf, whom he transmuted into 'Falstaff'. In the earlier play he had already portrayed him as an arrant coward, who had deserted the gallant Lord Talbot both at the battle of Patay and then again before Rouen, and had been stripped of his Garter and banished in consequence; but this too seems in retrospect to have been somewhat unfair. Fastolf had in fact fought bravely at Agincourt, and had later been appointed Governor of Maine and Anjou and Regent of Normandy. Only in 1429 at Patay had he failed: his men put to flight by Joan of Arc, had deserted him, and Talbot had been captured. But if there was a subsequent inquiry he had been exonerated, and he kept his Garter until his death.

So Oldcastle became Falstaff, though one or two hints of his former identity can still be found in *Henry IV Part I*. As early in the play as I.ii.41, Prince Hal calls him 'my old lad of the castle'; and II.ii.103, 'Away, good Ned, Falstaff sweats to death' would scan a good deal better with the substitution of the old name for the new. To avoid any similar misunderstandings, other drinking companions of the Prince were also given new identities. 'Harvey', the name of the third husband of the mother of Lord Southampton,[1] became 'Bardolph', and 'Russell', the family name of the Earls (later Dukes) of Bedford, was changed to 'Peto'. Now at last Shakespeare could promote his two plays without fear of opposition and even – almost certainly in deference to a wish expressed by the Queen herself to see Falstaff as a lover – add a third, written in two or three weeks and first performed before her on 23 April 1597: *The Merry Wives of Windsor*.

The first three acts of *King Henry IV Part I* are essentially antiphonal: serious political discussions are interspersed with comic scenes between Falstaff and Prince Hal, some set in in the latter's apartments at Rochester and Gadshill, others at the Boar's Head Tavern, Eastcheap. Quite apart from *The Famous Victories*, there was plenty of good evidence for Hal's riotous living: according to one contemporary source, the Prince 'was in his youth a diligent follower of idle practices, much given to instru-

---

1. Henry Wriothesley, thought by many to be the 'Mr W.H.' to whom the First Quarto of the Sonnets is dedicated.

ments of music, and fired with the torches of Venus herself,'[1] and many other chroniclers tell the same story. Shakespeare, in fact, lets him off remarkably lightly. He allows only a single oblique reference to the popular (if almost certainly baseless) story of the Prince's physical assault on the Chief Justice Sir William Gascoigne[2] – though there will be more of this, introduced for very different reasons, in *Part II*; and he makes no mention at all of young Henry's unaccountable appearance before his father in what Holinshed describes as 'a gowne of blew satten, full of small oilet holes, at euerie hole the needle hanging by a silke thred with which it was sewed'. It seems, in short, that he is anxious to emphasize throughout that Hal's youthful follies were, in the words of the great nineteenth-century historian William Stubbs, 'the frolics of a high-spirited young man, indulged in the open air of the town and camp; not the deliberate pursuit of vicious excitement in the fetid atmosphere of a court'. Such habits can be cast aside when the moment comes and, as early as the second scene in the play, the Prince's final soliloquy leaves us in no doubt that they will be. Later, in III.ii, he gives a similar reassurance to his father:

> For the time will come
> That I shall make this northern youth exchange
> His glorious deeds for my indignities.

What Shakespeare does not tell us – and the King himself seems to forget – is that the Prince's life was by no means entirely dissolute. As early as September 1400 he had accompanied his father into Wales on his first expedition against Glendower and had remained all the winter at Chester, where the rebels were summoned to present themselves before him on 30 November. In April 1401 he had advanced into Wales with Hotspur, recovering Conway Castle in May and securing the submission of Merioneth and Carnarvon shortly afterwards. In August – Hotspur having departed – he had led another attack, and was still on campaign when the King joined him in October. The following year was admittedly quiet enough, and would have left him plenty of

---

1. Titus Livius Forojuliensis, an Italian in the service of Humphrey of Gloucester, writing *c.* 1437.
2. 'Thy place in Council thou has rudely lost', III.ii.32.

time for the Boar's Head, though even in those days he might have
been thought a little young: on 9 August he celebrated his fifteenth
birthday. On 7 March 1403, however, he was appointed by the Council
to represent his father in Wales, and in May he invaded the country
yet again, destroying two of Glendower's principal castles. He was still
there in July, when he received word to meet Henry at Shrewsbury:
the Percys had risen in rebellion.

Precisely why they did so remains a mystery. The King himself was
taken by surprise – when he heard the news at Lichfield on 16 July he
had actually been on his way north to assist them. There were probably
several reasons. Doubtless the affair of the Homildon prisoners played
its part, as did Henry's continuing refusal to ransom Mortimer; but
the greatest grievance of all was the non-payment of the considerable
expenses, amounting to some £20,000, that the Percys had incurred
doing his work for him along the border. As recently as 26 June
Northumberland himself had written to the King, setting out the
situation and requesting urgent payment so that the realm would not
be disgraced at the next encounter with the Scots. Though strongly
worded it contained no hint of disrespect, far less of disloyalty, and
some historians have concluded that the Earl still had no thought of
rebellion in his mind, and had allowed himself to be persuaded only at
the last moment by his ever-impetuous son.

One can only say that it seems unlikely. Four years before, Northumberland had not hesitated to swear an oath to King Richard that he
would be permitted to retain his crown;[1] and even if he were not
himself a prime mover, he cannot have been unaware of the conspiracy
that his son had devised with the help of the Archbishop of York
Richard Scrope, Owen Glendower and his son-in-law Mortimer, who
had married Owen's daughter a few months before. Its object was to
depose Henry in favour of Mortimer's son and Hotspur's nephew the
young Earl of March – now twelve years old – leaving Wales independent under Owen; and it was in pursuit of this aim that Hotspur
had arrived on 9 July in Chester with his uncle the Earl of Worcester,
his erstwhile captive Douglas, a number of other Scottish prisoners
whom he had set free and 160 horse. His claim that King Richard was
also with them had immediate effect in the old loyalist stronghold, and

1. See p. 120.

he was acclaimed with enthusiasm; a day or two later, however, on his march south to join Glendower, this last pretence was dropped. Edmund of March was declared the rightful King, while 'Henry of Lancaster' was accused of breaking the oath he had sworn at Doncaster[1] and starving Richard to death.

Henry, meanwhile, had acted fast. The important thing was to prevent the rebels joining up with Glendower. After a few days spent collecting troops, on 20 July he had led his army on a forced march to Shrewsbury. The Percys, arriving the next morning and finding the gates closed to them, withdrew some three miles to the north along the Whitchurch road, taking up a strong position on the slope of the Hayteley field in the parish of Albright Hussey. Henry followed, drawing up his own forces at the foot of the slope. At this point, the chroniclers tell us, Hotspur called for his favourite sword, only to be told that it had been left behind in the village of Berwick, where he had spent the previous night without being told exactly where he was. When he heard the name he immediately remembered the words of a fortune-teller that he would die in Berwick, which till then he had always assumed was Berwick-on-Tweed. 'Then,' he murmured, 'has my plough reached its last furrow!' Peace talks, mediated by the Abbot of Shrewsbury, came to nothing; and around noon the King gave the order to attack. The Prince of Wales, though wounded in the face by an arrow from one of the Cheshire archers, led his men up the slope and engaged the rebels hand-to-hand. Hotspur and Douglas meanwhile, with a band of thirty chosen followers, cut their way through to the royal standard and dashed it to the ground; but they failed to kill the King, who had by now dispatched thirty of the rebels on his own account, despite being forced three times to his knees. Shortly afterwards Hotspur, pressing on as always ahead of his men, was struck down. The word spread quickly among his followers. With Worcester and Douglas captured, they had no more stomach for the fight; and by nightfall the battle was over.

It was Saturday, 21 July. Two days afterwards Worcester, together with two other rebel knights, was executed as a traitor. The body of Hotspur was buried in the family chapel at Whitchurch, but it did not remain there long. To scotch the inevitable rumours that he was still alive it was brought back to Shrewsbury, rubbed in salt to preserve it

1. See p. 118.

as long as possible, and finally propped up between two milestones next to the town pillory. Later the head was cut off and fixed on one of the gates of York; the trunk was quartered, the four quarters being separately hung above the gates of London, Bristol, Chester and Newcastle.

Henry now hurried northwards to meet Northumberland, who submitted to him at York on 11 August. He was put into custody and made to surrender his castles, but his life was spared. The King then turned back towards the south-west for a short campaign in Wales, before returning to London for the winter. His problems were by no means over. After four attempts to crush it, Glendower's rebellion still prospered; the French were threatening – and occasionally raiding – the south coast, and the financial position was still desperate. His victory at Shrewsbury and his successes over the Percys had mildly increased his popularity, and his son had distinguished himself by his courage; but heaven, he believed, continued to frown on the usurper, and the future looked bleak.

Act III of *Henry IV Part I* is virtually all the work of Shakespeare's imagination. It begins with the conspirators: Hotspur, Worcester, Mortimer and Owen Glendower himself. The meeting does not augur well for the coming rebellion: Hotspur begins by announcing that he has forgotten the map; Glendower reassures him; and immediately the two begin to quarrel, the Welshman boasting of the dreadful portents that attended his birth,[1] his supernatural powers and his military exploits, while Hotspur mocks him and deliberately makes himself as objectionable as he can. Just in time, it seems, Glendower leaves the room, to return shortly afterwards with his daughter Lady Mortimer and Hotspur's wife, Lady Percy. (In line 190 Mortimer is made to refer to the latter as his aunt: she was in fact his sister.) Of these ladies the chroniclers tell us virtually nothing; it is Shakespeare who breathes life into them. He makes gentle fun of the Mortimers' problems of communication – they speak not a word of each other's languages – but gives Lady Mortimer Welsh songs to sing. Lady Percy, by contrast, whom we have met before in the previous act, is full of spirit, exchanging good-humoured badinage with her husband – although, despite his insistence, she refuses

---

1. These portents were said to have attended the birth of Mortimer, not Glendower. Shakespeare makes a common mistake in confusing the two.

to compete vocally with her sister-in-law. The scene ends without the conspirators' plans having been appreciably advanced.

It is followed by a confrontation between the King and the Prince of Wales. Henry berates his son for his dissolute life, the Prince claiming that the rumours are exaggerated. At the same time, however, he expresses his regrets for the pain he has given his father and promises not only to change his ways but to cover himself with glory. (That the time for this reform has not yet come is to be made all too clear by the third scene of the act, which is set in the Boar's Head.) Just before the end of this confrontation scene there appears Sir Walter Blunt – a good deal more important in the play than is the simple standard-bearer we know from Holinshed – with a report that the rebels are on the march. They were not, as Blunt reports, at Shrewsbury but at Chester, and the orders now given by the King – that his son should advance through Gloucestershire and meet him at Bridgnorth – are still more at variance with the facts, if only because, as we have seen, the Prince was already in the west when the news broke. But such minor inaccuracies fall well within the bounds of normal artistic licence and should not be taken too seriously.

The same cannot altogether be said of Shakespeare's account of the battle itself which, with its preliminaries and its immediate aftermath, takes up the two last acts of *Henry IV Part I*. Act IV begins on the eve of the encounter, Friday 20 July, with Hotspur and the recently released Douglas learning from a messenger that Northumberland is sick and unable to join them. According to Holinshed the earl's illness, whatever it may have been, had actually struck him earlier; by the time the rebellion began he had recovered, and on the day of the battle he was already on the way to join his son. But Shakespeare, building up his drama, is anxious to show us the situation in the Percys' camp deteriorating minute by minute. There now arrives Sir Richard Vernon – by Holinshed barely rated a mention – with news that the King himself is on the march, together with his younger son John of Lancaster,[1] the Earl of Westmorland, and of course the Prince of Wales himself:

---

1. Prince John was only thirteen at the time of the battle of Shrewsbury. There is no historical record of his having been present. Shakespeare presumably introduces him here, rather than his elder brother Thomas of Clarence, because of his importance in the Gaultree Forest scene (IV.i) of *Henry IV Part II*.

> I saw young Harry with his beaver on,
> His cushes on his thighs, gallantly arm'd,
> Rise from the ground like feather'd Mercury,
> And vaulted with such ease into his seat
> As if an angel dropp'd down from the clouds
> To turn and wind a fiery Pegasus,
> And witch the world with noble horsemanship.

Finally Vernon – who seems to take considerable pleasure in the delivery of bad news – reveals that Glendower and his men cannot be there for another fourteen days. This last report puts paid to Hotspur's optimism: his courage is undiminished, but he knows his cause is lost. 'Doomsday is near; die all, die merrily' – and, he suggests, the sooner the better. He even wants to launch the attack that same night, and Douglas and the rest are still trying to persuade him to wait till the morrow when Sir Walter Blunt – rather than the Abbot of Shrewsbury – arrives from the King in the hopes of negotiating a peace. He is sent back with a promise that Worcester will bring Henry terms in the morning; but that interview,[1] despite the King's offer to take no punitive action if the rebels will disband their forces, is no more successful than the first. 'To save the blood on either side', the Prince offers to meet Hotspur in single combat (a challenge for which there is no evidence anywhere in the chronicles), but Worcester ignores it. He returns to the rebel camp, having resolved not even to report the King's generous terms, which he does not for a moment believe;[2] and the two armies prepare for battle. Only old Falstaff confesses what all of them are feeling:

> I would 'twere bed-time, Hal, and all well.

Shakespeare's version of the battle of Shrewsbury begins with the killing by the Earl of Douglas of Sir Walter Blunt, one of the four knights who were, according to Holinshed, 'apparelled in the kings

---

1. V.i.9–114.
2. Cf. Holinshed: 'The earle of Worcester (vpon his returne to his nephue) made relation cleane contrarie to that the king had said, in such sort that he set his nephues hart more in displeasure towards the king than euer it was before.'

sute' – deliberate decoys, who by wearing the royal arms hoped to reduce the danger to Henry himself. Another of these seems to have been Lord Stafford, who has already been dispatched by Douglas before the scene opens; in both cases the latter believes that he has killed the King. When Hotspur identifies the dead man as Blunt, remarking as he does so that 'the King hath many marching in his coats', he receives the furious reply, 'I'll murder all his wardrobe, piece by piece'; and Douglas does indeed shortly afterwards find himself face to face with Henry. As they engage in a furious hand-to-hand struggle the King is forced to his knees, and saved only in the nick of time by the arrival of the Prince of Wales, who puts his assailant somewhat ignominiously to flight.[1] Oddly enough, Douglas reappears a few moments later, during the fight between the Prince and Hotspur, when he silently attacks – of all people – Falstaff, before disappearing from the play for good.

Not surprisingly, in his account of the battle, Shakespeare takes a few liberties in the interests of his drama. Holinshed suggests that Henry met Douglas at an early stage of the three-hour battle, after which the Prince was withdrawn from that side of the field, while Blunt and Stafford – and probably a third knight, Sir Hugh Shirley – remained, only to be slaughtered shortly afterwards. (There can, however, be no doubt that the King – who, it must be remembered, was still only thirty-six – fought with exemplary courage throughout.) Did the Prince really save his father's life? There is some evidence, but not much. Holinshed goes no further than to say that the Prince 'holpe his father like a lustie yoong gentleman'; Samuel Daniel asserts that he did indeed save the King; but Daniel was writing an epic, and was probably no more conscientiously accurate than Shakespeare himself.

Did Prince Hal kill Harry Percy? Possibly, yes. Most historians are sceptical; it has been pointed out that the true Hotspur – as opposed to the Shakespearean ideal – was twenty-three years older than the Prince, a seasoned general for whom Hal had a deep respect and who, on those early Welsh campaigns, had taught him all he knew. This is undoubtedly true as far as it goes; but Percy was now a dangerous and desperate rebel, and nothing that we read of either of them suggests that in such

1. Still more humiliating was the fate he subsequently suffered: 'The earle of Dowglas, for haste, falling from the crag of an hie mounteine, brake one of his cullions [testicles] and was taken.'

a situation either would have hesitated to kill the other. There is also an admittedly ambiguous passage in Holinshed – one of the many that makes us wish that he had written just one degree better than he did – which reads: 'the other on his part . . . fought valiantlie, and slue the lord Persie'; we are given no indication of who 'the other' may be, but in the previous sentence the chronicler is certainly speaking of the King, and the Prince surely seems a likelier candidate than anyone else.

Whoever may have been responsible for it, the death of Harry Hotspur ends not only the battle of Shrewsbury but, effectively, Shakespeare's play. Prince Hal makes his noble speech

> When that this body did contain a spirit,
> A kingdom for it was too small a bound;
> But now two paces of the vilest earth
> Is room enough. This earth that bears thee dead
> Bears not alive so stout a gentleman

during which he covers the dead man's face with the plumes from his own helmet; there follows a short comic interlude in which Falstaff scrambles to his feet – he has feigned death to escape Douglas – and boasts unwittingly to Hal that he has killed Hotspur himself; and we then move on to the final, even shorter, scene in which the King condemns Worcester and Vernon to death, while the Prince orders Douglas to be freed as a tribute to his valour. Henry's closing speech points the way to the play's sequel, and the curtain falls.

7

King Henry IV Part II
[1403–1413]

The second of Shakespeare's two Henry IV plays is even more episodic than the first. Since the decade it covers – from the aftermath of the battle of Shrewsbury to the death of the King in 1413 – occupies five times as much space in Holinshed's chronicle as do the three years covered by *Part I*, the author has had to be ruthlessly selective of the events he has decided to include. Just how selective, we shall see as we go on; first, however, we must briefly trace the course of the last ten years of Henry's unhappy reign.

The Parliament that met from January to March 1404 might have been expected to show some appreciation of a monarch who had risked his life – and very nearly lost it – in the defence of his crown. In fact it proved openly hostile, being principally concerned with securing an official pardon for the father of the rebel leader. The Earl of Northumberland appeared in person at Westminster, confirmed the submission he had made at York five months before and swore a public oath of loyalty, both to the King himself and to the Prince of Wales as heir apparent. Parliament then returned to the attack. It demanded the immediate removal of four members of the King's household, drastically cutting down on that of the Queen; it decreed the expulsion from the kingdom of all aliens and schismatics; it severely reproved Henry for his alleged extravagance, despite the fact that his expenses were in fact little more than a fifth of his predecessor's; it insisted that the ludicrously small sum of £6,500, voted for the defence of the realm, should be paid not directly to the King himself – for fear of misappropriation – but to specially appointed 'treasurers of war'; and it stipulated finally that no mention should be made of the last item in the official records, lest it be taken as a precedent for the future.

This defence grant in fact proved to be so inadequate that Henry was obliged to summon another Parliament only seven months later. His need was now urgent, largely owing to the activities of the French. For ten years already, Charles VI had been subject to periodic fits of insanity, which with the passage of time were becoming increasingly prolonged; he seems by now to have developed a pathological hatred of Henry, whom he had forgiven neither for the deposition of his son-in-law nor for his refusal to maintain Queen Isabelle in the style to which she was accustomed. It was ostensibly on her behalf that French ships had for some time been raiding the Channel coast: in the early summer of 1404 there had been a serious attack on Dartmouth. Fortunately this had been repelled, causing heavy losses to the would-be invaders; it was soon afterwards learnt, however, that the French court had given a warm welcome to envoys from Glendower, with whom it was even then negotiating an alliance. Meanwhile Maud, Countess of Oxford – mother of Richard's favourite Robert de Vere – together with the Duke of Orleans and the Count of Saint-Pol, was found to be planning another invasion, this time in Essex, in support of Richard – whom she firmly believed to be still alive – and Isabelle. This second landing failed to materialize only because the young Queen did not share the Countess's illusions, and at the critical moment announced her engagement to Orleans's son Charles Count of Angoulême. Maud herself, with several others involved – mostly churchmen – was sent to the Tower on a charge of treason, but was eventually pardoned.

The French, on the other hand, continued to make trouble. Orleans turned his attention to Guyenne, where he was soon marching on Bordeaux – still of course in English hands; and at the great council meeting which was held at Lichfield in August 1404 it was reported that no less than sixty ships were gathered at Harfleur, with men-at-arms and provisions intended for Glendower. Henry immediately sent letters to various points along the south coast, urging the local authorities to keep a close watch for this fleet, and to intercept it when possible. Ideally, he would have liked to lead another expedition into Wales in a combined operation with the Prince, who had been in command there since the beginning of the year; but he had no more money than his son, who had already complained in a letter to Archbishop Arundel that he had had to pawn his own plate in order to pay his expenses.

The second Parliament of the year met at Coventry in October. Known as the 'Unlearned Parliament' since all lawyers were excluded by proclamation, it seemed to be principally interested in attacking the Church. There had recently been a notable upsurge of feeling throughout the country in favour of the Lollards – those followers of John Wycliffe who, basing their faith on the Scriptures alone, opposed many of the fundamental principles and practices of the established Church, including transubstantiation, the celibacy of the clergy and the sale of indulgences. Angry calls were made for the confiscation of ecclesiastical estates; Archbishop Arundel is said to have spent his nights in prayers and tears. He and his colleagues finally won the day – some of the Commons actually sought absolution for their earlier attitude – but there is no doubt that they were severely shaken. Where the all-important defence grant was concerned, however, the assembly proved surprisingly generous; and it was with a somewhat less heavy heart that the King returned, by easy stages, to London in time for Christmas. With a determined effort in the following year, he might succeed in crushing Glendower once and for all.

But again he was doomed to disappointment. In early April 1405 he had issued a summons to all knights, squires and others who could be called upon to march against his enemies; and immediately after Easter he headed west with an army, reaching Hereford on 14 May. It was there that he received a long letter from his council. It began favourably enough. A loan had been raised for his son Thomas, who was in command of the fleet at Sandwich, and another for the defence of Calais; a third, for Guyenne, was being negotiated and should be in place within a few days. Other monies would be available for the forthcoming Welsh expedition. Then came the bad news. Thomas, Lord Bardolph, who had been ordered to Wales, had quietly slipped away to join his long-time friend and ally the Earl of Northumberland, and there were disquieting rumours of a new rising along the borders. So great was the council's concern that it had ordered the Chief Justice, Sir William Gascoigne, and Lord Roos post-haste to the north to see what was afoot.

The King took this report very seriously indeed. If it were true, there could be no possibility of a campaign in Wales. A few days later it was followed by another, from an unknown source, which seems to have confirmed his worst suspicions; indeed, he now saw the situation to be even more serious than the council had led him to believe. Northumberland, heedless of the oath he had sworn little more than a year before, had once again risen against him – together with not only Lord Bardolph but Thomas Mowbray the Earl Marshal[1] and, worst of all, the Archbishop of York, Richard Scrope. In the seven years that he had been in office, Scrope had shown no previous signs of ill will towards the King; now, however, violently hostile manifestos were appearing on the doors of the York churches and were believed by many to be the work of the Archbishop himself.

They contained all the usual accusations: Henry had broken his oath and deposed the rightful sovereign; he had put to death Harry Percy and others without trial; by imposing unjust levies he had extorted money from his subjects and brought them to misery. They called first for the removal of the King; then for the enthronement of Richard's rightful heir (whom they were careful not to name); next for the restoration of peace with the Welsh; and finally for the abolition of all unfair and unwarranted taxation. In support of these demands the Archbishop had gathered a small army, consisting for the most part of members of his own flock but commanded by the Earl Marshal and three local knights, with which he proposed to join up with Bardolph and Northumberland. Temporarily abandoning the Welsh expedition, Henry left Hereford on 23 May and himself set off for the north to fight, for the second time in less than two years, for his throne.

The fact that he was not finally obliged to do so was entirely due to the prompt action of Ralph Nevill, Earl of Westmorland. With Henry's third son, John of Lancaster, he too hastened to York, catching up with the Archbishop six miles from the city at Shipton Moor. At the ensuing parley on 29 May the rebels were promised immediate redress of all their grievances – excepting, presumably, those relating to the King himself – in return for disbanding their forces. They agreed; whereupon,

---

1. Thomas was the son of the first Duke of Norfolk, who had died in Venice in September 1399 (see p. 124). He had not been allowed to inherit his father's dukedom, but was allowed to retain the title of Earl Marshal, now dissociated from the office of Marshal of England.

the moment their men had returned to their homes, both the Archbishop and the Earl Marshal were arrested as traitors. On 3 June at Pontefract they were brought before the King, who took them to York to await his judgement; and there, at the Archbishop's palace of Bishopthorpe just to the south of the city, and despite the urgent intercession of Thomas Arundel – who had ridden throughout the day and night of Whit Sunday to plead for his fellow archbishop – Scrope, Mowbray and one of the knights, Sir William Plumpton, were condemned to death. All three were beheaded on the spot.

To the King's enemies – and to many of his friends – the murder of an Archbishop was an unspeakable sin; rumours began to spread of miracles at Scrope's tomb, and it was natural that when Henry's health began to fail not long afterwards his illness should be ascribed to the vengeance of God. On the other hand his throne was safe again; on hearing of the fate of his allies, Northumberland had given up his rebellion and fled with Bardolph to Scotland, leaving his two remaining castles, Warkworth and Alnwick, in the King's hands. But Glendower continued to threaten: the French fleet had finally arrived at Milford Haven in early August, Carmarthen was quickly captured, and by the time Henry reached Worcester on the 23rd French and Welsh together were little more than ten miles away to the west. At the end of the month, for the fifth and last time, the King invaded Wales, only to be attended by his usual ill fortune. Although he managed to relieve the long-beleaguered castle of Coyty in Glamorgan, most of his baggage train was swept away by sudden floods and much of the rest captured by Glendower. When he returned to London in early December he was in a state bordering on despair – and conscious, too, that he was now a very sick man.

The rest of the story of the reign of King Henry IV can be quickly told. His illness not only sapped his physical strength, but seems also to have demoralized him. Precisely what it was we shall never know, but what little evidence we have points to some form of heart disease, accompanied by a horrible skin complaint which, while almost certainly not leprosy as several chroniclers maintain, nevertheless became disfiguring to the point where his intimates could hardly bear to look at him. His customary progresses through the country were henceforth impossible: by Easter 1406 he was unable to ride even the short distance from Eltham to Windsor, and was obliged to travel by river. He fought no more campaigns and made only one more painful journey to the north. This was in 1408, after Northumberland, Bardolph and their men had made one last attempt at insurrection and had been soundly defeated by the Sheriff of Yorkshire, Sir Thomas Rokeby, on 19 February at Bramham Moor. Northumberland had been killed in the battle; Bardolph, taken prisoner, had died of his wounds that same evening. Somehow Henry dragged himself to Yorkshire where, at the palace near Selby of his friend and supporter the Bishop of Durham, he sentenced some of the rebels, pardoned others, and hanged the Abbot of Halesowen who had played a leading part in the rising. He was back in London by the end of May, never again – apart from one short visit to Leicester and one to Kenilworth – to leave the home counties.

Meanwhile more and more of the day-to-day business of government was entrusted to Archbishop Arundel, now Chancellor of the Realm, and – insofar as his responsibilities in Wales allowed – to the King's eldest son who, whatever the chroniclers may say, by this time had little time for dissipation. Now twenty-one, young Henry had been campaigning against the Welsh since the age of thirteen; for the past five years he had exercised effective command and gone a long way towards turning the tide. On St George's Day 1406, having finally brought the rebels to a direct encounter, he had fought a victorious battle in which one of Glendower's sons had been killed; soon afterwards he had surrounded and captured a considerable number of the French men-at-arms. Even when he was in London his visits to the stews were less frequent than before. Clearly he was beginning to settle down, and was already showing signs of being as gifted in the arts of statesmanship as he was in those of war.

For the rest, the pattern was largely unchanged. The King was, as always, in desperate need of money; in the summer of 1406 he had had to appeal for loans before he could find the £4,000 necessary to send his daughter Philippa in a respectable degree of state to her betrothed King Eric of Denmark, who had already agreed to take her without a dowry. He was consequently obliged to make every concession that a harsh and unyielding Parliament might demand. In that same year for example, at the Parliament's insistence, he had agreed on further expulsions of aliens, including the two daughters of Queen Joan herself and some forty humbler members of his own household – cooks, valets and grooms; had nominated a new council, whose approval would be necessary before he could make any grants of lands or revenues; and had given his consent, albeit reluctantly, to the auditing of the accounts of the 'treasurers of war' appointed at Coventry two years before.

But the Parliament's tight-fistedness was not confined to domestic matters; it also refused categorically to vote any money for the defence of Bordeaux. The capture of the greatest city of Guyenne had long been an obsession of the Duke of Orleans, and the army of King Charles VI was now steadily advancing upon it. On 30 June 1406, with the enemy already in the suburbs, the city's Archbishop wrote urgently to Henry. He had cried for help, he declared, until his throat was hoarse, but to no avail: his flock had by now almost given up hope. Meanwhile the mayor, Sir Thomas Swynbourne, was hurriedly preparing his fellow citizens to face a siege. Fortunately for them, however, the French – or at least the Duke of Orleans, who had hastened south to accept the surrender – had other ideas. Fearing that an English relief fleet might yet appear, he decided instead to occupy both banks of the Gironde, thus cutting off Bordeaux from the sea. This operation split the French army into two and gave the inhabitants just the opportunity they needed. Pouring out of the city on 23 December, they attacked the army on the eastern bank at Bourg and routed it. Shortly afterwards the entire invasion force withdrew. It seemed at first only a temporary reprieve; but when summer came and the French did not return, the people of Bordeaux began to breathe normally again, and when at the end of November 1407 there came the news of the Duke's assassination in a Paris street they knew that the danger was past.

The following year brought Henry equally welcome news from Wales, where the Prince was applying himself more vigorously than ever to the task in hand. The autumn of 1408 brought the fall, after a prolonged siege, of Aberystwyth; and in January 1409 Harlech followed – with results disastrous for Glendower. His son-in-law and most important ally, Edmund Mortimer, died during the siege; Owen's wife, two daughters and three Mortimer granddaughters were taken prisoner and sent to London; he himself was left without a stronghold or a headquarters. It was a blow from which he would never recover: in 1410 he launched one more major attack, in which his three principal captains – Rhys ap Griffith, Rhys ap Tudor and Philip Scudamore –

were all captured. He himself escaped, but his rebellion was effectively at an end.

The messengers who brought the news of the fall of Harlech to the King found him desperately ill. In 1408 he had summoned one of the most famous doctors of Europe, David di Nigarellis of Lucca, who was to remain with him until shortly before his death; and it was probably Nigarellis who nursed him through his worst crisis to date during the following winter. In December he was so ill that the Prince of Wales and his brother Thomas were both summoned to his bedside; but he rallied slightly after Christmas and was taken down the river to Greenwich for a change of air. This treatment seems to have been successful, for the improvement continued; and although at Greenwich he took the opportunity of making his will – the first royal will, incidentally, to be written in English – he was strong enough to return to Eltham in time for Easter. There, as a thank-offering for his recovery, he ordered a chantry chapel on the battlefield of Shrewsbury, with provision for eight chaplains to pray for the souls of the fallen.

For the Prince of Wales, the last five years of the King's life were a difficult time. Had his father been continuously incapacitated he himself would have been Regent of England, a post which, with his now considerable experience of command in Wales, would have suited him admirably. But Henry's mysterious disease was spasmodic in its effect, with prolonged bouts of unconsciousness alternating with periods when he was able at least partially to resume control of affairs. At these latter times he was impatient and dictatorial, determined to surrender nothing of his sovereignty, resenting any attempt by his son to involve himself and seldom even asking his advice. The Prince thus found himself in an almost impossible position, which was further aggravated by the fact that on foreign policy in particular he and his father violently disagreed.

Of the country's three most troublesome neighbours Wales was at last quiet, while with Scotland an uneasy peace was preserved by means of constantly renewed truces; France, on the other hand, constituted a growing problem. Its King, Charles VI, was by now in even worse state than Henry of England. He still had brief spells of lucidity, during which his considerable intelligence appeared almost undimmed; but these were steadily growing less frequent, and of ever shorter duration. Meanwhile

– and for some years past – there had been an unremitting struggle for power between two of his close relatives, the Dukes of Burgundy and of Orleans. The Duke of Burgundy was the king's first cousin John Sanspeur, 'the Fearless', consumed with ambition and totally without scruple, who had succeeded his father Philip the Fair in 1404; his rival Charles of Orleans, the King's nephew, had inherited the dukedom even more recently, when his father Louis had been assassinated – on John's orders – in 1407, near the Porte Barbette in Paris. Charles, as we have seen, had married Richard II's widow Isabelle in 1406, and after her death three years later had taken as his second wife Bonne, daughter of the formidable Count Bernard of Armagnac – a marriage which had allied the house of Orleans with one of the most powerful magnates in all France. Unlike the Duke of Burgundy he was a man of courage and integrity, and was later to prove one of the greatest poets of his day.

It was only natural that each of the two rivals was eager for English support; and each had a valuable prize to offer in exchange. Burgundy – which then extended from the Jura in the south as far north as the river Scheldt – could guarantee the safety of the vital bridgehead of Calais and its links with the weavers of Flanders; Orleans, on the other hand, with its Gascon ally, could give similar protection to Bordeaux and the all-important wine trade. The first to take the initiative was John the Fearless, who in July 1411 – at a time when the King lay gravely ill – appealed to England for help against Orleans and the Armagnacs, offering the Prince of Wales in return the hand of his daughter Anne. The Prince – who, having recently been appointed Captain of Calais as well as Warden of the Cinque Ports, instinctively favoured Burgundy – immediately sent out a small force of about 1,200 men under his friend the Earl of Arundel, which after a brief engagement at St Cloud secured Paris for the Duke and drove his enemies beyond the Loire. Meanwhile he opened negotiations to discuss the size of his bride's prospective dowry.

The expedition returned to England generously rewarded by Burgundy and much exhilarated by its success; as for the Prince, it must have given him just the encouragement that he needed for the later and far more ambitious expedition that was already germinating in his mind. Unfortunately, however, towards the end of the year King Henry rallied and, as usual at such moments, took grave offence at the way in which, as he saw it, he was being elbowed aside – not on this occasion by his eldest son alone but also by his own half-brothers the Beauforts,[1] the youngest of whom, Thomas, had succeeded Archbishop Arundel as Chancellor in January of the previous year. It seems quite possible that at the time of the opening of the last Parliament of his reign, in November 1411, Thomas's brother Henry Beaufort, Bishop of Winchester, may even have gone so far as to suggest the King's abdication in favour of the Prince of Wales; this would certainly have prompted a furious refusal, and made Henry still more determined to reassert his authority. In any case the Beauforts were dismissed from the council, while the Prince, shrinking from the prospect of an open breach with his father, yielded his place on it to his brother Thomas – who now became Duke of Clarence – and left London on an extended progress through the northern midlands.

He was still away when, at the beginning of 1412, there arrived at Eltham envoys from the Dukes of Orleans and Berry. Their purpose was to frustrate the proposed marriage and the Burgundian alliance; and to achieve it they were prepared to pay a price considerably higher than that offered by their rival. As well as various other marriage proposals with members of their own families, they now offered the Duchy of Aquitaine in full sovereignty, as well as their own personal service in arms, if England would agree to join them against the Duke of Burgundy. To the King the prospect was irresistible. On 18 May, in return for extensive territory in Guyenne and several towns in Angoulême and Poitou, he agreed to make available 1,000 men-at-arms and 3,000 archers, and even at one moment proposed to lead this army himself; but since by this time he was totally unable to walk and could hardly even ride, it was the Duke of Clarence who commanded the force which, three months later, left for Normandy.

This second expedition achieved little of the success of that led by the Earl of Arundel in the previous year. While it was still engaged in somewhat desultory raiding and pillaging in the Cotentin peninsula around Cherbourg, the Armagnacs unexpectedly concluded a truce with the Burgundians, paid off the English army and sent it home. Clarence, it appeared, had been made a fool of; the King scarcely less so. The Prince of Wales, on the other hand, had been vindicated; what

---

1. The sons of John of Gaunt by Katherine Swynford. See p. 100n.

was more, he had not only the Beauforts but virtually the whole of Parliament on his side. Relations between himself and his father grew worse than ever.

But did all the blame for this increasing estrangement lie with the King? Not, perhaps, entirely. If Bishop Beaufort had indeed suggested abdication – which, fourteen years later, he hotly denied – had the Prince of Wales been behind the suggestion? During his long absence in the midlands the Prince had taken the opportunity to raise a considerable armed force, which accompanied him when he returned to London in June 1412; and though he made no threats – and was indeed vociferous in his denials of the several accusations of conspiracy that had been made against him – his protestations that this force was intended to supplement Clarence's campaign against the Armagnacs deceived nobody. His followers were still with him when on 25 September he arrived at Westminster to defend himself against a charge of peculation at Calais – from which, in due course, he was completely exonerated. It was, incidentally, on this occasion that he is said to have forced his way into his father's presence in that extraordinary costume described by Holinshed,[1] for a moving scene of reconciliation and forgiveness.

In the autumn the King's health declined fast. As late as November he was still talking about the Crusade that he had so long contemplated, but by now his words carried little conviction; in early December came another period of unconsciousness, and although he recovered sufficiently to celebrate Christmas as usual at Eltham there could no longer be any doubt that the end was near. Soon afterwards he fell into an intermittent coma, and the Parliament that had been summoned for the following February came to nothing. In mid-March he asked to be taken to Westminster Abbey, to pray before the shrine of his saintly predecessor King Edward the Confessor; and it was there that he suffered the sudden seizure that was to kill him. He was carried to the Abbot's private drawing-room, known – from the inscription round the fireplace – as the Jerusalem Chamber. Holinshed relates that on regaining consciousness he inquired where he was; when he was told, he murmured: 'Now I know that I shall die here in this chamber, according to the prophecy of me declared, that I should depart this life in Jerusalem.'

1. See p. 141.

He lingered a little longer, finally dying on Monday 20 March 1413, a fortnight before his forty-sixth birthday.

His embalmed body lay in state at Westminster; then it was taken slowly down the river to Gravesend and thence by road to Canterbury for burial, as he himself had commanded, in the cathedral. There, in the Trinity Chapel where once stood the shrine of St Thomas à Becket, near the tomb of his uncle the Black Prince, Queen Joan built for her husband one of the most elaborate alabaster monuments ever created, a massive sarcophagus in which, just twenty-four years later, her body was to join his. Upon it, under canopied niches, lie their two recumbent effigies. Henry's at least, his head lying on a pillow smoothed by solicitous angels, is clearly a portrait. We see a heavy face, bloated by disease, with drooping moustaches and a short, forked beard. There is little enough evidence of the outstanding physical beauty on which he had prided himself in his youth; he looks nearer sixty than forty-five. In 1832 the tomb was opened and the face revealed. The beard, thick and surprisingly red, was still evident. The features at first glance showed less signs of the 'leprosy' which, according to the chroniclers, ravaged them during his last years; but, on being exposed to the air, the flesh almost immediately fell away into dust.[1]

To his family and friends, as well as to himself, the reign of Henry IV can only have been one long anticlimax. The *vaillant chevalier, aigre et subtil contre ses ennemis*, who had carried all before him in 1399, winning a kingdom without the loosing of a single arrow and establishing a new dynasty on the throne of England, had declined in just fourteen years into a hopeless, hideously disfigured invalid. At the time of his accession the richest man in England, he had almost immediately found himself in the desperate financial difficulties which had continued throughout his reign, throwing him on the mercy of a hostile and parsimonious parliament on which, thanks to the circumstances of his accession, he was never able to impose his authority. The ultimate irony

---

1. No credence should be given to the portrait of Henry that hangs in the National Portrait Gallery in London. When, at the end of the sixteenth century, it was thought desirable that there should be a complete run of portraits of all British sovereigns since William the Conqueror, this one was hastily adapted from a wood engraving of Charles VI of France. The adapter placed the red rose of Lancaster in his right hand in place of Charles's falcon, and gave him a beard and moustache; but he left him the *fleur-de-lys* sceptre.

was that when, after the death of Northumberland in 1408 and the collapse of Glendower two years later, he might at last have achieved his frustrated ambitions – including, perhaps, even his long-promised Crusade – disease should have reduced him, while still in his early forties, to virtual incapacity. His father had lived to be fifty-nine, his grandfather to sixty-four: given another fifteen years of health and vigour, he might have proved himself one of the greatest of our medieval kings. Instead, he died a broken and pathetic figure, lacking alike the tragedy of his predecessor and the dazzle of his son.

And what does Shakespeare make of him? Not, perhaps, as much as he might have; not, certainly, as much as he made of Richard. The fault, of course, lies with Falstaff. In *King Henry IV Part I* the swaggering old ruffian plays a prominent role; in *Part II* – written very soon afterwards, probably in the summer of 1598 – he comes dangerously near to taking over the play, with the result that the strictly historical element is reduced to only eight scenes, all fairly loosely connected one with another. It could be argued – indeed it frequently has been – that this is no disadvantage: that the rollicking old knight is a greater character than the dying king, and that through him we are given a unique vision of Elizabethan England, an England which is no longer confined to monarchs and magnates but which embraces the publicans, the tapsters and the whores of Eastcheap as well as the country squires and peasantry of Gloucestershire. All this is perfectly true; but the pathos of the final rejection of Falstaff – who obviously deserves all he gets – by the newly crowned King is surely nothing when compared with the tragedy of Henry Bolingbroke dying, after a brilliant youth, disappointed and disillusioned, at forty-five already an old man. Again and again in *Part II*, we feel we are watching, not as in *Part I* a play with a sub-plot, but two quite different dramas; and it leaves us at the end, like its royal protagonist, with a clear impression of promise unfulfilled.

But this is not a book of literary criticism. We are concerned here less with the artistic quality of Shakespeare's history plays than with their historical accuracy, and the very construction of *King Henry IV Part II* – the need to compress the business of a whole decade into those eight short scenes – makes strict accuracy impossible. Shakespeare does not falsify the facts to any great extent; but he is repeatedly obliged to compress the time scale, telescoping events together as the need arises and sometimes even taking them back to the previous play. Thus it is already in the closing lines of *Part I* that we see the King bidding his son accompany him to Wales immediately after the battle of Shrewsbury, and in the first act of *Part II* we have a clear indication that the Prince actually did so.[1] In fact, the chroniclers leave no doubt that he remained in the north-west of England for several weeks, dealing with the rebels and recovering from his wound; and when the King returned from his expedition to the north to receive the submission of Northumberland and marched against Glendower towards the end of September, his eldest son was not with him. On the other hand the years immediately following saw the Prince in command of the army on the Welsh border, and it is presumably his later service in Wales that Shakespeare had in mind.

The account of the rebellions by Northumberland and Archbishop Scrope is even more dramatically compressed. According to Holinshed – still Shakespeare's principal authority – Northumberland first considered rebellion immediately after the battle of Shrewsbury, but this came to nothing. He then hatched a conspiracy jointly with the Archbishop in 1405, but gave up as soon as he heard of the fate of Scrope and Thomas Mowbray, the Earl Marshal. Finally in 1408 he led a new rising, which ended with his death on Bramham Moor. In the plays, all three separate movements are telescoped together. Again, the story begins in the last scene of *Part I*, when the King sends his son John of Lancaster with the Earl of Westmorland

> To meet Northumberland and the prelate Scroop,
> Who, as we hear, are busily in arms.

Then, in *Part II* (IV.i and ii), we see their arrival at 'the Forest of Gaultree' (the ancient royal forest of Galtres, just to the north of York) where John and Westmorland trick them – by a piece of double-dealing so shameless that one cannot read the passage today without a shock of repugnance – into sending home their forces and then immediately place them under arrest. When the report is brought to the King – who is already in the Jerusalem Chamber at Westminster – it is followed within a few lines by the news of the victory at Bramham Moor;

1. I.iii.83.

whereupon Henry suffers that sudden seizure which in fact occurred five years later, but which in the play leads directly to his death.

Holinshed, it should be noted, ignores the early stages of the King's illness, mentioning it only in 1412 and suggesting that until that time Henry was still leading a vigorous military life: the clear inference is that he did not personally put down the rebellions of 1405 and 1408 only because they were already crushed before he could get to them. In the play, on the other hand – in which the King does not appear at all until the third act – Falstaff refers as early as I.ii to an 'apoplexy . . . a kind of lethargy'; and in II.ii we have further testimony of the sickness from Prince Hal himself. When finally the King makes his appearance – just before the Archbishop's rebellion of 1405 – he is not only sleepless but 'hath been this fortnight ill';[1] and the next time we see him, in IV.iv, he is already in the room where he is to die. It may well be that this is another example of the influence of Samuel Daniel, whose whole account of the period is coloured by the King's sickness; but Henry's decline certainly began soon after the execution of Scrope – with which, as we have seen, it was connected in the public mind – so there can be no doubt that in this respect it is Shakespeare and Daniel, rather than Holinshed, who have history on their side.

In II.ii we return to the curious affair of the Lord Chief Justice, who on his very first appearance is referred to by Falstaff's page as 'the nobleman that committed the Prince for striking him about Bardolph'. Later in the same scene Falstaff reminds him of the incident: 'For the box of the ear that the Prince gave you, he gave it like a rude prince, and you took it like a sensible lord.' The story of Hal's being sent to prison in consequence of threatening the Justice, Sir William Gascoigne, goes back to a book known as *The Gouernour*, written in 1531 by Sir Thomas Elyot for the instruction of Henry VIII and other princes.[2] Historically, it is almost certainly without foundation. Had the heir apparent to the throne been committed as Elyot maintains, the event would surely have been recorded at the time and noted by the lawyers

1. III.i.104.

2. Neither Elyot nor John Stow (who in his *Chronicles* and *Annales of England* reproduces the earlier work almost verbatim) report that the Prince actually landed a blow on Gascoigne, though Robert Redmayne (*Vita Henrici Quinti*, c. 1540) and the anonymous play *The Famous Victories of Henry the Fifth* both suggest that he did.

as a significant precedent. But Shakespeare has an excellent reason, none the less, for introducing it here. He does so not to show the Prince in an unfavourable light, but to illustrate his generosity of spirit when, after his succession, he confirms the Lord Chief Justice in his office:

> Therefore still bear the balance and the sword;
> And I do wish your honours may increase
> Till you do live to see a son of mine
> Offend and obey you, as I did.[1]

The only awkward point that must be recorded here is that Gascoigne did not in fact continue in office after the old King's death. Although he seems to have been summoned to the new Parliament on 15 May 1413, the patent of his successor, Sir William Hankford, is clearly dated 29 March of the same year. Whether or not young Henry removed him we cannot tell, but he was by this time well into his sixties and was certainly not disgraced: in 1414 a royal grant allowed him four bucks and four does annually from the forest of Pontefract.

For the rest, the play's inaccuracies – if inaccuracies they are – stem more from personal prejudice than from historical misconception. Shakespeare's instinctive dislike of Northumberland, for example, results in a blackening of his character to a quite unjustified degree. Not one of our sources accuses the Earl of being 'crafty-sick'[2] at the time of his son's last rebellion – in other words that he feigned illness to account for his non-appearance at Shrewsbury. Nor is there any suggestion elsewhere of his deliberately abandoning Archbishop Scrope in 1405, 'to ripe his growing fortunes' in Scotland; according to Holinshed, he took flight only when the rising had failed and all hope was lost. All the evidence suggests that Northumberland showed outstanding courage at Bramham Moor where, Holinshed tells us, he 'incountred his aduersaries with great manhood . . . for whose misfortune the people were not a little sorrie, making report of the gentlemans valiantnesse, renowme [sic], and honour'; but there is no mention of this in the play,

---

1. V.ii.103–6.
2. Induction, l. 37.

1. St George (right) hands Edward III a shield bearing the English coat of arms

2. Edward the Black Prince pays homage to his father, Edward III, for the duchy of Aquitaine, July 1362

3. The battle of Sluys, 24 June 1340

4. King Richard II. State portrait in Westminster Abbey, *c.* 1395

5. *Above* Richard II entertains the Dukes of York, Gloucester and Ireland at dinner

6. *Left* The Court of King's Bench in session at Westminster Hall

7. *Opposite page top* Richard II sends Mowbray and Bolingbroke into exile

8. *Opposite page bottom* The Death of Wat Tyler, 1381. Richard II looks on

9. *Left* Richard II, captive in the Tower of London

11. *Opposite page top* The coronation of Henry IV, 13 October 1399

12. *Opposite page bottom* The funeral procession of Richard II from Pontefract to London, his face exposed to prevent rumours that he might still be alive

10. *Below* Richard II yields his crown to Henry, Duke of Lancaster, 29 September 1399

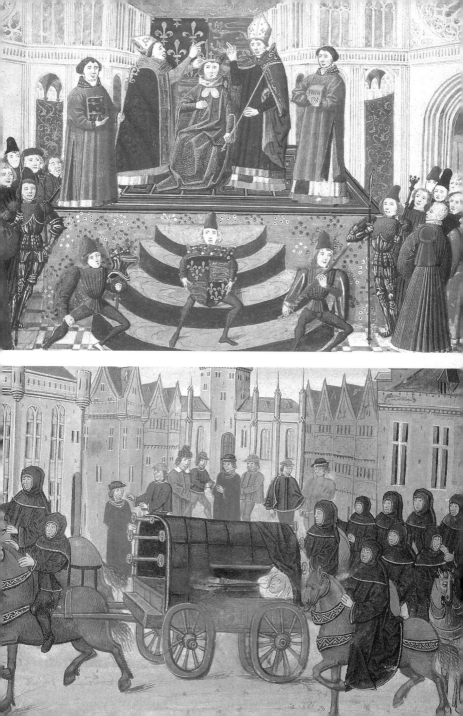

13. King Henry V

14. The battle of Agincourt, 25 October 1415

which emphasizes instead only the size of the rebel force and the relative inconsequence of the victor:

> The Earl Northumberland, and the Lord Bardolph,
> With a great power of English and of Scots,
> Are by the shrieve[1] of Yorkshire overthrown.

John of Lancaster also, whom we saw in *Part I* having distinguished himself at Shrewsbury, appears at Gaultree in a distinctly unpleasant light, being principally responsible for the shameless betrayal of trust by which the Archbishop and his fellow rebels were apprehended. This is the more surprising in that, although he may have formally accepted the surrender of the rebels as his father's representative, in Holinshed the negotiations are handled throughout by Westmorland. What prompts this gratuitous slur on young Lancaster is not entirely clear; the suggestion sometimes made that Shakespeare is trying to emphasize the cold-bloodedness of the Bolingbroke line is surely untenable: John was after all the full brother of the Prince of Wales, and the foremost scion of that line was Hal himself. Nor is it easy to accept the theory that the trick would have appeared perfectly legitimate to Elizabethan audiences, in whose eyes – it has been suggested – the end would have justified the means.[2]

And so we come to one of the most dramatic scenes of the play, Act IV scene v, in which the Prince, watching alone by the bedside of his father, picks up the crown from the pillow, places it on his own head and leaves the chamber. The sick man suddenly awakes, sees that the crown has gone and summons his attendants. They find Hal in the adjoining room and bring him back; and this allows Shakespeare his second great reconciliation scene – the first was in *Part I*, III.ii – in which the King first chastises his son:

> Dost thou so hunger for mine empty chair
> That thou wilt needs invest thee with my honours
> Before thy hour be ripe?

1. I.e. sheriff.
2. This point is debated at length in 'The "Dastardly Treachery" of Prince John of Lancaster', by P. A. Jorgensen (*Publications of the Modern Language Association of America*, Menasha, Wisconsin, Vol. lxxvi, Dec. 1961).

Henry, however, has his answer ready, and there is no suggestion that it is anything but sincere:

> I spake unto this crown as having sense,
> And thus upbraided it: 'The care on thee depending
> Hath fed upon the body of my father;
> Therefore thou best of gold art worst of gold' . . .
> Accusing it, I put it on my head,
> To try with it, as with an enemy
> That had before my face murder'd my father,
> The quarrel of a true inheritor.

His words have their effect. The King instantly accepts his explanation and gives his son

>   the very latest counsel
> That ever I shall breathe.

For him, the crown still imposes its load of guilt, but this will be expiated by his death:

> To thee it shall descend with better quiet,
> Better opinion, better confirmation,
> For all the soil of the achievement goes
> With me into the earth.

The story has a long pedigree, going back to recollections of the fourth Earl of Ormonde – on whom Henry V was to bestow a knighthood at Agincourt – and to the *Chroniques* of the near-contemporary Burgundian writer Enguerrand de Monstrelet, from whom it was adopted by the 1513 translator of Titus Livius, passing through him to Hall, Holinshed, *The Famous Victories* and Samuel Daniel. These two original sources – which are, so far as we know, unrelated – give to what would at first seem an obvious invention some claim to authenticity: Ormonde could quite possibly have heard something of the kind from Henry himself. But even if, like one of the King's more recent biographers,[1] we dismiss

1. Harold F. Hutchison, *Henry V: A Biography*, London 1967.

the whole thing as 'magnificent fiction', we have to agree that 'during the last few years of the reign of Henry IV his eldest son must frequently have considered how the crown of England would fit him'.

By the beginning of Act V, Henry V is already King. Of its five scenes, the first and third are set in the house and orchard of Justice Shallow in Gloucestershire; the remaining three are concerned, first, with the meeting between the King and the Chief Justice, discussed above; second, with the arrest of Mistress Quickly and Doll Tearsheet; third, with Henry's rejection of Falstaff. Of these the last is by far the most crucial to the drama – the rights and wrongs of it have been argued, very probably, since the first performance – but it bears little relevance to this book. Where history is concerned, this last act serves one purpose only: to emphasize the all-important fact that the young King has put his disreputable past behind him, once and for all.

> . . . I survive
> To mock the expectation of the world,
> To frustrate prophecies, and to raze out
> Rotten opinion, who hath writ me down
> After my seeming. The tide of blood in me
> Hath proudly flow'd in vanity till now.
> Now doth it turn, and ebb back to the sea,
> Where it shall mingle with the state of floods,
> And flow henceforth in formal majesty.

Both his reconciliation with the Chief Justice and his treatment of Falstaff make this same point, in their two very different ways. Even the arrest of the two women indicates clearly enough that the old order has changed: for them as for their beloved Sir John, life will never be quite the same again.

8

Harfleur and Agincourt

[1413–1415]

EXETER. . . . And bids you, in the bowels of the Lord,
          Deliver up the crown and to take mercy
          On the poor souls for whom this hungry war
          Opens his vasty jaws; and on your head
          Turning the widows' tears, the orphans' cries,
          The dead men's blood, the pining maidens' groans,
          For husbands, fathers and betrothed lovers
          That shall be swallowed in this controversy.
                                        KING HENRY V

With the doubtful exception of Richard the Lionheart, Henry V is the
only King of England who is still generally perceived as a hero. Whether
he deserved the title must be open to question. Much of his posthumous
reputation, inevitably, he owes to Shakespeare; but the fact remains
that, while still under thirty, he twice raised the largest and best-equipped
expeditionary force that the country had ever seen, transported it to
France – no mean achievement in itself – and on the first occasion, in
one of the most celebrated battles in English history, led it to a magnificent victory over an army many times its own size. On the other hand,
those invasions were planned and carried out on the basis of a claim
which, however much he tried to persuade himself to the contrary,
was without a shred of legal or moral justification; that battle – which,
at the last moment, he did his utmost to avoid – marked the climax of
a military adventure of almost criminal foolhardiness and irresponsibility;
and the pitiless brutality which he showed after its conclusion was
probably without parallel in English history.

    Henry was, first and foremost, a soldier. At the age of only twelve he
had accompanied Richard II on his second expedition to Ireland; later,
after Richard's deposition and his father's seizure of the throne, he had

fought valiantly at Shrewsbury and had commanded the army in successive campaigns against Owen Glendower in Wales. His personal courage was never questioned. By the time of his own succession at the age of twenty-five he was already a seasoned general, loved and trusted by his men, possessing a thorough knowledge of siegecraft, highly experienced both in pitched battles and guerrilla warfare. But his background was not exclusively military: his appointments as Constable of Dover and as Warden of the Cinque Ports had taught him something of ships and the sea, while during his father's long and incapacitating illness he had also had plenty of opportunity to test himself as a statesman.

It comes as no surprise to us to learn that the young King was strong and athletic – wearing his heavy armour, it was said, as if it were a light cloak – and more than usually good-looking: several of those who knew him well have left physical descriptions of him. He had, we read, thick brown hair, and eyes of much the same colour; his complexion was fresh and fair, his teeth perfectly even and sparkling white, his chin slightly cleft. A good deal more unexpected is what we know of his character, at least as it was after his accession. Riotous his early life may have been – stories about it were already in circulation during his lifetime – but those who knew him only after his accession found those stories hard to believe. When he inherited the crown, he put away childish things. On the day of his coronation – which took place on Sunday 9 April 1413, in a blinding snowstorm – he appeared solemn and unsmiling, and was observed to eat virtually nothing at the banquet which followed the ceremony. For ever afterwards he was known for his piety, which was exceptional even by the standards of the time and which more than once laid him open to charges of sanctimoniousness. It may be, of course, that his father's misdeeds weighed upon his conscience; this might account for his early reconstruction and completion of the nave of Westminster Abbey, financed – like so much else – with the assistance of Richard Whittington, who had been Mayor of London in 1397–8 and in 1406, and was to hold the same office again in 1419. It might also go some way to explain his many works of charity and piety, including his foundation for the poor at St Giles Cripplegate in London and his establishment at Twickenham in Middlesex of a Brigittine[1] monastery under the name of Syon – which was later,

---

1. An order founded *c.* 1346 by St Bridget of Sweden. A few of its houses still survive today.

ironically enough, to give its name to the great house of his old enemies, the Northumberlands.

From the outset, Henry was infinitely more popular than his father – a fact which was confirmed at his first parliament, which met in the Painted Chamber at Westminster on 15 May 1413 and willingly provided him with generous allowances, including no less than £10,000 which was granted specifically for the upkeep of the King's 'hostel, chamber and wardrobe'. A slightly chillier note was struck when it called for the expulsion from the realm of all Welshmen and Irishmen; but even the most rabid little-Englanders must have known that this would have been virtually impossible to achieve, and there were no protests when the motion was conveniently forgotten.

Perhaps the most important issue that the King had to face before he could devote all his energies to the coming struggle with France was that of the Lollards. In the last decade of the fourteenth century their numbers had shown a dramatic increase, particularly in the West Country and along the Welsh borders, where their leader was one of the closest of the King's former comrades-in-arms, Sir John Oldcastle.[1] In Henry IV's day Oldcastle – presumably because of his splendid military record and, later, the barony of Cobham which he had acquired through his second wife in 1409 – had largely escaped persecution; but with the accession of the new King a wave of book-burning had been instigated in St Paul's churchyard, and one of the most dangerous of the offending volumes – a collection of short but subversive tracts – proved to be his. Summoned peremptorily to Kennington to defend himself before the King and 'almost all the prelates and nobles of England', he maintained stoutly that although the volume belonged to him he had not even read it; but a number of bishops, headed by Archbishop Arundel himself, continued to insist that he should be forced to recant or take the consequences. When he refused, Henry undertook to discuss the matter personally with his old friend, but was quite unable to shake him; Oldcastle was excommunicated and imprisoned in the Tower pending a formal inquiry.

This inquiry was held in the chapter house of St Paul's on 23 and 25 September 1413; with Archbishop Arundel were Richard Clifford and Henry Beaufort, respectively Bishops of London and Winchester, with

1. See Chapter 6, pp. 139–40.

twelve doctors of law or divinity sitting as assessors. Oldcastle – who was at this time in regular correspondence with the Bohemian reformer John Hus – made a full statement of his beliefs, from which he once again refused to be shaken. He confirmed his belief in all the sacraments ordained by God, describing that of the Eucharist as 'Christ's body in the form of bread'; if the Church maintained that after consecration it was bread no longer, then the Church was wrong – infected, doubtless, by the poison of Popery. As to the act of confession, it might often be salutary but it was not necessary for salvation. The discussion grew increasingly heated, until finally Oldcastle denounced the Pope as Antichrist, with the prelates his members and the friars his tail. After that, there was no more to be said in his defence. Arundel reluctantly declared him a heretic and handed him over to the secular arm for punishment. Even then he was given the usual respite of forty days, during which both Henry and the Archbishop sent learned theologians to him in the Tower in a last effort to persuade him to recant; but he remained adamant.

Then, on the night of 19 October, he disappeared. How he did so we do not know. There was a persistent rumour that the King, or possibly Beaufort, was behind the escape, but from what we know of Henry this seems unlikely: he had sworn to crush the Lollards, Oldcastle was their leader, and it would have taken more than an old tie of friendship to prevent him from doing his duty. According to the royal chaplain, Oldcastle had pretended to capitulate, after which his fetters were removed and he seized the opportunity to flee. There seems in any case to have been some sort of conspiracy, in which many thousands of his co-religionists were involved; and the weeks that followed brought increasing signs of impending rebellion. The first plan – to seize the King in his palace at Eltham during a performance by a company of mummers on the Feast of Epiphany, 6 January 1414 – was revealed just in time to Henry. He returned at once to London, where he took up residence in the priory of Clerkenwell; and it was there that news was brought to him that some 20,000 armed Lollards from all parts of the kingdom were planning to assemble three days later in Fickett's Field (now Lincoln's Inn Fields), whence on the following day they proposed to march through London for a confrontation with 'the priests' prince'.

In his childhood Henry would surely have heard many stories of Wat Tyler's rebellion, only six years before his birth; and he had no desire for a repetition. On the evening of the 9th he ordered all the London gates to be closed, thus cutting off the demonstrators already within the city from those who were advancing upon it; then he himself, with a considerable armed force, moved to St Giles's Fields, a mile or two to the northwest of the assembly point, from where it was a simple matter to intercept the Lollard bands as they approached, disarm them and place them all under arrest. A special commission was appointed to sit in judgement over them; meanwhile, in sinister anticipation of the verdicts, four new sets of gallows were erected in St Giles's Fields. The precise intention of the rebels is unknown; their objectives may well have been peaceable enough, and limited to obtaining the right to practise their religion as they wished, without interference. But Henry was taking no chances. In the official indictment they were accused, ludicrously, of plotting to kill the King and his brothers, together with the principal prelates and other noblemen; to destroy and despoil cathedrals, churches and monasteries and to distribute the proceeds among themselves; to force all monks and nuns into secular employments; and to appoint Oldcastle regent of the kingdom.

Many of the Lollards may have understood in time what was happening and turned back; many others probably managed to escape in the darkness. Even then, over a hundred were executed at St Giles's alone, before the commission extended its work to the country as a whole. But the rising, such as it was, had been such an obvious fiasco that by the end of the month Henry ordered an end to the persecution, and in March he felt secure enough to declare a general amnesty. Those rebels who were still in custody were granted their freedom in return for heavy fines, and returned to their homes. As for their leader, Sir John Oldcastle, despite the reward of a thousand marks that had been offered for his recapture, he remained nearly four years at large – during which he continued, in the name of his faith, to make what trouble he could. Only at the end of 1417 was he finally run to ground in the Welsh marches and brought back, severely wounded, to the capital. By then he could expect no mercy, and received none. On 14 December he was summarily condemned as an outlawed traitor and convicted heretic, and on the same day was 'hung and burnt hanging' at St Giles – a fate similar to that suffered by his friend John Hus in Bohemia, just two and a half years before. But the blood of martyrs, as we have learnt, is the most effective of all fertilizers; and the faith for which Oldcastle and

Hus both died has lived on, only slightly transmuted to Protestantism, to the present day.

With the Lollard danger successfully averted, the King could turn his attention to what his second parliament – which met at Leicester on 30 April 1414 – was already referring to as his 'adversary of France'. The Hundred Years War still continued: the previous two reigns had marked only a lull, procured by a series of truces intermittently renewed – the most recent one, for twenty-five years, sealed by Richard II in 1396 when he married little Isabelle of France. But such truces bought only comparative peace. Even when there were no armies on foreign soil, neither the French or English coasts were safe from occasional incursions: both Rye and Winchelsea had been burnt to the ground by French raiding parties in the 1370s,[1] and thirty years later the ports and coastal villages of northern Brittany were being persistently harried by English pirates. The French attack on Bordeaux in 1406, with the expeditions of Arundel in 1411 and Clarence in 1412, had kept the pot boiling: throughout the country it was generally understood that full-scale war would be resumed before long, and Henry was determined to lose no time in winning what he seems genuinely to have believed was his birthright: the French crown.

As we have seen, the identical claim had been made the best part of a century before by his great-grandfather Edward III, on the grounds that Edward's mother Isabella was the rightful heir to the childless King Charles IV;[2] but it had been rejected by the French, who had pointed out that the old Salic Law of Charlemagne recognized male heirs only. The crown had therefore passed to Charles's first cousin, Philip of Valois. Three Kings had reigned over France since Philip; Henry was therefore now effectively claiming not only that he was the rightful sovereign, but that the last four rulers had been illegitimate. In fact, his claim was even less justifiable than his great-grandfather's: any right that might have existed would have passed to the Earl of March, Richard II's legitimate heir, rather than to a usurper's son. Such considerations,

1. It was as a defence against further forays of the same sort that Bodiam Castle in East Sussex was built during the following decade – the most complete and unspoilt late-medieval moated castle surviving anywhere in the country.
2. See p. 17.

however, were of little interest to Henry. 'No King of England, if not King of France!' – the words are Shakespeare's, but the sentiment was certainly his own. His character was straightfoward and direct, impatient of legal subtleties: he saw things in black and white, and by the early summer of 1414 he was preparing for the fray.

There could have been no more favourable moment to attack. France, virtually paralysed under an imbecile monarch, was split down the middle, with Charles of Orleans and the Armagnacs on one side and the Duke of Burgundy on the other. England, on the other hand, still possessed her two invaluable bridgeheads, Calais and Bordeaux – though in the event, neither would be used. There were domestic reasons, too, which made a foreign war desirable. The Lollard rebellion, hopeless failure as it had been, had occurred only ten months after Henry's accession and had severely shaken his confidence. He was not, it appeared, as popular as he had imagined. He needed now to burnish his own image, while distracting attention as far as possible from the dissatisfaction and dissent that had so unfortunately – some said omin- ously – marked the beginning of his reign. He was aware, too, of the vast numbers of idle soldiery who were roaming the kingdom – men whose courage and military skill made them virtually invincible in war, but who could cause havoc in the countryside when a protracted spell of peace, without opportunities for plunder or pillage, left them with no employment for their swords.

Early in 1415 the King sent his uncle Thomas Beaufort to the French court, at the head of an impressive company of high ecclesiastics and noblemen and armed with a list of still more formidable demands. It was a tactic as old as diplomacy itself: deliberately to ask of a weaker nation more than it could possibly perform, and then to use its inevitable refusal as an excuse for war. First on the list was the crown of France. When this was denied – as it clearly would be – Beaufort was to demand Normandy, Maine, Anjou, Touraine and all the territories ceded to Edward III by the Treaty of Brétigny in 1360.[1] Next he was to claim half of Provence, with the castles of Beaufort and Nogent, as being part of the Lancastrian inheritance through John of Gaunt. These territorial demands accounted for much of the French kingdom; but they were not all. Henry also insisted on the immediate payment of all the arrears

1. See p. 38.

of the ransom of John II, captured during the battle of Poitiers in 1356 – a sum which amounted to no less than 1,600,000 gold crowns. Finally he required the hand of Charles VI's daughter Katherine, on account of whom he professed himself ready to accept a dowry of a further 2,000,000 crowns.

France was not ready for war, and was willing to pay heavily to avoid it; but such demands were beyond the bounds of reason. The French negotiators, led by the Duke of Berry, offered a considerable territorial addition to the English duchy of Aquitaine and, for Katherine, an unprecedented dowry of 600,000 crowns, later increased to 800,000; but beyond that they could not go. Unhesitatingly Beaufort rejected the offer and returned with his retinue to England to inform his master. Henry could not conceal his satisfaction. It was exactly what he had expected. Diplomacy could have gained him valuable territory and a considerable increase in wealth; but only war could win him a crown.

With the return of the ambassadors, Henry began his preparations in earnest. Transportation would be one of his principal problems: he now sent out commissioners to every English port between Newcastle and Bristol, with orders to commandeer all ships above a certain capacity and to press sufficient sailors to crew them. Two of his knights were dispatched to the Low Countries to hire still more, with the result that in less than six months he had some 1,500 vessels lying at anchor along the south coast between Southampton and Portsmouth. Meanwhile he concentrated his own energies on the army, contracting for about 2,500 men-at-arms – fully armoured knights with their attendant esquires and pages – and perhaps 8,000 archers, together with gunners, sappers, armourers, grooms, surgeons, cooks, saddlers, smiths, fletchers, chaplains and even fifteen minstrels. With them were vast numbers of largely untrained hangers-on who could be mobilized as necessary. All were remunerated according to their rank and station, from dukes who were paid thirteen shillings and fourpence a day to the archers and other ranks who received sixpence. The cost, inevitably, was enormous: huge cash loans were raised from the wealthier private citizens, with virtually everything of value that the King possessed – including many of the crown jewels – being offered as security.

While this immense force was assembling, Henry set off on a pilgrimage to the shrine of St Winifred at Holywell in Flintshire – a distance of some 160 miles each way – returning in time for a solemn service at St Paul's on 16 June. Then he headed once again for the south coast, stopping briefly at Winchester to receive a delegation from the French court, dispatched in a desperate last-minute attempt to avert the coming invasion. He received the ambassadors with all the honour due to their high rank, and loaded them with presents; but he rejected their improved offer of 900,000 crowns for Katherine's dowry. The expedition, as he politely explained to them, was on the point of departure. There could be no turning back now.

If Henry did not in fact sail quite as soon as he had hoped, this was because on 31 July the Earl of March came to him at Portchester Castle near Portsmouth with disturbing news: a conspiracy was being hatched against him, and chief among the plotters was March's former brother-in-law Richard of Conisborough, Earl of Cambridge and younger brother of the Duke of York. After the death of his first wife, Anne Mortimer, Richard had married the sister-in-law of Harry Percy's daughter; he was thus in close contact with the family of Northumberland, and in particular with Hotspur's cousin, a certain Sir Thomas Grey. His intention – with the help of the Scots, of Glendower and his Welsh rebels, and of Oldcastle and his Lollards – was to assassinate Henry and his brothers on 1 August, replacing him with March, as Richard II's legal heir. The third member of the conspiracy was one of the King's most trusted confidants, 'whom he greatly loved and who had many times slept in his chamber':[1] Henry, Lord Scrope of Masham, nephew of that Archbishop Scrope whom Bolingbroke had executed ten years before. The three had approached March as early as 21 July; it was only ten days later that he had decided to expose them.

The King, on the other hand, lost no time. Summoning a council of his chief magnates – they included Cambridge, Grey and Scrope – he announced that rumours had come to him of a possible plot, almost incredible as it seemed to be. Perhaps he was looking hard at the three men as he spoke; in any case they all immediately confessed – Scrope maintaining that although he was aware of the plot he knew nothing of the intended assassination – and were immediately sentenced to be hanged, drawn and beheaded. By the royal prerogative the hanging was remitted, and so also, for Cambridge and Grey, was the drawing; only

1. St Rémy, *Chronique*, I, 224.

Scrope was drawn on a hurdle through the streets of Southampton to the north gate, where all three were executed just outside the city wall. Later Scrope's head was spiked on one of the gates of York, and Grey's on the Tower at Newcastle – a ghastly warning to the north that did not go unheeded. There remained the Earl of March. True, he had revealed the plot; but it had taken him ten days to do so, and he may have been thinking only to save his own skin. Not till 9 August was he granted a full pardon and restored to royal favour. And two days later, on Sunday the 11th, leaving as Regent his brother John, Duke of Bedford, and carrying such of the crown jewels as were not in pawn together with a hefty piece of the True Cross, the King boarded one of his 'great' ships, *La Trinité Royale*, and crossed the Channel to Harfleur.

From the moment that he had called his forces to Hampshire rather than to Kent, it had been clear that he had already decided against Calais as a port of disembarkation. Not only did he have in the Solent a superb natural harbour; his objective was not Picardy but the mouth of the Seine, less than a hundred miles of easily navigable river from Paris. The one serious obstacle in his way was Harfleur itself, whose great castle, towering above the harbour, was generally believed to be impregnable. Its walls ran some two and a half miles from shore to shore, protected by a broad, deep moat and no less than twenty-six towers. The fleet anchored in the estuary safely out of range of its cannon, while the army landed on the soft, marshy terrain a little to the east of the town and trundled its siege engines into position. On the following day the operation began.

It was to continue for the next five weeks – weeks which, to the besieging army, rapidly became a nightmare. The marshes, unhealthy at the best of times, swarmed with flies in the August heat; and the only available food supplies, which consisted largely of rotten fruit and dubious shellfish washed down with raw Normandy cider, led to fever and dysentery, which quickly spread through the whole army. Within a month the Bishop of Norwich and the Earl of Suffolk were dead, together with many of the leading knights and some 2,000 men; another 5,000, including the King's brother the Duke of Clarence and the Earls of March and Arundel, were sent back to England on stretchers. But life was equally hard for the people of Harfleur. They were by now running seriously short of food; and on 18 September the seigneur d'Estouteville, commander of the garrison, sent to the King asking for terms. Henry's first reaction was to insist on unconditional surrender; then, realizing that his own army could not long continue in its present condition, he relented and gave permission for a delegation from the town to appeal for help to the Dauphin in Rouen, on condition that if this were not forthcoming within four days, Harfleur would capitulate. The delegation set off, only to be informed that the French army was not yet ready for action; and on the 22nd, as promised, d'Estouteville surrendered. There followed a ceremonial entry into the town, with all the pomp and panoply that the King could muster; even then, however, he dismounted at the gates, removed his shoes and went barefoot into the church of St Martin to give thanks.

His treatment of the townspeople was severe rather than savage. Harfleur was not put to the sack, as it might easily have been. The chief citizens were captured and held to ransom. As for the rest, those who agreed to swear allegiance to the English crown were permitted to remain; those who refused – numbering some 2,000, including women and children – were driven from the city. (Most of them were later picked up by the French army and resettled in Rouen.) Henry, meanwhile, sent a messenger to the Dauphin bearing a challenge to single combat, the crown of France to go to the winner after the death of Charles VI; but this seems to have been rather a matter of form than anything else. The nineteen-year-old Dauphin, a confirmed debauchee who had already contracted the disease which was to kill him within the year, was hardly likely to measure himself against a professional soldier eight years his senior, in the prime of life and the pink of condition.

Harfleur had been, in a sense, a victory; it was certainly reported as one in London. But it had also been a catastrophe. Death or disease had deprived the King of almost a third of his men. Of the 2,500 men-at-arms who had sailed with him to France, there remained only some 900, with perhaps 5,000 archers. In such circumstances, the planned advance on Paris was obviously out of the question: the only sensible course for Henry would have been to return directly to England, leaving a strong garrison in the conquered town. Although his reputation might not have been enhanced by the expedition, at least he could have claimed another English bridgehead on French soil. But for him the adventure was not yet over. His spirits were largely unaffected by his losses, and he now announced to his surviving captains his intention of advancing to Calais.

To most of them, such a plan must have seemed little short of insane. Calais was separated from Harfleur by 150 miles of difficult country, studded with hostile castles and fortified towns and crossed by a number of rivers, many of which might soon be flooded by the autumn rains. The French army, meanwhile, was known to have received the Armagnac reinforcements it had long been expecting; it now easily outnumbered the sadly depleted English force and could confidently be expected to block its path. Of all this the King was well aware, but his mind was made up. On 8 October, leaving his uncle Thomas Beaufort, Earl of Dorset, with 1,200 men to garrison Harfleur, he gave the order to march.

The first week of the English advance went better than might have been expected. There was the occasional minor skirmish, but the French army continued to hold back, the walled towns along the way surrendered at once and the rivers Béthune and Bresle were negotiated without mishap. The first serious obstacle was the Somme. There was a well-known ford at its mouth, known as Blanche-Taque, where Edward III had crossed on his way to Crécy sixty-nine years before; but this the French army had rendered impassable with rows of sharpened stakes, while its approaches were defended by a company of cavalry. All Henry could do was to lead his men upstream in search of another crossing-point. For nearly sixty miles they followed the left bank, past Amiens and Abbeville – both formidably defended – until they eventually found a ford near the village of Béthencourt, where they crossed in safety. But many of them had set out in an already fragile state of health, they had now been ten days on the march, and they were dog-tired. Between them and Calais lay over a hundred miles of open road – and somewhere along it, almost certainly, the enemy.

They had not gone far beyond the Somme when the French heralds rode up and informed the King that that army was indeed a short distance ahead, and that he must prepare to face it in pitched battle, on ground – for such were the rules of medieval chivalry – favourable to neither side. Henry accepted the message cheerfully enough (unlike most of his men who, according to the royal chaplain, believed that their only hope lay in the mercy of God) and, assuming that the enemy would attack almost at once, immediately donned his armour, ordering his knights to do the same. In fact the two sides did not meet for another three days; but at last, on the morning of 24 October, the coming of dawn revealed the French army encamped on the opposite bank of the little river Ternoise. After some difficulty in securing the existing bridge, the English crossed in safety; but the King knew that he would not get much further without a fight, and it soon became clear just where the battle was to be – in the open country some thirty miles north-west of Arras, between the two neighbouring villages of Tramecourt and Agincourt.[1] As he watched the French army preparing for the fray, Henry seems at last to have recognized the gravity of his situation. He was, first of all, overwhelmingly outnumbered – perhaps by as much as five or six to one. Moreover the enemy was fresh and rested, while his own men were near exhaustion after two full weeks on the march. And so he suddenly took a decision which has always tended to be overlooked by the more patriotic or chauvinist historians, Shakespeare himself included: he sued for peace. Sending over to the French camp the handful of prisoners that he had taken on the road from Harfleur, he offered in addition the restoration of that town and all his other gains, with full compensation for all the damage caused by his troops, in return for their safe passage to Calais. There was little hope, as he well knew, that his offer would be accepted; but at least it would delay the start of the battle by some hours, giving his soldiers the chance of the night's rest that they so desperately needed.

For a week there had been almost incessant rain. All day the storm clouds had been gathering once again; and as evening fell there came yet another downpour, which continued for much of the night. Lying – as most of the English were – out in the open, few of them could have got much sleep. Fewer still could have realized, however, that where the coming battle was concerned, this almost unremitting rain was the best thing that could possibly have happened and would be seen, in retrospect, as a gift from God.

By the morning of Friday 25 October – it was the Feast of SS. Crispin and Crispinian – the rain had stopped, leaving the recently ploughed meadows between the woods of Tramecourt to the east and Agincourt

1. Now known as Azincourt.

to the west a waterlogged morass; but there had been no reply to Henry's offer of terms, and both sides now prepared for battle. The King drew up his army in three divisions, line abreast. He himself, wearing his surcoat on which the three leopards of England were quartered with the *fleurs-de-lys* of France, his helmet encircled by a slim gold crown, took command of the centre. The right wing he placed under his father's cousin Edward, the former Earl of Rutland and later of Albemarle, who had succeeded to the Duchy of York in 1402; the left was entrusted to one of his most faithful generals, Lord Camoys. All three wings, in which the men-at-arms fought dismounted, were supported on each flank by companies of archers.

The French commanders, the Constable of France Charles d'Albret and Marshal Jean Boucicault, followed a different plan. For an army as large as theirs, the limited space between the two woods on each side – some 1,200 yards – made a line formation impossible: they accordingly formed a column, deployed in three ranks one behind the other, similarly dismounted but with a body of heavy cavalry on each side of the front rank. Between the three were companies of crossbowmen – despite the lessons of the previous century, the longbow had never been generally adopted in France – and there seem also to have been a few light cannon, though these too were hardly used. Basically the French were putting their trust in their far superior strength, and in the impetus of the outflanking cavalry attack with which they intended to open the battle.

Oddly enough, they seem to have taken no account of the recent weather. A knight in full armour imposes a formidable weight on the strongest of horses, and for a successful cavalry charge hard ground was essential. At eleven o'clock the Constable gave the signal for the attack, and the chargers moved forward; but they soon sank up to their fetlocks in the soft mud, and the dismounted men-at-arms did very little better. Meanwhile the English archers loosed a deluge of arrows and took a fearsome toll of cavalry and infantry alike, before exchanging their bows for short swords, axes and clubs, with which they quickly accounted for the relatively few Frenchmen who managed to reach the English line. The second wave of the attack, under the Duke of Alençon, was no more successful than the first, the English scrambling over the piles of dead and wounded to continue the slaughter. The third wave, seeing the fate of its predecessors, turned tail and fled.

It was at this point, with victory already assured, that the King gave the order which in the eyes of posterity has been the darkest stain on his reputation. Only the highest-ranking noblemen – for whom valuable ransoms could be expected – were to be spared; all other prisoners, he commanded, were to be instantly put to death. What prompted such a reaction, utterly contrary as it was to all the traditions of medieval warfare? Was there, as it was later claimed, some sudden movement on the part of the French cavalry which led Henry to fear an attack from the rear? It is possible, though no such attack took place. Many of his men refused point-blank to obey the order, even after he had threatened to hang all those who held back; he was at last obliged to designate 200 of his own archers specifically for the task. Such was the aftermath of the victory that has gone down as one of the most glorious in English history.

By mid-afternoon there was nothing to do but to count and, where possible, to identify the dead. The French losses were enormous: out of some 20,000 men well over a third – some 7,000 – were gone, including the Constable, the Dukes of Alençon and Bar, and two brothers of the Duke of Burgundy, Anthony Duke of Brabant and Philip Count of Nevers. With them were some 1,560 knights, perhaps 5,000 men-at-arms and an unknown number of irregulars. Marshal Boucicault, with the Dukes of Orleans and of Bourbon, was a prisoner. By contrast the English losses were at the most 1,600, and probably a good deal less; some estimates suggest no more than a quarter of that figure. Only two noblemen lost their lives: the young Earl of Suffolk – whose father had been killed at Harfleur – and the forty-two-year-old Duke of York, who was seriously overweight and whose heavy armour seems to have brought on a heart attack. His body was subsequently taken back to England and buried at the castle of Fotheringhay.

Given the state of the ground and the tactics chosen by the French, the victory of Agincourt was a foregone conclusion; but there were other reasons too why the battle ended as it did. The English army was united under a single commander, who had already proved himself a superb leader of men and who fought like a tiger throughout the battle, personally saving the life of his brother the Duke of Gloucester. The French on the other hand were split, with none of their generals in undisputed control and their command structure, such as it was, riven by divided loyalties. Moreover – and this must be repeated since to us in retrospect it seems well-nigh inexplicable – despite their experience at Crécy and Poitiers they had still not accepted the superiority of the longbow and were consequently powerless against the English archers. For this alone they deserved to lose – though they certainly did not deserve the unspeakable brutality with which they were treated after their defeat.

The news reached London four days later, on 29 October, and was received with jubilation. The church bells rang all over the city as the Mayor led the citizens first to the shrine of Edward the Confessor in Westminster Abbey and then to St Paul's for a service of thanksgiving. On the same day King Henry V entered Calais with what was left of his victorious army. It took him a fortnight to muster a sufficient fleet to transport it back to England, during which time the men were obliged to exchange many of their prisoners – for whom they had expected large ransoms – for the bare necessities of life; but finally on the morning of 16 November he was able to set sail, landing the same evening at Dover, where the local magnates waded into the water and carried him triumphantly ashore. The next day he reached Canterbury, and from there rode by easy stages to the capital, where he arrived on the 23rd to a hero's welcome.

London had never witnessed such a procession as that which escorted the King from Blackheath to Westminster. It was led by the Mayor and Corporation, who were followed by all the principal merchants of the city and members of the guilds and crafts, carrying aloft their identifying banners and standards; the numbers involved have been estimated at well over 15,000. London Bridge was scarcely visible for flags and triumphal arches, which continued as far as St Paul's itself, and the conduit in Cheapside is said to have flowed with wine instead of water. After a brief ceremony at the cathedral Henry rode along the river to Westminster Abbey for another, longer, service at the shrine of the Confessor; all the way the streets were lined with excited crowds, cheering him to the echo.

One man only seemed unable to take part in the general rejoicing: the King himself. Just as he had at his coronation, he seemed withdrawn and preoccupied: not once during the five-hour journey from Black-heath to Westminster was he seen to smile. He had made it clear from the outset that he would accept no credit for the victory, which belonged to God alone – he would not even allow his battered helmet and armour to be displayed to the crowds – but there was more to his grimness than mere modesty. Was he perhaps wondering how much he had really achieved, what had been the true value of the prize for which the crown jewels were in pawn and some 3,000 men, at Harfleur and at Agincourt, had given their lives? He had won a great battle, certainly; but he had not won the war. The force that he had destroyed, considerable as it might have been, was by no means the whole French army: several thousand men remained at Rouen under the command of the Duke of Berry. Meanwhile John the Fearless of Burgundy had contrived to keep his own forces intact; he had not declared himself one way or the other, and if he chose he could prove a deadly enemy. As for the English army, it was now little more than a ghost of what it once had been. So far Henry had proved luckier than he had either expected or deserved; how long, however, would his luck hold?

9

The End of the Adventure

[1415–1422]

BURGUNDY.   . . . let it not disgrace me
                  If I demand before this royal view
                  What rub or what impediment there is
                  Why that the naked, poor and mangled peace,
                  Dear nurse of arts, plenties and joyful births,
                  Should not in this best garden of the world,
                  Our fertile France, put up her lovely visage?
                  Alas, she hath from France too long been chased,
                  And all her husbandry doth lie on heaps,
                  Corrupting in its own fertility.

                                        KING HENRY V

The months that followed the battle of Agincourt seemed to justify the
King's worst fears. On 29 November 1415 Charles VI and the Dauphin
entered Paris; almost immediately, however, the Duke of Burgundy
advanced with his army on the city and in little more than a fortnight
had reached Lagny, only sixteen miles away. Then, on 18 December,
Henry received a report that changed the entire situation: after a long
illness aggravated by his excesses, the Dauphin had died in his twentieth
year. His brother and successor, John, was married to the Duke's niece
and living in Burgundian territory; the Duke, his position immeasurably
strengthened, withdrew at once to Flanders. Three months later in
March 1416 the Earl of Dorset, who had been left in charge at Harfleur,
set off on a raiding expedition along the coast and was almost trapped
by the Count of Armagnac – now Constable of France in succession
to d'Albret – at Valmont, near Fécamp. Though himself badly wounded,
he and his men succeeded in marching the twenty miles back to the
port, and even in inflicting a small though dramatic defeat on the French
cavalry who caught up with them at dawn, just outside the walls; but

the incident had very nearly ended in disaster, and gave yet further proof of the precariousness of the English hold on Normandy.

Furious at this last-minute reversal, Armagnac now acquired a number of ships from Genoa and Castile and, having first launched for good measure one or two raids on Portsmouth and the Isle of Wight, established a total blockade of Harfleur by land and sea. Before many weeks had passed famine began to threaten the town and Henry, now seriously alarmed, sent off an expedition of 10,000 men under his brother the Duke of Bedford, who on 15 August, in an extraordinary seven-hour naval battle at the mouth of the Seine, soundly defeated the blockading fleet. Four of the huge Genoese carracks were sunk, and five other vessels were taken as prizes.

The King had not led this last expedition himself for a very good reason: he was entertaining the Holy Roman Emperor, Sigismund of Luxemburg.[1] Sigismund – the uncle of Richard II's first wife Anne of Bohemia – despite his reputation for cruelty and an insatiable appetite for women, took his imperial responsibilities seriously: he was determined on the one hand to heal the papal schism – to which end he had called a General Council of the Church at Constance – and on the other to settle the differences between France and England in preparation for a united front against the infidel. Henry, ever ambitious to cut a dash on the European stage, had had a representative at Constance from the start. (He had, incidentally, raised no protest when Sigismund, having promised John Hus safe conduct to the city, had had him arrested, condemned and burnt at the stake.) Where the Emperor's second objective was concerned, he was still more interested: with careful handling, Sigismund might be converted into a valuable ally. Three hundred English ships were sent to welcome him at Calais and, on 30 April, to escort him across the Channel; and the King himself, with a retinue of 5,000, received him a mile outside London and accompanied him to the Palace of Westminster, which had been put at his disposal for the duration of his visit.

The Emperor remained in England for no less than four months,

---

1. Technically a Holy Roman Emperor could not be so described until he had been crowned by the Pope in Rome; before that time his official designation was King of the Romans. Sigismund's coronation, however, had been delayed by the papal schism; he had therefore adopted the imperial title by declaration. He was eventually crowned Emperor by Eugenius IV on 31 May 1433.

during which Henry achieved all that he could have hoped, persuading him of the justice of the English claims on France and concluding with him an offensive and defensive alliance which was sealed at Canterbury on 15 August – the very day of the battle of the Seine. In a final effort to preserve the peace, the two monarchs then invited both the Armagnacs and the Burgundians to a conference at Calais in September. Little was achieved – there was too much distrust among all the parties – but to Henry it hardly mattered: the imperial alliance had greatly strengthened his hand, and he returned home at the end of October well satisfied with what he had done.

He was fully aware, however, that this was only the beginning; for by now he had decided on a new expedition into France, compared with which that of 1415 would seem little more than an exploratory raid. His objective would be Paris, his prize the French throne. Once more the crown jewels were put in pawn; once more carpenters and shipwrights – some of them as far away as Barcelona and Bayonne – were put to work. Those soldiers who had fought at Agincourt were summoned back to the colours; thousands more, rallied by promises of even greater glory and still more copious plunder, hastened to join them. To provide sufficient arrows for the longbowmen, six wing-feathers were demanded from every goose in England. The French and Genoese were still making trouble in the Channel; but a special squadron of eleven warships was prepared to deal with them and on 29 June 1417 John Holland, the young Earl of Huntingdon, defeated a combined fleet off La Hogue. A month later on 1 August, some 1,500 ships landed an army of perhaps 10,000 fighting men – with about three times that number of non-combatants and 20,000 horses – at Touques, on the left bank of the Seine a few miles beyond Honfleur.

This second expedition, though it led to no great military victory, was indeed to be of infinitely greater significance than the first. Caen – far smaller than Rouen, but larger than any English city except London – fell in a fortnight, thanks largely to the English artillery. The guns themselves, mounted high on the two great abbeys just outside the city walls,[1] were

1. The two abbeys – Saint-Etienne (the Abbaye aux Hommes) and La Trinité (the Abbaye aux Femmes) – were founded respectively by William the Conqueror and his wife Matilda. They still stand today, having miraculously survived two months of fighting during the summer of 1944.

relatively small and primitive, but had considerable psychological effect on a population who had never seen – or, more importantly, heard – such things before. Henry as usual showed no mercy after the surrender, ordering the massacre of the entire secular male population. The lesson was not lost on the neighbouring towns, and it was no surprise when, shortly afterwards, Argentan and Alençon gave in without a struggle. Falaise, however, proved a harder nut to crack. The town held out for a month, the castle – virtually impregnable on its towering cliff – for a further six weeks before its garrison was forced to submit. This time at least there was no massacre. By the spring of 1418 Henry was in effective possession of all Lower Normandy.

Meanwhile in France as a whole the situation was growing daily more chaotic. The Dauphin John had died in April 1417, little more than a year after his brother, and had been succeeded by the third brother, Charles; but whereas John's wife was Burgundian and he himself had been a virtual hostage of Burgundy, Charles had been married in childhood to the daughter of the Duke of Anjou and belonged firmly to the Armagnac faction. In May the Armagnacs had consequently felt strong enough to take action against Charles VI's Queen Isabella[1] – who had consistently intrigued against them – and banished her to Tours; but Isabella immediately appealed to John the Fearless of Burgundy, who had her rescued and brought to join him at Chartres. There she proclaimed herself Regent, shortly afterwards appointing Duke John 'Governor' of France; and the two of them settled down together to plan the capture of Paris. On 12 June 1418, as a result of their machinations, the Duke of Armagnac was murdered by the Paris mob; and on 14 July Isabella and John together entered the capital, where they received a warm welcome from the hopelessly demented King – though not from the Dauphin, who had fled the city to join the Armagnacs at Melun. The political pendulum had swung once more, so that when Henry crossed the Seine at Pont de l'Arche and marched on Rouen, it was to discover that the city's defenders were no longer the Armagnacs that he had expected: they were now Burgundians to a man.

1. The German form of her name is retained here, not only because she was the daughter of Duke Stephen of Bavaria but also to avoid confusion with her daughter Isabelle, the second wife of Richard II who was now married to Charles, Duke of Orleans.

But they did not defend the greatest city in Normandy any the less stoutly for that. The huge castle – built in the twelfth century by King Philip Augustus – had been strengthened and painstakingly provisioned, while the fields for miles around had been deliberately devastated to the point where every scrap of food for the besieging army had to be brought from England; so confident were the defenders of their success that they had even welcomed into the city thousands of refugees from Lower Normandy. Henry, however, was not discouraged. Surrounding the city with no less than five different camps, he closed the Seine with chain booms and ships roped together across the river. Then – making no attempt to take Rouen by storm – he settled down to wait. The siege began on 31 July 1418 and lasted nearly six months, the weather growing steadily colder until English and French alike found themselves in the grip of one of the most savage winters that any of them could remember. As food began to run short, the defenders attempted the occasional sortie; but they were always beaten back, the King playing his full part – as he always did – in the hand-to-hand fighting. For the rest of the time, we are told, he was constantly on the move between the camps, inspecting the armaments and weaponry, talking to his men, and 'passing menie a long wynter night without sleepe or repose'.

Some time in mid-December the captain of the garrison, Guy le Bouteiller, realizing that he could no longer feed those refugees who were unable to play an active part in the defence, turned some 12,000 of them out of the city. When Henry categorically refused to allow them through the English lines they were simply left in the surrounding fosse, there to die of cold or starvation – though a few days later he allowed a little food through so that those who were still alive could celebrate Christmas. Not till 19 January were the keys of Rouen finally surrendered, Henry making his formal entry on the following day for a thanksgiving mass at the cathedral and looking – as always on such occasions – pensive and sad. The citizens and garrison were treated sternly, but with none of the savagery he had shown to the people of Caen. They were made to pay a fine of 300,000 crowns at the rate of 80,000 a year, and to surrender their arms, armour and other military equipment, including horses. The Normans in the garrison were all taken prisoner: had they not, the King demanded, been resisting their rightful lord? The others were free to go.

★

Henry spent two months in Rouen, reorganizing both city and duchy, while his generals mopped up the few surviving pockets of resistance. Now in a strong position for negotiation, he arranged a meeting with the sixteen-year-old Dauphin in March 1419, and was furious when on the appointed day the young man failed to appear. Somewhat more successful was the meeting, held under a two-month truce, outside Meulan on 29 May, with Queen Isabella and the Duke of Burgundy. (Charles VI had come as far as Pontoise but was in no condition to go any further.) At last Henry was able to discuss terms personally with those in authority. He was, he told them, prepared to renounce his claims to the French throne; the price, however, would be all those territories ceded to Edward III at Brétigny in 1360, together with those that he himself had conquered since his landing at Touques. The agreement would be sealed by his own marriage with the Princess Katherine, whom he now met for the first time and by whom he seems to have been genuinely struck. Her family offered a dowry of 800,000 crowns – minus, however, the 600,000 which they maintained should have been returned to France with Richard II's widow, Queen Isabelle. Both sides had in fact overplayed their hands and the meeting ended in stalemate; but the ice had been broken, both knew where they stood, and the ground was now satisfactorily prepared for the more detailed negotiations that were planned for the following year.

By then, Henry's position was to be stronger still. The moment the truce expired after the Meulan meeting, his army attacked the Burgundian headquarters at Pontoise in an early-morning operation which took the garrison completely by surprise. The town was sacked, yielding provisions and stores valued at two million crowns and bringing the King within twenty miles of Paris. For the French, everything now depended on a united front. If the Burgundians and the Dauphinists could reach agreement between each other, there might yet be a hope of driving back the English; and it was finally agreed that Duke and Dauphin should meet on Sunday 10 September on the bridge at Montereau, some forty miles south-east of Paris, where the river Yonne flows into the Seine. Such was the mutual distrust that a special enclosure for the two of them was built in the middle of the bridge, with barricades at each end to restrain their followers; but the precautions proved useless. Hardly had the conversation begun when John the Fearless was felled by a battleaxe.

Who wielded the weapon, whether the assassination was the result of a premeditated plot, and if so whether the young Dauphin was a party to it, we shall never know. From the French point of view, however, it was a disaster, destroying as it did the last chance of uniting the country against the English invaders and playing straight into their hands. The Dauphin and his followers, after leaving a garrison in Montereau, retired south to Provence, Languedoc and Gascony, where they enjoyed the strongest support; meanwhile John's son and successor, the twenty-three-year-old Philip – later to be known as 'the Good' – swore vengeance on the Dauphinists and, six months afterwards on Christmas Eve, concluded an alliance with England against them, to be sealed by the marriage of one of his sisters to a brother of the King.[1]

To Henry, the truth was now unmistakable: ever since his landing at Touques he had known that God was on his side, and the murder of John the Fearless had proved it beyond all doubt. With Burgundy now firmly bound to him, there could no longer be any obstacle to the long-awaited alliance with France itself; and on 21 May 1420, at Troyes – despite a strong Dauphinist presence in the whole region of Champagne – the treaty was signed at last. It was agreed that Henry should immediately be appointed Regent of France, and that on the death of Charles VI the French throne should pass to himself and his heirs in perpetuity, the Dauphin being disinherited and hunted down. The two crowns, however, would remain separate: England and France would retain their own laws and customs, neither being subject to the other. King Charles, as usual, was absent from the negotiations; the Queen and the Duke took the oaths in his name. The treaty was proclaimed in Paris on 30 May; and on Trinity Sunday, 2 June, in the parish church of St Joan in Troyes – which still stands today – Henry and Katherine were declared man and wife.

But the fighting was not yet over. The return journey to Paris was held up for a week at Sens until the Dauphinist garrison surrendered; the town of Montereau was stormed, and the body of John the Fearless removed from its temporary grave to be reburied in all solemnity in the Charterhouse at Dijon;[2] and at Melun the royal party was delayed

1. It was in fact another three and a half years before John, Duke of Bedford, married Philip's sister Anne at Troyes.
2. The Charterhouse, built by Philip the Bold in 1383 to serve as a family mausoleum, was destroyed during the Revolution. The tombs themselves, however, were saved and can now be seen in the Salle des Gardes of the Musée des Beaux-Arts, formerly the ducal palace.

no less than four and a half months, the garrison eventually capitulating on 18 November. It included a small detachment of Scots mercenaries, whom Henry hanged – technically for having refused to obey orders to surrender given them by King James I of Scotland, who was his prisoner and whom he had brought over expressly for that purpose.[1] The remainder of the garrison were all taken prisoner and held to ransom, 600 of them being sent by river to Paris, where many died, being unable to raise the ransom money. That tendency towards cruelty – even brutality – which we see all too often throughout Henry's career had not, it seemed, been improved by success and marriage.

On 1 December the two Kings rode into Paris, Henry being the first – and indeed the last – English monarch to be welcomed in the French capital as a conqueror. With his wife and brothers, he occupied the most sumptuous apartments in the Louvre: accommodation which the French were not slow to compare with the relative squalor which Charles VI and Isabella were obliged to endure in the Hôtel de Saint-Pol. He remained there over Christmas; then, on the 27th, he and Katherine set off together for England. They delayed three weeks in Rouen – Henry was never less than deeply conscientious in the administration of his new duchy – before continuing their journey, finally arriving on 1 February 1421 at Dover, where the barons of the Cinque Ports waded once again into the waves to carry them safely ashore. Three weeks later the pair were officially welcomed by the City of London, and on the 23rd the young Queen was crowned at Westminster.

It says much for the stability of Henry's government that he had dared to remain abroad for three and a half years; his father, once King, could never have contemplated such an extended absence. His country needed him, and he would probably have done better to remain at home for the rest of his short life. But his work in France was not quite over. In March 1421 his younger brother Thomas, Duke of Clarence – whom he had appointed Captain of Normandy and Lieutenant of France – marched south with about 4,000 men against the Dauphinists, meeting

1. James had been captured by the English – probably in 1406, at the age of twelve – but had always been well treated and had received an excellent education. He was eventually to return to his kingdom in 1424, when on 21 May he was crowned at Scone.

them at Beaugé, some twenty-five miles east of Angers. Clarence may or may not have known that his enemy included a substantial contingent of Scots, recently arrived at the invitation of the French to help their old allies; in any event, in his eagerness for a victory to set beside Agincourt, he attacked at once, giving his archers no time to catch up with him. Not surprisingly, such rashness ended in disaster. He himself was killed – it was said, by the Scottish Earl of Buchan;[1] the Earls of Somerset and Huntingdon were captured. The effect of the battle on French morale was immense: the English, it seemed, were not invincible after all.

It was primarily in an attempt to minimize the damage done at Beaugé that, on 10 June 1421, Henry embarked for France on his last campaign. He brought with him a smaller army than on either of the two previous occasions – some 4,000 in all – having left a sizeable force in Normandy the previous year. By the end of the summer English prestige was restored; not, however, English popularity, for Henry now fell prey to some mysterious disease and, as his health declined, so his cruelty towards those who resisted him seemed to increase. After his capture of the castle of Rougemont he burnt it to the ground, hanged every member of the garrison and drowned every fugitive he caught. And Rougemont was not alone: the surrender of Meaux, after a siege which lasted throughout the winter and spring, provided opportunities for further inhumanity. Two weeks later, at the end of May 1422, Queen Katherine joined him in France, leaving behind at home their five-month-old son Henry, whom his father was never to see.

By now the King was clearly dying. Though no longer able to sit his horse, he made a last heroic effort to lead his army against the Dauphin, who was besieging the town of Cosne; but even by litter the journey proved too much for him. He was rowed down the Seine to Charenton and thence carried to Vincennes. There, on 31 August, he summoned his councillors and urged them to maintain the Burgundian alliance; then he begged them to forgive him for any injustices, took communion for the last time and died. Had he lived just six weeks longer he would have been King of France, for on 11 October his rival – the poor demented Charles VI – followed him to the grave. His body

---

1. It was perhaps in recognition of this that Buchan was appointed Constable of France in the following year.

lay in state at Saint-Denis, after which on 15 September the magnificent funeral procession started for home, arriving in London on 5 November. Two days later King Henry V was buried in Westminster Abbey, his three favourite chargers being led up to the altar with him. He was thirty-four years old.

Henry's tomb of Purbeck marble, at the far end of St Edward's Chapel just to the east of the crossing, has lost, alas, much of its splendour. It was originally surmounted – at the expense of his widow – by an effigy in oak, with the head, hands, sceptre and other regalia moulded in solid silver and the rest plated in silver gilt; but all the precious metal was stolen in 1546, and the new head of polyester resin, added in 1971, can hardly be considered an adequate substitute. For Henry, however, the tomb was only a beginning. He was the first English monarch also to insist on a chantry chapel, in which masses could be said in perpetuity for his soul; and this tremendous edifice towers above the tomb in a breathless display of arrogance, completely overshadowing not only the Plantagenet tombs below but even the shrine of the Confessor himself. It is covered with elaborate sculptures of remarkably high quality, including two representations of Henry on his charger and two more depicting his coronation. Most moving of all, on a wooden beam high above, are a shield and saddle, with a helmet which – although manifestly designed for tilting – is traditionally believed to have been worn by him at Agincourt.

And what of Katherine? In their tomb effigies, his two predecessors both lie beside their wives; Henry is alone. He had made no provision for his Queen, who some three years after her husband's death married the Welshman Owen Tudor and bore him a son, Edmund, the future father of King Henry VII. When she died in 1437, she was given a tomb in the Lady Chapel; and when her grandson demolished that chapel to make way for the one which now bears his name, her body was placed in a coffin of loose boards and laid beside Henry V's tomb, where it was regularly exposed to curious visitors.[1] Only in 1776 were the bones, still 'firmly united, and thinly cloth'd with flesh, like scrapings

---

1. 'Here did we see, by perticular favour, the body of Queen Katherine of Valois, and had her upper part of her body in my hands. And I did kiss her mouth, reflecting upon it that I did kiss a Queen, and that this was my birthday, 36 year old, that I did first kiss a Queen.' (Samuel Pepys, Diary, 23 February 1669).

of tann'd leather' at last removed from public view; and in 1878 they were laid beneath the altar slab in Henry's chantry chapel, where they remain today.

10

King Henry V

[1414–1420]

CHORUS.   Thus far, with rough and all-unable pen,
          Our bending author hath pursued the story,
          In little room confining mighty men,
          Mangling by starts the full course of their glory.

KING HENRY V

At the end of *King Henry IV Part II*, Henry V is already King of England. The play that bears his name consequently begins with the second year of his reign, and continues until the peace with France is sealed in 1420 and Henry marries the Princess Katherine at Troyes. We are told nothing of his second and third campaigns in France, for the excellent reason that after Agincourt even the second would have been an anticlimax, while the third proved to be little more than a prelude to his not particularly glorious death. *King Henry V* is primarily a celebration – of patriotism, of military glory and, in its last act, of true love as a means of reconciliation – and Shakespeare selected his material accordingly.

Perhaps in order to point up the difference between the play and its historical predecessors, he also gave it a Chorus – rather on the lines of Greek tragedy – who speaks directly to the audience. This Chorus provides not only a prologue and epilogue, together with separate introductions to each act after the first, but also two extremely significant clues as to dating. One of these is given in the opening lines:

> But pardon, gentles all,
> The flat unraised spirits that hath dared
> On this unworthy scaffold to bring forth
> So great an object. Can this cockpit hold
> The vasty fields of France? Or may we cram
> Within this wooden O the very casques
> That did affright the air at Agincourt?

There had been no apologies of this kind before the representation of the battle of Shrewsbury; and it has been plausibly suggested that these lines refer to the opening by Shakespeare's company, the Lord Chamberlain's Men, of their new playhouse, the Globe, on the Bankside in Southwark in 1599. This would certainly have been an event important enough to have deserved special mention if possible, and the presence of the Chorus would have provided a perfect opportunity.

The second clue lends strength to the first. In the introduction to Act V, we are given – for the only time in all the plays – a direct reference to current events:

> But now behold,
> In the quick forge and working-house of thought,
> How London doth pour out her citizens.
> The Mayor and all his brethren in best sort,
> Like to the senators of th'antique Rome
> With the plebeians swarming at their heels,
> Go forth and fetch their conquering Caesar in;
> As, by a lower but as loving likelihood,
> Were now the General of our gracious Empress,
> As in good time he may, from Ireland coming,
> Bringing rebellion broached on the sword,
> How many would the peaceful city quit
> To welcome him!

It is nowadays almost universally agreed that the General referred to here is Robert Devereux, Earl of Essex. On 27 March 1599, as Lieutenant and Governor-General of Ireland, Essex had left London to put down the rebellion by the Earl of Tyrone, and had been given a rousing send-off by the people. He was to return prematurely in September, having concluded an unjustifiable truce and in something very like disgrace; this would mean – if the basic supposition is correct – that *King Henry V* had its first performance some time between March and September 1599, in which case the play would have been written immediately after *Henry IV Part II*, which as we know was first performed in the previous year.

After the Prologue we have the conversation between the Archbishop of Canterbury and the Bishop of Ely about a proposed bill, first mooted under Henry IV, for the appropriation of Church lands by the Crown. The details of this bill are taken almost word for word from Holinshed; essentially, however, they are no more than a peg from which to hang a discussion – for the benefit of those of the audience who have not seen *Henry IV Part II* – of the King himself, and his extraordinary change of character since his accession. This first scene is thus in a sense an additional prologue; it is only with the entrance of the King in the second that the play really begins. At Henry's invitation, the Archbishop then launches into a long and almost ridiculously intricate justification of the English title to the throne of France – omitting, oddly enough, any reference to Edward II's Queen Isabella, sister of the French King Charles IV, on whom the whole case rested – and ending with an exhortation to the King, echoed by the Bishop of Ely and the assembled nobles, to claim his own. Henry needs no further encouragement:

> Now are we well resolved; and by God's help
> And yours, the noble sinews of our power,
> France being ours, we'll bend it to our awe
> Or break it all to pieces.

The arrival of the French embassy with the barrel of tennis balls only strengthens this resolve; Henry's answer to the ambassadors falls somewhere between a threat and a curse. When the curtain falls on the first act we are already on our way to the climax of Agincourt.

Is the incident of the tennis balls history or legend? It is reported both by Holinshed and Hall, and appears also in a contemporary ballad as well as in several other slightly later works. But Walsingham's chronicle – which would surely have included it if it had really occurred – makes no reference to it, and nor does any contemporary French historian. It certainly seems highly improbable. So gratuitous an insult must surely have led to a complete breach of diplomatic relations between the two countries, whereas we know that the negotiations continued. The story most likely had its origins in the Chronicle of one John Strecche, dating from only a few years after Henry's death in 1422, according to which in his boyhood the Armagnac ambassadors offered to send him 'little balls to play with, and soft cushions to rest on, until what time he should grow to man's strength'; Henry is said to have replied angrily that in a few months he would play such a game in the streets of France that it would cease to be a joke.

The second act of the play introduces the sub-plot, with the reappearance of the King's old Eastcheap companions: Bardolph, Pistol, his wife the former Mistress Quickly, her jilted suitor Nym – who does not figure in *Henry IV* but has been imported from *The Merry Wives of Windsor* – and, offstage, Falstaff himself, with the reports of his sickness and death. But since this book is concerned primarily with the historical accuracy of the plays, the fictitious characters need not detain us; we can pass on to Scene ii and the Southampton plot. Once again, Shakespeare's authority is Holinshed; he has not hesitated, however, to add a few touches of his own. The plot, when we first hear of it, has already been discovered, though the conspirators are not yet aware of the fact. The King plays them along, encouraging them to flatter him and to emphasize their own loyalty; he even goes so far as to suggest releasing

the man committed yesterday
That railed against our person

so that they may object, and urge instead that the offender should be severely punished. (This last is a little Shakespearean invention to increase the dramatic impact of the scene.) Only when they have condemned themselves with hypocrisy as well as treachery does Henry hand them the 'commission papers' (another invention) which reveal to them the truth. None of them – not even Scrope – makes any attempt to defend himself; they simply confess, express their contrition and beg for mercy – which, it need hardly be said, they do not receive.

After the brief scene in which the former Mistress Quickly tells of the death of Falstaff – Shakespeare thus in some measure fulfilling the promise made in the Epilogue of *Henry IV Part II* – the scene changes to the French court. King Charles VI is present, in full possession of his senses. Nowhere in the play is there any suggestion of his mental instability; indeed, in this scene his good sense stands out in marked contrast to the foolhardiness of his son the Dauphin, who persists in underestimating the English threat. (There is no historical evidence for supposing that this was the Dauphin's attitude, except for the earlier and equally suspect incident of the tennis balls.) The discussion is interrupted by the arrival of Henry's uncle the Duke of

Exeter[1] with his ultimatum: either Charles gives up his throne or, 'in thunder and earthquake, like a Jove', the English will come and get it. Exeter makes it clear, too, that his master has a particular contempt for the Dauphin, whose pride and arrogance are continually emphasized so that it is he, and not his father, who becomes the villain of the play; Charles, however, remains the principal spokesman, and it is he who closes the scene – and the act – with his dismissal of the ambassador and his promise of a full answer on the morrow.

The substance of that answer is left to our imagination. By the opening of Act III we are at Harfleur, and the siege has begun.

> Once more unto the breach, dear friends, once more,
> Or close the wall up with our English dead.
> In peace there's nothing so becomes a man
> As modest stillness and humility;
> But when the blast of war blows in our ears,
> Then imitate the action of the tiger;
> Stiffen the sinews, conjure up the blood,
> Disguise fair nature with hard-favoured rage.
> Then lend the eye a terrible aspect;
> Let it pry through the portage of the head
> Like the brass cannon; let the brow o'erwhelm it
> As fearfully as doth a galled rock
> O'erhang and jutty his confounded base,
> Swilled with the wild and wasteful ocean.
> Now set the teeth and stretch the nostril wide . . .

Recognizing the limitations of his 'wooden O', Shakespeare confines his account of the siege of Harfleur to Henry's famous exhortation and a brief scene with Pistol, Nym and their ill-fated Boy in which he also introduces both the Welshman Fluellen – thought to be a portrait either of the soldier Sir Roger Williams, a follower of the Earl of Essex, or of the Welsh poet and courtier Ludovic Lloyd – and the Irishman Macmorris. In scene iii the city surrenders, the Governor explaining to the King that since the Dauphin had not been able to send help he had no

---

1. Thomas Beaufort was not to be made Duke of Exeter until 1416. At this time he was still Earl of Dorset. But Shakespeare calls him Exeter, so Exeter he shall be.

alternative but to yield. We are given no indication of Henry's treatment of the citizens, except for his injunction to Exeter to 'use mercy to them all'; interestingly, however, there is a reference to the appalling English losses through disease:

> The winter coming on and sickness growing
> Upon our soldiers, we will retire to Calais.

At this point in the play we meet the Princess Katherine for the first time. Born on 27 October 1401, in the summer of 1415 she was fourteen years old – not perhaps too young, in the late Middle Ages, to have understood both of the agonizing *double-entendres* (foot = *foutre*, gown = coun = *con*) in her conversation with her companion Alice – to some of us, among the most embarrassing scenes in all Shakespeare. It is with considerable relief that we return to the court of France, imaginary though the ensuing conversation must be. Line 64 of scene v reveals that it is set in Rouen, although by this time, only a few days before Agincourt, with the English already across the Somme, the Constable d'Albret would surely have been with his army. (Holinshed and Hall, incidentally, both confuse Louis the Dauphin with his cousin Louis of Anjou, King of Sicily, and Shakespeare seems to have been led into the same trap.) It is a short scene, which serves only to emphasize the French determination to bring the invaders quickly to battle before they reach home ground at Calais – or possibly to extort from them an appropriate ransom. Holinshed tells us that at the French council of war – which was attended also by 'the dukes of Berry and of Britaine [Brittany], the earle of Pontieu the kings yoongest sonne, and other high estates' – the voting was thirty to five in favour; 'and so Montioy king at armes was sent to the king of England to defie him as the enemie of France, and to tell him that he should shortlie haue battell.'

Before the herald can deliver his message, Henry hears from Fluellen of the successful crossing of the Ternoise in the face of strong French opposition. (In the play – though not in Holinshed – the credit for this is wrongly given to Exeter, who had as we know been left in charge at Harfleur.) At this point, too, he learns from the same source of the arrest and impending execution of Bardolph, who has been caught robbing a church. Clearly he has it in his power to pardon his old drinking companion; instead, he unhesitatingly confirms the sentence,

Shakespeare's text – as opposed to most modern productions of the play – giving no indication that he even remembers him. The incident may be fictitious, but it accurately illustrates not only the King's mood but his extraordinary change of character since his accession. Accurate too, as far as it goes, is his answer to Montjoy's challenge. He does not – as the historical Henry did – sue for peace; indeed he even injects one or two gratuitous insults. At the same time he makes no secret of the condition of his army:

> My people are with sickness much enfeebled,
> My numbers lessened, and those few I have
> Almost no better than so many French . . .
> My ransom is this frail and worthless trunk,
> My army but a weak and sickly guard.
> Yet, God before, tell him we will come on,
> Though France himself and such another neighbour
> Stand in our way.

By now, as the last scene of Act III makes clear, the French can hardly wait for the battle to begin.

Act IV forms the climax of the play. Its first scene, in which the King makes his round of the English camp on the night before the battle, is – for its poetry, for the opportunity it gives to a great actor, and for the extraordinary atmosphere that Shakespeare manages to evoke – perhaps one of the best-known that he ever wrote. There is no historical evidence that Henry did any such thing; nor, on the other hand, is it in any way unlikely. All great generals – and though Henry's strategy was occasionally at fault there can be little doubt of his greatness – show a care for their men, and his immense popularity with his troops proves that he could have been no exception to the rule. Something must have occurred during those long, sodden hours before the dawn to infuse into the exhausted army the spirit to turn almost certain defeat into victory; and 'a little touch of Harry in the night' is surely the most probable explanation. The three soldiers – John Bates, Alexander Court and Michael Williams – are Shakespeare's creations; 'old' Sir Thomas Erpingham, however, is a historical figure; at the time of Agincourt he was fifty-eight. It is he who, at the end of the scene, leaves the King alone on the stage to speak his final prayer before the coming conflict:

> O God of battles, steel my soldiers' hearts

and this immediately leads us back to that moral burden that the House
of Lancaster could never entirely shake off – the guilt that Henry will
always feel for his father's usurpation of the throne.

'The sun doth gild our armour; up, my lords!' With this magical
line, and more vainglorious speeches from the French side, the dramatic
representation of the battle effectively begins. The scene then changes
to the English camp, and leads to the great St Crispin's Day speech that,
sixty years ago, every English schoolboy had sooner or later to learn by
heart: the King's indignant retort to the Earl of Westmorland's surely
comprehensible wish that

> we now had here
> But one ten thousand of those men in England
> That do no work today!

There is good historical evidence for this incident, which is included
by Holinshed – who does not, however, specify the figure and who
makes no mention of Westmorland by name. Interestingly enough, the
story is also told by Henry's unknown chaplain, in whose *Gesta Henrici
Quinti* the retort is made not to Westmorland but to Sir Walter
Hungerford, who had wished for 'another ten thousand of the best
English archers'. Whether the chaplain's account was known to Shakespeare we shall never know: if it was not, the choice of the figure ten
thousand could easily have been coincidental; if it was, the transfer of
the speech to an existing character in the play would surely have been
legitimate in the circumstances. Certainly from Holinshed is the second
appearance of Montjoy, giving the King his last chance of paying a
ransom to deliver himself and his army from almost certain destruction;
but the herald receives – predictably – the same response as before.

In his introduction to Act IV the Chorus has given us warning of
how

> we shall much disgrace
> With four or five most vile and ragged foils
> Right ill-disposed in brawl ridiculous
> The name of Agincourt.

The action of the battle is in fact compressed into three short scenes, of which the second already presents the French lords as fully conscious of their defeat and the third – of a mere thirty-eight lines – is almost entirely given over to the deaths of the only two English noblemen to have fallen, the Duke of York and the Earl of Suffolk. (The affecting story of their deaths as told by Exeter is plainly fabricated: Exeter was not even present at Agincourt – despite Holinshed's affirmation to the contrary – and York's death, as we have seen, was probably due to heart failure.) Just before the end of the scene, however, the mood changes: the King gives his terrible order to kill all the French prisoners. In his antepenultimate line he makes his reason clear: the noise of a distant alarum has persuaded him that 'the French have reinforced their scattered men'.

Strangely enough, however, at the beginning of scene vii only a few lines further on, Captain Gower attributes the decision to the King's anger on hearing of a French raid on the English tents, which ended in a massacre of the boy servants who had been left in charge of them; and when Henry enters again with the words

> I was not angry since I came to France
> Until this instant

he seems to confirm Gower's view. If we go back to Holinshed we find a still more confused account; and Shakespeare evidently shares the confusion. But for him, unlike Holinshed, there is an additional important consideration: he must at all costs keep the sympathy of his audience for the King. Gower and Fluellen are obviously speaking for the entire army when they express their disgust at the French atrocity – which, as Fluellen points out, is 'expressly against the law of arms' – and their support of Henry's order.

By contrast, the beginning of the following scene with Montjoy the herald is taken almost word for word from Holinshed: first the request to bury the French dead, then the King's demand for confirmation that the day is indeed his – which Montjoy immediately gives – and finally the naming of the battle after the neighbouring castle of Agincourt. The scene continues with Shakespeare's invented characters and the incident of the exchanged gloves; history reappears only towards the end of scene viii, with the English herald bringing Henry the list of the principal casualties on both sides. All these are taken directly from Holinshed, as is the thanksgiving to God with which the act ends:

> Let there be sung *Non nobis* and *Te Deum*,
> The dead with charity enclosed in clay,
> And then to Calais, and to England then,
> Where ne'er from France arrived more happy men.

The story of the King's triumphant return to London is given to the Chorus, in the introduction to Act V. We are told not only of the cheering crowds, 'Whose shouts and claps outvoice the deep-mouthed sea', but also of Henry's refusal to allow 'His bruised helmet and his bended sword' to be borne before him through the city.[1] The other function of the Chorus at this point is to bridge the five years between Agincourt and the Treaty of Troyes in May 1420. For Shakespeare it was essential that the great battle should form the climax of his play; there was no space for the King's second expedition, for the taking of Caen and Rouen or for the murder of the Duke of Burgundy. We must therefore

> omit
> All the occurrences, whatever chanced,
> Till Harry's back return again to France

and move directly on to the reconciliation of the two former enemies and Henry's marriage to the Princess Katherine, by which that reconciliation was sealed. There is in fact a short preliminary scene, in which Fluellen settles his score with Pistol; but this serves only to point up the pomp and ceremony which opens the final scene of the play. The first part of this is dominated by the great speech in praise of peace by the Duke of Burgundy – Philip the Good, now twenty-four, whose father John had been assassinated in the previous year. It is pure Shakespearean invention – and none the worse for that.

The scene continues with the second long conversation, in a mixture

---

1. Holinshed adds: '. . . neither would he suffer any ditties to be made and soong by minstrels of his glorious victorie, for that he would wholie haue the praise and thanks altogither giuen to God'.

of English and French, between the King and his bride-to-be. Less embarrassing than its predecessor, it nevertheless shows a distressing lack of consideration on Henry's part for the Princess's extremely limited English, to say nothing of several more *double-entendres*[1] which do not sound wholly appropriate in this context. (True, they are mild enough in comparison with the King's exchanges with Burgundy that follow;[2] one can only hope that the pair have moved beyond the hearing of poor Katherine, who remains onstage throughout.) The two Kings – Charles VI still apparently in perfect possession of his faculties – then confirm that there are now no longer any outstanding matters between them. There is even agreement on the official formula by which the English King is in future to be addressed by the French court, a formula which leaves no one – including the audience – in any doubt of Henry's most important single achievement: recognition by the French as Charles's heir, *héritier de France*. Pious hopes and good wishes are expressed on both sides and the Chorus speaks a short epilogue, pointing the audience both forward to Henry's son and successor and back to the Henry IV plays 'which oft our stage has shown' – they having been already written several years before.

Much critical ink has been spilt over the question of what sort of play its author intended *King Henry V* to be. Is it the nearest thing he ever wrote to a patriotic pageant, an epic celebration of English glory, or is it a diatribe against war and the abuse of power? The answer, surely, is that it is both. Shakespeare would have seen no contradiction between the two. One approach or the other alone would have made it two-dimensional; by combining them, he gave his play fullness and depth. Essentially, it is about conflict, but not only the obvious conflict between the English and the French. There is also the age-old moral conflict about the justification for aggressive war, to say nothing of Henry's own inner struggle in which his energy and ambition are set against the vicarious guilt he feels for the murder of Richard and

1. For example line 140, 'I could quickly leap into a wife'; or line 260, 'I cannot tell vat is *baiser* en Anglish'. (The colloquial meaning of *baiser*, delicately described in one dictionary as 'going all the way', has been current in French since the days of Clément Marot (1496–1564) or even before.)

2. 'A mean dialogue for princes' is how Dr Johnson described it; how right he was.

> the fault
> My father made in compassing the crown.

Seen from the historical point of view *Henry V* is, like its three predecessors, surprisingly accurate as far as it goes – seldom straying far from the available sources, and then nearly always for perfectly justifiable dramatic reasons. Its principal sins are those of omission, and there again the Chorus is swift to apologize:

> For 'tis your thoughts that now must deck our kings,
> Carry them here and there, jumping o'er times,
> Turning th'accomplishment of many years
> Into an hour-glass.

In his closing lines, however, he has one more task: to admit, for the first time in the play, that all Henry's achievements are to be set at nothing. Under his son England will be made to bleed as never before – and France will be lost.

11

King Henry VI: His Childhood and Youth

[1422–1445]

EXETER.   But howsoe'er, no simple man that sees
          This jarring discord of nobility,
          This shouldering of each other in the Court,
          This factious bandying of their favourites,
          But sees it doth presage some ill event.
          'Tis much when sceptres are in children's hands;
          But more when envy breeds unkind division:
          There comes the ruin, there begins confusion.
                              KING HENRY VI PART I

England had never had so young a King. Henry VI had been born at
Windsor on 6 December 1421; when he was proclaimed on 1 September
of the following year – the day after his father's death, the concept of
a seamless succession being still unknown – he was not quite nine
months old. The dying wishes of Henry V had been to entrust the
regency to Philip of Burgundy if he were to claim it – which, fortunately, he did not – and otherwise to his own brother John, Duke of
Bedford; and it was Bedford who, in one of his first ceremonial duties
as Regent, attended the funeral of Charles VI in Saint-Denis, a naked
sword being carried before him as a symbol of his royal authority. Now
thirty-three and strikingly handsome, he possessed none of Henry's
meteoric brilliance, nor the wide culture of his younger brother Humphrey; but he was more reliable than either – intelligent, prudent, blameless
in his private life and in battle a fearless fighter.

Since it was clear that for the foreseeable future the Regent would
be obliged to spend most of his time in France, Humphrey of Gloucester
was confirmed as Warden of the Realm and Protector, with overall
responsibility for English affairs. This appointment was a good deal less
well advised. 'The good Duke Humphrey' – as he was universally

known – seemed on first acquaintance to be the nonpareil of princes: courteous and charming, a patron of the arts with a genuine love of literature and a library which was to provide the nucleus of the Bodleian at Oxford. Shakespeare's portrait of him follows, in the main, this popular conception; there is little indication of the faithlessness and irresponsibility which Humphrey was to show throughout his life, or of the dissipation and debauchery that were to ruin his health before he was thirty, or of the overriding personal ambition for which he was repeatedly to sacrifice the nation's interests.

The guardianship of the infant King, meanwhile, was entrusted to a nobleman of the older generation: Thomas Beaufort, Duke of Exeter, the youngest of the three sons of John of Gaunt by Katherine Swynford. But Exeter was already an old man by the standards of the time – he was to die when his charge was still only five years old – and his character was anyway largely eclipsed by that of his elder brother Henry, Bishop of Winchester and after 1426 a cardinal of the Church. The richest man in England – he was an active dealer in wool – and one of the most influential figures in Europe, in 1417 the bishop had been seriously considered as a candidate for the papacy; he would certainly have been a far better choice as Warden than his nephew Humphrey of Gloucester, whom he cordially detested and opposed at every opportunity. His haughty arrogance was bound to antagonize many of his contemporaries; but he was to remain absolutely loyal to the young King, not only giving him wise and disinterested advice but also helping him with substantial loans whenever the need arose.

Where France was concerned, Henry V had left to his successors an impossible situation. The kingdom was on its knees: not only politically after Henry's victories, but economically and morally as well. The war had already been continuing sporadically for the best part of a century, and much of the north and west lay depopulated and desolate. Bedford did his best, and for the first few years after Henry's death achieved a fair measure of success. In 1422 the line of English garrisons had stretched from the border of Brittany to Abbeville and thence south to Paris; by the end of 1425 it embraced Champagne and Maine and extended as far as the Meuse. Conscientious governor that he was, Bedford was not personally unpopular in any of these conquered territories. He was careful to maintain French institutions and, wherever possible, to appoint Frenchmen to key positions; he also reformed the administration of justice, and even on occasion struck a strong coinage. But like most of his compatriots he knew full well that the cause was ultimately hopeless. England – also exhausted by war, neglected by her major landowners (many of whom had spent the better part of their adult lives fighting in France), her agriculture and population alike ravaged by successive visitations of the Black Death, could never wholly conquer France, far less hold it if conquered.

And the French knew it too. For many of them – and particularly the aristocracy – the death of Charles VI had radically changed the situation. Charles had bid them give their loyalty to Henry V, but now both he and Henry were dead. His son and namesake the Dauphin had grown up a weak and feckless youth; he had, however, been crowned after his father's death at Poitiers, and was now widely acknowledged south of the Loire as far as the borders of Guyenne. It was therefore hardly surprising that more and more French noblemen should have rallied to his banner: so many indeed that early in 1423 an increasingly anxious Bedford ordered a re-proclamation of the Treaty of Troyes, obliging many Frenchmen to swear allegiance to 'le Roy Henri II' – an oath which many of them took, we are told, only with extreme reluctance.

The boy King, meanwhile, was growing up fast. On the last day of April 1425, at the age of three and a half, he opened Parliament and then rode through London in triumph, being 'judged of all men to have the very image, lively portraiture and lovely countenance of his famous father'; and on 6 November 1429, St Leonard's Day, he was crowned at Westminster. The ritual seems to have been impressive enough, as was the banquet that followed; but none of the principal witnesses saw it as being much more than a necessary preliminary to the infinitely more important ceremony that was becoming ever more imperative: Henry's coronation in France, where the situation had once again been transformed – this time by a girl of seventeen.

The story of Joan of Arc has been told too often in the past for anything but a short summary to be necessary here; but her curious appearances in *King Henry VI Part I* make some reference to her essential. Born of peasant stock at Domrémy in Lorraine, she first heard her 'voices' at the age of thirteen; and four years later, in the early spring of 1429, she left her home village – first for the neighbouring fortress of Vaucouleurs and thence, against formidable opposition, for the Dauphin's court at Chinon. On 8 March, having been instantly identified by her as he hid among a group of courtiers, he granted her an audience, in the course of which she informed him of her divine mission: to raise the siege of Orleans and to escort Charles to his true coronation at Rheims. Still unconvinced, he sent her to Poitiers for examination by a body of senior ecclesiastics; only after they had given her their unqualified approval did he dispatch her to Orleans.

Orleans had been under siege since the previous October by an English army initially under the command of Thomas Montagu, Earl of Salisbury, who had recently returned to France with a private army of 2,700 men raised at his own expense. (Bedford, who had had his doubts about the wisdom of the operation – though he had not forbidden it – had remained at his headquarters at Chartres.) In November, however, Salisbury had been killed by a French cannon ball as he stood at a window; his place had been taken by two joint commanders, William de la Pole, Earl of Suffolk, and John Talbot, Earl of Shrewsbury, who had determined to starve out the city. The winter that followed had not been uneventful. An armed convoy of provisions led by Sir John Fastolf had been attacked on 12 February by 4,000 French and Scots. The assailants had been repelled, but not before their cannon had shattered the supply casks, which had spewed vast quantities of salted fish all over the field. Shortly after this 'Battle of the Herrings' the defenders of Orleans, now running seriously short of food, suggested the surrender of the city to the Duke of Burgundy, who had joined the siege with an army of his own; Bedford not unnaturally refused,[1] but Burgundy took grave offence and immediately withdrew with all his men.

It was at this point, or very soon afterwards, that Joan arrived in the city. Her appearance put new spirit into the citizens, and on 4 May the counter-attack began. She herself, though wounded in the neck by an arrow, refused to leave the battle till it was won. A day or two later the English were in full retreat, the French in pursuit. Suffolk was taken prisoner during fierce street fighting in the nearby village of Jargeau,

---

1. 'The Regent answered the dukes ambassadors, that it was not honorable nor yet consonaunte to reason, that the kyng of England should beate the bushe and the duke of Burgoyne should haue the birdes' (Hall, 147).

Talbot a few days later at Patay. Joan, now believed on all sides to be invincible, met Charles at Tours and pressed him no longer to delay his second coronation at Rheims – where, by long and hallowed tradition, all French Kings were crowned. This ceremony took place, in her presence, on 17 July 1429. Her work done, her voices now silent, her mission accomplished, she longed to return to her village, and had she been allowed to do so it might well have saved her life; but the people refused to let her go and she bowed, disastrously, to their will, urging Charles to march on Paris. He did so in September, but his attempt to capture it was unsuccessful and Joan was wounded for the second time.

All was not yet lost; the English, still in retreat, had already evacuated the Loire valley, most of the Ile-de-France and virtually all Champagne; a concerted French push into Picardy might yet have driven them back to Calais. But the chance was thrown away. The French commander La Trémouille (who detested Joan) now took it upon himself to disband the army, giving Bedford the perfect opportunity to regroup and recover – and finally to bring his young sovereign over to France for his own coronation. Henry, by now nine years old, reached Calais in April 1430 in the company of Cardinal Beaufort and 10,000 men, but such was the prevailing anarchy that he was forced to remain there for a further three months; not till the end of July was he able to travel, and then only as far as Rouen. He was lodged in the castle, and was still there five months later when Joan arrived, in chains. She had been taken prisoner on 23 May during an attempt to relieve Compiègne, which was under siege by the Burgundians; but she had spent the interim in several other prisons while her captor John of Luxemburg haggled over her price with Philip of Burgundy and the Duke of Bedford. Finally she had been handed over to the English for 10,000 francs. Did she and Henry ever meet? They certainly could have; but Richard Beauchamp, Earl of Warwick – who had succeeded Exeter as the King's guardian and tutor, and who happened also to be Governor of the castle, kept her guarded day and night by five English soldiers. He is unlikely, to say the least, to have permitted his young charge to come in contact with a woman whom he believed to be an evil witch, 'the disciple and limb of the Fiend'.

Joan's examination began on 21 February 1431; five weeks later, on 27 March, she appeared at her trial, during which she was allowed no defence counsel or spiritual adviser; and on Wednesday 30 May she was declared excommunicated and a heretic and burnt at the stake in the market place of Rouen – the pyre having been prepared well in advance of the sentence. Her ashes were cast into the Seine. But she had done her work well. She had delivered Orleans; she had had the Dauphin crowned, as his ancestors had been crowned before him, in the cathedral of Rheims; above all, she had given her compatriots a new spirit, and a new strength. From the moment of her first appearance English fortunes had begun to decline. They were never to recover. True, the ten-year-old Henry VI finally reached Paris where, alone of all the English monarchs, he was crowned in the French capital – by Cardinal Beaufort, according to the English liturgy, in Notre Dame on 16 December; but if Bedford had hoped to impress the French by this ceremony, he failed. The service was poorly attended, the subsequent banquet proved a fiasco, no amnesty was declared, no alms were distributed to the poor, and two days after Christmas the King was slipped almost furtively out of Paris to return to England.

By now there were few people on either side of the Channel who had much stomach for the war. To the pious young King, hostility between fellow Christians was a cause of continual grief; Bedford, knowing that the cause was hopeless, longed to put an end to the fighting and found strong support in Parliament, which actually presented a petition to that effect. The Burgundians, too, were increasingly eager for peace. Only Humphrey of Gloucester – who had been steadily building up his position during the long absence in France of his enemy the Cardinal – continued to argue furiously for a continuation of the war, sabotaging every attempt at negotiation. Finally, in 1435, Philip of Burgundy lost patience and convened, on his own initiative, a peace conference at Arras.

The English, whose delegation was led by the Archbishop of York but was strongly influenced by Duke Humphrey, refused to renounce the royal title to France and ultimately withdrew altogether from the negotiations. Almost at once, however, they had reason to regret this departure. A week later, on 21 September, they were horrified to learn that France and Burgundy had effected a reconciliation. King Charles had agreed to make a public apology for the assassination of John the Fearless and to surrender those responsible; Philip had then been formally absolved by the attendant cardinals from his oath of allegiance to the

English King. When Henry heard the news, he wept; for Humphrey of Gloucester and his militants, on the other hand, there was a great wave of support as the people of London expressed their anger at the Burgundian betrayal by firing and looting the houses of all the Flemish merchants in the city.

Bedford, too, would have shed tears to see much of his life's work brought to nothing; but a week before the Franco-Burgundian peace, on 14 September 1435, he had died aged forty-six at Rouen – where, a day or two later, he had been buried in the cathedral. He had served his father, his elder brother and his nephew with unswerving loyalty, never once – in marked distinction to his brother Humphrey – putting his own interests before his duty: if his life ultimately ended in failure, it was no fault of his. His wisdom and selflessness were sorely to be missed in the years that followed.

At the time of Bedford's death, King Henry VI was three months short of his fourteenth birthday and – as was by now painfully clear to all who knew him – totally unfitted for the crown. Though never particularly intelligent, in his youth at least he was by no means simple-minded, as has occasionally been claimed; on the contrary he was well educated and exceptionally well read, and from an early age took a precocious interest in political affairs. His piety was unusual, even by the standards of his time. He attended divine worship often two or three times a day, said grace 'like a monk' before each meal, and on the great feasts of the Church invariably wore a hair shirt beneath his robes of state. At all other times he dressed simply, paying no heed to style or fashion. His chief fault was that he was impressionable and almost pathetically easily led, putty in the hands of men like Cardinal Beaufort or Duke Humphrey; more dangerous still, he soon showed himself to be alarmingly lacking in political judgement, using such power as he enjoyed with a recklessness and irresponsibility that caused serious concern. After the departure – without replacement – of his guardian, the Earl of Warwick, to France in 1437, he began to play a steadily more important part in the administration, with almost invariably disastrous results. His mindless generosity made ever greater demands on the exchequer, as did his continual remission of fines and penalties; few petitioners were sent empty away, however unscrupulous their characters or unfounded their claims. At the same time the steep decline in wool exports, combined with the dishonesty of most of the tax collectors, had resulted in a dramatic decline in the revenue, while the exceptionally rainy weather which marked the three years between 1437 and 1440 led to the worst famine for well over a century.

And still the war dragged on. In April 1436 Bedford had been succeeded by Richard, Duke of York, now twenty-four,[1] who was accompanied by his brother-in-law Richard Nevill, Earl of Salisbury since the death of his father-in-law, killed before Orleans. Barely fourteen months later York had been replaced by Warwick, but had been reappointed after the latter's death in 1439. Meanwhile Charles VII had made his triumphal entry into Paris in November 1437, and a somewhat half-hearted peace conference near Calais in 1439 had come to nothing. The following year saw the release of Charles of Orleans, who had been taken prisoner at Agincourt and held in comfortable captivity for the past quarter of a century. His ransom of 80,000 écus, with a further 160,000 within six months, was largely paid by Philip of Burgundy, who gave him his fourteen-year-old niece, Mary of Cleves, in marriage.[2]

That same year, 1440, saw a sharp decline in the fortunes of Duke Humphrey of Gloucester. He had violently opposed giving freedom to the captive Charles of Orleans, despite the latter's oath on the sacrament never to bear arms against England; and Charles's subsequent release had been a bitter blow, not only to Humphrey's personal self-esteem but to his national prestige. He had also ill-advisedly brought quite unfounded charges of treachery and dishonesty against Cardinal Beaufort and the Archbishop of York, John Kemp, who had recently joined his friend Beaufort in the College of Cardinals. By now, in consequence, the Duke was generally discredited; and a further blow to his fortunes came in 1441 when his second wife Eleanor Cobham – 'a handsome,

1. Son of the wretched Earl of Cambridge who had been executed for complicity in the Southampton plot, he had inherited the title from his uncle, who had died (of natural causes) at Agincourt.

2. Charles's first wife – Richard II's widow, Isabelle of France – had died in childbirth at nineteen; his second, Bonne of Armagnac, had died childless during his captivity. Despite the thirty-two-year difference in age, this third marriage was to prove a remarkably happy one. Seventeen years later, in 1457, Mary was to present Charles with another daughter, also named Mary, almost half a century after the birth of his first.

greedy, sensual woman of doubtful antecedents'[1] who was formerly waiting-woman to his first wife, Jacqueline of Hainault – was accused of using sorcery against the King by making a wax image of him and melting it over a slow fire. Her motives were plain – Gloucester was heir to the throne – and the evidence incontrovertible. Of her two accomplices, one – Roger Bolingbroke, a known professor of the black arts – was hanged, drawn and quartered; the other, Margery Jourdain, was burnt at the stake. Eleanor, her life spared by the King, was sentenced to walk barefoot for three days through the City of London carrying a lighted taper, and to perpetual imprisonment thereafter; she was to die fourteen years later, at Peel Castle on the Isle of Man. Her husband, we are told, did not lift a finger to save her.

The eclipse of Gloucester left something of a vacuum on the political stage; but it was quickly filled. William de la Pole, fourth Earl of Suffolk, has already made his appearance in these pages. Born in 1396, he and his family had devoted their lives to the French wars. His father had died before Harfleur, from which he himself had been invalided home; his elder brother, the third earl, had been killed at Agincourt; another brother had met his death at Jargeau where, as we have seen, William had been taken prisoner. Having managed to pay his own ransom, he had returned to England in 1431 and married the Countess of Salisbury, the widow of his old chief.[2] Thenceforth his rise had been rapid. A close friend of Charles of Orleans – whose official custodian he became in 1432 – he was an active and influential member of Beaufort's peace party and consequently a bitter opponent of Gloucester; it came as no surprise when he was appointed one of the commissioners to inquire into the charges of sorcery made against the Duchess. His principal achievement of these years, however, was to engineer at Orleans's suggestion – and, it need hardly be said, in the teeth of vociferous objections from Duke Humphrey – the marriage of the King to Margaret, daughter of Count René of Anjou.

Margaret's name was not the first to have been proposed in this connection: among other candidates there had been the daughters of

---

1. *Dictionary of National Biography.*
2. She was the granddaughter of the poet Geoffrey Chaucer. Her extraordinary tomb, with its macabre *memento mori* beneath, stands in the church of Ewelme, Oxfordshire, and is well worth a visit.

the Holy Roman Emperor Albert II, of the King of Scotland and of the Count of Armagnac. The year 1438 even saw the beginning of negotiations for a daughter of Charles VII, but the French had proved so unenthusiastic that the English delegation had taken offence and gone home. Margaret, however, was different. Her father, known universally as *le bon roi René*, was not only Count of Anjou and Provence, Duke of Bar and Lorraine; he was also titular King of Naples, Sicily and Jerusalem and the brother-in-law of Charles VII, who had married his sister Mary. And even this was not all: through her mother, Isabella of Lorraine, Margaret was a direct descendant of Charlemagne. In 1444, though still only fifteen, she was already famous for her beauty and her intelligence. Her strong personality would, it was hoped, instil some backbone into her feckless husband; at the same time she was young enough to take direction from those in authority. Suffolk was deputed to lead an embassy, first to Charles VII to seek at least a temporary peace, and then to Count René to make a formal request for his daughter's hand. At first he seems to have been distinctly reluctant to accept these two tasks, demanding (and receiving) a formal indemnity in advance for any agreement he might make in the course of either set of negotiations; but both ultimately proved successful.

Reaching Harfleur in mid-March 1444, Suffolk and his train joined the Duke of Orleans a month later at Blois. Together they sailed down the Loire to Tours, where they were met by René and where Charles VII received them all on 17 April. Negotiations for both the marriage and a two-year truce proceeded smoothly enough and were virtually completed by early May, when Margaret and her mother arrived from Angers. On 24 May 1444 the betrothal of herself and Henry was solemnly celebrated in the church of St Martin at Tours, with Suffolk standing proxy for the absent King. Charles, we are told, took a prominent part in the ceremony, which was followed by a great feast in the Abbey of St Julien, Margaret being treated with all the respect due to a Queen of England.

Another year was to pass before bride and groom were united. The next winter Suffolk returned to France, this time to Lorraine where King and Count were together besieging Metz; not till the end of February 1445 did the city surrender, and only then did the French and Angevin courts return together to Nancy, where the final negotiations were completed. It was probably this unexpected delay that led to the widespread delusion in England that Charles and René had insisted on fresh concessions – including the surrender of all the territories that the English possessed, or claimed to possess, in Maine and Anjou. In fact there is no evidence that they did anything of the kind, still less that Suffolk agreed to any such demands; Henry's voluntary surrender of Maine to his new father-in-law at the end of the year seems to have been at the instigation of his young Queen alone. But the rumour was enough to destroy such popularity as Suffolk enjoyed, and was certainly a contributory cause of his downfall less than five years later.

Early in March 1445 the royal marriage was celebrated at Nancy by the Bishop of Toul, after which Margaret, escorted by Suffolk and a numerous following of her own, made her way by easy stages via Paris and Rouen to England, where she arrived at Portsmouth on 9 April, 'sick of the labour and indisposition of the sea'. She remained ill for a fortnight; not till the 23rd was she well enough to travel the nine miles to the Abbey of Titchfield, where Henry – now twenty-three – was anxiously awaiting her and where the two were quietly married by his confessor, the Bishop of Salisbury. Their movements over the next few weeks are unknown, but they entered London in triumph on 28 May, and two days later Margaret was crowned by the Archbishop of Canterbury, John Stafford, in Westminster Abbey.

Her compatriot Queen Isabella, who had been primarily responsible for the deposition of her husband Edward II one hundred and eighteen years before, had been known to her English subjects as 'the she-wolf of France'. For Margaret, as will soon become clear, such a description would have been an understatement.

12

King Henry VI Part I

[1422–1453]

> EXETER.　This late dissension grown betwixt the peers
> Burns under feigned ashes of forg'd love,
> And will at last break out into a flame;
> As fester'd members rot but by degree
> Till bones and flesh and sinews fall away,
> So will this base and envious discord breed.
> And now I fear that fatal prophecy
> Which in the time of Henry nam'd the Fifth
> Was in the mouth of every sucking babe:
> That Henry born at Monmouth should win all,
> And Henry born at Windsor should lose all . . .
>
> KING HENRY VI PART I

The First Part of King Henry VI is – with the arguable exception of *Titus Andronicus* – probably the earliest of Shakespeare's plays to have come down to us. Like its three sequels – for *Richard III* is so closely connected to the others that it can be considered part of a single series – it appears in the Stationers' Register after Spenser's *The Faerie Queene*, which is dated December 1589; on the other hand it must surely predate the reference to 'braue *Talbot* (the terror of the French) . . . that hee should triumphe againe on the Stage' in *Pierce Penilesse his Supplication to the Divell* by Thomas Nashe, registered on 8 August 1592. All three plays, therefore, are those of a young man, written when their author was still in his twenties. Perhaps partly for this reason, their authorship has been queried again and again, though the various arguments put forward have no place in this book. Suffice it to say that few modern scholars have any serious doubts that all are essentially from Shakespeare's pen. The question for us is, as always, how closely do the plays conform to historical truth?

This time the short answer is 'not very'. The young Shakespeare seems to have been a good deal less conscientious in these youthful productions than he was when he came to write those histories which come earlier in the chronological canon – and which have consequently been discussed in earlier chapters of this book. In his defence, however, it must be said that he was attempting something different, and a good deal more ambitious. His aim in these four plays is to portray not just the character of a King but a vast sweep of history. *Henry VI Part I* alone covers the period from the funeral of Henry V in 1422 to the death of John Talbot, Earl of Shrewsbury, in 1453. The need to compress over thirty years into the two-hour traffic of his stage obliges him to take considerable liberties with strict chronology, and the need to provide his audience with excitement and drama involves him in a good many more. But there: historical playwrights, like the authors of lapidary inscriptions, are not on oath; and few of us, I suspect, will find it in our hearts to blame him.

His two principal sources are once again Raphael Holinshed and Edward Hall; but since in the *Henry VI* plays his subject is above all the Wars of the Roses and the events which led up to them, it is hardly surprising that Hall's *Chronicle of the Vnion of the Two Noble and Illustre Famelies of Lancastre and Yorke* should make a rather larger contribution here than it does to the plays covering the earlier period. For Shakespeare as for Hall, the underlying theme is always retribution: the price that the House of Lancaster must continue to pay for the original sin of Henry IV in usurping the throne. His son Henry V, by a combination of personal glamour, high intelligence and astonishingly good luck, succeeded in almost all he set out to do; his grandson Henry VI, who possessed none of these attributes, was to prove a catastrophe.

It is hardly surprising that an English play about the Hundred Years War should reflect a degree of anti-French feeling:

> How are we park'd and bounded in a pale –
> A little herd of England's timorous deer,
> Maz'd with a yelping kennel of French curs!

Such feeling was, however, particularly strong in 1589, when the three parts of *King Henry VI* were being written. The Spaniards, smarting from the defeat of their Armada only a year before, were already planning a new invasion of England, this time using Brittany as a springboard. Meanwhile the Protestant Henry of Navarre was struggling – with the help of English arms and money – against the Catholic League in his ultimately successful attempt to gain the French throne. At this of all moments, Catholic France was fair game – it even offered a witch like Joan of Arc – and Shakespeare was not one to miss such an opportunity.

The very first scene of *Henry VI Part I* seems to contain the whole play in miniature. It is set in Westminster Abbey, against a background of the funeral procession of Henry V; but the dead King's body is scarcely cold before the two most powerful men in the realm are at loggerheads, with the Duke of Gloucester hurling insults at Bishop Beaufort – a quarrel which will all too soon be paralleled by that between York and Somerset and their two champions, Vernon and Basset. Bedford tries to calm them, but is almost immediately interrupted by the first of the three messengers who successively bring news of a whole series of military disasters across the Channel. Thus the three principal themes of the play – the inadequacy of the young King, with the consequent dissension among the nobles and ultimately the loss of France – are all introduced within the first sixty lines. At the same time we are given a particularly striking example of Shakespeare's technique of telescoping events. The first messenger announces the loss of Guyenne, Compiègne (which he confusingly calls 'Champaigne'), Rheims, Rouen, Orleans, Paris, Gisors and Poitiers – towns which in fact fell to the French at various times between 1427 and 1450; at the time of Henry V's funeral in November 1422 all of them were still firmly in English hands. With the second messenger comes the news of the Dauphin's coronation at Rheims, which occurred on 17 July 1429, just a month after the capture of Talbot ('Retiring from the siege of Orleans') at the battle of Patay on 18 June – not, as Shakespeare has it, 10 August – which is the subject of the third messenger's report. None of this of course would trouble the average audience, whether in the sixteenth century or the twentieth; some of us, on the other hand, may be a little bewildered to find Talbot, three scenes later, fighting on the walls of Orleans and very much at liberty.

Another source of surprise is the third messenger's report of the cowardice of Sir John Falstaff, an affecting account of whose death in 1415 is given by Mistress Quickly in the second act of *Henry V*. We have already seen in Chapter 6[1] how Shakespeare borrowed the name of this unfortunate knight in the two parts of *Henry IV* and in *Henry V*, when he found that he could no longer call him Oldcastle; it is nevertheless worth repeating here that in fact Fastolf–Falstaff had an unusually distinguished military career covering some forty years, during which he occupied many important posts and was awarded a number of honours – which included, in February 1426, the Order of the Garter. At Patay too he had displayed his usual gallantry; he was unfortunate, however, in that one of his tactical manoeuvres was misunderstood by his own men, who panicked and fled the field. According to Jean de Wavrin, an eyewitness, he himself continued to fight bravely on, retreating only when the day was seen to be irretrievably lost; the accusation of cowardice is made only by the chronicler Enguerrand de Monstrelet, who is also our sole authority for the story of his being stripped of his Garter. Even if, as seems possible, Bedford did order an inquiry into his conduct in the battle, Fastolf emerged from it fully vindicated; the offices in which he was later employed – Lieutenant of Caen, English ambassador to the Council of Basle, one of the chief negotiators of the Peace of Arras – were every bit as distinguished as those he had held before it. He certainly did nothing to deserve the character of a drunken poltroon which Shakespeare was so unfairly to foist upon him.

The third scene of the play contrasts the initial pride and confidence of the French – until they suffer an unpleasant reverse – with the despondency of the English; but it is chiefly notable for the introduction of Joan of Arc, *la Pucelle*, into the drama. Audiences in the eighteenth and nineteenth centuries were repelled by Shakespeare's portrayal of the simple and heroic Maid of Orleans as a witch and a harlot, and a good many in the twentieth have doubtless felt the same way. But the fault is hardly his. He had found this picture of her already fully developed in Holinshed and Hall; and in his own day it was still – on this side of the Channel – almost universally accepted. Of Joan's supernatural powers there is no doubt in his mind; immediately on her first appearance she recognizes the hidden Dauphin, and shortly afterwards overcomes him in the fight by which he insists on testing her claims. But whence do these powers come? Clearly, there are only two possible sources,

1. See p. 139–40.

God or the Devil; and for the English to have accepted that they came from God would have been tantamount to an admission of the injustice of their cause. Joan, therefore, was a witch; and the mildly ridiculous opening of Act V, scene iii – when she conjures up the fiends who have aided her in the past – merely confirms the fact.

A brief return to London enables us to witness an unpleasant confrontation between the Duke of Gloucester's men and those of the Bishop of Winchester, who refuse to admit the Duke to the Tower. Already, it appears, England has begun to suffer the consequences of the new reign: with the firm hand of Henry V no longer at the helm and his infant son altogether lacking in authority, the kingdom is already falling victim to dissension and internecine strife. A few minutes later, however, we are once more back at Orleans for the death of Salisbury, the most famous of the English captains and the most skilled in war. He had fought with distinction at Agincourt, since when – apart from a few brief intervals for diplomacy – he had ever been in the thick of the fray. Shakespeare's version of his death is remarkably close to Holinshed's: he even introduces the boy – son of the master gunner of Orleans – who was believed to have fired the fatal shot. The facts as we know them are essentially the following. On 24 October 1428, when the Earl was storming Tourelles, the fortification at the southern end of the bridge across the Loire, and surveying the situation from a high window, the stone window-frame was shattered by a cannon-ball and he was seriously wounded in the face, losing an eye. Carried to Meung, he died there ten days later. To his compatriots, his death came as yet another body-blow; to the French it was simply a further example of divine retribution.

The same scene also introduces us to John Talbot, first Earl of Shrewsbury, who is the real hero of the play. Talbot had already led campaigns on the Welsh borders, and had served two separate terms of office as Royal Lieutenant of Ireland. Now some forty years old, he seems to have been a Hotspur-like figure who made up in daring and general panache what he lacked in any real military brilliance. Quarrelsome and argumentative, he was not invariably popular among his peers; but he was a born leader, and his men adored him. He first appears in the play with an anachronism already on his lips, describing his recent ransom and exchange for the French knight Pothon – not, as he calls him, Ponton – de Santrailles; he was not in fact taken prisoner until the battle of Patay in May 1429, six months after Salisbury's death. The act ends with the obviously unhistorical hand-to-hand fight between the effective protagonists of the two sides: Talbot and the Pucelle. Thanks to her witchcraft she defeats him, while inflicting no serious harm – his hour, she tells him, is not yet come – and her victory is reflected by that of her followers. Orleans is relieved, and the furious Talbot gives his men the order to retreat.

Orleans was a symbol. To every loyal Frenchman the city stood for France, and the victory – which was unquestionably due in large measure to Joan – was seen as conclusive proof of her divine mission and of the truth of her message. It comes, therefore, as something of a surprise to find Shakespeare, at the very beginning of Act II, representing the quite unhistorical recovery of the city by Talbot and his men. He draws here on Hall's account of the taking of Le Mans, when 'the French men which wer scarce vp, and thought of nothyng lesse then of this sodain approchement, some rose out of their beddes in their shertes, and lepte ouer the walles, other ranne naked out of the gates for sauyng of their liues, leuyng behynde theim all their apparell, horsses, armure and riches'.

There follows Talbot's lament over Salisbury, for whom he vows to erect a tomb 'within the chiefest temple' of the French. (The body was in fact carried back to England and buried in the family priory at Bisham in Berkshire.) Scarcely has he completed his speech than a messenger arrives with an invitation for him from the Countess of Auvergne – which he suspects, rightly, of being a trap. Once again the source is Hall, but the story itself is clearly fictitious: such stories are common in the border ballads, as they are in the legends of Robin Hood. It is surely unthinkable that so experienced a soldier as Talbot should knowingly or unknowingly deliver himself into the hands of so powerful a woman as the Countess, who could easily have had him killed before he could summon his soldiers. And she for her part would have been fully conscious of the fact.

We return now to London, but simultaneously (as it later appears) go back a few years in time. The scene in the Temple[1] Garden is as

1. The Temple is the home of two of London's four Inns of Court – the Inner Temple and the Middle Temple – which have the exclusive right of admitting young lawyers to practise at the Bar.

imaginary as that of Talbot and the Countess; but it is of considerably more importance, since it introduces the incipient power struggle between the houses of Lancaster and York, identifying them for the first time with the red and the white rose respectively. For Lancaster, the protagonist is the Earl of Somerset, the grandson of John of Gaunt through John Beaufort – Gaunt's eldest son by Katherine Swynford – and consequently a first cousin of Henry V. (He appears later in the play as a Duke, which he became in 1443.) He picks a red rose for his badge, and the Earl of Suffolk plucks another after him. Chief spokesman for the house of York is the man who appears in the *dramatis personae* as 'Richard Plantagenet, *afterwards Duke of York*' – although in fact he had already succeeded to the dukedom on the death of his uncle at Agincourt. He picks a white rose, and is followed by the Earl of Warwick, the enthusiastic Yorkist Vernon,[1] and a lawyer.

Already in this scene – which, being fictitious, is undatable – we are reminded of Richard's claim to the throne, when Warwick points out that

> His grandfather was Lionel Duke of Clarence,
> Third son to the third Edward, King of England:

while Richard himself replies to Somerset's taunt that his father, the Earl of Cambridge, was executed for treason (after the Southampton Plot) with the words

> My father was attached, not attainted,[2]
> Condemn'd to die for treason, but no traitor.

Scene iii provides a further opportunity to emphasize the Yorkist claim, with Richard's last visit to the dying Edmund Mortimer, Earl of March, who has apparently been long imprisoned in the Tower. Here Shakespeare may once again be deliberately adjusting historical truth in the interests of his drama; it is possible, on the other hand, that Hall

---

1. It has been suggested that he may be the Sir Richard Vernon (d. 1452) who was Speaker of the House of Commons in the Leicester Parliament; but if so, why did Shakespeare not call him by his full name?

2. i.e. arrested, not convicted by a bill of attainder. This was in fact a quibble, since Cambridge had been executed summarily, on the direct orders of the King.

has led him astray. He was never very clear in his mind about the Mortimers: he confused them in *Henry IV Part I*, and was to confuse them again in *Henry VI Part II*.[1] There can be no doubt that the aged prisoner whom we see here is meant to be Edmund Mortimer, fifth Earl of March and uncle of the Duke of York, who on his deathbed passes on to his nephew his title to the throne; unfortunately the historic earl, born in November 1391, died of the plague in Ireland in January 1425, when he was only thirty-three and Richard of York just thirteen. Shakespeare's Mortimer reveals to his nephew that he has been imprisoned ever since the Southampton Plot; but, as we well know,[2] March – who was potentially the beneficiary of the plot – was also the one who revealed it; and although he was perhaps a little more hesitant in doing so than Henry V would have liked, the King soon restored him to favour and gave him his complete trust. It is perhaps significant in this connection that in his treatment of the conspiracy in *Henry V*, II.ii, Shakespeare makes no mention of March at all; he may well have remembered the dying prisoner whom he had invented a few years before and, rather than admitting that he was a fabrication, preferred to omit the character altogether from his new play.

'In the iiii. yeare [of the reign, i.e. 1426–7] fell a greate diuision in the realme of England, whiche of a sparcle was like to growe to a greate flame.' So wrote Edward Hall of the feud between Bishop Beaufort of Winchester and Duke Humphrey of Gloucester, which was now threatening the country with civil war. The specific incident represented at the beginning of Act III, in which Gloucester charges the Chancellor with having refused him admittance to the Tower (see I.iii), with attempting to have him murdered at London Bridge and even with having designs on the King himself, actually occurred during the parliament which met at Leicester on 18 February 1426; Shakespeare moves it to the Parliament House in London and conflates it with what had happened at London Bridge some four months previously, when the Duke had persuaded the Mayor to hold the bridge against the Bishop. Stones had been thrown, there had been a number of casualties, and the shops had been shut throughout the city. At Leicester the Lords

1. See Chapter 6, pp. 137–8 and Chapter 14, p. 273.
2. See Chapter 8, pp. 181–2.

ordered a reconciliation, and the two men were forced to take each other by the hand; but they did so with an ill grace, and Beaufort resigned the chancellorship shortly afterwards.

In the play it is not the parliament but King Henry himself, now making a curiously belated first appearance, who urges the two to make up their quarrel; he then goes on to restore Richard of York to his inheritance. Shakespeare's authority once again is Hall; but where did Hall find this totally untrue story? The attainder and execution of Richard's father, the Earl of Cambridge, would not have prevented his son from inheriting his estate, while the dukedom would have been his by the normal process of succession after his uncle's death at Agincourt. Eleven years later, on 19 May 1426, the fourteen-year-old Richard was knighted by the young King at Leicester; it is hard to see what more Henry could have done for him. The salient point here, however, is that by his public support of Richard he is, consciously or unconsciously, advancing the Yorkist claim to the succession.

And indeed Shakespeare himself is doing much the same: he is deliberately building up the character of Richard, in order to make him the chief protagonist in the coming plays that will portray the civil war. We have now watched this process in three consecutive scenes: in the Temple Garden, where the lines between York and Lancaster are first drawn; in Mortimer's cell, where the dying man confirms Richard as his heir; and now in the Parliament House, where the young prince is 'restored to his blood' and girded with 'the valiant sword of York'. It is important to remember, however, that Richard's claims extended well beyond those of his dukedom, for he was descended from Edward III through both his parents – his paternal grandfather being Edward's fifth son, Edmund of Langley, while his mother traced her descent through the Mortimers (Earls of March) to the third son, Lionel Duke of Clarence. Heir to the vast estates of York, March and Cambridge – which included property in virtually every county between Yorkshire and the English Channel – he was now, after the King himself, the greatest landowner in the realm. At this point in the play – with all allowances made for its cavalier chronology – he is still a boy in his teens; but Shakespeare is already grooming him for stardom.

The scene ends, none the less, on a note of menace. The Duke of Somerset – the foremost champion of the Lancastrian cause and the first to pick a red rose from the Temple Garden – has muttered his curse on York, in an aside worthy of the highest tradition of the stage villain, while the rest of those present are cheering the Duke to the echo; and a moment later the stage is empty of all but the King's great-uncle, the old Duke of Exeter, who speaks the sad words quoted at the head of this chapter. The play has run barely half its course, but we can no longer be in any doubt: catastrophe is on the way.

In France, meanwhile, the fighting continues. After three fairly long and static scenes the time has come once again for action, and we are treated to one of the most improbable representations of battle that even Shakespeare ever penned, in which Rouen is captured by the Pucelle and regained by the English in little more than a hundred lines. Joan, it need hardly be said, succeeds in entering the city only by a trick, infiltrating her men in the disguise of poor farmers going to market; but her magic, such as it is, has lost its potency. The Duke of Bedford, now mortally sick, has the satisfaction of seeing the final triumph of English arms and dies happy. The scene, short as it is, somehow contrives also to introduce a panic-stricken Sir John Falstaff in full flight from the enemy and, in contrast, the heroic Talbot – to whom, we are led to suppose, the victory is due.

For his version of the French capture of Rouen Shakespeare has turned either to Hall or, more probably, to an account by a certain Robert Fabyan – whose *New Chronicles of England and France* were published in 1516 – of the taking of the minor castle of Cornill, for which the Pucelle's unremarkable little ruse might have been more appropriate and even conceivably successful. As for his chronology, it is as cheerfully confused as ever. We cannot put even a putative date on the scene, since Rouen remained in English hands until 1449; but Joan was burnt in May 1431, 'Old Bedford' surviving her for well over four years until he died peacefully in his bed at the age of forty-six. There is some serious telescoping, too, in the scene that follows, in which Joan effortlessly persuades Philip of Burgundy to change sides. Change he did, as we saw in the previous chapter; but his alienation from the English was a long, slow process, prompted by several different considerations. Perhaps the most important of these was the readiness of the French King to make a public apology for the assassination of Philip's father, John the Fearless; Burgundy himself, moreover, had never quite forgiven the English for their refusal to allow him to accept the surrender of Orleans in 1429. Finally there were persistent rumours that the English were considering the early release – in return for a sizeable ransom – of Philip's old enemy Charles of Orleans, their prisoner since Agincourt. The one suggestion that can be confidently ruled out is that Philip suddenly yielded to the blandishments of Joan, whom it is extremely unlikely that he ever met. Even if he had, she could hardly have mentioned the liberation of Charles of Orleans, who was to remain a prisoner for nine and a half years after her death.

The act ends with a short scene, set in 'Paris, the Palace', in which King Henry creates Talbot Earl of Shrewsbury before moving on to his coronation. Once again the chronology is awry: Henry's French coronation took place in December 1431, Talbot's ennoblement – as Earl of Salop, incidentally, though he and his successors always took the name of Shrewsbury – not until May 1442. The true purpose of the scene seems to be to prepare the audience for the act to follow, which Talbot and his splendid son are to dominate – though Shakespeare actually brings down the curtain with another bad-tempered spat between Vernon and Basset, reminding us once again that however desperate the fight against the French, the growing breach between York and Lancaster is more significant still.

The opening scene of Act IV belongs, dramatically speaking, more properly to Act III. There is no interval of time; the location is unchanged, with Henry's French coronation taking place in the palace rather than in Notre Dame; Talbot's qualities are once again emphasized, the better to show up the cowardice of Sir John Falstaff, whose Garter is ripped by Talbot from his leg;[1] and the insufferable Vernon and Basset lay their differences before the King, supported this time by the protagonists themselves, York and Somerset. Henry's reaction is typically inept: first, with the words

> I see no reason if I wear this rose,
> That anyone should therefore be suspicious
> I more incline to Somerset than York

1. But see Chapter 6, p. 140 and above, p. 238. Monstrelet reports that Fastolf was stripped of his Garter by Bedford, not Shrewsbury; in fact it is far from certain that anyone but the King would have had the power to do so.

he pins to his robe a red rose; then, in an apparent attempt to oblige the two Dukes to forget their quarrel, he divides the army in France between them – giving Somerset the cavalry and York the regiments of foot. The insanity of this decision is made all too clear in the scenes covering the siege of Bordeaux which follow.

Unfortunately this sequence of cause and effect, however convincing on the stage, is set at naught by Shakespeare's cavalier chronology. The siege of Bordeaux took place in 1451, exactly twenty years after Henry's coronation in Paris; Talbot died two years later. The King never divided the army in the way that Shakespeare suggests, though in 1443 he did appoint Somerset Captain-General of Guyenne – much to the fury of York, who as Regent in France made a strong protest. Fortunately Somerset returned to England after a single ineffectual campaign and died a year later, probably by his own hand. It follows that Sir William Lucy's interviews with him and with York in scenes iii and iv are both fictitious, introduced purely to illustrate the seriousness of the breach between the two leaders. The scenes which come closest to historical truth are the fifth and sixth – which, with the first part of the seventh, cover the last hours of the Talbots, father and son. They died together, on 17 July 1453, not at Bordeaux as Shakespeare suggests – though he does not specifically say so – but at Castillon in the Dordogne, Shrewsbury having tried in vain (as he does in the play) to persuade his son, Lord Lisle, to save himself. They were the last heroes of the Hundred Years War.

The action of Act V is set essentially between the years 1442 – when the Count of Armagnac offered his daughter to King Henry as his bride – and 1444, when Henry sent the Earl of Suffolk to France to seek the hand of Margaret of Anjou. The passages in scenes ii–iv involving the Pucelle, however, can belong only to 1431. It would be tempting to describe them as flashbacks, but for the fact that Shakespeare obviously intends them to be nothing of the kind. He sees them as an integral part of a continuous story, and once again has no hesitation in sacrificing historical truth in the interests of his drama. The scenes themselves, it need hardly be said, though taken from Hall and Holinshed, merely reflect the prevailing sentiments of the English towards Joan; they are too grotesque to have any historical basis.

There is a curious moment in the opening scene of the act when

Exeter expresses surprise at seeing the Bishop of Winchester in his cardinal's robes:

> What! is my Lord of Winchester install'd,
> And call'd unto a cardinal's degree?
> Then I perceive that will be verified
> Henry the Fifth did sometime prophesy:
> 'If once he come to be a cardinal,
> He'll make his cap co-equal with the crown.'

Beaufort had in fact been a member of the Sacred College since 1417, and is plainly referred to as 'the Cardinal of Winchester' as early as Act I, scene iii. He has already appeared three times in the play, similarly attired and in Exeter's presence. This obvious inconsistency has been cited as an indication that the play may be by a number of different authors; all the stylistic evidence, on the other hand, points to a single, Shakespearean authorship of the play as a whole. What reason, then, can be found for this curious passage? It is difficult to accept that offered by the editor of the normally authoritative Arden edition that 'occasional errors and inconsistencies are to be expected, and are indeed character-istic, in authorial copy . . . It may be,' he continues, 'the author forgot what he had written earlier. The inconsistency is an argument for the authorial nature of the copy, since the prompter could be expected to iron out the discrepancy for the stage.' We can only say that he does not appear to have done so. Such a glaring contradiction might have escaped the printers of the First Folio, which was published only in 1623 – seven years after Shakespeare's death – and is our only text for the play; it is hard to imagine that it could have escaped Shakespeare himself as it apparently did. In the absence of any plausible explanation, the mystery remains.

Act V opens in London, with Humphrey of Gloucester informing his nephew of letters from the Pope and the Holy Roman Emperor Albert II – who had acceded to the imperial throne in 1438 – urging the restoration of peace between England and France. To further this end, the Count of Armagnac has offered the hand of his daughter in marriage, and Gloucester warmly recommends its acceptance. Henry is unenthusiastic at the thought of 'wanton dalliance with a paramour', but characteristically agrees to marry anyone his advisers think suitable. The court then retires and the Bishop of Winchester, left alone with the Papal Legate, makes it clear that he has bought his cardinal's hat – though there is no historical evidence that he did any such thing; Shakespeare may have been misled by a somewhat unclear passage in Hall, 139, which refers to Beaufort's 'purchase' – i.e. acquisition – of a 'Bull legatyne'. In fact the cardinal had long been one of the leading churchmen of Europe, and, as we have already seen, had even been considered a candidate for the papal throne during the long-disputed election of 1417.

The scene now shifts to France, where we see the Pucelle first forsaken by her familiar spirits – a serious challenge to any director – and then personally captured (another fiction) by the Duke of York. We also have the first appearance of Margaret of Anjou, the future Queen. Once again, Shakespeare has abandoned history altogether in the interests of his drama. The idea that Margaret had been taken prisoner by the Earl of Suffolk is little short of ludicrous, as is the suggestion that he had become infatuated by her; Suffolk's mission to France in the spring and early summer of 1444 had been undertaken at the command of the King – notwithstanding the vigorous objections of Gloucester – and was conducted with perfect propriety throughout. So too was his mission the following winter and spring (during which he was accompanied by his wife) to fetch Margaret from Lorraine and escort her to London, despite the unjustified accusations – taken up by Shakespeare in V.iii, where Suffolk and René (Regnier) discuss the marriage, and again in the opening scene of *Henry VI Part II* – of having surrendered Maine and Anjou.[1]

After yet another appearance of the Pucelle – over which, once again, it is kinder to pass without comment – Cardinal Beaufort appears at the English camp to announce the decision to conclude not a two-year truce but a full treaty of peace. York rounds on him angrily ('Is all our travail turn'd to this effect?') but accepts the inevitable when he hears the terms. So, after some initial reluctance, does Charles VII, who agrees henceforth to wear his crown as Henry's Viceroy. The final scene returns us to London, where Gloucester makes one last attempt to persuade his nephew to marry the Armagnac bride rather than the

1. See Chapter 11, p. 231.

Angevin. But Suffolk's arguments in favour of Margaret – together with the King's own inclinations, such as they are – carry the day. Gloucester warns of coming disaster, and Suffolk brings down the curtain with a cry of ominous if ungrammatical triumph:

> Thus Suffolk hath prevail'd; and thus he goes,
> As did the youthful Paris once to Greece;
> With hope to find the like event in love,
> But prosper better than the Trojan did.
> Margaret shall now be Queen, and rule the King;
> But I will rule both her, the King, and realm.

And so, for the next five years, he did.

King Henry VI: The Gathering Storm

[1445–1455]

KING. Thus stands my state, 'twixt Cade and York distress'd;
       Like to a ship that, having scap'd a tempest,
       Is straightway calm'd, and boarded with a pirate.

                        KING HENRY VI PART II

The truce of 1444 – which, with prolongations, continued effectively for five years – proved to be exactly what France needed. Whereas a quarter of a century before she had been largely incapacitated by a mentally unstable monarch while England was inspired to victory after victory by the greatest military leader ever to have occupied her throne, now the situations of the two countries had been neatly reversed: young Henry VI of England had proved a pious simpleton – if he were not yet clinically insane, he soon would be – while Charles VII of France, awoken to a sense of his responsibilities first by Joan of Arc, then by a number of brilliant and energetic captains and finally by his beautiful mistress Agnès Sorel, had revealed qualities of character which in his youth had remained unsuspected. He first used the breathing space to restore law and order throughout his domains; he then set about reorganizing his army, equipping it with modern artillery considerably more sophisticated than anything possessed by the English. By the time the truce came to an end, he – and it – would be ready for the last great effort: to drive his enemy back across the Channel once and for all.

England, meanwhile, remained preoccupied with her own affairs. A chapter ended in 1447, when Duke Humphrey of Gloucester and his old antagonist the Bishop of Winchester died within a few weeks of each other. Humphrey, as we have seen, had by now lost much of his power, having never really recovered from his wife's trial for witchcraft

in 1441. Ever since that time his nephew the King had been understandably suspicious of him, though for some years he was careful to press
no charges. Not till 1447 did the crisis finally come, when Parliament
met, on 10 February, at Bury St Edmunds. The Duke appeared a week
later, attended by eighty horsemen. He was met at the entrance to the
town and peremptorily ordered to go straight to his lodgings; and there,
that same evening, a number of high-ranking noblemen arrived to put
him under arrest. On 23 February he died, aged fifty-six. There were
the usual dark tales of smotherings, red-hot pokers and the like, but we
can probably accept the cause of his death that was officially announced
at the time – an apoplectic stroke. He was buried in the abbey of
St Albans, now its cathedral: probably the most cultivated man in
England, but with a character so fatally flawed that it was to prove his
undoing. To the young King he had been both a good example and a
bad one; but Henry's life-long enthusiasm for literature and learning
was almost certainly due, in very large measure, to him.

Two months later the Duke's arch-enemy Henry Beaufort followed
him to the grave. Twenty-one years a cardinal, Beaufort never became
an archbishop, preferring to retain his beloved see of Winchester until
his death. He was, however, the worldliest of prelates, for years dominat-
ing the political scene – despite the indefatigable opposition of Duke
Humphrey – as much as he did the ecclesiastical, working for peace
just as determinedly as the Duke had championed the continuation of
the war, if with rather less success. Much of his immense wealth he
spent on the rebuilding of his cathedral, and the re-founding and
enlarging of the Hospital of St Cross, which still survives today. The
sum of £2,000 from the residue of the estate he left to the King, but
Henry refused it. 'My uncle,' he said, 'was very dear to me, and did
me much kindness while he lived, may the Lord reward him! Do with
his goods as ye are bound to do: I will not have them.'

Government was thereafter effectively in the hands of Suffolk, now
at the summit of his power. In 1447 he was successively appointed
Chamberlain, Constable of Dover, Lord Warden of the Cinque Ports
and Admiral of England; in 1448 he became Governor of Calais and,
on 2 July, a duke. But all too soon he ran into trouble. He continued
to be blamed, however unjustly, for the loss of Maine – which had
been formally surrendered in February 1448 – and of Anjou; there were

difficulties, too, with Richard of York, whom the death of Duke Humphrey had brought a step nearer the throne and who now led the opposition party. It was almost certainly Suffolk who now relieved York of his command in France and had Henry nominate him royal Lieutenant in Ireland for the next ten years. Seeing this appointment – with good reason – as tantamount to banishment, a furious Richard delayed his departure for more than eighteen months. Even when he finally sailed in July 1449, there were few at court who believed that he would stay there long.

York's place in France was taken by Edmund Beaufort, Earl of Somerset, who had succeeded his elder brother in the earldom (though not the dukedom) four years before. By this time, thanks in large measure to the continued dissatisfaction among the English over the surrender of Maine and Anjou – which certain garrisons, such as that at Le Mans, flatly refused to evacuate until forcibly expelled by the French – the truce was being honoured as much in the breach as in the observance; and on 24 March 1449 one of the English detachments recently expelled from Maine crossed the frontier into Brittany, stormed the town of Fougères and put it to the sack. Charles VII and Philip of Burgundy lodged a furious protest; Somerset, however, instead of making reparation, foolishly refused to surrender the town or even to apologize for the incident; and a renewal of the war was the inevitable result.

But it was henceforth to be an unequal struggle. The English proved no match for the revitalized French army. Verneuil fell, despite the heroic efforts of Talbot, who fought 'like a boar enraged' to relieve it; Mantes and Lisieux followed, together with a number of other important towns and strongholds, until finally in October Charles drew up his men outside Rouen, where Somerset had taken refuge. Once again Talbot set an example of endurance and courage, but this time it was the people of Rouen themselves who eventually opened their gates and on 10 November Charles, accompanied by René of Anjou, entered the city in triumph. March 1450 saw the arrival of reinforcements from England; but on 15 April, at the little village of Formigny some twenty-five miles north-west of Caen, the French under the Comte de Clermont virtually exterminated them. Nearly 4,000 were killed, another 1,400 taken prisoner. After this, the spirit went out of the English. Vire, Avranches, Caen and Falaise soon surrendered;

Cherbourg fell on 12 August. In little more than a year, Henry's dominions in France had been reduced to the city of Calais – to remain for another century in English hands – and a sad remnant of Guyenne.

Responsibility for the catastrophe rested squarely on the shoulders of Somerset. It was he, as commander-in-chief, who had permitted the assault on Fougères; he who had refused to make reparations afterwards; he whose lack of energy, courage and leadership had led to defeat in every action in which he had been personally engaged. Yet it was not upon him but upon Suffolk that the storm broke. Long allied to the Beauforts, both in politics and also by marriage, it was he after all who had been responsible for Somerset's appointment. On 28 January 1450, accused by Parliament of having sold the realm to the French and treasonably fortified Wallingford Castle, he was committed to the Tower. Further charges followed: he had conspired to seize the throne for his son, husband of Margaret Beaufort, the infant heiress of the first Duke of Somerset; he had engineered the release of Charles of Orléans; he had forfeited Anjou and Maine, betrayed secrets to the French, failed to strengthen the English armies and antagonized Brittany and Aragon. He had promoted unworthy persons to high positions, and had been guilty of various acts of malversation and maladministration. Finally, in March, after repeated protestations of his innocence and without having been formally found guilty of any wrongdoing, he was sentenced to five years' banishment from 1 May.

On the last day of April Suffolk came to Ipswich, where he swore a further oath on the sacrament that he was innocent of all the charges laid against him. The following morning, having written a touching letter of farewell to his little son,[1] he set sail for France with two ships and a pinnace, which he sent off in advance to Calais to seek confirmation that he would be amicably received there. Almost at once, however, the pinnace was intercepted by another vessel, the *Nicholas of the Tower*, which had been purposely lying in wait. It then bore down on the other two ships – which seem to have offered no resistance – and took Suffolk on board. He was granted a day and a night in which to make his confession; then, on the morning of 2 May, he was rowed out in a small boat and beheaded – according to one account, with half a dozen strokes of a rusty sword. The

---

1. See the *Paston Letters*, i, 121–2.

body was brought back to England and buried in the family church at Wingfield, in the county which bears his name.[1]

The circumstances of his murder remain a mystery. The fact that the *Nicholas of the Tower* was a royal ship suggests that the crime was instigated by a person or persons of considerable influence – quite possibly Richard of York himself. As to motive, since Suffolk's career was obviously over it can hardly have been political; the obvious alternative was revenge. He had never courted favour, and had often quite unnecessarily antagonized those whom he would have been better advised to flatter or indulge. His death was largely unlamented by his contemporaries, and inspired a number of cruelly satirical verses. Later, his reputation was further stained by the certainly baseless allegations – made by both Hall and Holinshed, as well as Shakespeare – of adultery with Queen Margaret. Suffolk deserved better than this. His speech to Parliament of 22 January 1450 – to say nothing of his last letter to his son – both reveal in their very different ways a man of sincerity and genuine piety, who remained utterly loyal to his King. He gave Henry sterling service, and was ill repaid.

All too soon, Henry himself had reason to regret Suffolk's departure. Within three weeks of the Duke's death, at Whitsuntide 1450, the almost universal dissatisfaction at the weakness and incompetence of the government had brought the people of Kent, East Sussex, Essex and Surrey to the point of insurrection. Their leader was a man named Jack Cade, of whose origins we know next to nothing; it seems clear, however, that he was by no means the uneducated thug of Shakespeare's play. The fact that after the rebellion his 'goods, lands and tenements, rents and possessions' were forfeited and his blood declared corrupt suggests that he is more likely to have been a member of the local squirearchy; and this is further borne out by the obvious willingness of many landed gentry of the same or similar class to follow his banner. It

1. According to Hall, 'the capitayne of the same barke with small fight entered into the dukes shyppe, and perceyuyng his person present, brought hym to Douere Rode, & there on the one syde of a cocke bote caused his head to be stryken of, and left his body with the head vpon the sandes of Douer, which corse was there founde by a chapelayne of his, and conueyed to Wyngfield college in Suffolke, and there buried.' Oddly enough, however, while the collegiate church of Wingfield possesses fine tombs of his father the second Earl and his son the second Duke, of his own tomb there is no trace.

seems probable, too, that he had fought in the French wars, where he had acquired valuable military experience. In such circumstances it may seem surprising that he should have claimed to be John Mortimer, descendant through the Earls of March of Lionel, Duke of Clarence, third son of Edward III. He seems to have genuinely believed this himself; he certainly had no difficulty in convincing the vast majority of his followers.

Assembling at various points during the last days of May, the rebels – they included one knight, eighteen squires, seventy-four 'gentlemen', the Mayor of Queenborough and the Bailiff of Folkestone – marched on London and on 1 June pitched their camp at Blackheath. Henry, who had been attending a session of Parliament at Leicester, dissolved it at once and rode quickly to the capital, arriving six days later at St John's, Clerkenwell; and on 17 June he and his Council gave careful consideration to Cade's grievances. The King, it was claimed, had given away so many of the Crown lands that instead of living on their revenue he was forced to levy disproportionate taxes on his subjects. Moreover, those responsible for collecting these taxes bought and sold their offices instead of being appointed by Parliament. But Parliament itself was no longer properly representative, since elections were all too frequently managed by the local magnates, who imposed their own nominees. A yet greater degree of corruption was evident in the judiciary. Finally, the loss of the King's lands in France had been the result of criminal mismanagement, and the 'traitors' responsible were still unpunished. To remedy these ills the insurgents demanded that the King should resume possession of all the Crown lands; that the Dukes of York, Exeter, Norfolk and Buckingham should be relieved of their positions of power; that parliamentary elections and the administration of justice should be reformed; and that the Statute of Labourers, whereby those who demanded more than a certain wage were savagely penalized, should be repealed at once.

There was nothing unreasonable about any of this, and it should not have been impossible for the Council to have given a sufficiently encouraging reply to have persuaded the rebels to return contentedly to their homes. Instead, it rejected the demands out of hand and sent in the army to restore order. At this point, however, another serious mistake was made: the army was split in two. Several detachments were deputed to escort the King to Blackheath, and only a relatively small force to deal with Cade and his followers. This force pursued them as far as Sevenoaks – where, however, the rebels suddenly wheeled round and attacked, killing twenty-four of the King's men including the two leaders, Humphrey and William Stafford. When the news reached Blackheath the remainder of the army mutinied, and it was only with difficulty that Henry was able to retire with his attendant lords to Greenwich. A few days later he fled, seeking refuge at Kenilworth Castle in Warwickshire.

After this, the rebellion spread rapidly: northward to East Anglia, westward as far as Hampshire and even Dorset. In Wiltshire the Bishop of Salisbury, who had officiated at the King's wedding, was seized after mass and murdered by his own parishioners. Meanwhile on 3 July the self-proclaimed Mortimer, wearing a gown of blue velvet, a gilt head-piece and the gilded spurs of a knight, made his triumphal entry into London, a sword carried in state before him. On the day following he publicly beheaded two of the King's most hated advisers – whom, as a sop to the rebels, Henry had already sent to the Tower: Lord Say and his son-in-law Crowmer, the Lord Sheriff of Kent. All might still have been well for him had he not ill-advisedly allowed the plunder of the house of the staunch Lancastrian Philip Malpas, one of the few City Aldermen to have opposed his entry. The prospect of further profitable looting encouraged the rabble to join him, while law-abiding citizens grew anxious at this new turn of events and began to withdraw their support. They appealed for help to Lord Scales and Matthew Gough, who held the Tower in the King's name; and at ten o'clock in the evening of Sunday 5 July these two advanced with their garrison in an attempt to regain possession of London Bridge. The ensuing battle continued all night; Gough was killed, but neither side could prevail over the other. Finally the rebels set fire to the bridge and withdrew to Southwark, where they broke into the King's Bench and Marshalsea prisons and released all the inmates.

Now at last the government decided to negotiate, nominating for the task Archbishop Kemp – himself a man of Kent – and William Waynflete, who had succeeded Beaufort as Bishop of Winchester. These two met Cade at St Margaret's church, Southwark, where they received his petitions, granting to him – in the name of John Mortimer – and to all his followers a free pardon on condition that they should at once disperse peacefully to their homes. Many did so; a number of others, however, persuaded by Cade that their pardons were worthless until they had been ratified by Parliament, followed him to Rochester and attacked Queenborough Castle on the Isle of Sheppey. This was his second mistake. A bill of attainder was immediately issued against him, this time in the name of John Cade, his pardon being simultaneously declared invalid since it applied specifically to Mortimer. Suddenly, his support evaporated. He fled in disguise to East Sussex – where a few days later the recently appointed Sheriff, one Alexander Iden, ran him to earth in a garden at Heathfield. Cade defended himself as best he could, but was killed resisting arrest; on 15 July his body was delivered to the Council who ordered it to be drawn and quartered, the quarters being sent respectively to Blackheath, Salisbury, Gloucester and Norwich. The head was impaled on a lance and exhibited on London Bridge, facing towards Kent. Shortly afterwards a tribunal – which included both Archbishops – sat in judgement over the insurgent leaders at Canterbury. Eight of them were sentenced to death.

But Henry did not have long to enjoy his triumph. At the end of August Richard of York returned, without permission, from Ireland. On landing in Wales, he immediately summoned considerable numbers of retainers from the Welsh marches and advanced with them on London. His reception was anything but friendly: the panic-stricken Council denounced him as a traitor and even tried to hold him responsible for the recent insurrection, while more than one attempt was made to to waylay him on the road; but he now had some 4,000 men under his command, and such attempts were doomed to failure. Once in London he went straight to the palace and in face of heavy opposition forced his way into the King's chamber, where he complained angrily of the hostility with which he had been received. Henry could justifiably have retorted that his cousin had left his post without authorization, and had shown every sign of intending to bear arms against him; but that was not Henry's way. Instead, he expressed deep regret for what had occurred and instantly agreed to appoint a new Council, in which York himself should be included.

Unfortunately the King had recently taken another decision, of which few but he would have been capable: he had recalled Somerset from Calais, whither the unfortunate man had fled after his expulsion from Caen, and appointed him Constable of England. Now Somerset was, in the eyes of every Englishman, the man who had lost France; in

consequence he was perhaps the most hated figure in the country –
and he was particularly detested by Richard of York, who saw him as
a dangerous rival for the succession. Since the death of Duke Humphrey,
this had been far from clear. After five years of marriage, King Henry
was still childless: his three uncles – Clarence, Bedford and Gloucester
– had all died without issue. Of the House of Lancaster there remained
only the Duke of Somerset, grandson of John of Gaunt and Katherine
Swynford, and his little niece Margaret, the daughter of his late elder
brother. Normally, such distinguished lineage would have given
Somerset a virtually incontestable claim; the difficulty was that Henry
IV, when he legitimized his Beaufort half-brothers, had by special Act
of Parliament expressly disqualified them and their descendants
from the line of succession. The case for Richard of York, on the other
hand, though weaker in that he could boast descent only from Gaunt's
younger brother Edmund, was stronger in that it was untainted with
bastardy and free of legal embarrassments. Moreover, through his mother
Anne Mortimer, York could claim descent from Gaunt's elder brother,
Lionel Duke of Clarence. There was no doubt that the court favoured
the Lancastrians, but the unpopularity of the government in general
and of Somerset in particular had turned public opinion sharply towards
the Yorkists. Jack Cade had not adopted the name of Mortimer for
nothing.

As autumn turned to winter the hostility between the two parties
steadily increased, to the point where on 1 December Somerset was
physically attacked by a Yorkist mob, his life being saved only by the
providential appearance of the Earl of Devonshire, who in the nick of
time carried him off down the river by barge. Meanwhile his house,
together with those of several other leading Lancastrians, was sacked
and plundered. Fearing for his future safety, the King quickly appointed
him Captain of Calais; but even this did not prevent Parliament, in
January 1451, from demanding his banishment, with that of some thirty
other court favourites – demands which Henry largely ignored. Just
thirteen months later, in February 1452, Richard of York issued an
appeal from his castle at Ludlow. Somerset, he declared, having already
been responsible for the loss of Normandy and Guyenne, was using his
influence with the King in such a way that England itself was likely to
be destroyed; and he now called upon the people of Shrewsbury –
'though it is not my will or intent to displease my sovereign lord' – to

help him to remove the Duke from the scene once and for all. Many of them rallied to his banner, and with them he set off on his second armed march to London.

Careful as always to emphasize his loyalty, 'at about Shrovetide' York sent heralds to request formal permission to enter the city; and when, predictably, this was refused he crossed the Thames by Kingston Bridge and continued into Kent – where recent history suggested that he might find considerable popular support – pitching his camp at Dartford. Henry meanwhile advanced to Blackheath on 1 March, sending forward Kemp, Waynflete and the Bishop of Ely to negotiate an accord. They did so quite quickly; Somerset was becoming increasingly unpopular, and there were many on the King's side who were almost as eager as York to see the last of him. It was therefore agreed that he should be put under arrest, in return for which York immediately disbanded his army and rode to Blackheath to confirm the understanding personally with the King. Entering the royal tent, however, to his astonishment he found Somerset not only at liberty, but standing as usual at Henry's right hand. Despite the King's presence there was a furious altercation between the two men; but York, himself now virtually a prisoner, dared not go too far. He was obliged to return with Henry to London, and there in St Paul's to swear a solemn oath that he would never again assemble any body of men without the King's commandment or licence. Somerset's position, and his power, remained unchanged.

What was the reason for so blatant a breach of faith? Had the negotiating bishops exceeded their briefs, giving undertakings and making promises for which they had no authority? Had Queen Margaret, Somerset's principal supporter, put her foot down and positively forbidden her pathetic husband to dismiss her favourite? Or had Somerset himself somehow persuaded his royal master to change his mind? We shall never know. The only point on which we can be certain is that Richard of York considered, with good reason, that he had been deceived and betrayed. From that moment his much-proclaimed loyalty was weakened, and England was brought another step nearer to the inevitable war.

In the summer of 1453, taking advantage of a period of relative calm, King Henry VI went hunting at Clarendon in the New Forest; and it was there, in July or August – 'by a sudden and thoughtless fright', as one chronicler rather obscurely puts it – that he was stricken by a malady which left him both physically and mentally incapacitated, 'so lacking in understanding and memory and so incapable that he was neither able to walk upon his feet nor to lift up his head, nor well to move himself from the place where he was seated'. It did not escape those around him that these symptoms were all too similar to those displayed by his grandfather, Charles VI of France, during his own ever more frequent periods of insanity towards the end of his life – a fact which boded ill for the future. The King remained at Clarendon until early October, when he was carried by slow stages first to Westminster and then on to Windsor, still too apathetic to understand the great news that was brought to him on the 13th: that, after eight years of marriage, Queen Margaret had at last presented him with a son. Elsewhere, however, there was less cause for rejoicing. The previous July had seen the deaths at Castillon of the two brave Talbots, father and son, after which the English hold on Guyenne, already tenuous, had collapsed altogether. By the end of the year the whole province was back in French hands.

These two last developments dramatically changed the situation. The birth of the prince, who had been baptized by Bishop Waynflete with the name of Edward, came as a shattering blow to Richard of York. His hopes of a peaceful succession, which had seemed considerably brighter since the King's illness, were now destroyed. His only consolation was that those of Somerset had suffered a similar fate; but Somerset's star was anyway on the wane. With the loss of Guyenne by now inevitable he was rapidly losing influence, to the point where he was not even to be considered for the post of Regent which, with the King's continuing illness, was soon to be accepted as a necessity. Finally, in November 1453, at the insistence of York's ever-faithful ally the Duke of Norfolk, he was put under arrest and committed to the Tower.

By this time the King was at Windsor. His condition showed no improvement. When in January 1454 Queen Margaret and the Duke of Buckingham brought his son to his bedside for his blessing, he stared blankly at the baby but gave no sign of recognition or understanding. It was at this point that Margaret demanded that she should be entrusted with the government; the Council, however, would have none of it. As far as they were concerned the Queen was too young, too inexperienced and a great deal too ambitious; besides, she had identified herself too closely with Somerset. Two months later, however, after a committee of Lords had visited Windsor to report on Henry's health, it was decided that government could no longer continue without an official Act of Regency; and on 27 March York was appointed Protector until the King's recovery or the Prince's coming of age. Immediately he began to consolidate his position: as Chancellor, in place of the Cardinal-Archbishop William Kemp, who had died a few days before, he nominated his wife's brother, Richard Nevill, fifth Earl of Salisbury.[1] Another relation by marriage, Thomas Bourchier, Bishop of Ely – his brother, Lord Bourchier, was married to York's sister Isabella – became Archbishop of Canterbury.

Richard of York governed the kingdom wisely and well during his protectorship; but it did not last long. Around Christmas 1454 the King recovered from his illness, and on 30 December looked consciously upon his son – now fourteen months old – for the first time. Showing every outward sign of relief, York immediately resigned his office; but with the King once again in charge of affairs and the Queen behind him it was only to be expected that the pendulum should swing back towards the Lancastrians. Somerset was released from the Tower, all the charges against him having been dropped; Salisbury was dismissed as Chancellor in favour – somewhat surprisingly – of Archbishop Bourchier, who never hesitated to trim his sails when the need arose; while York, by a final stroke of irony, was obliged to relinquish the Captaincy of Calais to Somerset himself. Prudently, he and Salisbury retired to their Yorkshire estates. So too did Salisbury's son, Richard Earl of Warwick, whom York had appointed a Privy Councillor and who six years before had inherited through his wife, Anne Beauchamp, the first and by far the richest earldom of England.

As the weeks passed it became ever more clear that the King's restoration to sanity had been a national disaster; and in May 1455, with the country slipping slowly into chaos, Somerset – who had obviously learnt nothing from adversity – and the Queen called a Council at Leicester 'to provide for the safety of the King's person against his enemies'. Since they had pointedly omitted to summon York, Salisbury

---

1. Nevill had inherited his title through his wife Alice, the only child of the fourth Earl, who had died of a wound sustained before the walls of Orleans.

and Warwick to this assembly, there was little doubt as to whom they had in mind; and it was now that the three decided to act while they were still at liberty. Their army was already prepared, and a few days later they were on the march. From Ware in Hertfordshire the Duke of York dispatched a letter to the Chancellor, Archbishop Bourchier, protesting his loyalty and emphasizing that his only purpose was to remove Somerset; but the letter was intercepted and never reached its destination. On the very same day the King and Queen, with Somerset and Buckingham and a slightly smaller force of about two thousand, set out from London, resting for the night at Watford; and the following morning – it was Thursday 22 May – the two armies met at St Albans. For three hours York and his friends tried to convince the King of their loyalty, asking only that certain persons, whom they would accuse of treason, should be delivered into their hands – past experience having unfortunately shown that mere promises, even when made on oath, were not to be trusted. Only when they received the King's reply, to the effect that he would surrender no one and that all who resisted him would be executed as traitors, did York give the order to advance.

It was rare, in the late Middle Ages, to fight a battle within a city or a town; normally a neighbouring field was preferred. The first battle of St Albans was an exception. The royalist army was drawn up along St Peter's Street and Holywell Hill, running from St Peter's church to the river Ver. York's first attack – from what are now Hatfield Road and Victoria Street – failed, but Warwick attacked from the gardens between two inns (the Key and the Chequer, now the Cross Keys and the Queen's Hotel) and after an extremely bloody encounter put the King's men to flight. Somerset was killed outside the Castle Inn; two of his principal supporters, Northumberland and Clifford, fell close by. Buckingham, blood streaming from his face, sought sanctuary in the abbey (now the cathedral). Henry himself, totally bewildered, deserted by his men and wounded in the neck by an arrow, was left standing helplessly by his banner in the market place until he was eventually persuaded to seek refuge in a tanner's house nearby. There he was finally found by York, Salisbury and Warwick, who knelt before him and carried him to the abbey for safety. Their followers, meanwhile, were less respectful – terrorizing the city and pillaging it to their hearts' content, while three hundred men lay dead in the streets.

But the battle of St Albans was more than just a battle; it was the start of England's first civil war – that civil war that has gone down in history as the Wars of the Roses.

14

King Henry VI Part II

[1441–1455]

KING. Come, wife, let's in, and learn to govern better;
For yet may England curse my wretched reign.

KING HENRY VI PART II

The Second Part of King Henry the Sixth opens in April 1445, more than
eight years before the latest event covered by its predecessor – the death
of the Talbots in the high summer of 1453. It contrives, none the less,
to follow naturally on *Part I*, in the closing scene of which the Duke
of Suffolk prepares to leave for France to fetch King Henry's royal
bride; as the curtain rises on *Part II* he announces the successful outcome
of his mission and presents her to her bridegroom and the assembled
court. Almost immediately, however, the tension rises: Duke Humphrey
of Gloucester begins to read the terms of the truce, but when he comes
to the words '. . . that the duchy of Anjou and the county of Maine
shall be releas'd and deliver'd to the King her father' they appear to
choke him and he is unable to continue; it is left to Cardinal Beaufort
to finish the sentence.

As Beaufort points out a few moments later, Duke Humphrey was at
this point still the heir apparent; it was in his interest that the King should
remain unmarried and childless. Moreover, if marriage there had to be,
the Duke had long favoured the daughter of the Count of Armagnac
as a more suitable bride. To this extent he had good reason to be
annoyed at the choice of Margaret. On the other hand – and the point
cannot be too strongly emphasized – the surrender of Maine and Anjou,
though widely rumoured at the time and reported by Hall, was never part
of the truce.[1] The rest of the scene, therefore, after the departure of
Henry and Margaret for her coronation, is based on a misapprehension:

1. See pp. 230–31.

historically, Gloucester could never have made the loss of the two territories the main reason for his attack on Suffolk. The latter was consequently able to brush off the accusations made against him and – after the deaths in 1447 of the two arch-enemies Gloucester and Beaufort – to gain effective control of the kingdom. (It is perhaps just worth mentioning that Shakespeare considerably anticipates his investiture with the dukedom, which he received only on 2 July 1448.) During the three years before his fall, Suffolk was to prove himself a responsible statesman and an excellent administrator. Ambitious he may have been; but he was certainly not the power-hungry megalomaniac suggested by the closing lines of *Part I* and quoted at the end of Chapter 12.

Among the nobles echoing Gloucester's disgust is the Earl of Warwick, who claims to have been personally responsible for acquiring the provinces now lost:

> Anjou and Maine! myself did win them both;
> Those provinces these arms of mine did conquer:
> And are the cities, that I got with wounds,
> Deliver'd up again with peaceful words?
> *Mort Dieu!*

Since Salisbury specifically calls Warwick his son, there can be no doubt that the speaker is the young Richard Nevill – he who, with his father and the Duke of York, was to head the Yorkist forces at St Albans and later to be known as 'the Kingmaker'. But Nevill was born only in 1428 and did not inherit the earldom until 1449, four years after the arrival of Margaret in England: clearly Shakespeare is confusing him here with his wife's father, Richard Beauchamp, Earl of Warwick, from whom he derived his title. Beauchamp was a fine old warrior – in 1437 he had been appointed Lieutenant of France and Normandy – but even he could hardly have made the extravagant claim attributed to his son-in-law.

After Gloucester's exit, Cardinal Beaufort predictably does his best to discredit him:

> So, there goes our Protector in a rage.
> 'Tis known to you he is mine enemy;
> Nay, more, an enemy unto you all,
> And no great friend, I fear me, to the King . . .
> He will be found a dangerous Protector.

Those references, in the first line of his speech and again in the last, to Duke Humphrey as Protector come as something of a surprise. The Protectorate had been formally ended by Parliament in November 1429, only a week or two after Henry's coronation; and it may well be asked why Shakespeare decided to continue it for another sixteen years. Unless this was an oversight – which seems unlikely – he probably had three reasons. The first and most immediate would have been to lend additional force to Beaufort's speech, allowing the Cardinal to contrast the concept of protectorship with the veiled imputation of treason in his last two lines; later it would serve also to increase the dramatic impact of Gloucester's fall, the strange story of which begins – somewhat anachronistically – in the next scene; finally, it would strengthen the motive for the Duke's quite unhistorical assassination, which would otherwise have been based only on the unjustified suspicions that he was conspiring against the King.

The Cardinal now departs, and is immediately vilified by Somerset to the Duke of Buckingham in much the same way as he himself has just spoken of Duke Humphrey, being accused of personal ambition and the determination to assume the Protectorate for himself. Buckingham's reply could hardly be more direct:

> Or thou or I, Somerset, will be Protector,
> Despite Duke Humphrey or the Cardinal.

As these two leave in their turn, Salisbury turns to his son Warwick and to his brother-in-law Richard, Duke of York, and urges them to join him in support of the Duke of Gloucester

> In what we can, to bridle and suppress
> The pride of Suffolk and the Cardinal,
> With Somerset's and Buckingham's ambition;
> And, as we may, cherish Duke Humphrey's deeds,
> While they do tend the profit of the land.

Finally, the stage is left to Richard of York, whose closing soliloquy leaves no doubt of his own intentions:

> And therefore will I take the Nevils' parts
> And make a show of love to proud Duke Humphrey . . .

Then will I raise aloft the milk-white rose,
With whose sweet smell the air shall be perfum'd,
And in my standard bear the arms of York,
To grapple with the house of Lancaster;
And force perforce I'll make him yield the crown,
Whose bookish rule hath pull'd fair England down.

We are left as Shakespeare means us to be left, with a sentiment of bleak foreboding. The realm is being torn apart, with at least six separate factions intriguing for power under a weak, incapable King. It is perhaps unfortunate that the two principal themes running through this vitally important opening scene – the loss of the two French provinces and the office of Protector – should both be based on historical inaccuracies; but in a broader sense the scene carries its own truth. Dissatisfaction, resentment, personal ambition, spite: all these were real enough, and were running uncontrolled. It was a recipe for disaster, and that disaster was not to be long in coming.

With the second scene of Act I, Shakespeare begins to chronicle the slow succession of events which lead eventually to the death of Duke Humphrey. The disgrace of Humphrey's over-ambitious second wife, Eleanor Cobham – who is arrested in I.iv and sentenced in II.iii – had actually occurred in 1441, four years before the arrival of Queen Margaret in England,[1] and thus properly belongs to the first part of the trilogy; but to have included it there would have meant losing the impact of a steady dramatic crescendo, for which strict chronological accuracy was surely a small enough price to pay. All those named as being associated with the Duchess in the black arts – Margery Jourdain, Roger Bolingbroke, John Southwell and the odious *agent provocateur* Hume (called John by Hall and Shakespeare but Thomas in the earlier chronicles) are historic personages. Shakespeare ignores Hall's reference to the slow melting of the wax image of the King, concentrating instead on the spirit (which makes its brief appearance in scene iv), and its answers to Bolingbroke's three questions concerning the fate of the King, Suffolk and Somerset.

Three times, however, he interrupts his story – on two of those

1. See Chapter 11, p. 228–9.

occasions deliberately shifting the focus back to Richard of York. The first is in I.iii, when Peter, the armourer's apprentice, accuses his master of upholding York's claim to the crown. Clearly the Duke cannot be held responsible for a reported remark by someone else, which the accused in any case has indignantly denied; but his name is somehow tarnished and it is Somerset, in place of himself, who is appointed Regent in France.[1] (The same scene contains the highly enjoyable incident where the Queen gives the Duchess of Gloucester a box on the ear and the Duchess turns on her like a fishwife.) Richard steps still further towards the centre of the stage in II.ii, when − presumably in the interests of those members of the audience who had either missed the previous play or forgotten it − he reiterates the details of his claim,[2] with Warwick solemnly pledging his support.

The least important of these interruptions is the scene of the hawking party (II.i) which provides the nobles with yet another opportunity for quarrelling among themselves and showing their animosity towards Duke Humphrey. It comes as a distinct relief when their bickering is brought to an end by the arrival of Buckingham with the news of the Duchess's arrest. There follow her trial and judgement, the surrender by her husband of his Protectorship (which, as we have already seen, he had not in fact possessed for well over a decade) and, immediately afterwards, the duel between Horner the armourer and his apprentice, where the apprentice triumphs and the dying Horner confesses the truth of the accusation against him.

The second act ends with the scene of the Duchess's penance. Dressed in a white sheet and holding a taper in her hand, she pauses on her barefoot three-day march through the city streets to address her husband − who in the play is powerless, rather than unwilling, to help her. (The penance itself is a historic fact, though the conversation between the two must clearly be Shakespeare's invention.) The Duchess warns him of his imminent fall; he, with innocent optimism, reassures her:

> I must offend before I be attainted.

---

1. Somerset actually superseded Richard in this position in the summer of 1448.

2. As usual, muddling the Mortimers. See Chapter 6, p. 137−8 and Chapter 12, p. 241.

The two are still in conversation when he is accosted by a herald and summoned to the Parliament at Bury St Edmunds where, as we know, he is to meet his death.

But what form was that death to take? For Shakespeare as for Hall, there was no question: Duke Humphrey was murdered, with the unanimous approval of his enemies, all of them for once united against him. But Shakespeare and Hall were almost certainly wrong. The suddenness of Gloucester's death, following as it did so soon after his arrest, certainly looked suspicious; but those who knew him best were convinced that there was no foul play. He was admittedly only fifty-six, but years of drink and debauch had had their effect: the palsy was already upon him, and both his portraits[1] show a worn, tired old man. Besides, what by then would have been the purpose in killing him? He had had no real power, and very little influence, since his wife's disgrace of six years before; he was not standing in the way of any of the presumed conspirators, and was doing no real harm to anyone. True, he was widely suspected of conspiring against his nephew, but there was not a shred of evidence to support it. Where his own death was concerned, nothing that we know of the two principal suspects, Suffolk and Beaufort, suggests that they would have been capable of such a crime. And if indeed he did come to a violent end, it is to say the least surprising that when Suffolk fell just three years later and was charged with a long list of crimes, the murder of Duke Humphrey was not among them.

The entire action of the third act takes place in Bury St Edmunds. The first scene, in the abbey,[2] covers the late arrival and immediate arrest of Gloucester and the nomination of Richard of York to put down a new rebellion in Ireland. Historically, seven months separated these two events: Gloucester died on 23 February 1447, while Richard was 'retained' as the King's Lieutenant in Ireland on 29 September, his

---

1. There is one in the Oriel College MS of Capgrave's *Commentary on Genesis* (engraved in Doyle's *Official Baronage*, ii, 22) and another, from a window in Old Greenwich church, engraved in the *Catalogue of Manuscripts in the Bodleian*, 1697.

2. The great Benedictine abbey, once among the half-dozen most important in all England, was largely destroyed at the time of the Dissolution of the Monasteries, between 1536 and 1540. There remain only the two tremendous gateways, of the twelfth and fourteenth centuries respectively, giving into the precinct.

formal letter of appointment being dated as late as 9 December. As we know, he was extremely reluctant to accept the position and actually delayed his departure for a year and a half; but Shakespeare is certainly allowing full rein to his imagination when he gives the Duke of York the extraordinary soliloquy with which the scene ends, suggesting first that he has agreed to his appointment only as a means of obtaining an army to lead against the King, and then that he has personally engineered the coming insurrection under Jack Cade:

> 'Twas men I lack'd, and you will give them me:
> I take it kindly; yet be well assur'd
> You put sharp weapons in a madman's hands.

Richard showed on at least four occasions in his life that he was capable of raising an army whenever he wanted one, and although after his return from Ireland he was to be the subject of various wild accusations of association with Cade, no one either then or later took them very seriously.

Scene ii is set in 'a Room of State', presumably in the house of Cardinal Beaufort, to whose care Gloucester has been most unwillingly committed. The earliest version of the play, published in quarto form in 1594, includes at this point an opening stage direction: 'Then the Curtaines being drawne, Duke *Humphrey* is discouered in his bed, and two men lying on his brest, and smothering him in his bed. And then enter the Duke of *Suffolke* to them.' For some reason – possibly the insistence of the censor – these words were omitted from the version in the First Folio of 1623, in which the murder occurs offstage. A short conversation between the murderers and Suffolk makes it clear that it is he who has given them their orders, whereupon the King and Queen, accompanied by Beaufort and Somerset, enter on the scene. What brings them to the Cardinal's house is never explained, because they are apparently still unaware of Gloucester's death; when this is announced to them, the King falls in a swoon. He recovers only to launch a most uncharacteristically violent tirade against Suffolk, which gives rise to two still more passionate outbursts from Queen Margaret. The group is then joined by Warwick, leading an indignant delegation from the Commons; somehow they have already heard rumours of what has occurred, and it is Warwick who draws back the bed-curtains to reveal the body, pointing out as he does so that the Duke has died a violent death – for which, he alleges, Beaufort and Suffolk are responsible.

Beaufort leaves at once, not deigning to defend himself; Suffolk on the other hand angrily denies the charges and, after a furious and abusive exchange, he and Warwick draw their swords. Bloodshed is averted only by the arrival of Salisbury, demanding the immediate execution or exile of Suffolk; the King complies at once with a sentence of banishment, then withdraws. Now Suffolk and the Queen are left alone, and there follows a scene of parting which would have done credit to Romeo and Juliet themselves. It includes those haunting lines of Margaret's:

> So, get thee gone, that I might know my grief;
> 'Tis but surmis'd whiles thou art standing by.

Such tenderness comes as something of a surprise. True, in the somewhat ridiculous scene where Margaret first makes her appearance (*Part I*, V.v) Suffolk is seen to be infatuated with her; but the theme is not pursued, and up to this point in the present play the Queen has been represented as hard, bitter and vindictive. There has been no evidence until now that the two are anything more than political allies, and political allies is in fact all that they were. As we saw in the previous chapter,[1] Shakespeare cannot take the entire blame for a quite unjustifiable slur on both characters, based as it is on pure fable; both Hall and Holinshed – and even Michael Drayton, in his *Heroical Epistles* – make similar allegations. Still, he has given the pair some exquisite poetry – which is, perhaps, compensation of a kind.

The pair are interrupted by a messenger, Vaux, who brings news that Cardinal Beaufort is near death, thus preparing the ground for the third and final scene of Act III, which is set in his bedchamber. We have to assume that we are still at Bury, since the King, Salisbury and Warwick are all at the Cardinal's bedside;[2] we know for a fact, however, that Beaufort died on 10 April 1447 – two months after Duke Humphrey – in the Wolvesey Palace at Winchester. His terrifying delirium is also

---

1. See p. 257.
2. I can find no authority for the statement of Dr Andrew Cairncross, the distinguished editor of the Arden edition of the play, that 'the Cardinal dies in the same house, and bed, as his victim Gloucester.' The house, perhaps; but Beaufort is hardly likely to have given up his *bed* to his prisoner.

pure invention: an eyewitness reports that he spent his last days attending to his will. On the evening of 9 April it was read over to him, and he made such additions and corrections as were necessary. On the morning of the next day he confirmed it in an audible voice; then he took leave of all around him and died quietly and with dignity. He was buried in Winchester Cathedral, where his magnificent tomb may still be seen.[1]

Act IV of the play is concerned with two themes only: the murder of Suffolk and the rebellion of Jack Cade. On the face of it, Shakespeare makes no direct suggestion that Suffolk's captors are anything but common pirates; certainly they appear to have no idea of their prisoner's true identity until he himself reveals it. The pirate 'lieutenant', on the other hand, is clearly a man of considerable education. His first speech, with which the scene opens, begins with seven lines worthy of the most high-flown tragedy:

> The gaudy, blabbing, and remorseful day
> Is crept into the bosom of the sea,
> And now loud-howling wolves arouse the jades
> That drag the tragic melancholy night;
> Who with their drowsy, slow, and flagging wings
> Clip dead men's graves, and from their misty jaws
> Breathe foul contagious darkness in the air.

and the long diatribe which follows shortly afterwards – thirty-three lines of furious invective, obviously well-informed, embellished with classical allusion and even a Latin tag – strikes one as distinctly unpiratical. It could hardly provide a greater contrast with, for example, the language of Jack Cade and his followers in the following scenes. Is Shakespeare hinting that there may after all be something more in the Duke's capture than meets the eye, or is this merely a piece of literary self-indulgence?

With scene ii, set at Blackheath, we come to Cade's insurrection. George Bevis and John Holland, two minor characters whom we meet here for the first and last time, seem to have been actors in Shakespeare's company; he probably saw no reason to change their names. His account

---

1. It seems a little hard that a modern statue of Joan of Arc should have been placed opposite it, the idea apparently being that she can confront her persecutor for all eternity. In fact Beaufort was only marginally involved in her trial and condemnation.

of the rising is inevitably no more than an imaginative reconstruction; as we saw in the previous chapter, Cade is unlikely to have been the unlettered rabble-rouser depicted here, with his unconcealed contempt for literacy or learning. A brief, somewhat macabre parenthesis in scene iv introduces Queen Margaret grieving over Suffolk's head, and there is another short passage in scene ix in which a messenger reports the return of the Duke of York from Ireland; for the rest, the act essentially follows Cade's progress, with a fair degree of accuracy, until his final flight, capture and death. There is no suggestion in Hall that the garden in which he was found was actually the property of sheriff Iden, but it hardly matters.

> From Ireland thus comes York to claim his right,
> And pluck the crown from feeble Henry's head:
> Ring, bells, aloud; burn, bonfires, clear and bright,
> To entertain great England's lawful king.

These opening words of Act V leave Shakespeare's audience in no doubt as to the reason for Richard of York's unauthorized return, in August 1450, across the Irish Sea. It was not, however, as simple as that. For Shakespeare, as he has indicated many times before, York was a self-seeking villain consumed with personal ambition. In fact, from the moment of his arrival in Wales, Richard had never ceased to emphasize his personal loyalty to the King. His quarrel was with Somerset, who had returned from his disastrous regency in France and had been appointed – to almost universal dismay – Constable of England. Buckingham's assurance in the first scene that the King has already had Somerset arrested and imprisoned in the Tower is of course premature: it was only after Richard's second march on London – not from Ireland but from his northern estates – eighteen months later in the early spring of 1452, that the King promised to take action against his favourite, and even then failed to do so. Shakespeare is thus telescoping the events of two years into a single scene: Cade's death in July 1450, Richard's return from Ireland at the end of August and his interview with the King at Blackheath in early March 1452. In the circumstances, this seems reasonable enough; more seriously off-beam, however, is the second part of that scene, after the entrance of Somerset. The sight of

15. The battle of Agincourt. The miniature is inaccurate; the French relied on cavalry and crossbows, rather than longbows as suggested here.

16. The marriage of Henry V to Princess Katherine of France at Troyes, 2 June 1420

17. The infant Henry VI held by Richard Beauchamp, Earl of Warwick, who bears in his right hand his chantry chapel at Warwick

18. Ralph Nevill, Earl of Westmorland, with his twelve children

19. Joan of Arc

20. The Earl of Shrewsbury presents a book to Henry VI and his Queen, Margaret of Anjou

21. *Above* Anthony Woodville, Earl Rivers, presents a book to King Edward IV and Queen Elizabeth. The future Edward V stands beside them

22. *Left* King Edward IV

23. *Opposite page* The battle of Barnet, 1470

… vous que nostre souuerain
seigneur … d[e] … [edo]uart
par la grace de dieu Roy den
gletere et de francq et seigne
dirlande / departist du pais de zellande et

24. Edward IV leads his abortive military expedition to France, summer 1475

25. Stained glass in Canterbury Cathedral showing the Princes in the Tower

26. King Richard III; one of the
earliest known portraits

27. Margaret Beaufort, Countess of Richmond,
the mother of Henry Tudor

28. King Richard III and his Queen, Anne Nevill, in their coronation robes

the man who he had been assured was in prison throws York into a fury:

> King did I call thee? No, thou art not king;
> Not fit to govern and rule multitudes,
> Which dar'st not, no, nor canst not rule a traitor . . .
> Give place: by heaven, thou shalt rule no more
> O'er him whom heaven created for thy ruler.

A few moments later Salisbury and his son Warwick inform the King that they too must break their oath of allegiance and will henceforth look to York as their legitimate sovereign. The Duke of Buckingham and Lord Clifford remain loyal. The lines are drawn. War is now inevitable.

All this is, of course, a travesty of the truth. When he saw Somerset at Blackheath and realized that the King had broken his promise, Richard of York kept his head. To have behaved as Shakespeare describes, insulting both King and Queen ('O blood-bespotted Neapolitan!') and claiming the crown when surrounded by Henry's men, would have been suicidal. Instead, he wisely hid his resentment as best he could, returning with the King to London and swearing his oath in St Paul's. There followed Henry's mysterious illness and Richard's appointment as Protector, both events omitted altogether in the play. It was, as we know, only after Henry recovered and Somerset returned to power that the Duke of York reluctantly gave the call to arms, protesting to the last his own personal loyalty to his King.

Another curious feature of the scene is the introduction of York's children – or, more accurately, of the eldest and the youngest of his four sons, the future Edward IV and Richard III. In March 1452, the time of the meeting at Blackheath, young Edward was a month short of his tenth birthday – hardly a suitable age to stand surety for his father. As for Richard, he did not yet exist at all; he was to be born only on 2 October of that same year. Edward speaks but a single line; Richard, on the other hand, is already presented as a prematurely venomous youth, 'As crooked,' as Clifford unkindly points out, 'in thy manners as thy shape': the first reference in the canon of plays to Richard's deformity, to which Shakespeare gives so much prominence as his story continues.

The last two scenes cover the battle of St Albans. Clifford reappears at once. He is known to have played an important part in the engagement, fighting valiantly to keep the Yorkist forces out of the town; Shakespeare's account of his death at the hands of York himself is, however, based exclusively on a hint in Hall, who quotes Clifford's son as saying to York's second son, Edmund, the young Earl of Rutland: 'By God's blode, thy father slew mine, and so wil I do the and all thy kyn'. In the play, young Clifford is rather more articulate; the sight of his dead father inspires a long and savage speech before he sadly carries off the body. Poetic justice would dictate that York should also have dispatched his enemy Somerset, but Shakespeare rather surprisingly gives that task to young Prince Richard – who, at the time of the battle, was not quite three years old.

> So, lie thou there;
> For underneath an alehouse' paltry sign
> The Castle in St Albans, Somerset
> Hath made the wizard famous in his death.

The spirit called up for the Duchess of Gloucester in Act I, when asked about the fate of Somerset, had said, 'Let him shun castles'; that prophecy was now fulfilled.

Encouraged by the young Clifford, King Henry and Queen Margaret take flight – another fantasy of Shakespeare's, since in fact they spent the night at St Albans and returned to London only the following day. Meanwhile York, Prince Richard, Warwick, Salisbury and their followers congratulate themselves on their victory. Much emphasis is laid – as it was in V.i, when he withdrew his allegiance to King Henry – on Salisbury's advanced age:

> And like rich hangings in a homely house,
> So was his will in his old feeble body.

It comes as a mildly unpleasant shock to discover that at the time of the battle poor Salisbury was just fifty-five.

15

The Wars of the Roses

[1455–1475]

KING EDWARD.   Once more we sit in England's royal throne,
Repurchas'd with the blood of enemies.
What valiant foemen, like to autumn's corn,
Have we mow'd down in tops of all their pride!
Three Dukes of Somerset, threefold renown'd
For hardy and undoubted champions;
Two Cliffords, as the father and the son;
And two Northumberlands – two braver men
Ne'er spurr'd their coursers at the trumpet's sound;
With them, the two brave bears, Warwick and Montague,
That in their chains fettered the kingly lion
And made the forest tremble when they roar'd.
Thus have we swept suspicion from our seat
And made our footstool of security.

KING HENRY VI PART III

The opening scene of *The Third Part of King Henry VI*, beginning as it does with a post-mortem on the battle of St Albans by the Yorkist leaders and ending with the Duke of York's claim to the throne and what is tantamount to a declaration of war by Queen Margaret, covers a historical period of five and a half years. Those years were marked by two brief but extremely bloody battles, at Blore Heath and North-ampton, both ending in victory for the house of York; by various grand but ultimately unsuccessful gestures of conciliation; by a minor war in the West Country; by a Lancastrian attack on Calais and a Yorkist raid on Sandwich; by the increasingly rapid slide of the entire country into anarchy and civil war; and finally by the correspondingly growing authority and ambition of the Queen. Margaret of Anjou was, according to a contemporary, 'a great and intensely active woman, for she spares no pains to pursue her business towards an end and conclusion favourable to her power'. The loss of her most faithful ally the Duke of Suffolk seems only to have strengthened her resolve: realizing that nothing could be expected from her hopeless husband, she was gradually carving out an individual power base for herself and gathering the reins of government into her own ruthless but capable hands.

The other bright star clearly in the ascendant was that of the Earl of Warwick. He remained, during those five and a half years, the unswervingly loyal right-hand man of the Duke of York; but his sheer panache had earned him a reputation which far outshone that of his uncle. He had commanded the army at Northampton, when Richard had been once again away in Ireland; he seemed, moreover, to be equally at home on land and sea. What other Governor of Calais, refused by the Exchequer in London sufficient funds to pay his own garrison, would have built up a fleet of ten ships of his own and begun a new career as an outstandingly successful pirate, capturing six Spanish ships in the Channel and even daring to attack the great Hanseatic Bay Fleet on its annual journey between the Atlantic coast of France and the League towns of North Germany and the Baltic?

Not until October 1460 was the partnership of Warwick and Richard of York put under serious strain. In the previous month Richard had returned from Ireland, landing near Chester; and as he made his way south, gathering supporters as he went, he made it clear that this, his fourth march on the capital, was very different from its predecessors. Previously he had always emphasized his loyalty to the King; this time he had come openly to claim the crown. When he reached Abingdon, we are told, 'he sent for trumpeters and clarioners to escort him to London, and there he gave them banners with the royal arms of England without any diversity and commanded his sword to be borne upright before him.' Arriving on 10 October with 500 men at the Palace of Westminster, 'he went straight through the great hall until he came to the chamber where the king, with the commons, was accustomed to hold his parliament. There he strode up to the throne and put his hand on its cushion just as though he were a man about to take possession of what was rightfully his. He kept it there for a while, then, withdrawing it, he turned to the people and, standing quietly under the canopy of state, waited expectantly for their applause.'

There was none. Warwick in particular was furious. But York had

crossed his Rubicon. Laying before the House of Lords his formal claim
to the throne, based as it was upon his direct descent from Henry III,
he now demanded that Parliament should pass judgement on his case.
The Lords, much embarrassed but probably encouraged by Warwick,
pointed out that they themselves, as well as the Duke, had taken repeated
oaths of allegiance to King Henry VI. York retorted that Henry owed
his crown only to his grandfather, who was a usurper; it followed that
none of the last three monarchs had any legal right to the throne. Finally
he accepted a compromise, which was embodied in what was known
as the Act of Accord of 24 October 1460: Henry was to retain his
position during his lifetime, but would be succeeded on his death by
York and York's heirs in perpetuity. (The Duke was at this time
forty-nine, ten years older than the King; but Henry's precarious health
suggested that the succession would occur sooner rather than later.)

The King, predictably enough, accepted the arrangement without a
murmur; his wife, on the other hand, had no intention of standing by
while her young son was disinherited. Taking ship to Scotland, she
sought allies at the court of the eight-year-old James III – who had
succeeded his father some three months before – simultaneously summoning her adherents from all parts of the country to a general meeting
in the north. The outraged Lancastrians rallied to her standard. Jasper
Tudor, Earl of Pembroke, set out with his men from Wales; the Duke
of Somerset and the Earl of Devon marched up from the south-west;
in the north, the Earl of Northumberland with Lords Clifford and Roos
set to work raising forces of their own. Finally on 9 December, York
and Salisbury, together with their respective sons Edmund Earl of
Rutland and Sir Thomas Nevill, led the Yorkist army against them.
Near Worksop they were attacked by Somerset and lost a number of
men; but the remainder reached York's own castle of Sandal, just
outside Wakefield, on the 21st. There they spent Christmas, while the
Lancastrians closed in; and from there on 30 December, realizing that
the only alternative was a siege which he was ill-equipped to withstand,
Richard of York led his men out to meet his enemies.

It was a disastrous decision: the Yorkists were heavily outnumbered.
Richard himself was killed; his severed head – adorned, the Nevill
chronicler reports, with a paper crown – was impaled on a pike and
raised above the walls of York. Among the countless other casualties
were his son, the seventeen-year-old Earl of Rutland – dispatched by

Clifford in cold blood on the bridge at Wakefield – and Sir Thomas Nevill, whose father the Earl of Salisbury was captured, only to be executed at Pontefract on the following day. On receipt of the news Queen Margaret hurried south from Scotland, met her victorious captains at York and joined them in mid-January on their triumphal march to the capital – the rough northern soldiers wreaking, we are told, unspeakable havoc in the towns and villages through which they passed.

Reports of the battle of Wakefield soon reached Wales, where Richard's eldest son Edward, Earl of March, had been enjoying his first independent command. Now himself Duke of York, he at once set out with his locally engaged forces for London, but on hearing of the approach of Pembroke and the Earl of Wiltshire – who had recently landed in south Wales with an army of Frenchmen, Irishmen and Bretons – turned to intercept them and, in the first days of February 1461, defeated them soundly at Mortimer's Cross in Herefordshire. Pembroke's father, Owen Tudor – stepfather to the King, since he had married Queen Katherine after the death of Henry V – was executed at Hereford, in the market square; Pembroke himself, however, managed to escape, as did Wiltshire; and it was probably the knowledge that these two dangerous men were still at liberty that caused Edward to remain after all in the west.

The Yorkist army in the capital was thus in the hands of the Earl of Warwick, who had remained behind to supervise the government and keep a watchful eye on King Henry in the Tower. Setting out in mid-February with the King himself, the Dukes of Norfolk and Suffolk, the Earl of Arundel and his own brother John Nevill, Marquis of Montagu, he marched his considerable force – it included a formidable contingent of hand-gunners sent by Philip of Burgundy – to St Albans, scene of his and York's victory nearly six years before. That victory, however, was not repeated. The details of the second battle are as usual unclear, but much of the blame lay with Warwick himself. His reconnaissance, first of all, was hopelessly inadequate: Queen Margaret and her army arrived before he was ready for them, and by a different road. And his generalship, when the battle began, proved very little better. On being driven back from the market place by a hail of Yorkist arrows, the Lancastrians wheeled round to Barnet Heath a few miles to the north-east, where they came upon Warwick's vanguard – still in a state of hopeless disarray – and after a desperate struggle put them to flight. The remainder of the divided army, unsupported and outnumbered, took to its heels, as did its commander. King Henry, left alone, bewildered and frightened – here at least history seems to have repeated itself – was eventually picked up by his wife and son, who carried him off to the now familiar abbey.

After so humiliating a defeat, the Yorkists could not have prevented the King and Queen entering the capital, their jubilant army behind them. But Margaret had advanced no further than Barnet when she called her army to a halt. Why she did so we shall never know; perhaps she intended only a temporary delay while she negotiated with the city authorities. At all events the hesitation proved her undoing. Suddenly the people of London – among whom the stories of the northerners' barbarity, assiduously spread by Warwick, had lost nothing in the telling – rose up in violent opposition to the Lancastrians; Margaret, seriously alarmed, retreated to Dunstable. Young Edward of York, having made a rendezvous with Warwick at Burford in Oxfordshire, saw his chance: hurrying with his vast following of Welshmen to London, he entered the capital in triumph on 26 February and claimed the crown. Six days later on 3 March it was agreed by the Council, meeting at Baynard's Castle, that he was indeed the rightful ruler, Henry and Margaret having clearly acted in breach of the recent parliamentary settlement; and on the following day, seated on the royal throne in Westminster Hall and to the loud acclamation of all present, Edward declared himself King before moving across to the abbey to pray at the shrine of his namesake the Confessor. Finally, on 5 March, the royal proclamations were issued in his name: Edward IV, King of England.

Edward was King; but, significantly, he – or perhaps the bishops – had baulked at the idea of a formal coronation. The ceremony would surely have strengthened his hand; one is left with an uncomfortable feeling that he himself was not yet fully confident of his position. Besides, as he well knew, the war was by no means over. Queen Margaret, disappointed but undefeated, had withdrawn once again to her loyal fastness in the north, where she could still command the allegiance of well over half the country's nobility; there could be no peace in the land while she remained under arms, with Henry – ineffectual as he might be – at her side. After his proclamation Edward remained only ten more days in London before taking the road again, marching slowly northward via Cambridge to allow time for the hastily gathered contingents from East Anglia and the Midlands to rally to his standard. As he headed towards York the numbers of his army steadily increased; by the time he reached Pontefract he probably had as many as 50,000 men under his command.

But Margaret had also been raising forces. Her own army was every bit as formidable; and the battle of Towton, which was fought in bitterly cold weather on Saturday and Palm Sunday, 28 and 29 March 1461, proved to be on a dramatically different scale from any previous engagement. The first day saw a furious encounter as the Yorkist troops attempted to cross the river Aire at Ferrybridge, between Pontefract and York. The Lancastrians resisted with all their strength but were finally obliged to fall back. Warwick was wounded by an arrow in the leg, while the icy water claimed many victims on both sides. Shivering with cold – many of them were also soaked to the skin – and with practically no food to sustain them, Edward's men spent an agonizing night in the open, their leaders wondering how long the army would manage to hold together in such nightmare conditions; but Margaret's soldiers too were suffering, and by morning both sides were eager to come to grips as soon as possible.

It was Edward who attacked first. The lie of the land was against him, the Queen's army having occupied the higher ground on the road between Ferrybridge and Tadcaster. On the other hand the appalling weather was in his favour: it was blowing a blizzard but the wind was at his back, driving the snow straight into the eyes of Margaret's archers, slowing their arrows while speeding those of the Yorkists. The Lancastrians had no choice but to charge – perhaps 20,000 of them under Somerset, Lord Rivers and Sir Andrew Trollope, flinging themselves forward down the slope until it seemed that Edward's army must take flight or perish; yet somehow it stood its ground, and the next six hours saw one of the bloodiest and most ruthless battles ever fought on English soil. Edward himself remained in the thick of the fray, fighting on foot with immense courage, wielding in turn sword, axe and mace, encouraging and inspiring all those around him. Seeing his magnificent figure – he was six foot three inches tall, and his helmet probably added at least another six inches – Yorkists and Lancastrians alike could hardly fail to contrast him with the feeble, feckless Henry, cowering behind his wife in the rear.

The light was already beginning to fail when the Duke of Norfolk arrived with fresh troops to smash into the exposed Lancastrian flank, which finally broke and started the headlong flight of Queen Margaret's men. Hundreds of heavily armoured knights were drowned trying to cross the little river Cock; hundreds more of their followers were trapped at Tadcaster where, to block the Yorkist advance, they had themselves destroyed the only bridge two days before. Few prisoners were taken: for the vast majority, capture meant instant slaughter. Northumberland, Clifford and Nevill were among the royalist nobles who fell on the field; killed too was Sir Andrew Trollope, one of the bravest and most experienced of the Lancastrian leaders. Among the Yorkists Lord FitzWalter was the only noble casualty, but their losses too were horrendous. The snow is said to have been more crimson than white, while the river Wharfe and its tributaries ran red with blood. We need not necessarily believe the contemporary report that the heralds counted 28,000 dead on the field, but after ten hours of desperate hand-to-hand fighting even that figure is not impossible. Over an area six miles long by half a mile broad, the dead lay unburied for several days.

Edward entered York in triumph, removing from the walls the heads of his father and the other Yorkist nobles slain at Wakefield and replacing them with those of the Earl of Devon – captured alive but subsequently executed – and other Lancastrian leaders. He remained in the city for the next three weeks, consolidating his position. The great Lancastrian families of the north – the Percys, the Cliffords, the Dacres – were largely destroyed, their power shattered, their old loyalties severely shaken; now for the first time it seemed that there might be a chance of persuading the whole region to accept his authority. He also showed himself in Durham and Newcastle – where he witnessed the execution of one of his oldest enemies, the Earl of Wiltshire – finally returning in May to London, where on 28 June he was crowned at last in Westminster Abbey. His two brothers George and Richard, whom the Duchess of York had sent over to Utrecht for safety after her husband's death, returned in time for the ceremony and were awarded the dukedoms of Clarence and Gloucester respectively.

Queen Margaret, however, was not yet beaten. Having retreated once again to Scotland, she further ingratiated herself with the Scots by ceding to them the town of Berwick-on-Tweed; and early in 1462 she crossed to France, where she persuaded her cousin Louis XI – who, after two unsuccessful attempts to depose his father, Charles VII, had succeeded him naturally the previous July – to lend her money and send an expeditionary force to help her, promising him Calais in return. (Fortunately Philip of Burgundy refused point-blank to allow French troops to cross his territory, so this plan came to nothing.) In 1463 she tried again to establish a solid Lancastrian base in the far north, but with no greater success; then in the following year the young Duke of Somerset, whose father had been Richard of York's chief opponent but whom Edward had pardoned and befriended, reverted to his original cause and, with Sir Ralph Percy and Sir Humphrey Nevill, raised a revolt in Northumberland. On 25 April, at Hedgeley Moor near Alnwick, they attacked a Yorkist army under Warwick's brother, the Marquis of Montagu, but were soundly defeated. Percy was killed; Somerset escaped and tried to regroup his forces, but at Hexham on 15 May his army – which by now included all the Lancastrian notables in the north and had even been joined by King Henry in person – suffered a surprise attack by Montagu and was virtually annihilated. He himself, together with several of the other leaders, was captured and beheaded; the King escaped, only to spend nearly a year in disguise, wandering through the wild hill country of the north, taking refuge where he could at monasteries or in the homes of his supporters. At last he was recognized as he sat at dinner at Waddington Hall in Ribblesdale. Arrested and taken to London, he was imprisoned in the Tower – where he was to remain for the next five and a half years.

The pendulum had swung in favour of King Edward; but at Hedgeley Moor and Hexham he had played no part. His mind was on other matters. Early in the morning of 1 May 1464 he had paid a secret visit to Grafton, near Stony Stratford; it was the residence of the old Duchess of Bedford, widow of the Regent who had governed France some forty years before. After his death she had married Richard Woodville, Lord Rivers, and had borne him a daughter, Elizabeth, whose husband, the stalwart Lancastrian Sir John Grey of Groby, had been killed at the second battle of St Albans. The young widow was now twenty-seven, five years older than Edward and devastatingly attractive; he had been pursuing her for months, but it was widely believed that she had insisted on marriage before granting him her favours, even when he had held a dagger to her throat.[1] Finally he had given in, and by the time he left Grafton a few hours later the two were man and wife.

No public announcement was made. Other brides, a good deal more distinguished than Elizabeth,[2] had been suggested and had already been the subject of tentative diplomatic inquiries; they included the Princess Isabella of Castile – who was later to marry Ferdinand of Aragon and to send Christopher Columbus to the New World – and the sister-in-law of Louis XI, Bona of Savoy. Bona's cause was being industriously promoted by the Earl of Warwick as part of his policy to form an alliance with France and Burgundy, and Edward was well aware that the very idea of the Woodville marriage would drive him to fury. He kept his secret for four months, even from his closest friends, revealing it only in September 1464 when it could be kept no longer.

Warwick's reaction when he heard was even worse than the King had feared. The marriage meant not only the collapse of his political plans; it also affected him personally since, as soon became clear, Edward was marrying not just a beautiful woman but a highly ambitious clan. Over and above her own two sons by her first husband, Elizabeth possessed no less than five brothers and seven unmarried sisters, all of whom expected to be generously endowed. Three years earlier, they could have been satisfied without too much difficulty: Edward had had at his disposal all the vast Lancastrian estates confiscated from their former owners. Unfortunately, however, these had by now all been bestowed on the many Yorkist friends who had brought him to the throne. The only thing he could do for the Woodvilles was to arrange profitable marriages for them, and these followed thick and fast: over the next six years there was not a single heir to an English earldom who, on his marriage, did not choose a Woodville wife. Warwick

1. Such at least is the report of Dominic Mancini, a well-informed Roman visitor to London, who in December 1483 was to write a fascinating account of Richard III's *coup d'état* of the same year.

2. Elizabeth was in fact of extremely noble birth on her mother's side, the Duchess of Bedford being herself the daughter of Peter of Luxemburg, Count of St Pol, who claimed direct descent from Charlemagne. But the Duchess had married beneath her; her second husband, Richard Woodville, though generally believed to be the handsomest man in England, was by origin a simple country squire, and she had been obliged to pay a fine of £1,000 for marrying without the royal licence.

himself, who had no male heir but two daughters of his own to dispose of, saw them passed over again and again in favour of the Queen's innumerable relations; worse still, he was forced to stand by powerless while his own aunt Katherine Nevill, Duchess of Norfolk, was married off to one of the Queen's brothers, John Woodville – the groom being just twenty while his bride, as the Nevill chronicler records with heavy irony, was 'a slip of a girl almost four score years old'. He was, he felt, drowning in a sea of Woodvilles – and rapidly losing the prime position at court which he believed to be rightfully his.

For a man like Warwick such a situation was intolerable; before long he began looking around for other friends. He had never made any secret of his connections with the French court, and by 1467 there were rumours on both sides of the Channel that he was in communication with Queen Margaret, to whom Louis XI had given refuge. In fact, however, his principal ally was rather nearer home: the King's brother George, now Duke of Clarence and, for the moment, heir-presumptive to the throne. Warwick had long been determined on a marriage between Clarence and his own elder daughter Isabel; Clarence too had favoured the idea – the lady was, after all, the greatest heiress in England – and both of them had taken serious offence when Edward had rejected it out of hand on the grounds that Clarence's mother, Cecily of York, had been both Isabel's great-aunt and her godmother, and that the marriage consequently fell within the prohibited degrees.

Warwick, characteristically, refused to accept the King's decision. Having secretly obtained a special dispensation from Pope Paul II, early in July 1469 he suddenly summoned Clarence to Calais, where Isabel was waiting. The two were married on the spot by his brother George Nevill – now Archbishop of York – in the church of Notre Dame. They and Warwick together then issued a manifesto, announcing that they were coming to present to the King certain 'reasonable and profitable articles of petition' and calling upon all 'true subjects' to join them in an armed demonstration at Canterbury on Sunday 16 July to emphasize the need for reforms. The articles, which purported to be representations made to the confederates by men 'of diverse parties', were for the most part little more than the usual complaints of 'lack of governance' and 'great impositions and inordinate charges' that Warwick had so often levelled at the Lancastrians in the past; but there was no attempt to conceal his real grievance – that the King had antagonized and estranged the 'great lords of his blood' by his blatant favouring of the Woodvilles and other 'seducious persones'.

The people of Kent gave the Earl a warm welcome; and all the way to London he continued to protest his loyalty, much as Richard of York had done on his various marches to the capital some fifteen years before. Subsequent events, however, soon showed that his true intentions were far from peaceable. Already in Yorkshire an insurrection had broken out under a shadowy figure known as Robin of Redesdale – but who was very probably a landowner from Marske in Swaledale (and an old friend of Warwick) by the name of Sir William Conyers. Edward had marched north to deal with him, ordering the Earls of Pembroke[1] and Devon to gather troops in Wales and join him at Northampton. The first of these tasks they satisfactorily performed; but on 26 July, at Edgecote some six miles north-east of Banbury, they were intercepted and soundly defeated by Robin's men. That evening several hundred Welshmen lay dead on the field. Pembroke and his brother, Sir Richard Herbert, were taken to Northampton and beheaded, on Warwick's orders, the following morning.

King Edward was at the little town of Olney, on his way from Nottingham to his Northampton rendezvous, when he heard the news. What then occurred is not entirely clear; it seems, however, that many of his men deserted, and that he himself, perhaps bewildered by the events of the past month and the sudden reversal of his fortunes, relaxed his guard. At all events he somehow allowed himself to fall into the hands of the Archbishop of York, who had recently returned with his brother from Calais and who now dispatched the King – with every outward show of respect – first to Warwick Castle and then to the old Nevill fortress of Middleham in Yorkshire.

What, one wonders, were Warwick and his family trying to achieve? It was rumoured in many quarters that he was aiming to have Edward declared a bastard, so that the crown should devolve upon his new son-in-law Clarence; on the other hand he does not seem to have made any deliberate move in this direction, and any attempt would almost certainly have failed. It seems on the whole more probable that he was hoping to tame the King, to reduce him to the status of a willing tool,

1. Sir William Herbert had received the Earldom of Pembroke in 1468, after the attainder of Jasper Tudor.

happy to carry out such policies as he, Warwick, might dictate to him. If so, he had seriously misjudged his man: Edward, captive or free, took orders from no one.

It soon became clear that the King's arrest had been a serious mistake. When Warwick tried to raise forces in the north to put down a new Lancastrian rebellion by his distant kinsman Sir Humphrey Nevill of Brancepeth, he found himself unable to do so: while Edward remained a prisoner, the land was effectively ungovernable. He therefore proposed to the King that he should return to London, rejoin his wife and show himself to the people; and the Londoners for their part were told to prepare a suitable welcome. Edward – whose captivity had in fact been extremely comfortable, to the point where he regularly went out hunting – was only too happy to forgive and forget, and soon afterwards granted both Warwick and Clarence a general pardon for their offences.

All too soon, however, he was to have reason to regret it. His master of horse, Sir Thomas Burgh of Gainsborough in Lincolnshire, had for some time been at daggers drawn with his neighbour, Lord Welles and Willoughby; and early in 1470 Welles and his son attacked and destroyed Burgh's manor house, carrying off its contents. Feuds of this kind were frequent enough in the fourteenth and fifteenth centuries and were usually allowed to settle themselves; Burgh, however, was a member of the King's household, and Edward decided to go immediately to his assistance. For Clarence and Warwick, here was precisely the opportunity they had been seeking. Secretly allying themselves with the Welles faction, they put it about that the real reason for the King's visit to Lincolnshire was to take his revenge on the county for its part in Robin of Redesdale's insurrection; and on Sunday 4 March Welles's son, Sir Robert, issued a proclamation claiming that Edward intended 'to destroy the commons of Lincolnshire'. The King, knowing nothing of all this, had advanced only as far as Royston when he received a letter from Clarence to say that he and Warwick were riding up to meet him. He replied in all innocence with a handwritten letter of thanks, authorizing the two to raise troops in Warwickshire and Worcestershire.

On Monday 12 March he reached Stamford, where further letters from Warwick and Clarence informed him that they hoped to arrive the same evening. He also learned that a hostile army under Sir Robert Welles was only five miles away at the little village of Empingham, and instantly marched out to meet it. Edward's force may have been slightly outnumbered, but he was far superior in cavalry and artillery, and the fighting was soon over. Welles and his men were soon in headlong flight, tearing off their defensive clothing in such quantities that the place came to be known as 'Lose-coat Field'. But the battle had a consequence which far outweighed its military outcome. Among the dead was a man in Clarence's livery carrying a casket. It contained letters from the Duke to Welles, and left no doubt in Edward's mind that the insurrection, such as it was, had the full backing both of Clarence and of Warwick – a fact which was confirmed by Welles himself when he was captured a day or two later.

On 19 March, at Doncaster, Welles and his captain of infantry, Richard Warren, were publicly beheaded in view of the entire army. But what was to be done with Clarence and Warwick? Great as their treachery had been, Edward still had no taste for fratricide; and it was to Warwick, as he well knew, that he owed his throne. Several times he summoned the two of them to join him; on each occasion they assured him that they were on their way, then headed off in another direction. Finally he wrote to them that, even if they had indeed betrayed him, he was prepared to receive them 'with favour and pity, remembering their ties of blood and the old love and affection which had been between them'; but such vague assurances were not enough. They insisted on nothing less than free pardons and safe conducts for themselves and their followers, a demand to which he in his turn could not possibly agree. Finally, at York on 24 March, he issued a proclamation. If they appeared before him within four days, they would be received with grace and favour; if not, a price would be put on their heads and they could expect no mercy. Then he himself set off in their pursuit.

It was by now clear that the rebel lords had no intention of giving themselves up and, having failed to find any more English adherents, that they would try to seek refuge in France; and Edward reached Exeter on 14 April only to discover that they had sailed a few days before, taking with them Warwick's wife and daughter, the heavily pregnant Duchess of Clarence. By the time they reached Calais she was in labour; even so, they were refused entry to the town. Somehow the Duchess survived her ordeal, but the baby lived only a few hours and was buried a little further down the coast. At this point a large Flemish fleet entered the Channel from the north-east, and Warwick – who, even when his life was in danger, could never resist a little piracy – attacked and plundered it. He and the Clarences then sailed on to Honfleur, where they made a formal request to King Louis for protection.

Louis was only too pleased to agree. Now that King Edward had seemingly antagonized almost all the most important of his erstwhile supporters, there seemed at last to be a chance of restoring Henry VI and cementing an Anglo-French alliance against his arch-enemy Charles, Duke of Burgundy.[1] The principal stumbling-block was Queen Margaret. Could she ever be persuaded to overcome her hatred for Warwick and ally herself with him? Louis prepared his ground carefully; and at last, on 22 July 1470, the Earl of Warwick presented himself before Margaret and flung himself at her feet. She left him lying prone, we are told, for some considerable time before agreeing to forgive him, and even then insisted on a further public act of contrition at Westminster after her husband's restoration. But Warwick was finally permitted to rise to his feet and, to celebrate their reconciliation, Margaret's son the Prince of Wales was formally betrothed in the church of St Mary at Angers to Warwick's younger daughter, Anne Nevill, while all those present swore on a relic of the True Cross to remain faithful to Henry VI.

With this problem safely out of the way, Louis could now devote his energies to the next stage of his plan: the invasion of England. For some time already he had been preparing a war fleet, which Edward – who was well aware of his intentions – was doing his best to immobilize by setting up a blockade around the Channel ports of Barfleur and La Hogue where it lay. For most of the summer he was successful; but on 8 September a violent storm scattered the English ships – driving them, we are told, as far away as the Dutch and Scottish coasts – and Warwick saw his chance. His fleet put to sea the next day, making landfall at Dartmouth and Plymouth. Immediately he issued proclamations in the name of Henry VI, calling on all right-thinking Englishmen to rally to the cause of their true King; then, with Clarence and the Earl of Oxford at his side, he set off north-eastwards towards Coventry, gathering forces as he went.

Edward, who had been pacifying the north, rode south to meet him. He was not, as far as we can understand, unduly alarmed. He had already satisfied himself that the Marquis of Montagu, despite being Warwick's

---

1. Charles the Bold of Burgundy had succeeded his father Philip the Good in 1467; in the following year he had married, as his third wife, Edward IV's sister Margaret.

brother, would remain loyal; and with the addition of the northern levies that Montagu was in the process of raising he was confident that the Lancastrian forces would be comfortably outnumbered. He reached Doncaster, however, to find calamitous news awaiting him. His confidence had been misplaced. Six years before, he had rewarded Montagu for his loyalty by creating him Earl of Northumberland; unfortunately, however, and extremely unwisely, he had recently persuaded him to resign that earldom in favour of the heir of the Percys. To compensate him he had raised him to the dignity of a marquis; but since, as Montagu himself said, 'the King had given him but a magpie's nest to maintain his estate with', this had proved more a burden than anything else. And so, in his resentment, Montagu had betrayed him after all. Instead of riding down to his aid with his troops, he had at the last moment declared for Henry and was already at Pontefract, advancing against the Yorkist army.

Had Edward been given two or three days' prior warning of the betrayal, he might have saved the situation. He had several powerful lords on his side, including his brother Richard and his brother-in-law Lord Rivers, each with his own numerous following; but they were widely dispersed, and there was no hope of gathering them together in time to face Montagu's coming onslaught. To remain meant certain death or capture. His only hope lay in flight. With Gloucester, Rivers, his chamberlain Lord Hastings and about eight hundred men, he hurried south-east to the coast of Lincolnshire, commandeered a number of small boats and under cover of darkness crossed the Wash to King's Lynn; and from there, on 2 October, the party took ship for the Low Countries. They were sighted almost immediately, and were pursued all the way to the Dutch coast; but with the help of the Burgundian Governor of Holland they shook off their pursuers. Nine days later Edward was installed as the Governor's guest in his house at The Hague.

In London, the news of the King's flight caused chaos. Vast numbers of Lancastrians emerged from their various places of refuge and took to the streets, where they were joined by followers of the Earl of Warwick and, after the prisons were broken open, a whole rabble of criminals and cut-throats who went on the rampage. Elizabeth Woodville and her two daughters sought sanctuary at Westminster, where a month later she was to give birth to Edward's first-born son. On 5 October Archbishop Nevill, Warwick's brother, and old Bishop

Waynflete went down to the Tower, where they found King Henry, after over five years in captivity, 'not so worshipfully arrayed nor so cleanly kept as should seem such a prince'. They arranged for him to be dressed in more appropriate robes and then with great reverence brought him, 'mute as a crowned calf', to Westminster. Warwick and Clarence entered the capital on the following day, with the Earl of Shrewsbury and Lord Stanley behind them. The King, they saw, had declined both physically and mentally during his captivity; still less now could he ever hope to be anything but a figurehead, and a deeply uninspiring one at that. On 21 October, however, he wore his crown in public. Theoretically at least, as his subjects could see, he was back on the throne. And Warwick, appointed Lieutenant of the Kingdom, settled down to rule.

But not, as it turned out, for long. Warwick's hold on England was tenuous, and he knew it. Queen Margaret still viewed him with intense suspicion. Although she had refused to sail in his company to England she was bound to return there before long, together with her son the Prince of Wales, now seventeen. Would the old antipathy between her and Warwick flare up again, and if so what would be its outcome? Warwick's most important English ally, Clarence, was treacherous and utterly self-seeking; he could not be trusted an inch. There were of course other supporters, more reliable if less powerful; but sooner or later they too would expect rewards, and he had none to give them: after the recent events there were no great forfeited estates to be shared out among his friends. Meanwhile Edward IV, at liberty in Holland and still only twenty-eight, was anything but a spent force – particularly with his brother-in-law Charles the Bold of Burgundy to help him regain his throne.

Edward, however, had initially found Charles something of a disappointment. True, the Duke had put the Burgundian fleet at his disposal while he was in power and had been perfectly prepared to offer him a refuge after his flight; but the keystone of his foreign policy was his struggle with the King of France, for which he needed as an ally the effective King of England, not a refugee pretender. He had therefore entered into negotiations with Warwick, and it was only after these had broken down – Warwick was now, after all, firmly and inextricably bound to Louis XI – that he had even consented to grant his brother-in-law an audience. But then, fortunately for Edward, Louis began spoiling for war against Burgundy and the situation changed. Charles granted him a considerable sum of money for fitting out a fleet, which he was able to supplement with some two dozen other vessels from the Hanseatic League and elsewhere; and on Monday 11 March 1471, at the head of thirty-six ships and with an army of some 2,000 men, King Edward IV sailed for England. Three days later his ship, the *Anthony*, docked at Ravenscar on the Humber, exactly where Henry Bolingbroke had landed seventy-two years before. It seemed, on the whole, a favourable omen.

In another respect also Edward was to follow Bolingbroke. Finding that his country received him with little enthusiasm, he was obliged to give out that he had come to claim not the crown, but his dukedom only; to this at least his right was unquestioned. It was thus that he obtained permission to enter York – which was, paradoxically enough, by now firmly Lancastrian – from which he passed on to his family's own castle of Sandal, where his father had been killed eleven years before. Even in his home territories, however, he gathered relatively few adherents; only when he reached the Midlands, at Leicester and Nottingham, did appreciable numbers rally to his standard.

The Earl of Warwick, too, was recruiting in desperate haste. At the end of March he established his headquarters at Coventry, refusing all Edward's attempts to draw him on to the field until he received the reinforcements which he knew to be approaching under Oxford, Exeter, his brother Montagu and the Duke of Clarence. In little more than a week the first three had arrived – Exeter having had some trouble with a Yorkist detachment on the way – but then disaster struck. Almost predictably, Clarence decided once again to change sides and marched off, with 4,000 men behind him, to join his brother. At this point Edward, no longer troubling to conceal his true intentions, would have asked nothing better than a battle; but Warwick knew he was outnumbered. He knew too that Margaret, with the young Prince of Wales and the reinforcements sent by King Louis, would at any moment be arriving from France; why should he risk an engagement which might well prove disastrous?

On 5 April Edward headed for London. No general likes to advance in the knowledge that he is leaving a strong enemy force in his rear, but he had little choice: if he were ever to wrest the capital – and Henry VI himself – from Warwick's control, now surely was the moment to do so. Recognizing the danger, Warwick sent urgent messages to the Duke of Somerset and the other Lancastrian leaders in the city, enjoining them to hold fast until his arrival; by an ironic chance, however, reports had recently arrived to the effect that Margaret, her son and her army had finally set sail from Harfleur. They were expected from one day to the next on the south coast, and Somerset had already left to welcome them. Authority in the capital now lay with Warwick's brother, George Nevill, Archbishop of York. The poor man did his best, organizing on 9 April what he hoped would be an impressive parade of Lancastrian strength led by King Henry in person; but Henry, in a threadbare gown of blue velvet, barely able to sit his horse and tightly clutching the archbishop's hand, cut such a pathetic figure that the attempt did more harm than good. On the following day Nevill submitted, and on the 11th Edward entered London without opposition. After a hurried re-coronation at Westminster Abbey – Henry having returned to his former lodgings in the Tower – he went straight to the sanctuary to be reunited with his wife and daughters and to see his baby son for the first time.

But time was short: Warwick was on the march towards London and already approaching St Albans. It seems strange, in retrospect, that he had not waited for Margaret and her army to join him, but there were several uncertainties: how long she would be, where she would land, the strength of her army and – most doubtful of all – the extent to which she would trust him and treat him as an ally. His future position would be a good deal more secure if he could come to her as a victor, with a decisive battle behind him. Meanwhile Edward was growing stronger by the minute; the sooner the battle could be fought, the better.

The King, for his part, felt much the same way. He spent Good Friday 12 April in frantic preparations, and on Saturday afternoon – with Gloucester, Clarence, Hastings, Rivers and a number of other lords – led an army estimated at 10,000 men up the Great North Road towards St Albans. Henry too was with him, bewildered as always, but a valuable hostage in case of need. He found Warwick – with Montagu, Oxford and Exeter, and an army that appeared considerably larger than his own – sooner than he expected: on the high ground, a mile or so to the north of the little town of Barnet – and that night, under cover of darkness and in rapidly increasing fog, he drew up his troops opposite them, in what he intended to be a direct confrontation.

At first light on Easter Sunday, to a deafening blast of trumpets, he ordered the advance. The fog had grown thicker, to the point where it took him a little time to discover that he had slightly mistaken his position: his line outflanked Warwick's on the right and was itself outflanked on the left. One end of the Yorkist line, moreover, was unable to see the other – though this ultimately proved an advantage: when Edward's left wing was broken by the Lancastrians under the Earl of Oxford and took flight, the right remained unaware of the fact and fought on undismayed. Again the superbly armoured figure of the King himself, commanding the centre and towering above his soldiers, dominated the battle. He and they fought furiously for three hours, first wearing down Warwick's men and ultimately driving them back. By mid-morning it was all over, with perhaps a thousand men – Montagu among them – lying dead on the field. Warwick himself leaped on to his horse and fled; but he was captured in nearby Wrotham Park and cut down on the spot. His body and his brother's were carried to London and on the King's orders were exposed for two days, 'open and naked', in St Paul's, not as a grisly triumph but in order to refute any dangerous rumours that they might still be alive. King Henry, who had been fitted with armour and optimistically placed in the thick of the fighting, some-how escaped without a scratch and was taken back to the Tower.

That same evening, after three weeks during which she had been delayed again and again by contrary winds in the Channel, Queen Margaret – now forty-one – and her son Prince Edward landed at Weymouth. Next day she went to Cerne Abbey; it was there that she was joined by Somerset and the Earl of Devonshire, who told her of Warwick's defeat. She was, however, given a warm reception in the west country, where there was an immediate general rising in Dorset, Devon and Cornwall. At this point she had two choices before her. She could march directly on London, either taking the coast road or by way of Salisbury; alternatively she could head north to Lancashire and Cheshire, where her principal support was to be found and where there was a chance that she might meet up on her way with Jasper Tudor, who was believed to be rallying troops on her behalf. Either way, as she was well aware, Edward would not give her an easy journey.

Nor did he. His agents had watched her every movement since her arrival, and when she chose the second course of action he knew of her decision almost as soon as she knew of it herself. The several feints that she deliberately made in an attempt to put him off the scent were of no avail: on the very day – 29 April – that she arrived in Bath, he and his army reached Cirencester. Hearing of this she withdrew to Bristol, whence she advanced up the Severn valley, Edward following her on a parallel course through the Cotswolds. On 3 May, after an all-night march, she reached Gloucester, only to find its gates – and the Severn bridge behind them – firmly closed against her. Her troops, now scarcely able to drag one foot in front of the other – they had marched with full equipment nearly fifty miles in thirty-six hours, across difficult country, in unseasonably hot weather and with little water – were obliged to struggle on for another ten miles to Tewkesbury, where a shallow ford would enable them to cross the river.

Unfortunately for them, however, they were never able to make use of it. Arriving in the late afternoon, they and their horses were utterly exhausted. They could think of nothing but a few hours' rest; and the next morning, Saturday 4 May, Edward was upon them.

It was a hard-fought fight. The Yorkists had the advantage of vastly superior fire-power, from their archers and hand-gunners alike, and their adversaries soon found themselves cowering under a deluge of arrows and shot. Somerset, who was in command, had no choice but to go over to the offensive and launched a sweeping attack on Edward's left flank. Thanks to the wooded terrain with its hedges and sunken lanes, he was able to take the Yorkists momentarily by surprise; but Richard of Gloucester, commanding the vanguard, sped to his brother's aid. Just as they were beginning to drive back the attackers they were joined by a mobile column of 200 men-at-arms, who had been ordered off by Edward before the battle to guard against possible ambush in a wood. Swooping down from the higher ground, they made short work of the retreating Lancastrians. Young Prince Edward, who had been put in nominal command of the 'middle ward' of the army and had in consequence not been involved in the flanking attack, did his utmost to encourage his men to stay and fight; but they had seen the fate of their companions, and soon they too took to their heels.

The carnage at Tewkesbury was enough to earn the battlefield the name of Bloody Meadow – a name still locally current today; but it was nothing compared to the massacre that followed. Edward's men took no prisoners. Those of the defeated Lancastrians who failed to make their escape from the field were cut down where they stood;

others sought sanctuary in the great abbey that still dominates the town, but the Yorkists smashed down the doors and slaughtered every one of them, shedding so much blood that the building had to be closed for a month before it could be reconsecrated.[1] Somerset and several of his colleagues who, like him, had betrayed Edward not once but twice, were beheaded; those leaders who had never wavered from the Lancastrian cause were spared and pardoned.

The fate of Edward, Prince of Wales, is uncertain. According to most accounts he was killed in the battle; Hall, however, claims that he was taken prisoner by the King's former tutor Richard Croft, who delivered him up to the King as the result of a proclamation to the effect that anyone doing so would be rewarded with an annuity of £100, the Prince's life being guaranteed. He was brought before Edward, who asked him 'how he durst so presumptuously enter his realm with banner displayed?' The boy replied, 'To recover my father's kingdom', whereupon the King struck him with his gauntlet and Clarence, Gloucester, Dorset and Hastings, who were standing by, ran him through with their swords. He was seventeen years old.

His mother, Queen Margaret, had not been present at the battle. She had retired with her ladies to a 'poor religious place' on the Worcester road, and was still there three days later when she was taken prisoner. Brought before the King at Coventry, she was carried on to London, where on Tuesday 21 May, as part of Edward's triumphal entry into the city, she was paraded through the streets before her grimly smiling rival Elizabeth. For the next four years she was under what might be called house arrest, living in adequate style but constantly transferred from place to place. In 1475 Louis XI succeeded in ransoming her for 50,000 gold crowns and a renunciation of all rights to the English throne.

And what, finally, of King Henry himself? On the night of that same 21 May, he died in the Tower. Once again, the circumstances of his death are unclear. According to the subsequent proclamation, it was the result of 'pure displeasure and melancholy'; but both in England

1. Tewkesbury Abbey contains another curious relic of the battle: the door of the sacristy, which is actually the westernmost of the chevet chapels on the south side, is covered on its inner face with metal plates made from the armour worn by soldiers who were killed on the field. And immediately behind the high altar, an iron grating in the floor marks the vault in which the Duke of Clarence was buried after his murder seven years later.

and abroad it was an open secret that he had been murdered, almost certainly by Richard of Gloucester. The most circumstantial contemporary account (by John Warkworth, Master of Peterhouse, Cambridge, writing some twelve years later) reports that he

was put to death the 21st day of May on a Tuesday night betwixt xi and xii of the clock, being then at the Tower the Duke of Gloucester, brother to King Edward, and many other; and on the morrow he was chested[1] and brought to St Paul's and his face was open that every man might see him. And in his lying he bled on the pavement there; and afterwards at the Black Friars was brought, and there he bled new and fresh; and from thence he was carried to Chertsey Abbey in a boat and buried there in Our Lady's Chapel.

According to tradition, Henry was murdered in the Octagon Chamber on the first floor of the Wakefield Tower. His death seems to have been a violent one: when his coffin was opened in 1910, the skull was found to be 'much broken'.

Though widely hailed as a saint and martyr — and despite repeated overtures by Henry VII to Pope Julius II in Rome — Henry VI never received formal canonization. Nor, one suspects, did he deserve it. True, he was genuinely pious, unswervingly faithful to his wife, tender and solicitous to his family; but so are many men. Saints should be made of sterner stuff. In temporal rulers, too, there is no place for the innocence, unworldliness and humility that constituted so great a part of Henry's character. But for the accident of his birth, he would have led a quiet, uneventful life of scholarship and devotion; as King, he was a disaster — swayed by every breeze, puppet of every faction, totally unable to control or direct his kingdom as it drifted further and further into chaos. Having succeeded to the throne at the age of only nine months, he reigned for nearly fifty years — perhaps the saddest half-century in English history. His death, doubtless, was horrible; but it came not a moment too soon.

1. i.e. put in a coffin.

16

King Henry VI Part III

[1455–1475]

> Gives not the hawthorn bush a sweeter shade
> To shepherds looking on their silly sheep,
> Than doth a rich embroider'd canopy
> To kings that fear their subjects' treachery?

KING HENRY VI PART III

Nowhere is Shakespeare's extraordinary ability to turn a chronicle into a drama more impressively demonstrated than in the third part of *King Henry VI*. Its two predecessors both contain scenes of battle – in *Part I*, indeed, the fighting in France is portrayed with vigour and considerable brio – but it is only in the last play of the trilogy that the author is called upon to encapsulate in little more than two hours what is virtually the entire course of the Wars of the Roses, from the aftermath of the first battle of St Albans in 1455 to the defeat of Queen Margaret at Tewkesbury sixteen years later. Now at last, with all the inevitability of Greek tragedy, the House of Lancaster suffers retribution for the atrocity committed at the end of the previous century: the deposition and murder of Richard II and the usurpation of his crown by Henry IV are finally avenged. And the consequences of the outrage are visited not just on Henry and his successors but on the country as a whole: England loses France, is burdened with a detested French queen, and rapidly descends into anarchy. After Tewkesbury, however, it seems that Henry's crimes have been finally expiated. It will be another fourteen years before the sun of York suffers its final eclipse, but already the last of the Lancastrians, John of Gaunt's great-great-grandson Henry of Richmond, has made his appearance on the stage. He is described in the *dramatis personae* quite simply as 'a youth'; but it was he, as Shakespeare's audiences well knew, who was to inaugurate the great dynasty of the Tudors and, with it, well over a century of prosperity and peace.

Whatever those audiences might have felt, however, the opening of the play is not such as to fill the historian with confidence. 'I wonder how the King escap'd our hands!' says Warwick, after the first battle of St Albans. The short answer is that he did not escape: as we have seen, he and the Queen remained in the town for the night, and Warwick himself, with Salisbury and Gloucester, most deferentially escorted them back to London the following day. Within the first ten lines, too, Shakespeare has changed his own story: he allows York to report that his old enemy Clifford was 'by the swords of common soldiers slain', whereas at the end of *Part II* Clifford is killed by York himself.[1] Finally, he perpetuates the solecism of the earlier play in the matter of Prince Richard's age – to have 'best deserv'd of all [York's] sons' is a remarkable tribute to a two-year-old – but this is of course deliberate: now more than ever, historical time must be telescoped if it is to fit the two-hour traffic of the Shakespearean stage.

So drastic is this telescoping that, the play having begun in May 1455, by line 35 of the first scene we find ourselves already in October 1460 when York, having recently returned from Ireland, makes his first open claim to the crown, laying his hand on the cushion of the throne in Westminster Hall. It need hardly be said that the appearance of King Henry at this point is an invention. (Even had it not been, the King is unlikely to have said that he was crowned at the age of nine months; although this was indeed his age at his accession he received his first coronation, in London, shortly before his eighth birthday.) His presence, however – together with that of Queen Margaret, who enters a few minutes later with the seven-year-old Prince of Wales – allows a brilliant dramatization of the Act of Accord[2] and the Queen's furious protest at her son's disinheritance.[3]

Two months pass. Scene ii is set at York's castle of Sandal in Yorkshire, where he, with his eldest and youngest sons Edward and

---

1. See Chapter 14, p. 280. But Shakespeare soon returns to his earlier version: in *Part III*, I.i.166, young Clifford is made to refer to York as 'him that slew my father'.

2. See Chapter 15, pp. 284–5.

3. 'The feare yᵗ thei had of the quene, whose countenance was so fearfull, and whose looke was so terrible, that to al men . . . her frounyng was theyr vndoyng, & her indignation was their death' (*Hall*, 241).

Richard,[1] are about to engage Northumberland and the Lancastrians of the north. With them is John Nevill, Marquis of Montagu, who had in fact remained in London and who is unaccountably addressed by York throughout the scene as his brother – although he was in fact only his nephew by marriage. The likeliest explanation here is that Shakespeare substituted Montagu at the last moment for his father the Earl of Salisbury, who was certainly at Sandal but whom – since he was to be executed immediately after the coming battle – he had decided to leave out of the play altogether. The scene begins with a chilling conversation in which Richard (who in 1460 was still only eight years old) reveals his precociously Machiavellian nature by encouraging his father to seize the throne, on the grounds that the oath he has recently sworn to allow King Henry to reign in peace is technically invalid. A messenger then arrives to announce that Queen Margaret has arrived, with the northern lords and an army of 20,000, and is about to besiege the castle.

The last two scenes of Act I are given over to the battle of Wakefield. Like all Shakespeare's battles it is inevitably impressionistic, consisting as it does of two main episodes: first, the vengeful killing by young Clifford of York's second son, the seventeen-year-old Earl of Rutland ('Thy father slew my father; therefore die'); second, the capture and death of York himself, stabbed first by Clifford and then by the Queen in person. Shakespeare, of course, knew as well as we do that Margaret was not at Wakefield at all; at the time of the encounter she was still in Scotland, whence she was to join the triumphant Lancastrians at York only some three weeks later. Once again, however, her sudden appearance, her savage mockery of her captive (made to stand on a molehill with the paper crown on his head) and, worst of all, that terrible moment when she herself drives her dagger into York's heart – all this adds immeasurably to the drama, as well as casting a new and hideous light on her character.

The first scene of Act II – the opening line of which is curiously similar to that of Act I – is a masterpiece of concision, covering as it does two

---

1. Neither Prince was in fact with him. Edward was away in Wales, while the eight-year-old Richard was with his elder brother George, staying at Fastolf Place, the vast mansion built by the late Sir John Fastolf in Southwark, across the river from the Tower.

major battles, both fought within two weeks of each other in February 1461. The victory of York's son Edward – formerly Earl of March, now himself Duke of York – at Mortimer's Cross is briefly represented by the miraculous appearance, to him and his brother Richard (who with his other surviving brother George was actually in the Low Countries at the time) of three suns simultaneously in the sky; while the second battle of St Albans, in which the Lancastrians had their revenge, is reported by Warwick – who had joined the two princes after this last encounter – in a single speech (II.i.120ff). At this point, as we know, Edward and Warwick marched on London, where Edward claimed the throne before heading northwards to meet the Lancastrians, returning to the capital in May for his coronation the following month; but Shakespeare very sensibly streamlines the action by sending him off immediately after St Albans, telescoping the two London visits into one and bringing Edward to London only after the victory of Towton. This allows him to build up an impressive – if entirely unhistorical – confrontation scene at York between Edward, his two brothers (who were in fact still in Holland) and Warwick on the one hand and King Henry, Queen Margaret and the Lancastrians on the other. It is followed by the battle itself, which he somewhat uncharacteristically spreads over all four of the remaining scenes of the act.

The one glaring historical inaccuracy in Shakespeare's version of the battle of Towton is the continued presence of Edward's brothers George and Richard, who were actually brought back from Holland only in time for his coronation the following June. The first scene of the fight – in fact scene iii – opens with Warwick exhausted, Edward and George in despair. Then Richard arrives to report the death of Warwick's 'brother' – in fact his illegitimate half-brother, designated by Hall 'the bastard of Salisbury'. The news rouses Warwick to fury, filling him with a desire for revenge which enables him to breathe new spirit into the rest. Next, in the extremely short (and obviously invented) scene iv, we see Richard attacking Clifford as the man who has killed both his brother Rutland and his father Richard of York; Clifford, initially fearless, flees with the arrival of Warwick.

Scene v – which is equally imaginary and which, it has been pointed out, might have been taken from a medieval morality play – now introduces a completely different mood. Here we are at the still centre of the hurricane with King Henry, seated on a molehill – ironically enough, identical to that on which York had been mocked at Wakefield – reflecting first on the ever-changing fortunes of war and then on the miserable lives of monarchs when compared to those of the meanest of their subjects. He is joined by two symbolic figures, both illustrative of the horrors of civil war: 'a Son that hath kill'd his Father' and 'a Father that hath kill'd his Son'. He gives them his sympathy but insists – with rare insensitivity in the circumstances – that he is ten times unhappier than either of them. He is finally roused out of his self-pity by the arrival of his wife and son with the Duke of Exeter, who urge him to flee with them – for 'Warwick rages like a chafed bull'.

The last scene of the act introduces the dying Clifford, seen for the first time in the play as noble rather than vindictive, lamenting the overthrow of his beloved House of Lancaster more than his own imminent death. The three young princes come upon him as he expires, and agree that his head must now replace their father's on the battlements of York. (Hall records that the replacement heads were those of 'the erle of Devonshyre and iii. other'.) The scene ends with the victorious princes leaving for London and Edward's coronation, after which Warwick announces his intention of going to France to seek the hand of Bona of Savoy on behalf of the new King. Edward promises to give his brothers the dukedoms of Clarence and Gloucester, rejecting Richard's claim that 'Gloucester's dukedom is too ominous' – a reference, presumably, to the fate of his predecessor Duke Humphrey – and his request for that of Clarence instead.

And so to Act III, which opens with another imaginary scene in which Henry VI, wandering the countryside in disguise after the battle of Hexham, is finally recognized and arrested. For Shakespeare, this occurs not at Waddington Hall but in 'a chase in the north of England'. It hardly matters: his purpose is simply to provide another of those scenes of quietness – one might almost say religious quietism – during which the deposed King can reflect upon his fate. After just a hundred lines we are transported to London. Edward, now crowned and a dramatically different character from his predecessor on the throne, is obsessed by Elizabeth Grey (née Woodville) whom he is determined to take to his bed. She for her part holds out for marriage – Shakespeare has clearly read his Mancini[1] – to which he eventually agrees. The stage

1. See Chapter 15, p. 291n.

is then left empty but for Richard of Gloucester, who in a long and magnificent soliloquy makes his first clear declaration of his ambitions:

> I'll play the orator as well as Nestor,
> Deceive more slily than Ulysses could,
> And, like a Sinon, take another Troy.
> I can add colours to the chameleon,
> Change shapes with Proteus for advantages,
> And set the murderous Machiavel to school.
> Can I do this, and cannot get a crown?
> Tut! Were it further off, I'll pluck it down.

Scene iii brings us to the French court. Queen Margaret, still determined on revenge, has taken refuge with Louis XI, from whom she is seeking military assistance. Warwick, all unaware of recent developments, arrives to negotiate on behalf of his master for Princess Bona, whose hand Louis immediately grants – though not without another outburst of anger from Margaret, who bitterly accuses them both of disloyalty to her husband. At this point a messenger arrives from London with letters informing all three of them of Edward's marriage to Elizabeth Grey; and in a moment the entire situation is changed. Warwick instantly transfers his loyalties to Henry VI; the Queen is triumphant at this new proof of Edward's duplicity; and Louis hesitates no longer in promising her the aid she seeks. To seal the new alliance, Warwick and Margaret agree that his daughter shall forthwith be married to her son, Edward Prince of Wales.

Once again, history has been drastically compressed: the events related in this single scene cover some nine years. Warwick did indeed go to France to sue on Edward's behalf for the hand of Bona; but that was in 1461, three years before the King's marriage. The visit from which he returned in rebellion was in 1470, five years after it. It was in the later year, too, that Warwick's younger daughter, Anne (not the 'eldest', as the play has it), was betrothed to the young Prince – his elder, Isabel, having already been given to Clarence in 1469. In spite of everything, however, the diplomatic consequences of Edward's ill-advised marriage are admirably illustrated. Once again one is left with the conviction that, whatever liberties Shakespeare might take with strict historical truth, in the essentials he was almost invariably right. For the non-scholar, seeking merely an overall view of Plantagenet history, there are many worse guides to follow.

One of the inevitable consequences of Shakespeare's telescoping of time is that we are occasionally obliged to put back the clock; the opening of Act IV, in which King Edward asks his brothers their opinion of his 'new marriage', can be dated no later than 1464. Basically, its purpose is to emphasize the almost universal unpopularity of Edward's action. First the brothers themselves leave him in no doubt of their own feelings: they complain, in particular, about the heedless way in which he is marrying off all his new Woodville relations. Then, most conveniently, a messenger arrives from France to report the fury of King Louis, of the wronged and humiliated Bona and, as always, of Queen Margaret, who is 'ready to put armour on'. She has also, he continues, made up her differences with Warwick, whose daughter is to marry the young Prince of Wales. (Shakespeare's confusion between the Earl's two daughters is once again in evidence, expressed this time by Clarence.) At the end of the scene, as a result of the quarrel, Clarence and Somerset[1] leave to join Warwick; Richard of Gloucester, Hastings and Montagu assure the King of their support.

The next scene brings us forward again to 1469. Warwick has landed in Kent with his 'articles of petition' and has hurried north-westwards in the hopes of meeting up with the rebel Robin of Redesdale in the north. (The stage directions tell us that he is accompanied by French soldiers, but this is incorrect: King Louis's men did not in fact appear on the field until the battle of Tewkesbury, still two years in the future.) In Warwickshire he is joined by Clarence and Somerset and suspiciously inquires whose side they are on; reassured, he reiterates his promise that Clarence shall have his daughter to wife. Here again, however, Shakespeare errs: both enquiry and promise would have been unnecessary, since Clarence had already married Isabel Nevill a week or so before. Scene iii then follows straight on its predecessor, with what is

1. Three Dukes of Somerset were killed during the Wars of the Roses. Edmund Beaufort, second Duke, was killed at the first battle of St Albans; Henry, third Duke, at first a loyal Lancastrian, went over to Edward in 1462 but soon returned to his old allegiance and was executed by the Yorkists after the battle of Hexham in 1464; his brother Edmund, fourth Duke, who remained firmly Lancastrian, was also executed, two days after Tewkesbury. The present Somerset is a compound of the second two.

presumably the field of Edgecote in which, contrary to what we see on the stage, neither King Edward nor Warwick took part. Edward was indeed captured soon after the battle, but by the king-maker's brother, the Archbishop of York.

At this point we realize that Shakespeare has been telescoping again, and that King Edward's two successive defeats – the first his captivity after Edgecote, the second his flight to Holland fifteen months later – have been deliberately run into one. In scene iv Queen Elizabeth first tells Lord Rivers that her husband has been captured and is in the hands of the Archbishop; immediately afterwards, she tells him of her pregnancy and her determination to seek sanctuary. We can thus date the first half of this extremely short scene to July 1469, the second half to October 1470. This contrivance certainly streamlines the action, but it also raises new problems for the author: if Edward is a prisoner in England, how can he land from abroad with an army? Shakespeare's solution is to invent a totally fictitious rescue of the King by Richard of Gloucester and others, after which he takes refuge in Flanders. This enables Warwick to release Henry VI from the Tower and reinstate him on the throne – which did indeed occur when Edward was away in the Low Countries – and Edward to disembark at Ravenscar for the last triumphant chapter of his long battle against the Lancastrians.

And so, in scene vii, we find him with his small army before the walls of York. At first he demands his dukedom only; but when Sir John Montgomery threatens to leave him unless he proclaims himself King, he agrees to do so. (Historically, he delayed this proclamation until he reached Nottingham.) He then heads south, and the last scene of the act finds him entering the Bishop's palace in London. Before his arrival Warwick, Clarence and other lords are discussing their resistance with King Henry: each will go to his own particular territory to rally what troops he can, and they will all meet Warwick at Coventry. Edward then appears, with Richard of Gloucester, and summarily returns Henry to the Tower. Then he and his men themselves set off for Coventry, for what they hope and believe will be the final reckoning.

There was, as it turned out, no fighting at Coventry, and the confrontation in V.i at the walls of the city, in the course of which Edward challenges Warwick to come out and fight and Warwick refuses ('Alas, I am not coop'd here for defence!'), in fact occurred on 29 March, a fortnight before Edward's arrival in London. Shakespeare is right, on the other hand, in making Coventry the scene of Clarence's second betrayal – of Warwick this time – and of his return to his brother's allegiance; we learn from Polydore Vergil that he had first prevented Warwick from fighting by urging him to await his coming, and then on his arrival ordered the 4,000 men whom he had levied in the cause of Henry VI to espouse the Yorkist cause instead. When he and Edward met, the two brothers had 'right kind and loving language', swearing 'perfect accord for ever hereafter'. They were to fight side by side both at Barnet and at Tewkesbury.

The story of Barnet is quickly told. We hear nothing of the fighting, nor of the fog that shrouded the field and was as much a feature of the battle as the cold had been at Towton, almost exactly ten years before. For Shakespeare – and perhaps for us too – all that really matters is the death of Warwick, who lives just long enough to hear of the fate of his brother Montagu, and whose last words suggest a certainty of his own salvation that cannot have been shared by many of his hearers. A brief scene iii establishes that victory has been won, announces the landing of Margaret and her son and prepares us for Tewkesbury. Hall's account of the three weeks that followed stresses the Queen's despondency; and indeed she had good reason for gloom. But for the bad weather that had delayed her for three weeks in Normandy she would have been able to join Warwick before Barnet, and the result of that battle might have been very different. The news that her most powerful ally was dead had very nearly sent her straight back to France. Only the assurances of Somerset that Edward too had sustained heavy losses and that feeling in England was still overwhelmingly Lancastrian had persuaded her to stay, but they had not improved her spirits.

Shakespeare, on the other hand, stresses her courage. Addressing her son, Somerset, Oxford and her soldiers on 'the plains near Tewkesbury', she makes no attempt to conceal the gravity of the situation, but bids them take heart none the less; there can be no going back now:

> Great lords, wise men ne'er sit and wail their loss,
> But cheerly seek how to redress their harms.[1]

---

1. Compare *Richard III*, III.ii:
> My lord, wise men ne'er sit and wail their woes,
> But presently prevent the ways to wail.

What though the mast be now blown overboard,
The cable broke, the holding anchor lost,
And half our sailors swallow'd in the flood;
Yet lives our pilot still . . .

The young Prince of Wales follows in similar vein, inviting – like his grandfather before Agincourt – all those who have no stomach for the coming fight to depart,

Lest in our need he might infect another
And make him of like spirit to himself.

So begins the penultimate battle of the long and tragic civil war. Scene v represents its end: Margaret, Somerset and Oxford have all been captured. The two last are sentenced to execution and go bravely to their fate; Margaret's life is of course spared, but she is obliged to stand by while her son is murdered before her eyes, stabbed by Edward, Clarence and Gloucester in turn. At this point the dramatist in Shakespeare has once again taken over from the historian. He has chosen, quite legitimately, the alternative – and far more dramatic – version of the Prince's death as reported by Hall,[1] and has then subtly improved it. In Hall's account the King does no more than strike the boy with his gauntlet, while Dorset and Hastings use their daggers. Nor is it anywhere suggested that Queen Margaret was present, either during the battle or afterwards – still less that Gloucester was about to kill her too, but was restrained at the last moment by the King.

Edward was now supreme. The House of Lancaster was effectively destroyed, and would never again imperil his throne. True, one or two Lancastrian lords, Oxford in particular and his friend Lord Beaumont, would continue to amuse themselves with isolated raids and short bursts of irregular warfare – in September 1473 the two of them would actually seize St Michael's Mount in Cornwall and hold it for several months – but they scarcely affected the security of the realm. A more serious danger in the long term might be the fourteen-year-old Henry of Richmond, who soon after Tewkesbury would sail with his uncle Jasper Tudor to France. But heavy storms in the Channel would oblige them

1. See Chapter 15, p. 303.

to put in at one of the Breton ports; and Duke Francis of Brittany, fully aware of Henry's potential importance, would keep him under close watch.

There remained the sad, defeated Henry VI – by now more an inconvenience than a threat, but still theoretically a rival to the throne. Whether the King himself would ever have ordered his elimination is arguable: Henry was widely seen to be a saint, and to Edward his murder would certainly have had overtones of sacrilege. His brother Richard, however, had no such qualms. We may perhaps doubt whether he left Tewkesbury quite as precipitately as Shakespeare suggests, 'to make a bloody supper in the Tower'; but the events represented in scene vi are, so far as we can tell, substantially true. One would love to think that the doomed King showed as much spirit at his end as his last great vituperative speech suggests; alas, it seems unlikely.

It remains only for Shakespeare to draw the various threads together and to provide a suitable closing scene. Edward refers in generous terms to the slaughtered enemies through whose blood he has 'repurchas'd' the throne, discreetly refraining to mention that several of them were not killed in battle but executed by the Yorkists afterwards; he then turns affectionately to his son – the future Edward V:

> Young Ned, for thee thine uncles and myself
> Have in our armours watch'd the winter's night,
> Went all afoot in summer's scalding heat,
> That thou might'st repossess the crown in peace;
> And of our labours thou shalt reap the gain.

The irony would not have been lost on Shakespeare's audiences, even without Richard's two asides – in the second of which he cheerfully compares himself with Judas Iscariot. One tends to forget that at the time of King Henry's death the Duke of Gloucester was just eighteen years old.

A few lines before the end of this short scene we learn of the ransoming of Queen Margaret by her father and her return to France. This, as we have seen, did not actually occur until four years later, in 1475 – but where otherwise could it be reported? It forms, in any case, little more than a parenthesis. The true subject of the scene – even though it is covered in only nine lines – is Richard's villainy and duplicity:

> And, that I love the tree from whence thou sprang'st,
> Witness the loving kiss I give the fruit.
> [*Aside*] To say the truth, so Judas kiss'd his master
> And cried 'All hail!' when as he meant all harm.

It was this, above all else, that the Elizabethan audiences would carry home with them; it was to emphasize this that Shakespeare had been deliberately building up the character of Richard; and this that he was to make the theme of the last and greatest play of his series.

But to what extent was it justified historically? Was Richard really the ogre that we see before us on the stage? These questions have been asked for over four centuries, and are still being discussed today. The next two chapters of this book will attempt to answer them.

17

King Edward V

[1471–1483]

RICHARD. Sweet Prince, the untainted virtue of your years
          Hath not yet div'd into the world's deceit,
          Nor more can you distinguish of a man
          Than of his outward show, which – God He knows –
          Seldom or never jumpeth with the heart:
          Those uncles which you want were dangerous;
          Your Grace attended to their sugar'd words,
          But look'd not on the poison of their hearts.
          God keep you from them, and from such false friends!

PRINCE. God keep me from false friends – but they were none.

KING RICHARD III

For the twelve years between the battle of Tewkesbury on Saturday 4 May 1471 and his death on Wednesday 9 April 1483, King Edward IV ruled England wisely and well, while a prolonged period of internal peace allowed the country time to recover, at least in part, from its sufferings. True, in the summer of 1475 the King led an expeditionary force into France, terrifying Louis XI to the point where, according to the Milanese ambassador, 'he almost lost his wits'; but before a shot was fired Louis invited the entire English army to a three-day feast at Amiens, by the end of which the English soldiers were far too drunk to fight. He then met Edward at the nearby town of Picquigny, where the two Kings quickly reached agreement. In return for a down payment of 75,000 crowns and further annual payments of 50,000, Edward undertook peaceably to leave French soil – and, incidentally, negotiated the ransom of Margaret of Anjou.

At home, such dissension as we know of seems to have been largely confined to the royal princes, Clarence and Gloucester. The two brothers – now by far the most powerful magnates in the realm after the King himself – had much in common. In the first twenty years of their lives they had known nothing but war. Both had experienced victory and defeat, exile and betrayal; both had killed many men with their own hands, in hot blood and in cold; both, despite their high intelligence, were greedy and ambitious, utterly self-centred and devoid of principle. In other respects, however, they were very different. Clarence shared the magnificent physique and outstanding good looks, as well as the easy charm and eloquence, of his brother Edward. Gloucester, for his part, could never have been the hunchback that Shakespeare suggests; nor, given his undoubted prowess on the battle-field, could he have had a left arm withered 'like a blasted sapling'. But contemporary chroniclers are all agreed that he was unusually small and at least slightly deformed, with his right shoulder higher than his left; and the incident during the meeting of 13 June 1483 reported by Sir Thomas More[1] indicates that the left arm must certainly have been damaged in some degree. As to his looks, Polydore Vergil describes him as having 'a short and sour countenance' – though he too could be dangerously charming when he wished to be. Between such men it does not take much to start a quarrel; and by the end of 1471 they were at each other's throats – over what was, by any standards, a very major issue indeed: the enormous fortune of Warwick the King-maker.

Warwick, dying on the field of Barnet, had left two children, both daughters. Isabel, the elder, was the wife of Clarence; Anne, three years younger, had been betrothed to Edward, Prince of Wales, but he had been killed at Tewkesbury before they could be married. Though some of the vast estates were still technically the property of Warwick's widow – who had taken sanctuary at Beaulieu Abbey in Hampshire – Clarence expected eventually to inherit them all; Richard now decided to dispute this inheritance by marrying the sixteen-year-old Anne, who had been captured with her mother-in-law Margaret of Anjou after Tewkesbury. On hearing of his brother's intentions the furious Clarence determined to prevent him, taking possession of his sister-in-law and concealing her, disguised as a kitchen-maid, in the house of one of his retainers; but Richard found her, seized her back and removed her to sanctuary in the church of St Martin-le-Grand, where she was forced

1. See below, pp. 329–30.

to stay for several months. The two married in February or March 1472 – without the papal dispensation necessary for a marriage between cousins – after which Richard took his bride off to his favourite northern residence: Middleham in Yorkshire, one of the several castles formerly belonging to Warwick which the King had made over to him in the summer of 1471.

The quarrel rumbled on for three years until, in February 1475, a settlement was finally agreed. Even then, however, Clarence continued to sulk, believing – with some justification – that the King trusted him less than he did his brother; and towards the end of the following year he was given still greater cause for resentment. On 21 December his wife died of complications after childbirth, and the death of Charles the Bold of Burgundy a fortnight later led his widow to propose a marriage between Clarence and her daughter Mary, now mistress of all her father's dominions. The Duke was naturally enthusiastic, but King Edward would not hear of it. Such a marriage would not only have made his brother at least as rich and powerful as he was himself; it would also have caused serious difficulties in his relations with France. He absolutely forbade any further discussion of the matter – thereby antagonizing the Duke still further.

Clarence had always been unstable; henceforth his behaviour became distinctly paranoid. He began suggesting that Edward was illegitimate; in East Anglia, he deliberately incited riots against him. Next he put it about that his late wife had been bewitched by Queen Elizabeth and then poisoned, and actually had one of her former waiting-women – who was by then in the Queen's service – arrested, beaten, robbed of her jewellery and put on trial at Warwick, where he personally bullied the jury into finding her guilty and had her hanged within twenty-four hours. Clearly such conduct could not be allowed to continue, and Edward struck back hard. His first step was to arrest a celebrated astrologer and friend of Clarence's, a certain Dr John Stacey of Merton College, Oxford. Under torture, Stacey confessed that he had cast horoscopes of the King and the Prince of Wales to discover when they would die, and further implicated one Thomas Burdett, a member of the Duke's household. Both men were put on trial, and despite their pleas of not guilty were hanged at Tyburn on 20 May 1477. There could hardly have been a clearer warning, but Clarence ignored it. On the following day he forced his way into a meeting of the Privy Council accompanied by a Franciscan friar, whom he obliged there and then to testify to the two men's dying protestations of innocence. Edward had had enough. By the end of June his impossible brother was in the Tower.

The trial was held in January 1478 at Westminster. The Duke of Clarence was found guilty of what the King described as a 'more malicious, more unnatural and loathly treason than was ever before committed', and was condemned to death. His mother having begged that he be spared the horrors of a public execution, on 18 February he was put to death in the Tower – almost certainly by being drowned in a butt of malmsey wine.[1] He was buried next to his wife – ironically enough, in Tewkesbury Abbey. He was twenty-eight. Edward, we are told, ever afterwards regretted his brother's death and bitterly reproached himself for having allowed it; but Clarence had tried him sorely and had pushed his patience just a little too far.

Richard of Gloucester's feelings on the execution of his brother are uncertain. He certainly made a fine show of grief, but Sir Thomas More is not the only writer to suggest that his brother's death was not altogether unwelcome to him; and if indeed he ever personally interceded with the King on Clarence's behalf, his pleas have not been recorded. In his position he could hardly remain aloof; but as with the Picquigny agreement of 1475 – of which he had strongly disapproved – he tried to dissociate himself as much as possible. This was made easier by the fact that he was now spending nearly all his time in the north, which was still overwhelmingly Lancastrian – with concurrent and occasionally conflicting loyalties towards the Percys and the Nevills – and where Edward was determined to make him the effective successor to Warwick. It was to this end that Richard had been granted Warwick's castles of Middleham and Sheriff Hutton in Yorkshire and of Penrith in Cumberland, together with all their lands. He also owned the castles of Pontefract, Barnard Castle and Skipton-in-Craven, to say nothing of Sudeley Castle in Gloucestershire and his vast estates across the south.

1. The old story sounds improbable enough, but is confirmed by no less than three contemporary writers. (Except that Mancini reports that the wine was 'sweet Falernian'.) According to Philippe de Commynes, Clarence's daughter for ever afterwards wore a little wine-cask on her bracelet in memory of her father.

By 1482 he was probably the richest and most powerful magnate in English history, excepting only the monarchs themselves. And even this was not all; for when in June 1482, in his military capacity as Lieutenant-General of the North, he led some 20,000 men across the border into Scotland and briefly occupied Edinburgh without firing a shot, he also became – in the eyes of most Englishmen – a national hero.

His brother the King, meanwhile, was in sad decline. War had kept him in superb condition; with peace he had grown self-indulgent. Always strongly sexed – and despite the considerable charms of his mistress, Jane Shore, whom he had first taken to his bed as early as 1470 – he had now also become a compulsive womanizer. 'Married and unmarried,' writes Mancini, 'noblewomen and wenches, he made no distinction.' He drew the line only at rape: Edward 'made all his conquests through money and promises, and having had his way with them bade them farewell.' Had fornication been his only vice, it might have done him little enough physical harm; but he was also an equally compulsive glutton. As a result, the man who was once the handsomest prince in Europe had by the age of forty become immensely fat and prematurely aged by drink and debauch. The end came at Easter, 1483. Already on Good Friday he had suffered an agonizing fit of indigestion brought on, we are told, by a surfeit of fruit and vegetables; a day or two later, during an afternoon's fishing expedition on the river, he caught a chill which was followed soon afterwards by what seems to have been a stroke. He died on 9 April, less than three weeks before his forty-first birthday.

Edward's eldest son by Elizabeth Woodville – the new King Edward V – was now twelve. Eight years before, during his father's absence on the French expedition, the Woodvilles had ruled England; and they had every intention, during the young King's minority, of doing so again. Their leader Lord Rivers, the Queen's brother, was already his official Governor, while her eldest son by Sir John Grey, now Marquess of Dorset, was in charge of the Royal Treasury. The Lord Chamberlain, Lord Hastings, pointed out that the late King had insisted in his will that Gloucester should be made Protector; the Woodvilles merely replied that final authority must lie with the Council – on which, it need hardly be said, they enjoyed a comfortable majority.

But they had underestimated their adversary. Richard had plans of his own, and they did not include the Woodvilles. His principal ally was to be Henry Stafford, Duke of Buckingham. A nephew of the third and fourth Dukes of Somerset who had been executed within seven years of each other, Buckingham was not only a Beaufort: he was also handsome, rich and highly intelligent. No wonder Edward IV had mistrusted him. Moreover, having been forcibly – and disastrously – married to one of the Queen's innumerable sisters at the age of eleven, he detested the whole Woodville clan and was prepared to go to almost any lengths to destroy them. He and Richard now set about the systematic suborning of all members of the 'old nobility' and their adherents, alerting them to the threat of a complete Woodville takeover and deliberately spreading rumours, true and false, of the family's iniquities. Meanwhile Richard wrote to the Council in the most cordial and respectful terms, stressing his absolute loyalty to the new King but reminding them also of the terms of his brother's will and of his own just claim to a place in any future government. This letter he took care to have circulated as widely as possible throughout the kingdom, and since he was at this time at the peak of his popularity – his Scottish exploit in the previous year had not been forgotten – it had its effect.

With public opinion on his side, action could no longer be delayed. The coronation had already been fixed for Sunday 4 May. Once Edward V were crowned, the Woodvilles could claim that no Protectorate was necessary, since – as had happened after the crowning of Henry VI – the Protector's powers would automatically devolve on the Council. The ceremony must clearly be prevented at all costs. Fortunately for Richard, Edward was at Ludlow, a good week's journey from London; and more fortunately still the boy's uncle, Lord Rivers, who was to escort him to the capital, had decided to celebrate St George's Day before their departure. This meant that they could not leave Ludlow till 24 April; the Duke of Gloucester had plenty of time to make his plans. He wrote to Edward saying that he and Buckingham would naturally wish to accompany him on his formal entry into London, and would therefore meet him at Northampton to continue the journey together.

When the two Dukes reached Northampton on the 29th, they found that the royal party was already at Stony Stratford, fourteen miles further south; but Rivers and Lord Richard Grey – the Queen's younger son by her first marriage and thus the King's half-brother – immediately rode back to explain that they had gone on only because there was insufficient accommodation in Northampton for both retinues. That evening all four men had a convivial supper together before Rivers and Grey retired to bed in the next-door inn; they awoke early the next morning, however, to discover that all the outer doors were locked and that bands of the Dukes' men were blocking the road to the south. When they had finally freed themselves they sought out Richard and demanded an explanation; he replied by accusing them of turning his nephew against him, and had them both put under arrest. He and Buckingham then hurried to Stony Stratford, took possession of the King and rode back with him to Northampton, where they explained to him that the Woodvilles had deliberately destroyed his father and were determined to destroy him in the same way. Tearfully young Edward tried to defend his mother and her family, but to no avail. The noblemen around him were arrested, the serving men and women dismissed. Rivers himself, with certain of his colleagues, was sent to Richard's castle of Sheriff Hutton; later he was transferred to Pontefract, where he was executed, apparently without trial, on 25 June. He did not deserve his fate. His support for his own family was natural and perfectly legitimate. A man of wide culture, he had travelled extensively in Italy; he was also a writer and poet, several of whose works were to be produced by William Caxton – one of them, his translation of *The Dictes and Sayings of the Philosophers* (from Jean de Téonville's French version of the Latin original) being the first book ever printed in England. At the time of his execution he was found to be wearing a hair shirt next to the skin.

Richard of Gloucester, his nephew Edward V and their entourage reached London on 4 May to find that the news of the *coup* had arrived before them. The Queen, with her nine-year-old son the Duke of York and her five daughters, had already taken sanctuary in the Abbot's Lodgings at Westminster, bringing with her a vast quantity of furniture and all her possessions that could somehow be accommodated. But the ordinary citizens too were growing nervous. The Duke's men seemed to be everywhere – standing in threatening groups at key points in the city, roaming the streets, even patrolling the river in boats. And rumours, as always at such moments, were spreading fast: that Richard was planning to seize the throne, and that he was acting not only against the Woodvilles but against the young King himself.

The Londoners were reassured, first by the universally respected Hastings who told them, in absolute good faith, that they had nothing to fear, and then, a few days later, by Richard himself in the King's ceremonial procession to St Paul's Cathedral. Riding beside the beautiful, fair-headed youth, he would repeatedly bow low to the crowds lining the streets, calling to them as he did so: 'Behold your Prince and Sovereign Lord!' Impressed by the obvious pride that he showed in his nephew, they once more took him to their hearts. At the next meeting of the now seriously depleted Council, the Duke of Gloucester was confirmed as Protector of the Realm and of the King. Meanwhile a new date, 22 June, was fixed for the long-awaited coronation.

It could be claimed, with all the wisdom of hindsight, that Richard gave the first sign of his true intentions when, some ten days after his arrival in the capital, he removed the young King from the palace of the Bishop of London adjoining St Paul's and transferred him to the Tower. As we have seen often enough in this history, the Tower was not, in the fifteenth century, the grim prison of popular imagination; it too was a palace, boasting a fine banqueting hall and several sumptuously furnished apartments in which most of the Plantagenet kings had lodged at one time or another. But it also contained other, less desirable accommodation; and its formidable walls effectively cut it off from the outside world. With Edward safely installed, Richard's next concern was to bring his younger brother to join him. The little Duke of York was, after all, technically heir to the throne: it would be pointless to dispose of one of the two Princes without the other. The difficulty was their mother. The Queen and her family were still in sanctuary at Westminster, and she would not let him out of her sight. It was explained to her that the King was lonely without his brother; that he was calling for him again and again; that it was doing the boy no good to be virtually incarcerated in the Abbey in the exclusive company of 'old and ancient persons'; and that sanctuaries were designed for criminals rather than for princes of the blood. Elizabeth refused to listen. It was only when the Archbishop of Canterbury, the seventy-nine-year-old Cardinal Bourchier, went personally to see her, pointed out that her son would anyway have to be released to attend his brother's coronation and finally suggested that, if she maintained her attitude, he might have to reconsider the question of her own sanctuary, that she yielded at last.

With the two boys now together in the Tower, Richard's position was immeasurably strengthened; but there remained one further potential obstacle to the realization of his plans. The Lord Chamberlain, Lord Hastings, had no particular love for the Woodvilles, but as Edward IV's closest friend he would certainly have been prepared to ally himself with them or anyone else on behalf of the young King. Another friend, Lord Stanley, seems to have warned him of possible danger, but Hastings remained unconcerned; he and Richard, he claimed, had always been on excellent terms. Besides, he was constantly kept informed by one of his most trusted retainers – a certain William Catesby, who enjoyed Richard's confidence – of all the Duke's regular meetings with his associates, and was certain that nothing could be plotted against him without his knowledge. Here, unfortunately, he deceived himself: Catesby was in fact a double agent, who was being paid good money by Richard to keep his master in ignorance until the plot was sprung.

It was Friday 13 June when the Duke of Gloucester summoned a meeting at the Tower to discuss the final details of the coming coronation. By this time he was increasingly reluctant even to sit down with the Woodvilles, and had consequently split the Council into two parts. This particular gathering consisted largely of his own adherents; also present were Hastings and Stanley, together with Thomas Rotherham, Archbishop of York, and John Morton, Bishop of Ely.[1] Richard arrived at about nine in the morning in what appeared to be a genial mood, asking Morton to get him some strawberries from the garden of his palace in Holborn. Soon after the discussion had begun, however, he suddenly left the room, reappearing an hour and a half later frowning and withdrawn. The table fell silent. What did people deserve, he asked very quietly, for having plotted 'the destruction of me, being so near of blood unto the King, and Protector of his royal person and his realm'? Hastings replied at once such men should be punished as traitors. Only then did the Duke identify those to whom he referred: 'yonder sorceress, my brother's wife, and others with her . . . You shall all see,' he continued, 'in what wise that sorceress and that other witch of her counsel, Shore's wife, with their affinity have by their sorcery and

---

1. Morton later became Archbishop of Canterbury and a Cardinal. It was almost certainly his eyewitness account of the meeting which formed the basis for that of Sir Thomas More, the fullest and most circumstantial that we have.

witchcraft wasted my body.' With that he pulled up his left sleeve to show his withered arm.

Had Richard been seriously concerned to prove his sincerity, this would have been a serious mistake: all those present were well aware that his arm had been damaged since his birth. But perhaps he hardly cared. Suddenly he turned on Hastings who, having kept Jane Shore for some years as his mistress, had ill-advisedly attempted to defend her. 'They have so done!' he shouted. 'And that will I make good upon thy body, traitor!' His fist crashed down on the table; outside there were cries of 'Treason!'; and a body of armed men burst into the chamber. One attacked Stanley, who dived under the table, blood streaming down his face. He was arrested, together with Rotherham and Morton. But Richard's eyes were on Hastings, whom he told to find a priest and confess himself at once, 'for by St Paul I will not to dinner till I see thy head off.' The poor man was beheaded within the hour, on Tower Green.[1] As to the other accused, the Queen was still in sanctuary and could not be touched; Jane Shore was arrested and put on trial, first for witchcraft and then – when not a shred of evidence could be found against her – for harlotry, where admittedly she was on somewhat weaker ground. She was condemned, as the Duchess of Gloucester had been condemned forty-two years before,[2] to walk barefoot through the streets of London carrying a lighted taper in her hand; but the punishment seems to have misfired. She looked so beautiful that every male heart in the crowd went out to her; and it was Richard of Gloucester, rather than Jane Shore, whose reputation suffered.

Having dealt to his satisfaction with the Woodvilles and with the two little Princes now firmly in his power, Richard could proceed with the second half of his plan. His first action was once again to postpone his nephew's coronation. The next task – a good deal harder – was to persuade the people that he, Richard of Gloucester, was their rightful King. Since there could be no doubt that Edward V was the legitimate heir of Edward IV, this meant accusing the latter – his own brother – of bastardy, even at the cost of dishonouring their mother, the old

---

1. Hastings was buried in St George's Chapel, Windsor, in a tomb close to that of Edward IV – as the King had specifically asked.
2. See Chapter 11, p. 228–9.

Duchess of York, who was still very much alive. The propaganda campaign began with a sermon preached at St Paul's Cross, just outside the cathedral, on Sunday 22 June 1483 by a certain Dr Ralph[1] Shaa, or Sha, or Shaw, brother of the mayor of London. Dr Shaa, not content with claiming that Edward IV, Rutland and Clarence had all been bastards and that only Richard was legitimate, also held that Edward's marriage to Elizabeth Woodville was invalid, he having already plighted his troth to Lady Eleanor Butler, the daughter of the Earl of Shrewsbury, who had borne him a child. Both Lady Eleanor and the child were long since dead, but they had been alive at the time of the marriage to Elizabeth and canon law in those days held the ceremony of 'troth-plight', unless formally dissolved, to be as binding as matrimony itself; it would certainly have been enough to have invalidated the marriage.

Several other noted preachers took up the theme, but the Londoners as a whole were not persuaded. They disliked being patronized; and Shaa's allegations were, so far as they were concerned, an insult to their intelligence. They at least could no longer fail to see Richard for what he was: a man devoid of conscience or principle, who would stop at nothing to achieve his ambition. He might dress as regally as he liked, parade through the city with a dazzling retinue of a thousand men or more, entertain hundreds every day to his table; his popularity evaporated until it was as if it had never been. Two days after Shaa's sermon, Buckingham himself addressed the mayor, aldermen and all the leading citizens at Guildhall, telling them of the injustices and iniquities they had suffered during the previous reign, blaming Edward IV for the recent wars as well as for the murder of his own brother Clarence, and castigating him for his endless womanizing from which, he maintained, no female in the city had been safe. Would not now all his dear friends present stand up and call for 'this noble prince, now Protector,' to be their King? They would not. The only sound to be heard in the great hall was a low whispering, 'as of a swarm of bees'.

But there was no going back now: if Richard could not make himself King by popular acclamation, he would have to do so without it. On Wednesday 25 June Buckingham and his principal followers, together with the Mayor and corporation – who by this time were well aware

---

1. More and Holinshed call him John, but Ralph – or Raffe, according to Hall and Fabyan – seems to have been his proper name.

of what was expected of them and of what was in store for them if they failed to deliver – visited Richard at his London palace, Baynard's Castle. The Protector feigned first astonishment, then reluctance; he impressed all those present with his histrionic abilities, though he deceived no one. At last, with much hesitation he gave his consent. That evening, to confirm and ratify the agreement, a formal petition was drawn up by the lords, knights and burgesses who had come to London for the now-cancelled Parliament. Its words are hard indeed to reconcile with what we know of the ordered and peaceable later reign of Edward IV:

... the prosperity of this land daily decreased, so that felicity was turned into misery ... [Owing to the] murders, extortions and oppressions, namely of poor and impotent people ... no man was sure of his life, land nor livelihood, nor of his wife, daughter nor servant, every good maiden and woman standing in dread to be ravished and defouled ...

The said King Edward during his life and the said Elizabeth lived together sinfully and damnably in adultery against the law of God and of his Church ... It appeareth evidently and followeth that all the issue and children of the said King Edward be bastards and unable to inherit or to claim anything by inheritance by the law and custom of England.

That same day, Earl Rivers with three of the principal Woodville supporters – Lord Richard Grey, Sir Thomas Vaughan and Sir Richard Haute – were beheaded on the Protector's orders at Pontefract; their naked corpses were thrown into a common grave.

The final stage of the *coup* took place on Wednesday 26 June, when Richard rode in state from Baynard's Castle to Westminster Hall. On his arrival, in the presence of the assembled Justices of King's Bench and of Common Pleas, he formally seated himself on the marble throne – that same traditional seat of the King as dispenser of justice to which his father had vainly stretched out his hand twenty-three years before. There he took the royal oath, after which he delivered what must have seemed to his audience a remarkably sanctimonious lecture, charging them to administer justice without fear or favour and reminding them that all men were equal in the sight of the law. The reign of King Richard III had begun.

★

The coronation took place on Sunday 6 July 1483. Richard, in a doublet of blue cloth of gold and a purple velvet gown trimmed with ermine, rode from the Tower – into whose most sumptuous apartments he had moved a few days before – to the Palace of Westminster, accompanied by Queen Anne in a magnificent litter, escorted by five ladies-in-waiting on horseback. There followed the Duke of Buckingham and most of the English peerage, attended by a vast retinue of knights and gentlemen. After a brief pause at the palace, the King and Queen walked barefoot to the abbey, where they were duly crowned. Despite the obvious reluctance of Archbishop Bourchier to perform the ceremony – underlined by his refusal to attend the coronation banquet afterwards – all those present agreed that no more impressive ceremony could ever have been staged in London.

Yet no one could have failed to note the absentees. Edward IV's widow, Queen Elizabeth, was still in sanctuary with her daughters at the Abbot's Lodging, where the music of the coronation service must have been clearly audible to them. More significant still was the absence of her two sons. Early in the previous month, soon after the little Duke of York had joined his brother in the Tower, the two boys had been seen on several occasions playing together and practising their archery; more recently, however, there had been no sign of them. Bastards they might be, though few people really believed it; they remained the King's nephews, and as such might have been expected to take their seats in the abbey, where their very presence might have been seen as an indication that they had accepted their new position and were now loyal subjects of their uncle. It would also have successfully scotched the rumours already circulating that they had been quietly done away with.

If we are to believe Dominic Mancini – whose account, with its wealth of circumstantial detail, certainly suggests a remarkable degree of inside knowledge – immediately after the execution of Hastings on 20 June the two Princes 'were taken into the innermost rooms of the Tower, and as the days went by began to be seen more and more rarely behind the bars and windows, until at length they ceased to appear altogether'. Mancini adds that according to his friend Dr John Argentine, the royal physician who had been called to the Tower to see young Edward, the Prince was going to confession daily and doing penance 'because he believed that death was facing him'. We shall never know for certain precisely how the boys met their fate – but there is no doubt at all that they were killed and very little that the King was responsible. The first full reconstruction of the affair is that of Sir Thomas More. It is by no means universally accepted, but it is professedly based on the reports 'of them that much knew and little cause had to lie', and despite repeated attempts by the highly articulate defenders of Richard to prove it false it still carries more conviction than any other.[1] Rumours of the murders were already circulating at the time of the coronation, when the King must certainly have been turning the possibility over in his mind; the weight of the evidence, however, suggests with More that the fatal decision was taken only when he was at Warwick in mid-August, and that it was then prompted by reports of a plot to free the Princes and spirit them abroad, probably to Holland. The man first ordered to do the deed was the Constable of the Tower, Sir Robert Brackenbury; but Brackenbury, to his eternal honour, refused outright and it was only then that Richard turned to a knight from Suffolk named Sir James Tyrell, whom he knew to be ambitious, efficient and entirely loyal to himself. Tyrell, writes More,

devised that they should be murdered in their beds. To the execution whereof he appointed Miles Forest . . . a fellow flushed in murder beforetime. To him he joined one John Dighton, his own horsekeeper, a big broad strong square knave. Then all the others being removed from them, this Miles Forest and John Dighton about midnight (the innocent children lying in their beds) came into the chamber and suddenly lapped them up among the clothes – so bewrapped them and entangled them, keeping down by force the featherbed and pillows hard unto their mouths, that within a while, smothered and stifled, their breath failing, they gave up to God their innocent souls into the joys of heaven, leaving to the tormentors their bodies dead in the bed. After the wretches perceived them – first by the struggling with the pains of death and after, long lying still – to be thoroughly dead, they laid their bodies naked out upon the bed and fetched Sir James to see them, Who, upon the sight of them, caused those murderers to bury them at the stairfoot, meetly deep in the ground under a great heap of stones.

1. This is not the place for a detailed discussion of the various arguments that have been put forward. Readers avid for more information are referred to *Richard III* by Desmond Seward, revised edition (1997), pp. 143–55.

Nearly two centuries later, in 1674, workmen demolishing a staircase in the White Tower came upon a wooden chest. Inside it were the bones of two children, which Charles II ordered to be transferred to an urn in the Henry VII Chapel of Westminster Abbey. When this was opened in 1933 the bones were found to be of males, of four feet ten inches and four feet six and a half inches; their ages were given respectively as about twelve and ten.

18

The Final Reckoning

[1483–1485]

K.RICH.   Remember whom you are to cope withal:
A sort of vagabonds, rascals, and runaways;
A scum of Bretons and base lackey peasants,
Whom their o'er-cloyed country vomits forth
To desperate adventures and assur'd destruction.
You sleeping safe, they bring to you unrest;
You having lands, and bless'd with beauteous wives,
They would restrain the one, distain the other.
And who doth lead them but a paltry fellow,
Long kept in Bretagne at our brother's cost?
A milksop! One that never in his life
Felt so much cold as over-shoes in snow.

KING RICHARD III

From Warwick the King travelled by way of Coventry, Leicester and
Nottingham to York, where he was given a magnificent reception. He
was genuinely popular in the north, of which he had been the effective
governor during the last years of his brother Edward's reign and where
he had ruled with firmness and justice. Whether or not the quickly
spreading rumours about the fate of the little Princes had reached
Yorkshire before him we do not know; but they were unproven and
certainly in no way diminished the warmth of his welcome. On what
appears to have been the spur of the moment, he decided to invest his
nine-year-old son Edward of Middleham as Prince of Wales in York
Minster; the ensuing ceremony is said to have been almost as impressive
as his own coronation two months before. All too soon, however,
messengers arrived with news as serious as it was surprising: his oldest
friend and the most powerful of his subjects, Henry Stafford Duke of
Buckingham, had risen in open revolt against him.

Why Buckingham should have acted as he did remains a mystery. According to Shakespeare, he was furious at the King's refusal to grant him the earldom of Hereford which he had been promised. But Buckingham already possessed titles and estates in plenty; and in any case there was no reason to think that he would not be granted the earldom later, when Richard might be in a more generous mood. We should remember, on the other hand, that the atmosphere in the south was by now very different from that in the north. As the truth about the Princes had gradually dawned upon the people, London in the late summer of 1483 had come alive with plots and rumours of plots; and it may well be that Buckingham had become seriously alarmed at the strength of feeling against the King. If Richard were to be overthrown – as seemed increasingly likely – his own survival would obviously depend on breaking with him as soon as possible. Sir Thomas More goes so far as to suggest that ambition too played its part: that Buckingham might have considered making his own bid for the crown. He was after all a Beaufort, a grandson on his mother's side of that Edmund, second Duke of Somerset, who had been killed at St Albans in 1455, and consequently a great-great-grandson of John of Gaunt; his claim was arguably every bit as good as that of Richard III himself.[1]

But if the young man – we do not know exactly when Buckingham was born, but he was probably still under thirty – ever had any delusions about his own succession, these were quickly cast aside. The rightful heir to Edward IV was now unquestionably the eldest of his seven daughters, Elizabeth of York; though in these troubled times the choice of an eighteen-year-old girl – who was, incidentally, still in sanctuary with her mother – would have been disastrous. If an able, energetic man was required, capable of leading armies in war, there remained only the Beauforts. Buckingham was admittedly of Beaufort stock through his mother, but she traced her descent only from the youngest of John of Gaunt's grandsons. Henry Tudor, Earl of Richmond, being descended from the latter's elder brother, had indubitably the better

---

1. It is true that Henry IV had done his best to bar the Beauforts from the succession by adding to Richard II's patent of legitimation the words *excepta dignitate regali* (see Chapter 13, p. 261); but he had failed to make these words law by means of a subsequent act of parliament. The exclusion was therefore by now generally considered to have no legal validity.

claim; and if he were to marry Elizabeth this claim would be stronger still. The additional fact that his grandmother, Katherine of Valois, had been the widow of the ever-glorious Henry V may have had no legal relevance; but it certainly took nothing from his reputation.

What seems virtually certain – and is confirmed by More – is that Buckingham was greatly encouraged by Dr John Morton, Bishop of Ely. Morton had been arrested at the same time as Hastings; but after a brief period in the Tower he had been transferred at Buckingham's request to the latter's castle at Brecon in Wales. Already in his early sixties, he had a firmly Lancastrian background: taken prisoner at Towton, he had escaped from the Tower to join Queen Margaret in France and had accompanied her to Tewkesbury. Only after the battle was lost and the young Prince of Wales killed did he transfer his allegiance to Edward IV, whom he then served with similar devotion.[1] He could not, however, show the same to Richard. Perhaps he already knew, or suspected, the truth about the Princes; perhaps his long experience told him that the new King was simply too unpopular to maintain himself on the throne. At any event he seems to have become something of a father figure to Buckingham and to have directed him, during their long discussions at Brecon, towards the course of action which he subsequently took.

Morton's first action after winning Buckingham's support for his plan was to contact Henry's mother Margaret Beaufort. Though still only forty and deeply devout – she is said to have heard six masses every day – the daughter of John Duke of Somerset and great-granddaughter of John of Gaunt was a powerful, even formidable woman. She had given birth to Henry in January 1457 after the death of his father, Edmund Tudor, Earl of Richmond, and shortly before her fourteenth birthday; she had then married first Lord Stafford, Buckingham's uncle, and then Lord Stanley, later to be Earl of Derby. True, she had not seen her son – who had been brought up in Wales by his uncle Jasper Tudor, Earl of Pembroke – since he was two years old, a quarter of a century before; but she, like Morton, had no doubt in her mind that

---

1. It is unfortunate for Morton, and more than a little unfair, that he should be best known for the eponymous 'Morton's Fork' – a form of taxation devised under Henry VII, whose Chancellor he later became. This in fact was not his invention at all; on the contrary, he always did his best in the Council to restrain the King's avarice.

he was best qualified for the throne. Already she had been in secret contact with the former Queen in her Westminster sanctuary, proposing the marriage between her son and the Princess Elizabeth; on hearing from Morton of Buckingham's support for the conspiracy, she sent at once to Henry in Brittany to tell him the news, urging him to leave as quickly as possible to join the Duke in Wales.

The rebel forces gathered fast. Among them were virtually all the Woodvilles, who could have asked nothing better; then there were the many Lancastrians in Wales, the west country and the south-east; and finally a vast number of honest men who had simply been disgusted by Richard's murder of his nephews and his usurpation of the throne and were determined that he should be somehow brought to justice. With so many different and disparate groups, co-ordination was difficult; but there was a general plan that they should all rise simultaneously on 18 October. Had they been able to do so they might, with a modicum of good luck, have succeeded. Unfortunately those in the south-east were unable to wait and acted prematurely; the Duke of Norfolk, who was in London and like the majority of Londoners had remained – however reluctantly – loyal to Richard, managed to prevent the men of Kent from crossing the Thames and joining their fellows; and the rebels withdrew to Guildford, there to await the main spearhead which was marching from Wales under Buckingham himself.

The Duke left Brecon on the 18th as planned, but got no further than the Forest of Dean. On the very day of his departure the heavens opened. The deluge continued uninterruptedly for over a week, during which both the Severn and the Wye burst their banks, flooding the countryside for miles around. After ten days of waiting it was clear that the rebellion was doomed. The army dispersed and Buckingham himself fled in disguise to Shropshire, where he sought refuge with one of his old retainers, a certain Ralph Bannister; but he was soon discovered, and the £1,000 which Richard had put on his head proved too strong a temptation for Bannister, who surrendered him to the authorities. His request for an audience with the King was refused, and on All Souls' Day, Sunday 2 November, he was beheaded in the market place at Salisbury. In the weeks that followed, many of his fellow insurgents met a similar fate, their lands and estates being confiscated and shared out among Richard's northern henchmen – making the King more unpopular in the south than ever.

Fiasco as it turned out to be, Buckingham's rebellion had one vitally important consequence: it turned the political spotlight firmly on Henry, Earl of Richmond. Previously almost unknown, Henry was now the generally accepted Lancastrian contender for the crown, with a wide and enthusiastic following. Sailing from Paimpol in Brittany towards the end of October, he had run into the same storm that had shattered Buckingham's hopes; and when he had eventually arrived at Poole in Dorset it was plain to him from the number of armed troops around the harbour that the projected rising had failed. Without hesitation he had ordered his captains to turn about, and had returned to Brittany to find his suspicions confirmed. Some of the rebels, however – they included Thomas Grey, Marquis of Dorset – had managed to escape across the Channel, and these he summoned to Rennes for a discussion of future plans. It was there in the cathedral, early in the morning of Christmas Day 1483, that they knelt before him and did him homage, just as if he were already an anointed King; he in return swore to marry Elizabeth of York and to lead them back to England and victory.

By the beginning of the year 1484, King Richard III was a seriously worried man. True, he was living like a Renaissance prince, in greater splendour than any English King before him; but, as Sir Thomas More wrote,

he never had quiet in his mind, he never thought himself sure. Where he went abroad, his eyes whirled about, his body secretly armoured, his hand ever on his dagger, his countenance and manner like one always ready to strike back. He took ill rest a-nights; lay long waking and musing, sore wearied with care and watch; rather slumbered than slept, troubled with fearful dreams – suddenly sometimes started up, leapt out of his bed and ran about his chamber.

Buckingham's treachery had shaken him profoundly. Whom now could he trust? Lord Stanley, to whom he had given Buckingham's former office of Constable of England, was for the moment loyal but, as he well knew, ready to turn his coat at any moment; the Earl of Northumberland, now Lord Great Chamberlain, was scarcely more reliable. Only old John Howard, whom he had created Duke of Norfolk a few months before, was tried and true; but he was by now well into his fifties, by the standards of the day an old man.

It was perhaps in a vain attempt to ease his conscience that Richard was by now spending vast sums of money on chantries and chapels in which requiems could be sung for the dead. The Grey Friars of Richmond in Yorkshire were paid generously to say 1,000 masses for the soul of Edward IV; similar payments were made to the abbeys of Tickhill and Knaresborough, and the King even had plans for a vast chantry with six altars and a hundred priests to be attached to York Minster, in which masses could be said in perpetuity round the clock. About Henry VI – whom, it must be remembered, he had almost certainly murdered with his own hands – he seems to have been particularly uneasy. Henry was considered by most Englishmen to be a saint, and a considerable pilgrim traffic had grown up around his grave in Chertsey Abbey, which was already said to have been the scene of several miracles. Some time during the summer of 1484 Richard decided that the body should be transferred from the abbey to some more appropriate shrine, and in August he made a special journey down from the north to attend its reburial in St George's Chapel, Windsor Castle, just to the south of the high altar.

For his own troubled spirit, however, there was to be no rest. His only son, Edward of Middleham, had died on 9 April at the age of ten: once again, the King found himself without an heir. And wherever he looked, he saw enemies. For a surprisingly long time he had continued to ignore the most dangerous of them: in the general proclamation that he had issued on 23 October 1483 after Buckingham's abortive rising, the name of Henry of Richmond was conspicuous by its absence from the list of the leading insurgents. It was to be several more months before he would begin to take Henry seriously. He had no delusions, on the other hand, about the general insecurity of his position. Throughout 1484 he did everything possible to improve his image – making progresses through the country, performing ostentatious acts of generosity, publishing high-minded and sanctimonious declarations of intent, bestowing privileges, distributing offices and estates with a lavish hand; but it was useless. Already by the spring of 1484 the truth about the Princes was known throughout the kingdom. The people could not – and would not – forget.

Now, and only now, did Richard begin to see the Earl of Richmond as a force to be reckoned with. Henry's supporters were increasing fast. Dorset was not the only powerful magnate to have joined him; by this time there were also his uncle Jasper Tudor, Earl of Pembroke; Edward Courtenay, Earl of Devon; Richard Lord Rivers, eager to avenge his brother's execution the previous year; the Bishop of Exeter and the future Bishop of Winchester Richard Fox; and a large number of less distinguished knights and gentlemen – perhaps as many as 500 altogether. Morton, though remaining in Flanders, was in constant touch. It was probably some time in April that the King first approached Duke Francis of Brittany to suggest some arrangement whereby the Earl of Richmond might be prevented from making any more trouble; we know that in May 1484 the agents of the Duke's chief minister, the deeply corrupt Pierre Landois, came to England to negotiate. The result was a treaty with several secret clauses, signed on 8 June at Pontefract, by the terms of which the King agreed to pay a very considerable sum – including all the revenues of the earldom of Richmond – in return for an undertaking that Henry Tudor would be kept in strict confinement until further notice.

Since Duke Francis was by now suffering periodic fits of insanity, we can be fairly sure that the money paid went into Landois's own pocket; for a small additional sum the minister might even have agreed to surrender Henry into Richard's hands. Fortunately, however, he never had a chance to do so. According to Polydore Vergil, Bishop Morton – who had spies everywhere – got wind of the treaty and warned Henry in the nick of time, simultaneously arranging for him to be received in France. Some time in the late summer Henry succeeded in escaping across the border into Anjou, just an hour ahead of the troops sent by Landois to arrest him.

He was lucky, too, in that relations between France and Brittany were at that moment particularly strained. Duke Francis had no son to succeed him, and it was generally believed (with good reason) that on his death the French King would attempt to annex his duchy – a move which the King of England in his turn would do his best to prevent. In such circumstances Henry of Richmond might be a useful ally; the thirteen-year-old Charles VIII and his elder sister Anne de Beaujeu – who effectively ruled in her brother's place – accordingly gave him a warm reception, promising to help him financially when the need arose. By yet another stroke of good fortune, Henry was joined soon after his arrival in France by one of the doughtiest champions of the Lancastrian cause, John de Vere, Earl of Oxford. With his friend Lord Beaumont,

Oxford had captured St Michael's Mount in Cornwall in 1473[1] and held it for over four months; but it had been a quixotic enterprise at best, and he had spent the next ten years a prisoner in the castle of Hammes near Calais until, a week or two before Henry's escape from Brittany, he had persuaded the captain, James Blount, to release him and accompany him to join the exiles at the French court. A former Lord High Constable of England, he was a fine commander who had shown outstanding courage in battle. Not surprisingly, Henry welcomed him and Blount with open arms, the more so when he heard that the latter had left his wife in command of the garrison of Hammes, with orders to hold it against Richard. She did so, magnificently, throughout an ensuing siege by royalist troops, surrendering at the end of January 1485 only after the promise of free pardons for herself, her husband and the entire garrison.

The turn of events at Hammes added considerably to Richard's now rapidly increasing alarm. On 7 December he issued his first proclamation against 'Henry Tydder', who by reason of his 'insatiable covetousness' intended to perpetrate 'the most cruel murders, slaughters and robberies and disinheritances that ever were seen in any Christian realm'. The next day he dispatched commissions of array to most of the counties of England, and on the 18th he ordered his commissioners to report immediately on how many nobles, gentry and men-at-arms could be raised at half a day's notice. He kept Christmas at Westminster with characteristic pomp and splendour, but the festivities must have had a hollow ring: no one present could have forgotten the imminent danger of invasion and a renewal of the civil war, or could have ceased for a moment to ponder the all-important question of which side offered the best chances of survival.

There was further concern over the Queen, who was obviously dying. She had never recovered from the death of her son eight months before; but her pallor and skeletal thinness could not be accounted for by bereavement alone. Inevitably, there were rumours that she was being slowly poisoned by her husband, who – although he now treated her with studied callousness and refused, on what he claimed were doctors' orders, to share her bed – had been frequently heard to complain of her inability to give him another child. It was also common knowledge that he was eager to marry his niece, Elizabeth of York; he

1. See Chapter 16, p. 316.

had recently introduced her into his court where, although officially proclaimed a bastard, she had played a leading role that winter. The most charitable explanation of his attentions was that he wished simply to frustrate the designs of the Earl of Richmond;[1] but the Croyland chronicler refers darkly to 'many other matters as well, which are not written down here for shame', and it cannot be ruled out that his relations with Elizabeth – who was by now an unusually attractive girl of nineteen – may have gone somewhat beyond the avuncular.

Queen Anne died, aged twenty-eight, on 16 March 1485. Despite her husband's barely concealed hostility and although on that same day, to the consternation of all who witnessed it, the sun went into eclipse, her death is less likely to have been due to poison than to pulmonary tuberculosis. Richard, however, did not marry Elizabeth. Once again according to the Croyland chronicler, he gave up the idea on the advice of his two closest counsellors, William Catesby and Sir Richard Ratcliff, who told him bluntly that his subjects would never stand for it. If, they warned him, he did not make a public denial of any such intention, even the people of the north would rise against him, accusing him of killing the Queen – the daughter of their hero the Earl of Warwick – merely in order to satisfy his own incestuous lust. And so, on 30 March 1485 – barely a fortnight after his wife's death – Richard made a public statement at the Priory of the Knights of St John at Clerkenwell, declaring that 'it never came into his mind to marry [his niece], nor willing or glad of the death of the Queen, but as sorry and in heart as heavy as man might be.' Elizabeth was packed off to his castle at Sheriff Hutton, where she remained – with the young Earl of Warwick, Clarence's son – until after the battle of Bosworth.

The same chronicler also tells us that during the celebrations of Twelfth Night in Westminster Hall an urgent dispatch was brought to the King by 'his spies from beyond sea', informing him that his enemies would, beyond all doubt, invade the realm in the course of the summer following. Richard is said to have replied that 'nothing could have been more pleasing to him than this news'. He probably meant it. His nerves must have been at breaking point, but in a few months the agony of waiting would be over.

*

1. Polydore Vergil tells us that Henry was 'pinched to the very stomach' when he heard of Richard's rumoured intentions.

Henry of Richmond spent the spring and early summer of 1485 bringing together his army and the ships that were to carry it to England. It was not a large force: between two and three thousand at the most, perhaps half of it made up of trained professionals – mostly Welshmen – and the remainder what Commynes describes as 'the most unruly men that could be found and enlisted in Normandy'. By July all was ready; on 1 August the expedition set sail; and six days later, shortly before sunset on Sunday the 7th, the little fleet dropped anchor at Milford Haven in South Wales. Since the early spring Richard had had two flotillas patrolling the Channel; but somehow Henry had managed to give them both the slip, and his landing was unopposed. On the other hand there was no sign of the immensely influential Welsh nobleman Rhys ap Thomas, nor of Sir John Savage, a kinsman of the Stanleys, nor of Sir Gilbert Talbot, uncle of the young Earl of Shrewsbury, all three of whom Henry had expected to find awaiting him; and rumours of the imminent approach of Richard's army were already having their effect on the French soldiers' morale. Clearly, delay would be dangerous: early the following morning Henry led his army north-east, intending to cross the Severn at Shrewsbury.

And there, suddenly, his luck turned. The gates of the town were immediately opened to him; to Buckingham, they had remained closed. At Newport, on the Staffordshire border, Rhys ap Thomas joined him with 1,000 men; a day or two later there appeared Sir Gilbert Talbot with another 500. The arrival of this latter force was particularly significant for Henry. Apart from the Norman contingent, the vast majority of his army had been composed of Welshmen; here, for the first time, was a substantial body of local Shropshire yeomen. If they were ready to rally to his banner of the red dragon, how many of their compatriots might not be prepared to follow? On he marched, to Lichfield and thence to Tamworth, where his numbers swelled still further. The first new arrivals were Sir Walter Hungerford and Sir Thomas Bourchier, two former members of Edward IV's household who had been implicated in Buckingham's rebellion. Richard had formally pardoned them, but had not yet returned to them their confiscated estates; their positions, if he continued to reign, would remain uncertain to say the least. Soon afterwards arrived the long-awaited Sir John Savage of Cheshire – formerly one of Richard's closest henchmen – with another sizeable retinue.

The King was now at Nottingham. Though concerned at the speed of Henry's advance, he still seems to have found it difficult to see this unknown Welshman as a serious threat to his throne. The forces against him were growing rapidly; but they were still only a fraction of what he, as England's legitimate King, could surely summon at will. The first defection to bring him to his senses was that of Thomas, Lord Stanley. As Henry's stepfather Stanley might have been an obvious suspect; but Richard had loaded him with honours and his son, Lord Strange, who was being kept at court as an unofficial hostage for his father's good behaviour, never ceased to assure the King of his family's loyalty. Then, one day at about this time, Stanley sent word to Richard that he was sick of a fever and unable to join the royal army as he had promised; and a day or two later Strange was caught trying to escape. Under torture, he quickly admitted that he, his uncle Sir William Stanley and several other lords had indeed been planning to transfer their allegiance to Richmond, but insisted that this group did not include his father. Richard did not believe him for a moment. To his ever-devious mind it was plain that Strange was out to save his own skin: as the son of a rebel he would be worthless, but while his father's position remained ambiguous he would continue to be a valuable security. Stanley had refused to join him; that, to him, was treason enough.

And now, as he marched south from Nottingham to Leicester where the bulk of his army was being mustered, he realized that Stanley's example was being all too widely followed. The peers, knights and landed gentry of England might not be going over to the Earl of Richmond; but neither were they rallying to the colours of their King. They were, quite simply, staying at home. Thirty-three noblemen had attended his coronation, only two years before. Now, apart from Norfolk, Northumberland and the obviously unreliable Strange, the only others in his army were Norfolk's son the Earl of Surrey and the Lords Lovell, Ferrers and Zouch – though one or two more would be waiting for him at Leicester. With the knights and gentry it was much the same story. Emotionally, most of them sided with Henry Tudor. Even though Richard remained their King, crowned and anointed, they were terrified of him: of his ruthlessness, his cruelty and his vengeance.

Early in the morning of Sunday 21 August, King Richard III marched out of Leicester at the head of an army of about 12,000 men, with as much pomp and ceremony as he could muster. On his head, as so often, was a slim gold crown. It was a symbol not only of his royalty but of his constant insecurity; no other English ruler has ever felt the need to wear the badge of kingship so insistently. In the late afternoon, hearing that Richmond was near, he chose his battlefield – on rising ground, some two miles south of the present town of Market Bosworth.[1] Henry was in fact about three miles away to the south-east, with an army of perhaps 5,000. He knew that he could not avoid the coming encounter; overwhelmingly outnumbered as he was, however, he cannot have been looking forward to what was to be the first battle of his life. His only hope lay in Lord Stanley and his brother Sir William, with whom he had had long discussions at nearby Atherstone a day or two before. They had been cordial enough, but had still not declared themselves. (Their son and nephew Lord Strange was, it must be remembered, still a royal hostage.) Now that they had arrived at Bosworth with about 8,000 men, they might easily tip the scale – if he could only persuade them to join him.

The sun rose on the 22nd to reveal the two armies already drawn up in line of battle. The King's vanguard occupied the top of the hill. Commanded by the Duke of Norfolk, it contained both cavalry and infantry, both archers and gunners. Behind this was Richard, his helmet ringed by a golden circlet, surrounded by a corps of picked men-at-arms and another detachment of cavalry. In the rear were the troops of the Duke of Northumberland, 3,000 strong. The army of Henry Tudor was in a much inferior position at the foot of the slope. Commanding his centre was the Earl of Oxford, with Sir John Savage on the left wing and Sir Gilbert Talbot on the right. Henry himself was behind Oxford, with a small troop of horsemen and a few men-at-arms on foot. He had already dispatched an urgent appeal to the Stanleys for assistance, but had received a characteristically evasive answer. As it happens, Richard had sent them a similar message at about the same time, threatening to kill Strange if his father did not rally at once to the royal standard; Henry would have been considerably cheered had he known

1. We know little, if anything, more of the battle of Bosworth than we do of its predecessors in the Wars of the Roses. Apart from a very brief mention in the Croyland chronicle, our only source is Polydore Vergil – who did not arrive in England till 1502, although he certainly seems to have talked to a number of eyewitnesses. The present 'Battlefield Centre' on what is believed to be the site gives a vivid picture of the encounter, but its historical accuracy must be open to doubt.

that Stanley had still refused to be drawn, replying ominously that Strange was not his only son: he had others.

It was clear that the Stanleys would not move until they saw the turn the battle was taking; and also that the beginning of that battle could no longer be delayed. Oxford, fully aware of his disadvantage, knew that he must not wait for the enemy's downhill charge; he must seize the initiative while there was still time. He gave the order to advance up the slope – and immediately Norfolk attacked. With his numerical superiority, he might have carried the day with a single charge; but Oxford, drawing on his long experience, ordered his men to group themselves into a tight wedge, so that not one of them was more than ten feet away from the standards. The very density of their mass split the charge in two, breaking its momentum. Norfolk was obliged to regroup his men; and the hand-to-hand fighting began.

From this point onwards the picture becomes impossibly confused. An early casualty seems to have been Norfolk himself, shot through the throat by an arrow after Oxford had smashed his gorget. It seems too that Henry, determined to make one last appeal to the Stanleys, suddenly rode off towards them; and that Richard, recognizing his banner, led his men against him in a direct attack. As the two households struggled with each other in the fearful slogging match that constituted so much of medieval warfare, Henry found himself, for the first time, fighting for his life. He fought, we are told, with considerable courage; but his men were heavily outnumbered, and before long it looked as though he – and the whole Tudor cause – was doomed.

He was saved by Sir William Stanley. His elder brother still refused to move; but Sir William, who had been closely following the progress of the fighting from his own position perhaps half a mile away, finally made up his mind. He gave his men the order they had so long been awaiting, spurred his horse and galloped to Henry's rescue. This sudden arrival of 3,000 men, fresh and ready for the fray, changed the entire course of the battle. Richard, whose white charger had been shot from under him, was still fighting desperately on foot. Seeing that their cause was lost, his men urged him to flee; but he refused to listen to them, continuing to swing his heavy mace with manic energy until he was finally himself struck down. It was his army that took to its heels. He himself, shouting 'Treason! Treason!' with his last breath, died as he was determined to die, King of England to the end.

*

Bosworth was a small battle as battles go. It lasted only two hours – it was probably over by eight o'clock in the morning. If we include the fleeing remnants of the royal army, pursued by the Earl of Oxford and hacked down as they ran, it saw the death of well under 1,000 men. None the less, it was a turning-point of English history. It marked the end not only of the Plantagenets and the Wars of the Roses, but also of the Middle Ages. The England of Henry Tudor and his successors would be a very different – and happier – place.

Tradition tells us that Henry VII was first crowned on the battlefield, when Stanley removed his predecessor's gold coronet from his helmet and placed it on his head. One of his first acts as King was to order the arrest of the Duke of Northumberland. In fact, he had good cause to be grateful to him: Northumberland, despite having shown Richard every sign of loyalty beforehand, when the fighting began had refused the King's order to advance and had remained with his men motionless at the top of the hill while the battle raged below him. Now he knelt before Henry and did him homage; but the King was not satisfied. The Duke, he probably felt, had betrayed both sides. He had sat too long on the fence. He was taken prisoner for a time, but was soon restored to all his old offices.

Where Henry himself deserves censure is in the treatment of Richard's body. According to the author of *The Great Chronicle of London*,

Richard late King, as gloriously as he was by the morning departed from town, so irreverently was he that afternoon brought into that town, for, his body despoiled to the skin and nought being left about him so much as would cover his privy member, he was trussed behind a pursuivant . . . as an hog or other vile beast. And so, all too bestrung with mire and filth, was brought to a church in Leicester for all men to wonder upon. And there lastly indifferently buried.

Much later, Henry VII ordered a tombstone for the hitherto unmarked grave in the church of the Grey Friars in Leicester. It cost him just a shilling over ten pounds.

19

King Richard III

[1471–1485]

K. RICH.   I, that am curtail'd of this fair proportion,
          Cheated of feature by dissembling Nature,
          Deform'd, unfinish'd, sent before my time
          Into this breathing world scarce half made up –
          And that so lamely and unfashionable
          That dogs bark at me, as I halt by them –
          Why, I, in this weak piping time of peace,
          Have no delight to pass away the time,
          Unless to spy my shadow in the sun,
          And descant on mine own deformity.
          And therefore, since I cannot prove a lover
          To entertain these fair well-spoken days,
          I am determined to prove a villain . . .

                                        KING RICHARD III

King Richard III, the only English ruler since the Norman Conquest
to have been killed in battle, is also the only one to have become a legend.
That legend, due first to Sir Thomas More and then to Shakespeare, is
of the lame and twisted hunchback whose misshapen body reflects the
evil heart within it. To satisfy his own all-consuming ambition, he
murders the royal saint King Henry VI and the latter's son Edward
Prince of Wales, seduces Edward's Lady Anne while her husband's
body is still warm, engineers the death of his own brother Clarence
and finally disposes of his two child nephews – one of them the rightful
King of England – in the Tower of London. He quite probably poisons
his wife, and would almost certainly have married his niece had he not
been persuaded that public opinion would never stand for it. He acts,
in short, more like one of those ogres of the Italian Renaissance, of
whom his contemporary Cesare Borgia was perhaps the most obvious

example and another contemporary, Niccolò Machiavelli, the most characteristic voice. For all of them, ends invariably justified means: to ensure the proper maintenance of the ruler's authority, no crime was too unspeakable, no treachery too abhorrent.

More recently, however, there has grown up another legend, which has come a long way towards supplanting the first. This is the legend of the great and good man of perfectly normal physique, the fine administrator and far-sighted law-giver who, had he been allowed the time and the opportunity, would have restored peace and good government to his realm; but who, instead, has been made the victim of one of the most contemptible campaigns in the history of personal defamation. His character has been blackened, deliberately and system-atically, while appalling crimes of which he was completely innocent have been laid at his door. The man who was potentially one of the greatest of English monarchs has been branded as being incomparably the vilest.

The proponents of this second school of thought may not be quite in the league of More and Shakespeare; but they include a number of admirable writers beginning with Horace Walpole and continuing with historians like Paul Murray Kendall and even novelists like Josephine Tey, whose brilliant *The Daughter of Time* has probably done more than any other single work in the past half-century to reinstate Richard in the ranks of the blessed. For them, the arch-villain is of course King Henry VII, himself every bit as much of a usurper as his predecessor, and with far less reason. Only by presenting Richard as a fiend, they point out, could Henry have hoped to justify his own action in deposing him. And why, having deposed him, should he himself not have killed the two princes? He would have had just as strong a motive, and he was certainly never to shrink from other executions – even, in 1495, that of Sir William Stanley, who ten years before had saved both his life and his cause at Bosworth.

The trouble about this second legend is that it flies in the face of our best witness, Sir Thomas More. To accept it, we have to demolish him as thoroughly as he demolishes Richard; and this is not easy to do. First of all, More was not, as some have argued, a 'later historian'. Born in the reign of Edward IV, he was seven years old at the time of Bosworth; and he certainly knew many of Richard's contemporaries, including several who had held high office under the late King. Indeed his immediate predecessor as Under-Treasurer, Sir John Cutts, had been Richard's Receiver of Crown Lands. More's own father, a leading London lawyer, would have been able to give him first-hand evidence in plenty of what had really occurred in that short and disastrous reign. Was he then simply an unscrupulous propagandist for his master, Henry VII? Surely not: nothing that we know of his character suggests that he would have sold his integrity in such a way, or have deliberately written what he knew in his heart to be untrue. We are speaking, after all, of a formally canonized saint who, according to no less an authority than Erasmus, possessed the finest legal brain in Europe. And again and again the truth of what he writes is confirmed by contemporary writers whose work has come to light only many years after his death. Dominic Mancini, Philippe de Commynes, the author of the Continuation of the Croyland Chronicle – who was almost certainly John Russell, Bishop of Lincoln and Chancellor of Oxford University – all, though they may differ on points of detail, substantially agree with More. The same applies to Polydore Vergil who, though he arrived in England only in 1502, tells us that he personally interviewed 'every elderly man pointed out to me as having once held an important position in public life'. All these sources, and much other evidence besides, leave no doubt that Richard's reputation had already reached its nadir during his lifetime; no subsequent blackening of it was possible.[1]

Shakespeare, as we know, always had a cavalier approach to chronology; and there can be no more revealing illustration of it than in the opening of *King Richard III*. In Act I scene i, the famous soliloquy ('Now is the winter of our discontent') leads directly to the arrest of Clarence and his committal to the Tower; this places the action firmly in the early summer of 1477. The next scene, however – Richard's wooing of Lady Anne – is set against the funeral of Henry VI, six years before, and here too the timing is distinctly awry. Henry died on 21 May 1471; his funeral can have been held only a day or two later. Yet in line 245 Richard specifically refers to his own stabbing of the Prince of Wales, which must have occurred immediately after Tewkesbury, as being

---

1. A more detailed discussion of the two legends will be found in the Introduction to *Richard III*, by Desmond Seward – perhaps the best, and certainly the most readable, of recent biographies.

'some three months since' – which would make the date of this scene some time around the beginning of August. It is of course far from certain that Richard was involved in the Prince's death; and it is perhaps worth repeating, too, that while Anne had been betrothed to the young man in 1470, he was never her husband.

Where Clarence is concerned, Richard proudly – though, in the eyes of history, quite unjustifiably – claims responsibility for his brother's downfall. We cannot doubt that he would have been capable of such villainy had the need arisen; but Clarence saved him the trouble. He had always been his own worst enemy and, as we have seen, brought his destruction very largely on himself. There had indeed been a prophecy, much talked about at the time, that King Edward's heirs would be disinherited by a man whose name began with the letter G – the Duke's Christian name was George – but there were far stronger reasons than this for the King to move against him. Another inaccuracy – though perhaps a relatively unimportant one – is Shakespeare's introduction here (and again in scene iv) of Sir Robert Brackenbury. Brackenbury was appointed Lieutenant of the Tower only in 1483; he was never responsible for Clarence, and was to play no part in his death.

The dating of scene iii poses a major problem; indeed, it is only if we accept the appearance of old Queen Margaret of Anjou as a historical fact that we can date it at all, and even then our conclusion can never be more than approximate. Margaret was taken prisoner after Tewkesbury and spent the next four years in semi-captivity, until her ransom by Louis XI in 1475; this is therefore the latest date at which she could, even theoretically, have shown herself at the English court. But would she ever have been permitted to do so? It seems unlikely. The mystery deepens in lines 167–9, when Richard asks her

> Were you not banished on pain of death?

to which she answers

> I was, but I do find more pain in banishment
> Than death can yield me here by my abode.

Margaret, as we know (and as Shakespeare himself surely knew) was never banished. The fact that he brings her back again in IV.iv, after the death of the Princes and therefore also after her own – for she died in 1482 – makes it virtually certain that he is using her presence in both scenes purely for dramatic effect and with no thought for historic truth.

The fourth and last scene of Act I is given over to the death of Clarence. The Duke first tells of a dream:

> Methoughts I saw a thousand fearful wrecks;
> Ten thousand men that fishes gnaw'd upon;
> Wedges of gold, great anchors, heaps of pearl,
> Inestimable stones, unvalu'd jewels,
> All scattered in the bottom of the sea . . .
> I pass'd, methought, the melancholy flood
> With that sour ferryman which poets write of,
> Unto the Kingdom of perpetual night . . .
>   Then came wandering by
> A shadow like an angel, with bright hair
> Dabbled in blood; and he shriek'd out aloud,
> 'Clarence is come: false, fleeting, perjur'd Clarence,
> That stabb'd me in the field by Tewkesbury!'

and later pleads for his life with the two murderers, one determined, the other conscience-stricken. It is a superb scene, full both of exquisite poetry and of high drama; only as a piece of history can it be faulted. At the end of scene iii we saw Richard giving his instructions to the two hired murderers; here they speak of him time and again as their paymaster and indeed identify him as such to their incredulous victim. Shakespearean audiences were therefore left in no possible doubt that, in addition to all his other crimes, Richard had been guilty of fratricide – which, as we know, he was not. The story of the butt of malmsey[1] is of course retained – clearly it was too good to miss – but the actual immersion occurs, disappointingly for audiences but blessedly for the actor concerned, off-stage.

The only problem that Shakespeare has to face in advancing the fratricide theory is that already, at his trial in January 1478, Clarence had been condemned to execution. He deals with this in the first scene of Act II, when Richard reveals his brother's death to the dying King

1. See p. 324 and fn.

Edward and his court. The King objects that 'the order was revers'd', to which Richard replies:

> But he, poor man, by your first order died,
> And that a winged Mercury did bear;
> Some tardy cripple bore the countermand,
> That came too lag to see him buried.

The 'tardy cripple' was, we are surely to assume, a wry joke against himself. Historically, there was never any question of a reprieve; this passage is sheer dramatic invention, designed to pin the blame more firmly on the Duke of Gloucester than would otherwise have been possible. It also enables Richard to injure the King – who, having negotiated a general reconciliation between his family and the Wood-villes, was expecting to die happy. Now, on hearing the news, he is consumed with guilt and terrified of divine retribution.

Both the guilt and the sickness are Shakespearean inventions. Apart from being somewhat overweight, at the time of Clarence's death Edward seems to have been in excellent health; and it is doubtful whether the removal of his insufferable brother would have caused him more than the faintest twinge of conscience. He was in fact to survive Clarence more than five years – a fact which necessitates some serious telescoping in scene ii. This scene opens in 1478, with Clarence's two small children – Margaret Plantagenet was in fact five years old at the time, her brother Edward three – being told by their grandmother of their father's death, then leaps without warning to 1483 with the widowed Queen, 'her hair about her ears', entering with her brother Rivers and her son Dorset to bewail that of her husband. The ensuing show of what can be described only as competitive lamentation – a contest won hands down by the old Duchess of York, who succeeds in simultaneously mourning not only the late King but a husband who has been in his grave for twenty-three years and another son who has been dead for five – is interrupted by the entry of Richard, Buckingham and others. Buckingham suggests the departure of a delegation for Ludlow to fetch the new young King; Rivers agrees; and Richard and Buckingham are left alone to make their plans.

There follows the short scene of the three citizens, illustrative of public concern at the King's death. The First Citizen's history proves shaky; Henry VI had not been 'crown'd in Paris but at nine months old'. His Westminster coronation took place when he was eight, its repetition in Paris two years later.[1] Scene iv begins with the announcement by the Archbishop of York that Edward V and his train are approaching Northampton, and continues with a short conversation during which the King's younger brother the Duke of York is revealed as an unusually tiresome child. At this point a messenger brings news of the arrest of Rivers and Grey and their imprisonment at 'Pomfret'. In fact they were first sent to Richard's castle of Sheriff Hutton, being moved to Pontefract only for their executions the following month; but this hardly matters. Far more important – and of course true – is the Queen's decision to take sanctuary with her son. (No mention is made of the five daughters who also accompanied her.)

It seems mildly surprising that Shakespeare should make so little of Richard's first *coup* against the Woodvilles. Here, one might have thought, was a superb opportunity for a playwright. He could have imagined the night at Northampton, with Richard and Buckingham plying Rivers and Grey with wine before, the following morning, showing themselves in their true colours; another fine scene might have covered their subsequent meeting with the young King at Stony Stratford, when they accused the Woodvilles of treason and brushed aside all his attempts to defend them. Instead the whole story is told, briefly and undramatically, by a messenger. Doubtless Shakespeare had his reasons; but these incidents are wonderfully illustrative of Richard's character – his quickness, his deviousness and his total lack of scruple – and it is difficult to pass on to Act III without some slight feeling of disappointment, and regret at a fine chance missed.

This act opens with the arrival in London, on 4 May, of the young King; and in his short dialogue with his uncle we are given at least a taste of what that scene at Stony Stratford might have been. In the play – which here is very probably accurate enough – Edward shows unwillingness to reside at the Tower: not because of its grim reputation (which it was to acquire only in later centuries) but, we may assume, because it had all too recently

---

1. It is only fair to point out that Shakespeare's King Henry labours under the same delusion: see Chapter 16, p. 308.

seen the deaths of a King and a Prince of the Blood.[1] This is certainly the response of the young Duke of York, when he joins his brother later in the scene and they go off to the Tower together. (Historically, as we know, they did no such thing, Cardinal Bourchier having taken several days to persuade Queen Elizabeth to release her son from sanctuary.) The scene ends with Richard and Buckingham instructing their hench-man, Sir William Catesby, to sound out Hastings on his probable reaction to Richard's seizure of the throne and to tell him of the execution, on the following day at Pontefract, of 'his ancient knot of dangerous adversaries': Rivers, Grey and two of their followers, Sir Thomas Vaughan and Sir Richard Haute.

In scene ii Catesby carries out his orders. Hastings, replying to his question, does not mince his words:

> I'll have this crown of mine cut from my shoulders
> Before I'll see the crown so foul misplac'd.

He remains, none the less, confident of Richard's and Buckingham's goodwill towards him, and mocks the anxious Lord Stanley who tries to persuade him to flee. His confidence is still undiminished two scenes later – scene iii, in which the condemned men at Pontefract bid each other farewell, being little more than a brief parenthesis – when we come to the Council meeting which ends with his arrest. Here Shake-speare sticks closely to More and Hall (who incorporates More's history in his own chronicle), using indeed their very words whenever possible: the reference to the Bishop's strawberries, the sudden accusations, the revealing of the withered arm – all these details are faithfully retained. Once again the only confusion – and this is to a large extent inevitable – is in the chronology. Edward V entered London, as we know, on 4 May; the Council meeting was held on 13 June; and the beheadings at Pontefract took place on 25 June, nearly a fortnight after Hastings's execution.[2] Historically, then, Hastings would never have had the

---

1. The building was, incidentally, begun by William the Conqueror and not, as Buckingham maintains, by Julius Caesar.

2. More and Hall, however, claim that the captives at Pontefract were executed 'the same day that the lord Chamberlayne was headed in the towre of London and about the same houre.'

satisfaction − as he has in the play − of knowing that his enemies had preceded him to the block.

The remaining scenes of the act show, if anything, still more fidelity to More and Hall. Shakespeare introduces the gullible mayor to represent the 'many substancial men out of the cytie' to whom Richard and Buckingham, 'harnessed in olde evill favoured briganders', explain the sad necessity which has obliged them to kill Hastings; he makes Richard dispatch Buckingham to Guildhall to spread the word of his brothers' illegitimacy; another henchman, Lord Lovell, is sent to fetch the mayor's brother Dr Shaa − he who is shortly to preach the sycophantic sermon − while his trusted Sir Richard Ratcliffe goes off to find Friar Penker,[1] Provincial of the Augustinian Friars − 'bothe great preachers, bothe of more learnyng then vertue, of more fame then learnyng, & yet of more learnyng then trueth'. In scene v, which contains only fourteen lines, we even have a scrivener illustrating More's point that the proclamation of Hastings's death was so long and elaborate that it could only have been prepared many hours in advance. This brings us to the final scene of the act, which falls into two parts. In the first, which can be dated to 24 June, Buckingham tells Richard of his fruitless efforts to persuade the citizens of London to acclaim him at Guildhall; instead of which

> they spake not a word,
> But like dumb statues or breathing stones
> Star'd each on other, and look'd deadly pale.

The second part covers the visit − which actually took place on the following day − of Buckingham, the mayor and a group of citizens to the Protector at Baynard's Castle to beg him to take the crown as of right. Twice he refuses; finally, with every show of reluctance, he accedes to their wishes:

> But if black scandal, or foul-fac'd reproach,
> Attend the sequel of your imposition,
> Your mere enforcement shall acquittance me
> From all the impure blots and stains thereof:
> For God doth know, and you may partly see,
> How far I am from the desire of this.

1. Holinshed's spelling; Hall calls him Pynkie.

In the play, the mayor and citizens are genuinely deceived by Richard's attitude: by the prayer book in his hand, and by the two reverend churchmen flanking him. Historically speaking, however, we can be fairly sure that the leaders of the delegation were by now fully aware that they were participating in a cold-blooded charade.

With the beginning of Act IV we are back once more in the world of Shakespeare's imagination. Stanley's first speech, bidding Queen Anne to go straight to Westminster for her coronation, makes it clear that the first scene is set on Sunday 6 July; the widowed Queen Elizabeth, who is seen on the way to the city to visit her sons, was then still in sanctuary. It is true, on the other hand, that at this time – and probably for at least a fortnight before – no access was allowed to the two little Princes in the Tower. As for the Marquess of Dorset, Elizabeth's son by her first marriage, he too had taken sanctuary, but escaped at about this time; we read that although Richard sought him with dogs, 'after the manner of hunstsmen', he eventually managed to escape to France. Even if his mother, emboldened by her anxiety for her sons' safety, had ventured to the Tower, he would certainly not have been able to accompany her.

Scene ii once again shows us Richard at his most villainous. First he discusses with Buckingham how best to rid himself of the Princes; next he arranges with Stanley to spread the word of his wife's sickness, so that he may more easily dispose of her also and marry his niece; then he whispers his deadly instructions to Sir James Tyrell; and finally he refuses to listen when Buckingham claims the promised earldom of Hereford. In essence this and the succeeding scene iii are simply a dramatization of More's account; the only important difference is that Shakespeare brings forward the death of Queen Anne by nearly two years, making it roughly contemporary with the murder of the Princes. It is immediately after Tyrell confirms their deaths that he soliloquizes:

> The sons of Edward sleep in Abraham's bosom,
> And Anne my wife hath bid this world good night.

By this time, one feels, Stanley could scarcely have begun to spread the rumour that she was sick. In fact, as we know, the poor Queen survived till March 1485 – dying possibly of slow poison, but more probably of natural causes.

★

In the first part of scene iv the reappearance of the ghastly Queen Margaret is of course unhistorical; but by now she is hardly Queen Margaret at all. Her character, since the battle of Tewkesbury, has been transformed. What we see before us is a figure scarcely human, belonging more to Greek tragedy than to English, a personification of malignant vengeance who is capable of expressing satisfaction even over the death of the Princes. The second part of the scene on the other hand, during which Richard demonstrates once again his remarkable powers of persuasion in inducing Queen Elizabeth to press his suit with her daughter, makes historic sense so long as we accept – and, as Shakespeare's audience, accept we must – that his first wife Anne is already dead. In the third part the King is informed first of the imminent arrival of Henry Tudor in alliance with Buckingham, and then of the failure of their insurrection and Henry's return to Brittany. Since Buckingham is obviously still alive and we know that he was executed on 2 November, this enables us to date the end of the scene confidently to late October 1483.

The curious little scene v which brings the act to an end – and in which Lord Stanley explains that he cannot actively support Richmond while Richard holds his son as a hostage – might more appropriately be transposed with its successor, V.i: it belongs quite clearly to August 1485, when Richmond had made his landing. (He did so, incidentally, not at Haverfordwest or Pembroke as Sir Christopher Urswick maintains, but at Milford Haven.) With Act V we briefly return to 1483 and Buckingham's execution after the botched rebellion; then, with scene ii, we are back again in 1485 – Shakespeare having passed over the events of 1484 in silence – where we remain to the end of the play. This short scene with Richmond and his principal followers, somewhere on the road towards Bosworth, is a precursor to the fight. The three scenes which follow, iii to v, are all set on the field of battle; and it is on this, after Richard's death and a suitable concluding speech by Richmond – now King Henry VII – that the final curtain falls.

Of the three, scene iii is by far the longest and the most important, inescapably reminiscent of the finest scene (IV.i) of *King Henry V*, the night before Agincourt. In the early part at least, the two enemy camps share the stage as Richard and Richmond make their dispensations for the morrow. Both show their concern for Stanley, uncertain as they are both of his precise position and of his intentions; but it is to

Richmond that Stanley presents himself under cover of night, to explain for the second time how the King's possession of his own son as hostage makes it impossible for him to side openly with his stepson as he would otherwise have done. (The visit is obviously unhistorical; it should be noted too that – perhaps to simplify the story, or even to economize in casting – Shakespeare presents us with one Stanley only; he makes no mention of Sir William, whose last-minute intervention was to decide the battle.) It is at this point that the ghosts appear – eleven of them, each speaking first to Richard, cursing him, and then passing on to the sleeping Richmond, to whom they wish victory. Then Richmond and Richard deliver their orations to their men, and the battle begins.

Scene v, apart from containing the most famous line in the play[1] – twice delivered – serves to emphasize the King's valour in battle as he determinedly seeks out Richmond to engage him in single combat. It also suggests that the latter protected himself by dressing a number of others in similar armour:

> I think there be six Richmonds in the field:
> Five have I slain today instead of him.

This appears to be an invention of Shakespeare's. The use of doubles was a well-known trick of medieval warfare,[2] but there is no suggestion of it at Bosworth, where Richard is known to have worn the regal circlet on his helmet. Hall claims on the contrary that Richmond 'perceyved wel the kyng furiously commyng towarde him, and by cause the hole hope of his welth and purpose was to be determined by battaill, he gladlye proferred to encountre with hym body to body and man to man'. But the encounter takes place at last, at the beginning of scene v, and Richard is killed. We shall never know at whose hands he met his death; we can be confident they were not those of Richmond, since if he had personally struck the fatal blow the fact would almost certainly have been recorded. Here of all places, however, a little dramatic licence can surely be forgiven.

The story of the presentation of the crown by one of the Stanleys to the victorious Richmond on the field of Bosworth was a venerable

1. 'A horse! A horse! My kingdom for a horse!'
2. See Chapter 6, pp. 146–7.

tradition long before Shakespeare's day. In the circumstances it can only have been Sir William, since his brother had refused to engage himself or his men in the battle. Richmond's closing speech is unhistoric but unexceptionable – unless we take issue with his description of himself and Elizabeth as 'the true succeeders of each royal house'. Elizabeth, whom he was shortly to marry, was indeed the heir to the house of York, although after the death of Richard's only son in 1484 (unmentioned by Shakespeare) he had in fact adopted his nephew John de la Pole as his heir; but to that of Lancaster – even of what was left of it – Henry's claim was legally a good deal more questionable. No matter: in the immediate aftermath of Bosworth there would have been few men in all England who would not have knelt before Henry Tudor as their rightful King.

Epilogue

This book has covered, very sketchily, a century and a half of English history, forming the framework of Shakespeare's nine greatest historical plays. The story is one of almost incessant fighting: first comes the Hundred Years War with France, and then those three further decades of the Wars of the Roses during which Englishmen confronted not the French but their own compatriots. Both conflicts are misleadingly named. The former lasted a good deal longer even than its epithet implies, while the second possessed neither beauty nor romance – and, to those involved, smelt anything but sweet. On the other hand, they did the country comparatively little material harm. These were still medieval wars. The armies were tiny by modern standards. For the individual soldiers there was, as there has always been, the risk of being killed or wounded; but the survivors of the fighting in France quite often returned with their pockets stuffed with ransom money, dragging behind them whole cartloads of plunder. Civil war admittedly exacted a heavier price on the domestic population, especially in the regions through which the armies marched; but the fighting, nightmarish as much of it must have been, continued for a total of only thirteen weeks. To the vast majority of the King's subjects the rival claims and counter-claims, the conflicts and ambitions of the nobility must have seemed remote indeed. They too had their struggles, as they had always had – against the elements, against economic depression, against the inquity of a landlord or the injustice of a magistrate; but life for them continued largely unchanged, and would continue to do so for many years to come.

The true cost of the wars was not material but moral. Under the old feudal system the vassal had given his service to his lord, for a fixed number of days per year, in return for the land which the lord allowed him to farm; but the old feudal system was slowly breaking down, and as it did so there was an increasing need for professional or semi-professional armies, who would stay in the field over a protracted campaign, and who sold their services for money – and the hope of plunder – not necessarily to their lord but to the highest bidder. Thus there grew up private militias who owed their allegiance to whoever was prepared to pay them and who, when the fighting was over and they could no longer find legitimate occupation for their swords, turned into armed bands of marauders who would devastate one village after another, helping themselves to its food and its women and then moving on to the next.

A strong ruler could have done much to limit the damage; it was England's misfortune, in the fourteenth and fifteenth centuries, to suffer some of the worst kings who have ever disgraced a throne. Edward III was quite obviously not one of them: he had at least succeeded in re-establishing the prestige of the monarchy after the deposition and murder of his contemptible father. But his decision (taken largely for the sake of providing employment and occupation for the turbulent magnates who threatened to make trouble at home) to mount an aggressive war for the French throne was to cause untold suffering to the people of France and to cost, over the next 120 years, countless thousands of English lives. Moreover – and this, in the long run, was to prove almost as catastrophic – he had far too many children. For a king to have seven sons, in an age when the laws of succession were vague and unwritten, was a virtual recipe for disaster; and it was the slow, relentless unfolding of that disaster that gave Shakespeare his theme.

The premature death of the Black Prince was another tragedy. Had the Prince kept his health and outlived his father, his son Richard II might still have succeeded him; but it would have been an older Richard, perhaps even a wiser one – a Richard who might, with any luck, have outgrown that mercifully rare combination of fecklessness and arrogance that caused his downfall. He might even, one would have thought, have learnt a lesson from the fall of his great-grandfather Edward II; instead, with his worthless, self-seeking favourites and his ill-concealed contempt for the barons on whom his crown depended, he seemed almost wilfully to copy him – thereby precipitating another revolution and forfeiting, as Edward had forfeited, both his throne and, ultimately, his life. Henry IV, who deposed him, was by no means incapable; but he never managed to live down his usurpation of the throne, and he was hamstrung by a series of parliaments more uncooperative than any before the seventeenth century. His son Henry V sought, as Edward III had sought before him, to bury his domestic problems by renewing the war with France. A courageous and inspiring leader of men though a remarkably indifferent general, he won a glorious but largely undeserved victory and thereby immense popular acclaim; but he died at thirty-four, leaving the country in no better state than he found it.

Once again an early death exacted its toll, and a far greater one than before: Richard II on his accession had been a boy of ten: Henry VI was a babe in arms. More serious still, he effectively remained one for the rest of his life. A strong hand at the helm might, at this point, have averted catastrophe; under Henry, and under the baleful influence of his councillors and his Queen, the Wars of the Roses were inevitable. The King's life was to prove, to everyone's surprise, not so much too short as very much too long; even so it was plain, in the absence of any suitable Lancastrian successor, that the throne must pass to the House of York. That it should have done so during Henry's lifetime, and should then have been returned to him at the whim of a jumped-up nobleman, says all that needs to be said about the depths to which the monarchy had fallen. Could Edward IV, after his second coronation, have redeemed it as successfully as his great-great-grandfather and namesake, a hundred and fifty years before? Quite possibly – he possessed many of the qualities necessary for the task. But he made one calamitous mistake: he married a Woodville. As a direct result of that marriage the Yorkists were split in two: and thus, with Edward's early death while his sons were still defenceless children, the way was laid open for the usurpation of Richard III – and, indirectly, for the accession of Henry Tudor.

It was said of Henry that he had never been young; but a military upbringing at the hands of an uncle, followed by an adolescence and early manhood spent largely in exile and in constant danger of capture and execution, are hardly conducive to *joie-de-vivre*. Seldom if ever did Henry show any of the passions, the overwhelming emotions, the terrible rages of his son and granddaughters. Cruel and inflexible he could be, but his decisions were always ruled by the head rather than the heart; far more frequently he amazed his advisers by his mercy and tolerance – which sprang, however, not from any deep wells of kindness or compassion but from the conviction that his primary task must be to reconcile the old factions and, slowly and patiently, to bring the aristocracy to its senses. At long last, the country had a superb King; it had waited, heaven knows, long enough.

The history of England in the late fourteenth and fifteenth centuries is tragic indeed, but it is never lacking in drama; no wonder Shakespeare saw it as fit material for his pen. There were of course danger areas, of which the most perilous was probably religion. Only forty years before he wrote his plays, under Bloody Mary, English men and women were being martyred for their Protestant faith; Elizabeth had to some degree restored the equilibrium, but feelings were still running high on both sides. Shakespeare solved this particular problem by ignoring it: there are few contemporary writers, in England or even in Europe, in whose work the affairs of the spirit play so insignificant a part. Except for the speech of the Bishop of Carlisle in Act IV of *Richard II* and the doggerel quatrain[1] on his tomb – which it is almost impossible to believe that he wrote himself – there is scarcely a line in all his work that mentions, uncorrupted and in a serious context, the name of Jesus Christ.

More inescapable were the dethronements of Richard II and Henry VI. The Queen was known to be sensitive on such matters, and it must always be borne in mind that these plays, written for the most part while Shakespeare was still in his twenties, are Elizabethan rather than Jacobean. Besides, as things turned out, Her Majesty had good reason to be uneasy: on Friday 6 February 1601 did not a party of supporters of the Earl of Essex demand a special performance of *Richard II*, promising to pay forty shillings for it and to indemnify the players against any loss? Two days later Essex was proclaimed a traitor and the same evening gave himself up.

The overall message of the plays, on the other hand, was one which the Queen would have taken instantly to her heart: the supreme importance – and the ultimate triumph – of the state. When Edward III came to the throne in 1327, there had been only one competent

---

1. GOOD FREND FOR IESVS SAKE FORBEARE,
   TO DIGG THE DVST ENCLOASED HEARE.
   BLESTE BE YE MAN YT SPARES THES STONES,
   AND CVRST BE HE YT MOVES MY BONES.

monarch since the death of Henry II in 1189;[1] though at last tolerably well governed, that state was still woefully immature. The tribulations and indignities which it was soon afterwards called upon to undergo, the dangers by which it was to be threatened, even the inanity of all too many of its rulers – against which Elizabeth's and her grandfather's formidable abilities stood out in a contrast which was itself dramatic enough – could all be seen in retrospect as necessary stages in the tempering of the national steel.

In what is essentially a pageant embracing five or more generations, the only possible hero – or heroine – can be England herself: blameless, as all good heroines should be, but disgracefully put upon by those in authority over her. They it is who ruin her, ravish her and ultimately tear her apart – a process which continues, almost without interruption, from the first rising of Shakespeare's curtain until a few minutes before it finally falls. In those few minutes Richard III is killed on Bosworth Field, Henry of Lancaster is acclaimed as his successor, and the country emerges, suddenly and spectacularly, out of its long darkness into the Tudor sun. There – in the very contrast between the chaos wrought by the Plantagenets and the peace and tranquillity introduced by Henry and his successors – was a subject fit for the Queen.

And Shakespeare knew it. His sources may have been few, and not invariably satisfactory; but where they were found wanting he always had his imagination to fill the gaps. He would never have claimed historical accuracy – and to establish just how close to it he came has been one of the principal purposes of this book – but then he was not a historian; he was a dramatist. The play was the thing; and if he could amuse, inspire and perhaps very modestly educate his audiences, that was enough. He did so, and he has continued to do so for four hundred years. He rests his case.

---

1. Edward's grandfather, Edward I. Before him, Henry III and John had both proved disasters; while John's predecessor and brother Richard I (*Coeur de Lion*), despite a ten-year reign, spoke hardly any English, took absolutely no interest in England and spent less than a year there in his entire life.

Chronological Table

1327 Murder of Edward II; accession of Edward III
1328 Death of French King Charles IV; accession of Philip VI
1329 Edward does homage to Philip at Amiens
1330 Birth of the Black Prince
1332 Scots capture Berwick
1337 Philip confiscates Gascony; Edward claims French throne;
Hundred Years War begins
1339 Edward invades France
1340 Battle of Sluys; truce signed at Espléchin; birth of John of
Gaunt
1341 Scots capture Newcastle
1346 Battle of Crécy; Siege of Calais begins; King David of Scotland
captured
1347 Capture of Calais
1348 Black Death strikes France
1349 Black Death strikes England
1350 Death of Philip VI, accession of John II
1356 Battle of Poitiers
1357 King David of Scotland ransomed
1360 Peace of Brétigny
1362 Edward makes over Gascony and Poitou to Black Prince
1364 Death of John II; accession of Charles V
1367 Birth of Richard II; and of Henry IV; battle of Najera
1368 Resumption of war
1369 Death of Queen Philippa
1370 Black Prince, already sick, besieges Limoges
1375 Truce signed at Bruges
1376 Death of Black Prince
1377 Mob attacks John of Gaunt's Palace of Savoy; death of Edward
III; accession of Richard II

1381 Peasants' Revolt; death of Edmund Mortimer, third Earl of
March

1382 Marriage of Richard II and Anne of Bohemia

1383 Expedition to Flanders under Henry Despenser, Bishop of
Norwich

1385 Death of Queen Joan; Richard's expedition to Scotland

1386 John of Gaunt's Spanish expedition; 'Great and Continual
Council' appointed

1387 Gloucester, Arundel and Warwick defy King; de Vere defeated
by Bolingbroke at Radcot Bridge

1388 Appellants and 'Merciless' Parliament bring Richard to heel;
executions; Scots defeat English at Otterburn (Chevy Chase)

1389 John of Gaunt returns to England

1394 Four-year truce with France; death of Anne of Bohemia;
Richard leaves for Ireland

1395 Richard returns from Ireland

1396 Richard marries Isabelle of France; truce with France (lasts 25
years)

1397 Coronation of Isabelle; Gloucester, Arundel and Warwick
eliminated

1398 Parliament at Shrewsbury; Bolingbroke denounces Mowbray;
both sentenced

1399 Death of John of Gaunt; Richard sails for Ireland; Bolingbroke
lands in England; Richard is deposed; Bolingbroke crowned as
Henry IV

1400 Risings in Scotland and Wales

1402 Henry marries Joan of Brittany; battle of Homildon Hill

1403 Coronation of Joan; Percys rebel; battle of Shrewsbury

1404 Death of Philip the Fair of Burgundy; accession of John the
Fearless

1405 Rising in north under Northumberland and Archbishop of
York

1407 Assassination of Duke Louis of Orleans; succession of son
Charles

1408 Battle of Bramham Moor; Northumberland killed

1409 Fall of Harlech

1411 Expedition sent by Prince of Wales to help Burgundy in
France

1412 Expedition under Clarence sent by King to help Orleans

1413 Death of Henry IV; accession of Henry V

1414 Lollard rebellion

1415 Henry invades France; Cambridge plot; siege of Harfleur; Agincourt

1416 Relief of Harfleur; visit of Emperor Sigismund

1417 Henry's second expedition; capture of Caen

1418 Capture of Rouen after long siege

1419 Murder of John the Fearless

1420 Treaty of Troyes; marriage of Henry and Katherine; Henry rides into Paris

1421 Coronation of Katherine; battle of Beaugé; Henry's last campaign; birth of Henry VI

1422 Henry's death; accession of Henry VI; death of Charles VI; accession of Charles VII

1428 Siege of Orleans begins; death of Salisbury

1429 Coronation of Henry at Westminster; coronation of Charles VII; battle of Patay

1431 Burning of Joan of Arc; Henry crowned in Paris

1437 Charles VII enters Paris

1441 Duchess of Gloucester accused of witchcraft

1444 Truce with France; formal betrothal of Henry and Margaret of Anjou

1445 Marriage (by proxy) of Henry to Margaret

1447 Death of Duke Humphrey of Gloucester; death of Cardinal Beaufort

1448 Maine surrendered to France

1449 Sack of Fougères by Somerset; French regain Rouen; Richard of York goes to Ireland

1450 Battle of Formigny; disgrace of Suffolk; his death; Jack Cade's rebellion; Richard of York returns from Ireland without permission

1452 Richard of York marches on London

1453 Henry seriously ill; birth of son; arrest of Somerset

1454 Richard of York appointed Protector of Realm; Henry recovers

1455 Somerset back in power; first battle of St Albans

1460 Richard of York makes fourth march on London and formally

claims throne; Act of Accord; battle of Wakefield; death of
Richard

1461 Battle of Mortimer's Cross; second battle of St Albans;
Londoners rise against Lancastrians; Edward IV claims throne;
battle of Towton; death of Charles VII, accession of Louis XI

1462 Queen Margaret appeals to Louis XI

1464 Revolt in the north; battles of Hedgeley Moor and Hexham;
Henry VI escapes, wanders through north for almost a year;
Edward marries Elizabeth Woodville

1469 George Duke of Clarence marries Isabel, daughter of Warwick;
revolt under Robin of Redesdale; battle of Edgcote; capture of
King Edward by Warwick and Clarence

1470 Battle of Erpingham ('Lose-coat Field'); Warwick and Clarence
flee to France; Margaret's reconciliation with Warwick;
Warwick lands in Devon calling for restitution of Henry VI;
Edward, betrayed by Montagu, takes refuge in Holland; Henry
VI reinstated, with Warwick in power

1471 Edward returns to England; his recoronation; battle of Barnet;
death of Warwick; Margaret and her son Edward land at
Weymouth; battle of Tewkesbury; death of King Henry in
Tower

1475 Edward leads army to France; agreement at Picquigny;
Margaret ransomed

1478 Trial and death of Clarence

1482 Richard of Gloucester leads army into Scotland, occupies
Edinburgh

1483 Death of Edward IV; *coup* at Northampton; Richard transfers
two Princes to Tower; Richard arranges to be asked to assume
crown; his coronation; death of the Princes; revolt of
Buckingham

1484 Death of Richard's son, Edward of Middleham

1485 Death of Queen Anne; Henry Tudor lands at Milford Haven;
battle of Bosworth

Bibliography

THE PLAYS

The Arden Shakespeare. London, various editors and dates.
(For *Edward III*: *Elizabethan History Plays* (ed.) William A. Armstrong,
   OUP 1965.

CONTEMPORARY WORKS

Adam of Usk. *Chronicle, 1377–1421.* Tr. and ed. E. M. Thompson,
   London 1904.
Anon. *The Famous Victories of Henry the Fifth.* 1594?–8.
Anon. *The First English Life of Henry V.* Ed. C. L. Kingsford, Oxford
   1911.
Anon. *Gesta Henrici Quinti.* An account by an unknown chaplain to
   Henry V, ed. B. Williams for the English Historical Society, London
   1830.
Anon. *Historie of the Arrivall of King Edward IV.* Ed. J. Bruce, Camden
   Society, London 1838.
Chandos Herald, The. *Life of the Black Prince.* Tr. and ed. M. K. Pope
   and E. C. Lodge, London 1910.
Commynes, Philippe de. *Mémoires.* Ed. J. Calmette and G. Durville, 3
   vols, Paris 1924–5.
Croyland Chronicle, The. *Historiae Croylandensis Continuatio.* Tr. H. T.
   Riley as *Ingulph's Chronicles*, London 1893.
Daniel, Samuel. *The First Fowre Bookes of the ciuile warres between the two
   houses of Lancaster and Yorke.* In *Complete Works in Verse and Prose*, ed.
   A. B. Grosart, London 1885.
Fabyan, Robert. *The New Chronicles of England and France.* 1516, repub-
   lished by Sir Henry Ellis, 1816.
Fox, John. *Actes and Monuments.* Repr. 1843–9.
Froissart, Jean. *The Chronicle of Froissart translated out of French by Sir John*

Bourchier Lord Berners. With introduction by W. P. Ker, London 1903.

—*Chronicle*. Eng tr. abridged by G. Brereton, London 1968.

Great Chronicle of London, The. Ed. A. H. Thomas and I. D. Thorney, London 1938.

Hall, Edward. *Chronicle of the Vnion of the Two Noble and Illustre Famelies of Lancastre and Yorke*. 1542, 1548, 1550. (Reprinted London 1809)

Holinshed, Raphael. *The firste volume of the chronicles of England, Scotlande and Irelande*. 2nd edn, 1587. (*See* Nicoll, below)

Jean de Venette. *Chronicle*. Tr. J. Birdsall. Ed. R. A. Newhall, New York 1953.

Knighton, Henry. *Compilatio de eventibus Angliae*. Ed. J. R. Lumby. Rolls Series, London 1889–95. (Fifth book, by another author, covers the reign of Richard II.)

Mancini, Dominic. *De occupatione Regni Angliae per Riccardum Tercium*. Tr. and ed. C. A. J. Armstrong, Oxford 1969.

Monstrelet, Enguerrand de. *Chronique*. Ed. L. Douët d'Arcq for the Société de l'Histoire de France, 6 vols, Paris 1857–62.

More, Sir Thomas. *The History of King Richard the Third*. In *The Complete Works of Sir Thomas More*, vol. II. Ed. R. S. Sylvester, Yale 1963.

Paston Letters, 1422–1509. Ed. J. Gairdner, Rolls Series, 1858.

Polydore Vergil. *Three Books of Polydore Vergil's English History*. Ed. H. Ellis, Camden Society, London 1844.

—*The Anglica Historia of Polydore Vergil, AD 1485–1573*. Tr. and ed. D. Hay, Camden Series 1950.

Saint-Rémy. *Chronique de Jean le Fèvre, Seigneur de Saint-Rémy*. Ed. F. Morand, Paris 1876.

Titus Livius Forojuliensis. The 1st English Life of Henry V, written 1513 by 'the Translator of Livius'. Ed. C. L. Kingsford, Oxford 1911.

Walsingham, Thomas. *Historia Anglicana, 1272–1422*. Ed. H. T. Riley, 2 vols, Rolls Series, London 1863–4.

—*Chronicon Angliae, 1322–88*. Ed. E. M. Thompson, Rolls Series, London 1874.

—*Annales Ricardi Secundi*. Ed. H. T. Riley, Rolls Series, London 1866.

Waurin, Jean de. *Recueil des chroniques*. Ed. W. and E. Hardy, London 1872–3.

MODERN WORKS

Bagley, J. J. *Margaret of Anjou, Queen of England*. London.

Barber, Richard. *Edward, Prince of Wales and Aquitaine: A Biography of the Black Prince*. London 1978.

Black, M. W. *The Sources of Richard II*. J. Q. Adams Memorial Studies, Washington 1948.

Bullough, Geoffrey. *Narrative and Dramatic Sources of Shakespeare*. London 1960.

Burgess, Anthony. *Shakespeare*. London 1970.

The Cambridge Medieval History, vol. vii. Cambridge 1932.

Campbell, Lily B. *Shakespeare's 'Histories': Mirrors of Elizabethan Policy*. San Marino, California, 1947.

Christie, Mabel E. *Henry VI*. London 1922.

Churchill, G. B. *Richard III up to Shakespeare*. Berlin 1900.

Clarke, M. V. *Fourteenth Century Studies*. Oxford 1937.

The Dictionary of National Biography.

Elton, G. R. *England under the Tudors*. 3rd edn, London 1997.

Gillingham, John. *The Wars of the Roses: Peace and Conflict in Fifteenth-Century England*. London 1981.

Goodman, Anthony. *A History of England from Edward II to James I*. London 1977.

Hanham, A. *Richard III and His Early Historians*. Oxford 1975.

Hutchison, Harold F. *The Hollow Crown: A Life of Richard II*. London 1961.

—*Henry V: A Biography*. London 1967.

Jacob, E. F. *The Fifteenth Century, 1399–1485*. Oxford 1961.

Johnson, Paul. *The Life and Times of Edward III*. London 1973.

Kantorowicz, E. H. *The Kings's Two Bodies*. Princeton 1957.

Kendall, P. M. *Warwick the Kingmaker*. London 1957.

—*Richard III*. London 1955.

Kirby, J. L. *Henry IV of England*. London 1970.

The London Encyclopaedia. Ed. Ben Weinreb and Christopher Hibbert, London 1983.

McKisack, May. *The Fourteenth Century, 1307–1399*. Oxford 1959.

McLeod, Enid. *Charles of Orleans: Prince and Poet*. London 1969.

Mathew, Gervase. *The Court of Richard II*. London 1968.

Metz, G. Harold. *Sources of Four Plays Ascribed to Shakespeare*. London 1989.

Murray, Margaret. *Witchcraft in Western Europe*. Oxford 1921.

Nicoll, A. & J., eds. *Holinshed's Chronicle as Used in Shakespeare's Plays*. London 1927.

Packe, M. and Seaman, L. C. B. *King Edward III*. London 1983.

Pollard, A. J. *The Wars of the Roses*. London 1988.

—*Richard III and the Princes*. London 1991.

Ross, C. *Edward IV*. London 1974.

—*The Wars of the Roses*. London 1976.

—*Richard III*. London 1981.

Rowse, A. L. *The Annotated Shakespeare*. London 1978.

—*Bosworth Field and the Wars of the Roses*. London 1966.

Saul, Nigel. *Richard II*. London 1997.

Senior, Michael. *The Life and Times of Richard II*. London 1981.

Seward, Desmond. *Richard III*. London 1982.

A Shakespeare Encyclopaedia. Ed. O. J. Campbell and E. G. Quinn. London 1966.

Sprague, A. C. *Shakespeare's Histories: Plays for the Stage*. London 1964.

Steel, A. *Richard II*. Cambridge 1941.

Stubbs, William. *A Constitutional History of England*. 3 vols, Oxford 1874–8.

Tillyard, E. M. W. *Shakespeare's History Plays*. London 1944.

Trevelyan, G. M. *England in the Age of Wycliffe*. 4th edn, London 1909.

Tuchman, Barbara. *A Distant Mirror*. London 1978.

Walpole, Horace. *Historic Doubts on the Life and Reign of Richard III*. London 1768.

Weir, Alison. *The Wars of the Roses*. London 1995.

—*The Princes in the Tower*. London 1992.

Wilson, J. Dover, ed. *Richard II*. Cambridge 1951.

Wylie, J. H. *History of England under Henry the Fourth*. 4 vols, London 1884–98.

Ziegler, P. *The Black Death*. London 1969.

Appendix

Shakespeare's *Edward III*

The following text of *Edward III* is an early version taken from *Elizabethan History Plays*, William A. Armstrong (ed.), Oxford 1965.

DRAMATIS PERSONAE

EDWARD THE THIRD, King of England
EDWARD, Prince of Wales, his Son
EARL OF WARWICK
EARL OF DERBY
EARL OF SALISBURY
LORD AUDLEY
LORD PERCY
LODWICK, Edward's Confidant
SIR WILLIAM MONTAGUE
SIR JOHN COPLAND
Two Esquires, and a Herald, English
ROBERT, styling himself Earl, of Artois
LORD MOUNTFORD (or MONTFORT)
GOBIN DE GREY
JOHN, King of France
CHARLES,
PHILIP, } his Sons
DUKE OF LORRAINE
VILLIERS, a French Lord
King of Bohemia
A Polish Captain } Aids to King John
Two Citizens of Calais
A Captain, and a poor Inhabitant, of the same
Another Captain; a Mariner
Three Heralds, and four other Frenchmen

DAVID, King of Scotland
EARL DOUGLAS
Two Messengers, Scotch
PHILIPPA, Edward's Queen
COUNTESS OF SALISBURY
A French Woman
Lords, and divers other Attendants; Heralds, Officers, Soldiers, etc.
SCENE – dispersed; in ENGLAND, FLANDERS, and FRANCE

THE REIGN OF KING EDWARD THE THIRD

ACT I
SCENE I

London. A Room of State in the Palace.
Enter King Edward, Derby, Prince Edward, Audley, and Artois.

K. ED.   Robert of Artois, banish'd though thou be
From France, thy native country, yet with us
Thou shalt retain as great a signiory;
For we create thee Earl of Richmond here.
And now go forwards with our pedigree;
Who next succeeded Philip Le Beau?
ART.   Three sons of his; which all, successively,
Did sit upon their father's regal throne,
Yet died and left no issue of their loins.
K. ED.   But was my mother sister unto those?
ART.   She was, my lord; and only Isabel
Was all the daughters that this Philip had:
Whom afterward your father took to wife;
And, from the fragrant garden of her womb,
Your gracious self, the flower of Europe's hope,
Derived is inheritor to France.
But note the rancour of rebellious minds.
When thus the lineage of Le Beau was out,
The French obscur'd your mother's privilege;
And, though she were the next of blood, proclaim'd
John, of the house of Valois, now their king:
The reason was, they say, the realm of France,

(I, i) Replete with princes of great parentage,
    Ought not admit a governor to rule
    Except he be descended of the male;
    And that's the special ground of their contempt
    Wherewith they study to exclude your grace:

K. ED. But they shall find that forged ground of theirs
    To be but dusty heaps of brittle sand.

ART. Perhaps it will be thought a heinous thing
    That I, a Frenchman, should discover this:
    But Heaven I call to record of my vows;
    It is not hate nor any private wrong,
    But love unto my country and the right,
    Provokes my tongue thus lavish in report:
    You are the lineal watchman of our peace,
    And John of Valois indirectly climbs:
    What then should subjects, but embrace their king?
    Ah, wherein may our duty more be seen,
    Than striving to rebate a tyrant's pride
    And place the true shepherd of our commonwealth?

K. ED. This counsel, Artois, like to fruitful showers,
    Hath added growth unto my dignity:
    And, by the fiery vigour of thy words,
    Hot courage is engendered in my breast,
    Which heretofore was rack'd in ignorance,
    But now doth mount with golden wings of fame,
    And will approve fair Isabel's descent
    Able to yoke their stubborn necks with steel
    That spurn against my sov'reignty in France.—

              Sound a horn

    A messenger? – Lord Audley, know from whence.

     Enter, as messenger, Lorraine

AUD. The Duke of Lorraine, having cross'd the seas,
    Entreats he may have conference with your highness.

K. ED. Admit him, lords, that we may hear the news. –
    Say, Duke of Lorraine, wherefore art thou come?

LOR. The most renowned prince, K[ing] John of France,
    Doth greet thee, Edward: and by me commands,
    That, for so much as by his liberal gift
    The Guyenne dukedom is entail'd to thee,
    Thou do him lowly homage for the same:
    And, for that purpose, here I summon thee
    Repair to France within these forty days,
    That there, according as the custom is,

(I, i)   Thou may'st be sworn true liegeman to our king;
Or, else thy title in that province dies,
And he himself will repossess the place.

K. ED.   See, how occasion laughs me in the face!
No sooner minded to prepare for France,
But straight I am invited, nay, with threats,
Upon a penalty, enjoin'd to come:
'Twere but a childish part to say him nay. —
Lorraine, return this answer to thy lord:
I mean to visit him as he requests;
But how? not servilely dispos'd to bend,
But like a conqueror, to make him bow,
His lame unpolish'd shifts are come to light,
And truth hath pull'd the vizard from his face
That set a gloss upon his arrogance.
Dare he command a fealty in me?
Tell him, the crown, that he usurps, is mine,
And where he sets his foot, he ought to kneel:
'Tis not a petty dukedom that I claim,
But all the whole dominions of the realm;
Which if with grudging he refuse to yield,
I'll take away those borrow'd plumes of his
And send him naked to the wilderness.

LOR.   Then, Edward, here, in spite of all thy lords,
I do pronounce defiance to thy face.

PR. ED.   Defiance, Frenchman? we rebound it back,
Even to the bottom of thy master's throat:
And, — be it spoke with reverence of the king
My gracious father, and these other lords, —
I hold thy message but as scurrilous,
And him that sent thee, like the lazy drone
Crept up by stealth unto the eagle's nest;
From whence we'll shake him with so rough a storm,
As others shall be warned by his harm.

WAR.   Bid him leave off the lion's case he wears,
Lest, meeting with the lion in the field,
He chance to tear him piecemeal for his pride.

ART.   The soundest counsel I can give his grace
Is to surrender ere he be constrain'd.
A voluntary mischief hath less scorn,
Than when reproach with violence is borne.

LOR.   Degenerate traitor, viper to the place
Where thou wast foster'd in thine infancy,
Bear'st thou a part in this conspiracy?

He draws his sword

K. ED.   Lorraine, behold the sharpness of this steel:

Drawing his

    Fervent desire, that sits against my heart,
    Is far more thorny-pricking than this blade;
    That, with the nightingale, I shall be scar'd,
    As oft as I dispose myself to rest,
    Until my colours be display'd in France.
    This is thy final answer; so be gone.

LOR.   It is not that, nor any English brave,
    Afflicts me so, as doth his poison'd view,
    That is most false, should most of all be true.

Exeunt Lorraine

K. ED.   Now, Lord, our fleeting bark is under sail;
    Our gage is thrown, and war is soon begun,
    But not so quickly brought unto an end. –

Enter Montague

    But wherefore comes Sir William Montague?
    How stands the league between the Scot and us?

MON.   Crack'd and dissever'd, my renowned lord.
    The treacherous king no sooner was inform'd
    Of your withdrawing of your army back,
    But straight, forgetting of his former oath,
    He made invasion on the bordering towns.
    Berwick is won; Newcastle spoil'd and lost;
    And now the tyrant hath begirt with siege
    The castle of Roxborough, where enclos'd
    The Countess Salisbury is like to perish.

K. ED.   That is thy daughter, Warwick – is it not? –
    Whose husband hath in Britain serv'd so long,
    About the planting of Lord Mountford there?

WAR.   It is, my lord.

K. ED.   Ignoble David! hast thou none to grieve,
    But silly ladies, with thy threat'ning arms?
    But I will make you shrink your snaily horns. –
    First, therefore, Audley, this shall be thy charge;
    Go levy footmen for our wars in France:
    And, Ned, take muster of our men at arms:
    In every shire elect a several band.
    Let them be soldiers of a lusty spirit,
    Such as dread nothing but dishonour's blot:
    Be wary therefore; since we do commence
    A famous war and with so mighty a nation.
    Derby, be thou ambassador for us.

(I, i)   Unto our father-in-law, the Earl of Hainault:
           Make him acquainted with our enterprise;
           And likewise will him, with our own allies
           That are in Flanders, to solicit to
           The Emperor of Almaine in our name.
           Myself, whilst you are jointly thus employ'd,
           Will, with these forces that I have at hand,
           March and once more repulse the trait'rous Scot.
           But, sirs, be resolute; we shall have wars
           On every side: and, Ned, thou must begin
           Now to forget thy study and thy books
           And ure thy shoulders to an armour's weight.
PR. ED.   As cheerful sounding to my youthful spleen
           This tumult is of war's increasing broils,
           As at the coronation of a king
           The joyful clamours of the people are
           When, 'Ave, Cæsar!' they pronounce aloud.
           Within this school of honour I shall learn,
           Either to sacrifice my foes to death
           Or in a rightful quarrel spend my breath.
           Then cheerfully forward, each a several way;
           In great affairs 'tis naught to use delay.

                                                                      Exeunt

SCENE II

Roxborough. Before the Castle.
Enter the Countess above.

[COUNT.]   Alas, how much in vain my poor eyes gaze
           For succour that my sovereign should send!
           Ah, cousin Montague, I fear, thou want'st
           The lively spirit sharply to solicit
           With vehement suit the king in my behalf:
           Thou dost not tell him, what a grief it is
           To be the scornful captive to a Scot;
           Either to be woo'd with broad untuned oaths,
           Or forc'd by rough insulting barbarism:
           Thou dost not tell him, if he here prevail,
           How much they will deride us in the north;
           And, in their wild, uncivil, skipping jigs,
           Bray forth their conquest and our overthrow,
           Even in the barren, bleak, and fruitless air.

                   Enter David and Douglas, Lorraine
           I must withdraw; the everlasting foe

(I, ii) Comes to the wall: I'll closely step aside,
And list their babble, blunt and full of pride.

K. DAV. My Lord of Lorraine, to our brother of France
Commend us, as the man in Christendom
Whom we most reverence and entirely love.
Touching your embassage, return and say
That we with England will not enter parley
Nor never make fair weather or take truce,
But burn their neighbour towns, and so persist
With eager rods beyond their city York.
And never shall our bonny riders rest,
Nor rusting canker we have the time to eat
Their light-borne snaffles nor their nimble spurs;
Nor lay aside their jacks of gimmaled mail;
Nor hang their staves of grained Scottish ash
In peaceful wise upon their city walls;
Nor from their button'd tawny leathern belts
Dismiss their biting whinyards, till your king
Cry out, 'Enough; spare England now for pity.'
Farewell, and tell him, that you leave us here
Before this castle; say, you came from us
Even when we had that yielded to our hands.

LOR. I take my leave, and fairly will return
Your acceptable greeting to my king.

Exit Lor.

K. DAV. Now, Douglas, to our former task again,
For the division of this certain spoil.

DOUG. My liege, I crave the lady, and no more.

K. DAV. Nay, soft ye, sir, first I must make my choice;
And first I do bespeak her for myself.

DOUG. Why, then, my liege, let me enjoy her jewels.

K. DAV. Those are her own, still liable to her,
And, who inherits her, hath those withal.

Enter a Scot [as Messenger] in haste

MESS. My liege, as we were pricking on the hills,
To fetch in booty, marching hitherward
We might descry a mighty host of men;
The sun, reflecting on the armour, show'd
A field of plate, a wood of pikes advanc'd.
Bethink your highness speedily herein:
An easy march within four hours will bring
The hindmost rank unto this place, my liege.

K. DAV. Dislodge, dislodge, it is the King of England.

(I, ii)   DOUG.   Jemmy my man, saddle my bonny black.

K. DAV.   Mean'st thou to fight, Douglas? We are too weak.

DOUG.   I know it well, my liege, and therefore fly.

COUNT.   My lords of Scotland, will ye stay and drink?

K. DAV.   She mocks at us; Douglas, I can't endure it.

COUNT.   Say, good my lord, which is he, must have the
            lady,
    And which, her jewels? I am sure, my lords,
    Ye will not hence, till you have shar'd the spoils.

K. DAV.   She heard the messenger and heard our talk;
    And now that comfort makes her scorn at us.

Another messenger

MESS.   Arm, my good lord! O, we are all surpris'd!

COUNT.   After the French ambassador, my liege,
    And tell him that you dare not ride to York;
    Excuse it, that your bonny horse is lame.

K. DAV.   She heard that too; intolerable grief! –
    Woman, farewell: although I do not stay, –

                                            Exeunt Scots

COUNT.   'Tis not for fear, and yet you run away. –
    O happy comfort, welcome to our house!
    The confident and boist'rous boasting Scot, –
    That swore before my walls, they would not back
    For all the armed power of this land, –
    With faceless fear that ever turns his back,
    Turn'd hence again the blasting north-east wind
    Upon the bare report and name of arms.

Enter Montague

    O summer's day! see where my cousin comes.

MON.   How fares my aunt? we are not Scots;
    Why do you shut your gates against your friends?

COUNT.   Well may I give a welcome, cousin, to thee,
    For thou com'st well to chase my foes from hence.

MON.   The king himself is come in person hither;
    Dear aunt, descend, and gratulate his highness.

COUNT.   How may I entertain his majesty,
    To show my duty and his dignity?

                                    Exit, from above

Enter King Edward, Warwick, Artois, with others

K. ED.   What, are the stealing foxes fled and gone
    Before we could uncouple at their heels?

(I, ii)   WAR.   They are, my liege; but, with a cheerful cry,
Hot hounds and hardy chase them at the heels.

Enter Countess

K. ED.   This is the countess, Warwick, is it not?

WAR.   Even she, my liege; whose beauty tyrant's fear,
As a May blossom with pernicious winds,
Hath sullied, wither'd overcast, and done.

K. ED.   Hath she been fairer, Warwick, than she is?

WAR.   My gracious king, fair is she not at all,
If that herself were by to stain herself,
As I have seen her when she was herself.

K. ED.   What strange enchantment lurk'd in those her eyes
When they excell'd this excellence they have,
That now her dim decline hath power to draw
My subject eyes from piercing majesty
To gaze on her with doting admiration?

COUNT.   In duty lower than the ground I kneel
And for my dull knees bow my feeling heart,
To witness my obedience to your highness;
With many millions of a subject's thanks
For this your royal presence, whose approach
Hath driven war and danger from my gate.

K. ED.   Lady, stand up: I come to bring thee peace,
However thereby I have purchas'd war.

COUNT.   No war to you, my liege; the Scots are gone,
And gallop home toward Scotland with their hate.

[K. ED].   Lest yielding here I pine in shameful love,
Come, we'll pursue the Scots; – Artois, away!

COUNT.   A little while, my gracious sovereign, stay
And let the power of a mighty king
Honour our roof; my husband in the wars,
When he shall hear it, will triumph for joy:
Then, dear my liege; now niggard not thy state;
Being at the wall, enter our homely gate.

K. ED.   Pardon me, countess, I will come not near;
I dream'd to-night of treason, and I fear.

COUNT.   Far from this place let ugly treason lie!

K. ED.   No farther off than her conspiring eye,
Which shoots infected poison in my heart
Beyond repulse of wit or cure of art.
Now in the sun alone it doth not lie
With light to take light from a mortal eye;
For here two day-stars, that mine eyes would see,

(I, ii)   More than the sun, steals mine own light from me.
Contemplative desire! desire to be
In contemplation, that may master thee!
Warwick, Artois, to horse, and let's away!

COUNT.   What might I speak, to make my sovereign stay?

K. ED.   What needs a tongue to such a speaking eye
That more persuades than winning oratory?

COUNT.   Let not thy presence, like the April sun,
Flatter our earth and suddenly be done.
More happy do not make our outward wall.
Than thou wilt grace our inner house withal.
Our house, my liege, is like a country swain,
Whose habit rude and manners blunt and plain
Presageth nought, yet inly beautified
With bounty's riches and fair hidden pride:
For, where the golden ore doth buried lie,
The ground, undeck'ed with nature's tapestry,
Seems barren, sere, unfertile, fruitless, dry;
And where the upper turf of earth doth boast
His pride, perfumes and parti-colour'd cost,
Delve there, and find this issue and their pride
To spring from ordure and corruption's side.
But, to make up my all too long compare,
These ragged walls no testimony are
What is within; but, like a cloak, doth hide,
From weather's waste, the under-garnish'd pride.
More gracious than my terms can let thee be,
Intreat thyself to stay a while with me.

K. ED.   *[Aside]* As wise as fair; what fond fit can be heard
When wisdom keeps the gate as beauty's guard? –
Countess, albeit my business urgeth me,
It shall attend while I attend on thee. –
Come on, my lords, here will I host to-night.

                                                      Exeunt

ACT II
SCENE I

The same. Gardens of the Castle.
Enter Lodwick

LOD.   I might perceive his eye in her eye lost,
His ear to drink her sweet tongue's utterance;
And changing passion, like inconstant clouds
That rack upon the carriage of the winds,

(II, i)   Increase and die in his disturbed cheeks.
Lo, when she blush'd, even then did he look pale,
As if her cheeks, by some enchanted power,
Attracted had the cherry blood from his:
Anon, with reverent fear when she grew pale,
His cheeks put on their scarlet ornaments,
But no more like her oriental red,
Than brick to coral or live things to dead.
Why did he then thus counterfeit her looks?
If she did blush, 'twas tender modest shame,
Being in the sacred presence of a king;
If he did blush, 'twas red immodest shame,
To vail his eyes amiss, being a king:
If she look'd pale, 'twas silly woman's fear,
To bear herself in presence of a king:
If he look'd pale, it was with guilty fear,
To dote amiss, being a mighty king:
Then, Scottish wars, farewell! I fear, 'twill prove
A ling'ring English siege of peevish love.
Here comes his highness, walking all alone.

Enter King Edward

K. ED.   She is grown more fairer far since I came hither;
Her voice more silver every word than other,
Her wit more fluent: what a strange discourse
Unfolded she of David and his Scots!
'Even thus,' quoth she, 'he spake,' – and then spoke broad,
With epithets and accents of the Scot;
But somewhat better than the Scot could speak:
'And thus,' quoth she, – and answer'd then herself;
For who could speak like her? but she herself
Breathes from the wall an angel's note from heaven
Of sweet defiance to her barbarous foes.
When she would talk of peace, methinks, her tongue
Commanded war to prison; when of war,
It waken'd Cæsar from his Roman grave,
To hear war beautified by her discourse.
Wisdom is foolishness, but in her tongue,
Beauty a slander, but in her fair face:
There is no summer, but in her cheerful looks,
Nor frosty winter, but in her disdain.
I cannot blame the Scots that did besiege her,
For she is all the treasure of our land;
But call them cowards, that they ran away,

(II, i)   Having so rich and fair a cause to stay. –
        Art thou there, Lodwick? give me ink and paper.
LOD.   I will, my liege.
K. ED.   And bid the lords hold on their play at chess,
        For we will walk and meditate alone.
LOD.   I will, my sovereign.

                                      [Exit]

K. ED.   This fellow is well read in poetry
        And hath a lusty and persuasive spirit:
        I will acquaint him with my passion;
        Which he shall shadow with a veil of lawn,
        Through which the queen of beauty's queens shall see.
        Herself the ground of my infirmity. –

              Enter Lodwick
       Hast thou pen, ink, and paper ready, Lodwick?
LOD.   Ready, my liege.
K. ED.   Then in the summer arbour sit by me,
        Make it our council–house, or cabinet;
        Since green our thoughts, green be the conventicle
        Where we will ease us by disburd'ning them.
        Now, Lodwick, invocate some golden muse
        To bring thee hither an enchanted pen
        That may, for sighs, set down true sighs indeed;
        Talking of grief, to make thee ready groan;
        And, when thou writ'st of tears, encouch the word,
        Before and after, with such sweet laments,
        That it may raise drops in a Tartar's eye,
        And make a flint–heart Scythian pitiful:
        For so much moving hath a poet's pen;
        Then, if thou be a poet, move thou so,
        And be enriched by thy sovereign's love.
        For, if the touch of sweet concordant strings
        Could force attendance in the ears of hell;
        How much more shall the strains of poet's wit
        Beguile and ravish soft and human minds?
LOD.   To whom, my lord, shall I direct my style?
K. ED.   To one that shames the fair and sots the wise;
        Whose body is an abstract or a brief,
        Contains each general virtue in the world.
        Better than beautiful, thou must begin;
        Devise for fair a fairer word than fair;
        And every ornament, that thou wouldst praise,
        Fly it a pitch above the soar of praise:

(II, i)   For flattery fear thou not to be convicted;
For, were thy admiration ten times more,
Ten times ten thousand more the worth exceeds,
Of that thou art to praise, thy praise's worth.
Begin, I will to contemplate the while:
Forget not to set down, how passionate,
How heart-sick, and how full of languishment,
Her beauty makes me.

LOD.   Write I to a woman?

K. ED.   What beauty else could triumph over me;
Or who, but women, do our love-lays greet?
What, think'st thou I did bid thee praise a horse?

LOD.   Of what condition or estate she is,
'Twere requisite that I should know, my lord.

K. ED.   Of such estate, that hers is as a throne,
And my estate the footstool where she treads:
Then may'st thou judge what her condition is,
By the proportion of her mightiness.
Write on, while I peruse her in my thoughts.
Her voice to music, or the nightingale:
To music every summer-leaping swain
Compares his sun-burnt lover when she speaks:
And why should I speak of the nightingale?
The nightingale sings of adulterate wrong;
And that, compar'd, is too satirical:
For sin, though sin, would not be so esteem'd;
But, rather, virtue sin, sin virtue deem'd.
Her hair, far softer than the silkworm's twist,
Like to flattering glass, doth make more fair
The yellow amber: 'like a flattering glass'
Comes in too soon; for, writing of her eyes,
I'll say, that like a glass they catch the sun,
And thence the hot reflection doth rebound
Against my breast, and burns my heart within.
Ah, what a world of descant makes my soul
Upon this voluntary ground of love! –
Come, Lodwick, hast thou turn'd thy ink to gold?
If not, write but in letters capital
My mistress' name, and it will gild thy paper.
Read, lord, read;
Fill thou the empty hollows of mine ears
With the sweet hearing of thy poetry.

LOD.   I have not to a period brought her praise.

K. ED.   Her praise is as my love, both infinite,

(II, i)   Which apprehend such violent extremes
        That they disdain an ending period.
        Her beauty hath no match but my affection;
        Hers more than most, mine most, and more than more:
        Hers more to praise than tell the sea by drops;
        Nay, more, than drop the massy earth by sands,
        And, sand by sand, print them in memory:
        Then wherefore talk'st thou of a period,
        To that which craves unended admiration?
        Read, let us hear.

LOD.   'More fair and chaste than is the queen of shades,' –

K. ED.   That line hath two faults, gross and palpable:
        Compar'st thou her to the pale queen of night,
        Who, being set in dark, seems therefore light?
        What is she, when the suns lifts up his head,
        But like a fading taper, dim and dead?
        My love shall brave the eye of heaven at noon,
        And, being unmask'd, outshine the golden sun.

LOD.   What is the other fault, my sovereign lord?

K. ED.   Read o'er the line again.

LOD.   'More fair and chaste,' –

K. ED.   I did not bid thee talk of chastity,
        To ransack so the treasure of her mind;
        For I had rather have her chas'd, than chaste.
        Out with the moon-line, I will none of it,
        And let me have her liken'd to the sun:
        Say, she hath thrice more splendour than the sun,
        That her perfections emulates the sun,
        That she breeds sweets as plenteous as the sun,
        That she doth thaw cold winter like the sun,
        That she doth cheer fresh summer like the sun,
        That she doth dazzle gazers like the sun:
        And, in this application to the sun,
        Bid her free and general as the sun;
        Who smiles upon the basest weed that grows,
        As lovingly as on the fragrant rose.
        Let's see what follows that same moon-light line.

LOD.   'More fair and chaste than is the queen of shades;
        More bold in constancy' –

K. ED.   In constancy! than who?

LOD.   – 'than Judith was.'

K. ED.   O monstrous line! Put in the next a sword,
        And I shall woo her to cut off my head.
        Blot, blot, good Lodwick! Let us hear the next.

(II, i) LOD.   There's all that yet is done.

K. ED.   I thank thee then, thou hast done little ill;
But what is done, is passing passing ill.
No, let the captain talk of boist'rous war;
The prisoner, of immured dark constraint;
The sick man best sets down the pangs of death;
The man that starves, the sweetness of a feast;
The frozen soul, the benefit of fire;
And every grief, his happy opposite:
Love cannot sound well, but in lovers' tongues;
Give me the pen and paper, I will write. —

Enter Countess

But, soft, here comes the treasurer of my spirit. —
Lodwick, thou know'st not how to draw a battle;
These wings, these flankers, and these squadrons
Argue in thee defective discipline:
Thou shouldst have plac'd this here, this other here.

COUNT.   Pardon my boldness, my thrice-gracious lords;
Let my intrusion here be call'd my duty,
That comes to see my sovereign how he fares.

K. ED.   Go, draw the same, I tell thee in what form.

LOD.   I go.

[*Exit*]

COUNT.   Sorry I am, to see my liege so sad:
What may thy subject do, to drive from thee
Thy gloomy consort, sullen melancholy?

K. ED.   Ah, lady, I am blunt, and cannot straw
The flowers of solace in a ground of shame:
Since I came hither, countess, I am wrong'd.

COUNT.   Now, God forbid, that any in my house
Should think my sovereign wrong! Thrice-gentle king,
Acquaint me with your cause of discontent.

K. ED.   How near then shall I be to remedy?

COUNT.   As near, my liege, as all my woman's power
Can pawn itself to buy thy remedy.

K. ED.   If thou speak'st true, then have I my redress:
Engage thy power to redeem my joys,
And I am joyful, countess; else, I die.

COUNT.   I will, my liege.

K. ED.   Swear, countess, that thou wilt.

COUNT.   By Heaven, I will.

K. ED.   Then take thyself a little way aside,
And tell thyself, a king doth dote on thee:

(II, i)
Say that within thy power [it] doth lie
To make him happy, and that thou hast sworn
To give him all the joy within thy power:
Do this; and tell me, when I shall be happy.

COUNT.   All this is done, my thrice-dread sovereign:
That power of love, that I have power to give,
Thou hast with all devout obedience;
Employ me how thou wilt in proof thereof.

K. ED.   Thou hear'st me say, that I do dote on thee.

COUNT.   If on my beauty, take it if thou canst;
Though little, I do prize it ten times less:
If on my virtue, take it if thou canst;
For virtue's store by giving doth augment:
Be it on what it will, that I can give
And thou canst take away, inherit it.

K. ED.   It is thy beauty that I would enjoy.

COUNT.   O, were it painted, I would wipe if off
And dispossess myself, to give it thee.
But, sovereign, it is solder'd to my life;
Take one, and both; for, like an humble shadow,
It haunts the sunshine of my summer's life.

K. ED.   But thou may'st leave it me, to sport withal.

COUNT.   As easy may my intellectual soul
Be lent away, and yet my body live,
As lend my body, palace to my soul,
Away from her, and yet retain my soul.
My body is her bower, her court, her abbey,
And she an angel, pure, divine, unspotted;
If I should leave her house, my lord, to thee,
I kill my poor soul, and my poor soul me.

K. ED.   Didst thou not swear, to give me what I would?

COUNT.   I did, my liege; so, what you would, I could.

K. ED.   I wish no more of thee than thou may'st give,
Nor beg I do not, but I rather buy;
That is, thy love; and, for that love of thine,
In rich exchange, I tender to thee mine.

COUNT.   But that your lips were sacred, my lord,
You would profane the holy name of love.
That love, you offer me, you cannot give,
For Cæsar owes that tribute to his queen:
That love, you beg of me, I cannot give,
For Sara owes that duty to her lord.
He that doth clip or counterfeit your stamp
Shall die, my lord: and will your sacred self

(II, i)   Commit high treason against the King of Heaven,
To stamp his image in forbidden metal,
Forgetting your allegiance and your oath?
In violating marriage' sacred law,
You break a greater honour than yourself:
To be a king, is of a younger house
Than to be married; your progenitor,
Sole-reigning Adam on the universe,
By God was honour'd for a married man,
But not by him anointed for a king.
It is a penalty to break your statutes,
Though not enacted with your highness' hand:
How much more, to infringe the holy act
Made by the mouth of God, seal'd with his hand?
I know, my sovereign – in my husband's love,
Who now doth loyal service in his wars –
Doth but to try the wife of Salisbury,
Whether she will hear a wanton's tale, or no;
Lest being therein guilty by my stay,
From that, not from my liege, I turn away.

Exit

K. ED.   Whether is her beauty by her words divine,
Or are her words sweet chaplains to her beauty?
Like as the wind doth beautify a sail,
And as a sail becomes the unseen wind,
So do her words her beauty, beauty words.
O, that I were a honey-gathering bee,
To bear the comb of virtue from his flower;
And not a poison-sucking envious spider,
To turn the juice I take to deadly venom!
Religion is austere, and beauty gentle;
Too strict a guardian for so fair a ward.
O, that she were, as is the air, to me!
Why, so she is; for, when I would embrace her,
This do I, and catch nothing but myself.
I must enjoy her; for I cannot beat,
With reason and reproof, fond love away.

Enter Warwick

Here comes her father: I will work with him,
To bear my colours in this field of love.

WAR.   How is it, that my sovereign is so sad?
May I with pardon know your highness' grief,
And that my old endeavour will remove it,

(II, i)   It shall not cumber long your majesty.

K. ED.   A kind and voluntary gift thou proffer'st,
That I was forward to have begg'd of thee.
But, O thou world, great nurse of flattery,
Why dost thou tip men's tongues with golden words
And peise their deeds with weight of heavy lead,
That fair performance cannot follow promise?
O, that a man might hold the heart's close book,
And choke the lavish tongue when it doth utter
The breath of falsehood not character'd there!

WAR.   Far be it from the honour of my age
That I should owe bright gold and render lead!
Age is a cynic, not a flatterer:
I say again, that, if I knew your grief,
And that by me it may be lessened,
My proper harm should buy your highness' good.

K. ED.   These are the vulgar tenders of false men,
That never pay the duty of their words.
Thou wilt not stick to swear what thou hast said;
But, when thou know'st my grief's condition,
This rash-disgorged vomit of thy word
Thou wilt eat up again, and leave me helpless.

WAR.   By Heaven, I will not, though your majesty
Did bid me run upon your sword and die.

[K. ED].   Say, that my grief is no way med'cinable,
But by the loss and bruising of thine honour?

WAR.   If nothing but that loss may vantage you,
I would account that loss my vantage too.

K. ED.   Think'st that thou canst unswear thy oath again?

WAR.   I cannot; nor I would not, if I could.

K. ED.   But, if thou dost, what shall I say to thee?

WAR.   What may be said to any perjur'd villain
That breaks the sacred warrant of an oath.

K. ED.   What wilt thou say to one that breaks an oath?

WAR.   That he hath broke his faith with God and man
And from them both stands excommunicate.

K. ED.   What office were it to suggest a man
To break a lawful and religious vow?

WAR.   An office for the devil, not for man.

K. ED.   That devil's office must thou do for me;
Or break thy oath or cancel all the bonds
Of love and duty 'twixt thyself and me.
And therefore, Warwick, if thou art thyself,
The lord and master of thy word and oath,

(II, i)   Go to thy daughter, and in my behalf
            Command her, woo her, win her any ways,
            To be my mistress and my secret love.
            I will not stand to hear thee make reply;
            Thy oath breaks hers, or let thy sovereign die.

                                                                    Exit

WAR.   O doting king! O detestable office!
       Well may I tempt myself to wrong myself.
       When he hath sworn me by the name of God
       To break a vow made by the name of God.
       What if I swear by this right hand of mine
       To cut this right hand off? the better way
       Were to profane the idol than confound it:
       But neither will I do; I'll keep mine oath
       And to my daughter make a recantation
       Of all the virtue I have preach'd to her.
       I'll say, she must forget her husband Salisbury,
       If she remember to embrace the king;
       I'll say, an oath may easily be broken,
       But not so easily pardon'd, being broken;
       I'll say, it is true charity to love,
       But not true love to be so charitable;
       I'll say, his greatness may bear out the shame,
       But not his kingdom can buy out the sin;
       I'll say, it is my duty to persuade,
       But not her honesty to give consent.

                        Enter Countess

       See, where she comes: was never father, had
       Against his child an embassage so bad.
COUNT.   My lord and father, I have sought for you:
         My mother and the peers importune you
         To keep in presence of his majesty
         And do your best to make his highness merry.
WAR.   How shall I enter in this graceless errand?
       I must not call her child; for where's the father
       That will, in such a suit, seduce his child?
       Then, 'Wife of Salisbury', – shall I so begin?
       No, he's my friend; and where is found the friend,
       That will do friendship such endamagement? –
       [*To the Countess*]   Neither my daughter, nor my dear friend's wife,
       I am not Warwick, as thou think'st I am,
       But an attorney from the court of hell;
       That thus have hous'd my spirit in his form,

(II, i)   To do a message to thee from the king.
The mighty King of England dotes on thee:
He hath power to take away thy life
Hath power to take thine honour; then consent
To pawn thine honour, rather than thy life:
Honour is often lost and got again;
But life, once gone, hath no recovery.
The sun, that withers hay, doth nourish grass;
The king that would distain thee will advance thee.
The poets write that great Achilles' spear
Could heal the wound it made: the moral is,
What mighty men misdo, they can amend.
The lion doth become his bloody jaws
And grace his foragement, by being mild
When vassal fear lies trembling at his feet.
The king will in his glory hide thy shame;
And those that gaze on him to find out thee
Will lose their eyesight, looking in the sun.
What can one drop of poison harm the sea,
Whose hugy vastures can digest the ill
And make it lose his operation?
The king's great name will temper thy misdeeds,
And give the bitter potion of reproach
A sugar'd-sweet and most delicious taste:
Besides, it is no harm, to do the thing
Which without shame could not be left undone.
Thus have I, in his majesty's behalf,
Apparell'd sin in virtuous sentences,
And dwell upon thy answer in his suit.

COUNT.   Unnatural besiege! Woe me unhappy,
To have escap'd the danger of my foes
And to be ten times worse envir'd by friends!
Hath he no means to stain my honest blood,
But to corrupt the author of my blood
To be his scandalous and vile solicitor?
No marvel, though the branches be then infected,
When poison hath encompassed the root:
No marvel, though the leprous infant die,
When the stern dam envenometh the dug.
Why then, give sin a passport to offend,
And youth the dangerous rein of liberty:
Blot out the strict forbidding of the law;
And cancel every canon, that prescribes
A shame for shame or penance for offence.

(II, i)   No, let me die, if his too boist'rous will
Will have it so, before I will consent
To be an actor in his graceless lust.

WAR.   Why, now thou speak'st as I would have thee speak:
And mark how I unsay my words again.
An honourable grave is more esteem'd,
Than the polluted closet of a king:
The greater man, the greater is the thing,
Be it good or bad, that he shall undertake:
An unreputed mote, flying in the sun,
Presents a greater substance than it is:
The freshest summer's day both soonest taint
The loathed carrion that it seems to kiss:
Deep are the blows made with a mighty axe:
That sin doth ten times aggravate itself,
That is committed in a holy place:
An evil deed, done by authority,
Is sin and subornation: deck an ape
In tissue, and the beauty of the robe
Adds but the greater scorn unto the beast.
A spacious field of reasons could I urge
Between his glory, daughter, and thy shame:
That poison shows worst in a golden cup;
Dark night seems darker by the lightning-flash;
Lilies that fester smell far worse than weeds;
And every glory that inclines to sin,
The shame is treble by the opposite.
So leave I, with my blessing in thy bosom;
Which then convert to a most heavy curse,
When thou convert'st from honour's golden name
To the black faction of bed-blotting shame!

COUNT.   I'll follow thee; and, when my mind turns so,
My body sink my soul in endless woe!

                                   Exeunt

SCENE II

The same. A room in the castle.
Enter at one door Derby from France: at another door Audley
with a drum.

DER.   Thrice-noble Audley, well encounter'd here:
How is it with our sovereign and his peers?

AUD.   'Tis full a fortnight since I saw his highness,

(II, ii) What time he sent me forth to muster men;
    Which I accordingly have done, and bring them hither
    In fair array before his majesty.
    What news, my Lord of Derby, from the Emperor?

DER. As good as we desire: the Emperor
    Hath yielded to his highness friendly aid;
    And makes our king lieutenant-general
    In all his lands and large dominions:
    Then *via* for the spacious bounds of France!

AUD. What, doth his highness leap to hear these news?

DER. I have not yet found time to open them;
    The king is in his closet, malcontent,
    For what, I know not, but he gave in charge,
    Till after dinner, none should interrupt him:
    The Countess Salisbury, and her father Warwick,
    Artois, and all, look underneath the brows.

AUD. Undoubtedly then something is amiss.

            [Trumpet within]

DER. The trumpets sound; the king is now abroad.

       Enter the King

AUD. Here comes his highness.

DER. Befall my sovereign all my sovereign's wish!

K. ED. Ah, that thou wert a witch, to make it so!

DER. The emperor greeteth you:

K. ED.   Would it were the countess!

DER. And hath accorded to your highness' suit.

K. ED. Thou liest, she hath not; but I would, she had!

AUD. All love and duty to my lord the king!

K. ED. Well, all but one is none: – what news with you?

AUD. I have, my liege, levied those horse and foot,
    According to your charge, and brought them hither.

K. ED. Then let those foot trudge hence upon those horse,
    According to our discharge, and be gone. –
    Derby, I'll look upon the countess' mind anon.

DER. The countess' mind, my liege?

K. ED. I mean the emperor: leave me alone.

AUD. What's in his mind?

DER.   Let's leave him to his humour.

            Exeunt

K. ED. Thus from the heart's abundance speaks the tongue;
    Countess for emperor: and, indeed, why not?
    She is as imperator over me;
    And I to her

(II, ii)   Am as a kneeling vassal that observes
The pleasure or displeasure of her eye. –

Enter Lodwick

What says the more than Cleopatra's match
To Cæsar now?

LOD.   That yet, my liege, ere night
She will resolve your majesty.

[*Drum within*]

K. ED.   What drum is this, that thunders forth this march,
To start the tender Cupid in my bosom?
Poor sheep-skin, how it brawls with him that beateth it!
Go, break the thund'ring parchment-bottom out,
And I will teach it to conduct sweet lines
Unto the bosom of a heavenly nymph:
For I will use it as my writing-paper;
And so reduce him, from a scolding drum,
To be the herald and dear counsel-bearer
Betwixt a goddess and a mighty king.
Go, bid the drummer learn to touch the lute,
Or hang him in the braces of his drum;
For now we think it an uncivil thing,
To trouble heaven with such harsh resounds:
Away. –   *Exit Lodwick*
The quarrel, that I have, requires no arms
But these of mine; and these shall meet my foe
In a deep march of penetrable groans;
My eyes shall be my arrows; and my sighs
Shall serve me as the vantage of the wind,
To whirl away my sweet'st artillery:
Ah but, alas, she wins the sun of me,
For that is she herself; and thence it comes
That poets term the wanton warrior blind;
But love hath eyes as judgment to his steps,
Till too-much-loved glory dazzles them. –

Enter Lodwick

How now?

LOD.   My liege, the drum that struck the lusty march
Stands with Prince Edward, your thrice-valiant son.

[*Exit*]

Enter Prince Edward

K. ED.   I see the boy. Oh, how his mother's face,
Modell'd in his, corrects my stray'd desire

(II, ii)   And rates my heart and chides my thievish eye;
                Who being rich enough in seeing her,
                Yet seeks elsewhere: and basest theft is that,
                Which cannot cloak itself on poverty. –
                Now, boy, what news?

PR. ED.   I have assembled, my dear lord and father,
                The choicest buds of all our English blood
                For our affairs in France; and here we come,
                To take direction from your majesty.

K. ED.   Still do I see in him delineate
                His mother's visage; those his eyes are hers,
                Who looking wistly on me make me blush;
                For faults against themselves give evidence:
                Lust is a fire, and men, like lanthorns, show
                Light lust within themselves, even through themselves.
                Away, loose silks of wavering vanity!
                Shall the large limit of fair Brittany
                By me be overthrown? and shall I not
                Master this little mansion of myself?
                Give me an armour of eternal steel;
                I go to conquer kings; and shall I not then
                Subdue myself and be my enemy's friend?
                It must not be. – Come, boy, forward, advance!
                Let's with our colours sweet the air of France.

Enter Lodwick

LOD.   My liege, the countess with a smiling cheer
                Desires access unto your majesty.

K. ED.   Why, there it goes! that very smile of hers
                Hath ransom'd captive France, and set the king,
                The Dauphin, and the peers, at liberty. –
                Go, leave me, Ned, and revel with thy friends.

Exit Prince

                Thy mother is but black; and thou, like her,
                Dost put into my mind how foul she is. –
                Go, fetch the countess hither in thy hand
                And let her chase away those winter clouds;
                For she gives beauty both to heaven and earth.

Exit Lodwick

                The sin is more to hack and hew poor men,
                Than to embrace in an unlawful bed
                The register of all rarities
                Since leathern Adam till this youngest hour.

(II, ii)   *Enter Countess [and Lodwick]*

    Go, Lodwick, put thy hand into my purse,

    Play, spend, give, riot, waste; do what thou wilt,

    So thou wilt hence a while and leave me here.

                             [Exit Lodwick]

    Now, my soul's playfellow! art thou come,

    To speak the more than heavenly word of *yea*

    To my objection in thy beauteous love?

COUNT.   My father on his blessing hath commanded –

K. ED.   That thou shalt yield to me.

COUNT.   Ay, dear my liege, your due.

K. ED.   And that, my dearest love, can be no less

    Than right for right and tender love for love.

COUNT.   Than wrong for wrong and endless hate for hate.

    But, – sith I see your majesty so bent,

    That my unwillingness, my husband's love,

    Your high estate, nor no respect respected

    Can be my help, but that your mightiness

    Will overbear and awe these dear regards, –

    I bind my discontent to my content,

    And, what I would not, I'll compel I will;

    Provided that yourself remove those lets

    That stand between your highness' love and mine.

K. ED.   Name them, fair countess, and, by Heaven, I will.

COUNT.   It is their lives, that stand between our love,

    That I would have chok'd up, my sovereign.

K. ED.   Whose lives, my lady?

COUNT.   My thrice-loving liege,

    Your queen, and Salisbury my wedded husband;

    Who living have that title in our love

    That we can not bestow but by their death.

K. ED.   Thy opposition is beyond our law.

COUNT.   So is your desire: if the law

    Can hinder you to execute the one,

    Let it forbid you to attempt the other:

    I cannot think you love me as you say

    Unless you do make good what you have sworn.

K. ED.   No more; thy husband and the queen shall die.

    Fairer thou art by far than Hero was;

    Beardless Leander not so strong as I:

    He swum an easy current for his love;

    But I will through a Hellespont of blood

    To arrive at Sestos where my Hero lies.

COUNT.   Nay, you'll do more; you'll make the river, too,

(II, ii) With their heart-bloods that keep our love asunder,
     Of which my husband and your wife are twain.
  K. ED. Thy beauty makes them guilty of their death
     And gives in evidence that they shall die;
     Upon which verdict, I, their judge, condemn them.
  COUNT. O perjur'd beauty! more corrupted judge!
     When to the great star-chamber o'er our heads
     The universal sessions calls to count
     This packing evil, we both shall tremble for it.
  K. ED. What says my fair love? is she resolute?
  COUNT. Resolute to be dissolv'd; and, therefore, this, –
     Keep but thy word, great king, and I am thine.
     Stand where thou dost, I'll part a little from thee,
     And see how I will yield me to thy hands.
     Here by my side doth hang my wedding knives:
     Take thou the one and with it kill thy queen
     And learn by me to find her where she lies;
     And with this other I'll despatch my love,
     Which now lies fast asleep within my heart:
     When they are gone, then I'll consent to love.
     Stir not, lascivious king, to hinder me;
     My resolution is more nimbler far
     Than thy prevention can be in my rescue,
     And, if thou stir, I strike: therefore stand still,
     And hear the choice that I will put thee to:
     Either swear to leave thy most unholy suit,
     And never henceforth to solicit me;
     Or else, by Heaven, this sharp-pointed knife
     Shall stain thy earth with that which thou wouldst stain,
     My poor chaste blood. Swear, Edward, swear,
     Or I will strike and die before thee here.
  K. ED. Even by that Power I swear, that gives me now
     The power to be ashamed of myself,
     I never mean to part my lips again
     In any words that tends to such a suit.
     Arise, true English lady, whom our isle
     May better boast of, than e'er Roman might
     Of her, whose ransack'd treasury hath task'd
     The vain endeavour of so many pens:
     Arise; and be my fault thy honour's fame,
     Which after-ages shall enrich thee with.
     I am awaked from this idle dream; –
     Warwick, my son, Derby, Artois, and Audley,
     Brave warriors all, where are you all this while?

(II, ii)   *Enter all*

Warwick, I make thee Warden of the North: —
Thou, Prince of Wales, and Audley, straight to sea;
Scour to Newhaven; some there stay for me: —
Myself, Artois, and Derby, will through Flanders
To greet our friends there and to crave their aid:
This night will scarce suffice me, to discover
My folly's siege against a faithful lover;
For, ere the sun shall guide the eastern sky,
We'll wake him with our martial harmony.

Exeunt

ACT III
SCENE I

Flanders. The French Camp.
Enter King John of France; his two Sons, Charles of Normandy,
and Philip; and the Duke of Lorraine.

K. JOHN.   Here, till our navy of a thousand sail
Have made a breakfast to our foe by sea,
Let us encamp to wait their happy speed. —
Lorraine, what readiness is Edward in?
How hast thou heard that he provided is
Of martial furniture for this exploit?
LOR.   To lay aside unnecessary soothing
And not to spend the time in circumstance,
'Tis buried for a certainty, my lord,
That he's exceeding strongly fortified;
His subjects flock as willingly to war
As if unto a triumph they were led.
CHAR.   England was wont to harbour malcontents,
Bloodthirsty and seditious Catilines,
Spendthrifts, and such as gape for nothing else
But changing and alteration of the state;
And is it possible,
That they are now so loyal in themselves?
LOR.   All but the Scot; who solemnly protests,
As heretofore I have inform'd his grace,
Never to sheathe his sword, or take a truce.
K. JOHN.   Ah, that's the anch'rage of some better hope!
But, on the other side, to think what friends
King Edward hath retain'd in Netherland,
Among those ever-bibbing Epicures,
Those frothy Dutchmen, puff'd with double beer,

(III, i)   That drink and swill in every place they come,
            Doth not a little aggravate mine ire:
            Besides, we hear, the Emperor conjoins,
            And stalls him in his own authority:
            But, all the mightier that their number is,
            The greater glory reaps the victory.
            Some friends have we beside domestic power;
            The stern Polonian, and the warlike Dane,
            The King of Bohemia and of Sicily,
            Are all become confederates with us,
            And, as I think, are marching hither apace.

                                        [*Drum within*]

            But, soft, I hear the music of their drums,
            By which I guess that their approach is near.

                Enter the King of Bohemia, with Danes, and a
                Polonian captain, with other soldiers, another way.

K. BOH.   King John of France, as league and neighbourhood
            Requires when friends are anyway distress'd,
            I come to aid thee with my country's force.

POLE.   And from great Moscow, fearful to the Turk,
            And lofty Poland, nurse of hardy men,
            I bring these servitors to fight for thee
            Who willingly will venture in thy cause.

K. JOHN.   Welcome, Bohemian king; and welcome, all:
            This your great kindness I will not forget.
            Besides your plentiful rewards in crowns,
            That from our treasury ye shall receive,
            There comes a hare-brain'd nation, deck'd in pride,
            The spoil of whom will be a treble game.
            And now my hope is full, my joy complete:
            At sea, we are as puissant as the force
            Of Agamemnon in the haven of Troy;
            By land, with Xerxes we compare of strength
            Whose soldiers drank up rivers in their thirst:
            Then, Bayard-like, blind over-weening Ned,
            To reach at our imperial diadem
            Is either to be swallow'd of the waves
            Or hack'd a-pieces when thou com'st ashore.

                        Enter [Mariner]

MAR.   Near to the coast I have descried, my lord,
            As I was busy in my watchful charge,
            The proud Armado of King Edward's ships:
            Which at the first, far off when I did ken,

(III, i) Seem'd as it were a grove of wither'd pines;
But, drawing near, their glorious bright aspect,
Their streaming ensigns wrought of colour'd silk,
Like to a meadow full of sundry flowers,
Adorns the naked bosom of the earth.
Majestical the order of their course,
Figuring the horned circle of the moon:
And on the top-gallant of the admiral,
And likewise all the handmaids of his train,
The arms of England and of France unite
Are quarter'd equally by herald's art.
Thus, tightly carried with a merry gale,
They plough the ocean hitherward amain.

[K. JOHN].   Dare he already crop the flower-de-luce?
I hope, the honey being gather'd thence,
He, with the spider, afterward approach'd,
Shall suck forth deadly venom from the leaves. —
But where's our navy? how are they prepar'd
To wing themselves against this flight of ravens?

MAR.   They, having knowledge brought them by the scouts,
Did break from anchor straight; and, puff'd with rage
No otherwise than were their sails with wind,
Made forth, as when the empty eagle flies
To satisfy his hungry griping maw.

K. JOHN.   There's for thy news. Return unto thy bark;
And, if thou scape the bloody stroke of war
And do survive the conflict, come again
And let us hear the manner of the fight. —

Exit Mariner

Mean space, my lords, 'tis best we be dispers'd
To several places, lest they chance to land:
First, you, my lord, with your Bohemian troops,
Shall pitch your battles on the lower hand;
My eldest son, the Duke of Normandy,
Together with this aid of Muscovites,
Shall climb the higher ground another way;
Here in the middle coast, betwixt you both,
Philip, my youngest boy, and I will lodge.
So, lords, be gone, and look unto your charge;
You stand for France, an empire fair and large.—

Exeunt

Now tell me, Philip, what is thy conceit,
Touching the challenge that the English make?

PHIL.   I say, my lord, claim Edward what he can,

(III, i)   And bring he ne'er so plain a pedigree,
'Tis you are in possession of the crown,
And that's the surest point of all the law:
But, were it not, yet, ere he should prevail,
I'll make a conduit of my dearest blood
Or chase those straggling upstarts home again.

K. JOHN.   Well said, young Philip! Call for bread and wine,
That we may cheer our stomachs with repast,
To look our foes more sternly in the face.

The battle heard afar off

Now is begun the heavy day at sea.
Fight, Frenchmen, fight; be like the field of bears,
When they defend their younglings in their caves!
Steer, angry Nemesis, the happy helm;
That with the sulphur battles of your rage
The English fleet may be dispers'd and sunk!   *Shot*

PHIL.   O, father, how this echoing cannon-shot,
Like sweet harmony, disgests my cates!

K. JOHN.   Now, boy, thou hear'st what thund'ring terror 'tis,
To buckle for a kingdom's sovereignty.
The earth, with giddy trembling when it shakes,
Or when the exhalations of the air
Breaks in extremity of lightning flash,
Affrights not more than kings when they dispose
To show the rancour of their high-swoln hearts.

Retreat

Retreat is sounded; one side hath the worse:
O, if it be the French! – Sweet Fortune, turn;
And, in thy turning, change the forward winds,
That, with advantage of a favouring sky,
Our men may vanquish and the other fly!

Enter Mariner

My heart misgives: – say, mirror of pale death,
To whom belongs the honour of this day?
Relate, I pray thee, if thy breath will serve,
The sad discourse of this discomfiture.

MAR.   I will, my lord.
My gracious sovereign, France hath ta'en the foil,
And boasting Edward triumphs with success.
These iron-hearted navies,
When last I was reporter to your grace,
Both full of angry spleen, of hope and fear,
Hasting to meet each other in the face,

(III, i)   At last conjoin'd, and by their admiral
             Our admiral encounter'd many shot.
             By this, the other, that beheld these twain
             Give earnest-penny of a further wrack,
             Like fiery dragons took their haughty flight;
             And, likewise meeting, from their smoky wombs
             Sent many grim ambassadors of death.
             Then gan the day to turn to gloomy night;
             And darkness did as well enclose the quick
             As those that were but newly reft of life.
             No leisure serv'd for friends to bid farewell;
             And if it had, the hideous noise was such,
             As each to other seemed deaf and dumb.
             Purple the sea; whose channel fill'd as fast
             With streaming gore that from the maimed fell
             As did her gushing moisture break into
             The crannied cleftures of the through-shot planks.
             Here flew a head, dissever'd from the trunk;
             There mangled arms and legs were toss'd aloft,
             As when a whirlwind takes the summer dust
             And scatters it in middle of the air.
             Then might ye see the reeling vessels split
             And tottering sink into the ruthless flood
             Until their lofty tops were seen no more.
             All shifts were tried both for defence and hurt.
             And now the effect of valour and of force,
             Of resolution and of cowardice,
             We lively pictur'd; how the one for fame,
             The other by compulsion laid about.
             Much did the Nonpareille, that brave ship;
             So did the Black-snake of Bullen, than which
             A bonnier vessel never yet spread sail:
             But all in vain; both sun, the wind and tide
             Revolted unto our foeman's side,
             That we perforce were fain to give them way,
             And they are landed: thus my tale is done;
             We have untimely lost, and they have won.
K. JOHN.   Then rests there nothing, but with present speed
             To join our several forces all in one,
             And bid them battle ere they range too far. –
             Come, gentle Philip, let us hence depart;
             This soldier's words have pierc'd thy father's heart.

                                                    Exeunt

413

(III, ii)

SCENE II

Picardy. Fields near Cressy.
Enter two Frenchmen; a woman and two little children
meet them, and other citizens.

1 [FR.] Well met, my masters: how now? what's the news?
    And wherefore are ye laden thus with stuff?
    What, is it quarter-day, that you remove
    And carry bag and baggage too?

[1 CIT.] Quarter-day? ay, and quartering day, I fear:
    Have ye not heard the news that flies abroad?

1 [FR.] What news?

[2 CIT.] How the French navy is destroy'd at sea
    And that the English army is arriv'd.

1 [FR.] What then?

[1 CIT.] What then, quoth you? why, is't not time to fly,
    When envy and destruction is so nigh?

1 [FR.] Content thee, man; they are far enough from hence;
    And will be met, I warrant ye, to their cost,
    Before they break so far into the realm.

[1 CIT.] Ay, so the grasshopper doth spend the time
    In mirthful jollity, till winter come;
    And then too late he would redeem his time
    When frozen cold hath nipp'd his careless head.
    He, that no sooner will provide a cloak
    Than when he sees it doth begin to rain,
    May, peradventure, for his negligence,
    Be throughly wash'd down when he suspects it not.
    We that have charge and such a train as this
    Must look in time to look for them and us,
    Lest, when we would, we cannot be reliev'd.

1 [FR.] Belike, you then despair of all success
    And think your country will be subjugate.

[2 CIT.] We cannot tell; 'tis good to fear the worst.

1 [FR.] Yet rather fight, than like unnatural sons
    Forsake your loving parents in distress.

[1 CIT.] Tush, they that have already taken arms
    Are many fearful millions in respect
    Of that small handful of our enemies.
    But 'tis a rightful quarrel must prevail;
    Edward is son unto our late king's sister,
    Where John Valois is three degrees remov'd.

WOM. Besides, there goes a prophecy abroad,

(III, ii) Publish'd by one that was a friar once
      Whose oracles have many times prov'd true;
      And now he says, 'The time will shortly come,
      When as a lion, roused in the west,
      Shall carry hence the flower-de-luce of France':
      These, I can tell ye, and such-like surmises
      Strike many Frenchmen cold unto the heart.

Enter a Frenchman

[3 FR.] Fly, countrymen and citizens of France!
      Sweet-flow'ring peace, the root of happy life,
      Is quite abandon'd and expuls'd the land:
      Instead of whom, ransack-constraining war
      Sits like to ravens upon your houses' tops;
      Slaughter and mischief walk within your streets,
      And, unrestrain'd, make havoc as they pass:
      The form whereof even now myself beheld,
      Upon this fair mountain, whence I came.
      For so far off as I directed mine eyes,
      I might perceive five cities all on fire,
      Corn-fields and vineyards burning like an oven;
      And, as the reeking vapour in the wind
      Turn'd but aside, I likewise might discern
      The poor inhabitants, escap'd the flame,
      Fall numberless upon the soldiers' pikes.
      Three ways these dreadful ministers of wrath
      Do tread the measures of their tragic march.
      Upon the right hand comes the conquering king,
      Upon the left his hot unbridled son,
      And in the midst our nation's glittering host;
      All which, though distant, yet conspire in one
      To leave a desolation where they come.
      Fly, therefore, citizens, if you be wise,
      Seek out some habitation further off.
      Here if you stay, your wives will be abus'd,
      Your treasure shar'd before your weeping eyes.
      Shelter you yourselves, for now the storm doth rise.
      Away, away! methinks, I hear their drums.
      Ah, wretched France, I greatly fear thy fall;
      Thy glory shaketh like a tottering wall.

                 Exeunt

(III, iii)

SCENE III

The Same.
Enter King Edward, and the Earl of Derby,
with soldiers and Gobin de Grey.

K. ED.   Where's the Frenchman, by whose cunning guide
We found the shallow of this river Somme,
And had direction how to pass the sea?

GOB.   Here, my good lord.

K. ED.   How art thou called? tell me thy name.

GOB.   Gobin de Grey, if please your excellence.

K. ED.   Then, Gobin, for the service thou hast done,
We here enlarge and give thee liberty;
And, for recompense, beside this good,
Thou shalt receive five hundred marks in gold. –
I know not how we should have met our son,
Whom now in heart I wish I might behold.

Enter Artois

ART.   Good news, my lord; the prince is hard at hand,
And with him comes Lord Audley and the rest,
Whom since our landing we could never meet.

Enter Prince Edward, Lord Audley, and soldiers

K. ED.   Welcome, fair prince! How hast thou sped, my son,
Since thy arrival on the coast of France?

PR. ED.   Successfully, I thank the gracious heavens:
Some of their strongest cities we have won,
As Harflew, Lo, Crotaye, and Carentine,
And others wasted; leaving at our heels
A wide apparent field and beaten path
For solitariness to progress in:
Yet, those that would submit, we kindly pardon'd;
But who in scorn refus'd our proffer'd peace,
Endur'd the penalty of sharp revenge.

K. ED.   Ah, France, why shouldst thou be thus obstinate
Against the kind embracement of thy friends?
How gently had we thought to touch thy breast
And set our foot upon thy tender mould,
But that in froward and disdainful pride
Thou, like a skittish and untamed colt,
Dost start aside and strike us with thy heels? –
But tell me, Ned, in all thy warlike course
Hast thou not seen the usurping King of France?

(III, iii) PR. ED.   Yes, my good lord, and not two hours ago,
With full a hundred thousand fighting men,
Upon the one side of the river's bank,
And on the other both his multitudes.
I fear'd he would have cropp'd our smaller power:
But, happily, perceiving your approach
He hath withdrawn himself to Cressy plains;
Where, as it seemeth by his good array,
He means to bid us battle presently.

K. ED.   He shall be welcome, that's the thing we crave.

Enter King John, Dukes of Normandy and Lorraine,
King of Bohemia, young Philip, and soldiers.

K. JOHN.   Edward, know, that John, the true King of France, —
Musing thou shouldst encroach upon his land,
And, in thy tyrannous proceeding, slay
His faithful subjects and subvert his towns, —
Spits in thy face; and in this manner following
Upbraids thee with thine arrogant intrusion.
First, I condemn thee for a fugitive,
A thievish pirate, and a needy mate;
One, that hath either no abiding place,
Or else, inhabiting some barren soil,
Where neither herb nor fruitful grain is had,
Dost altogether live by pilfering:
Next, — insomuch thou hast infring'd thy faith,
Broke league and solemn covenant made with me, —
I hold thee for a false pernicious wretch:
And last of all, — although I scorn to cope
With one so much inferior to myself;
Yet, in respect thy thirst is all for gold,
Thy labour rather to be fear'd than lov'd, —
To satisfy thy lust in either part,
Here am I come, and with me have I brought
Exceeding store of treasure, pearl and coin.
Leave therefore now to persecute the weak;
And, armed ent'ring conflict with the arm'd,
Let it be seen, 'mongst other petty thefts,
How thou canst win this pillage manfully.

K. ED.   If gall or wormwood have a pleasant taste,
Then is thy salutation honey-sweet:
But as the one hath no such property,
So is the other most satirical.
Yet wot how I regard thy worthless taunts; —

(III, iii)   If thou have utter'd them to foil my fame
Or dim the reputation of my birth,
Know that thy wolvish barking cannot hurt:
If slily to insinuate with the world,
And with a strumpet's artificial line
To paint thy vicious and deformed cause,
Be well assur'd the counterfeit will fade
And in the end thy foul defects be seen:
But if thou didst it to provoke me on, –
As who should say, I were but timorous,
Or coldly negligent did need a spur, –
Bethink thyself how slack I was at sea;
How, since my landing, I have won no towns,
Enter'd no further but upon the coast,
And there have ever since securely slept.
But if I have been otherwise employ'd,
Imagine, Valois, whether I intend
To skirmish, not for pillage, but for the crown
Which thou dost wear; and that I vow to have,
Or one of us shall fall into his grave.

PR. ED.   Look not for cross invectives at our hands
Or railing execrations of despite:
Let creeping serpents hid in hollow banks
Sting with their tongues; we have remorseless swords,
And they shall plead for us and our affairs.
Yet thus much, briefly, by my father's leave:
As all the immodest poison of thy throat
Is scandalous and most notorious lies,
And our pretended quarrel is truly just,
So end the battle when we meet to-day;
May either of us prosper and prevail
Or, luckless curst, receive eternal shame!

K. ED.   That needs no further question, and, I know,
His conscience witnesseth, it is my right. –
Therefore, Valois, say, wilt thou yet resign,
Before the sickle's thrust into the corn
Or that enkindled fury turn to flame?

K. JOHN.   Edward, I know what right thou hast in France,
And ere I basely will resign my crown
This champion field shall be a pool of blood
And all our prospect as a slaughter-house.

PR. ED.   Ay, that approves thee, tyrant, what thou art:
No father, king or shepherd of thy realm;
But one that tears her entrails with thy hands

(III, iii)   And, like a thirsty tiger, suck'st her blood.

AUD.   You peers of France, why do you follow him
That is so prodigal to spend your lives?

CHAR.   Whom should they follow, aged impotent,
But he that is their true-born sovereign?

K. ED.   Upbraid'st thou him, because within his face
Time hath engrav'd deep characters of age?
Know that these grave scholars of experience,
Like stiff-grown oaks, will stand immovable,
When whirlwind quickly turns up younger trees.

DER.   Was ever any of thy father's house
King, but thyself, before this present time?
Edward's great lineage, by the mother's side,
Five hundred years hath held the sceptre up: —
Judge then, conspirators, by this descent,
Which is the true-born sovereign, this, or that.

PHIL.   Father, range your battles, prate no more;
These English fain would spend the time in words,
That, night approaching, they might escape unfought.

K. JOHN.   Lords and my loving subjects, now's the time
That your intended force must bide the touch:
Therefore, my friends, consider this in brief, —
He that you fight for is your natural king;
He against whom you fight, a foreigner:
He that you fight for, rules in clemency
And reins you with a mild and gentle bit;
He against whom you fight, if he prevail,
Will straight enthrone himself in tyranny,
Make slaves of you, and with a heavy hand
Curtail and curb your sweetest liberty.
Then, to protect your country and your king,
Let but the haughty courage of your hearts
Answer the number of your able hands,
And we shall quickly chase these fugitives.
For what's this Edward but a belly-god,
A tender and lascivious wantonness,
That th' other day was almost dead for love?
And what, I pray you, is his goodly guard?
Such as, but scant them of their chines of beef
And take away their downy feather-beds,
And, presently, they are as resty-stiff
As 'twere a many over-ridden jades.
Then, Frenchmen, scorn that such should be your lords,
And rather bind ye them in captive bands.

(III, iii)   FRENCH.   Vive le Roy! God save King John of France!
        K. JOHN.   Now on this plain of Cressy spread yourselves, –
        And Edward, when thou dar'st, begin the fight.

                        [*Exeunt King John, Charles, Philip,*
                            Lorraine, Bohemia, and Forces]

        K. ED.   We presently will meet thee, John of France: –
        And, English lords, let us resolve to-day
        Either to clear us of that scandalous crime
        Or be entombed in our innocence. –
        And, Ned, because this battle is the first
        That ever yet thou fought'st in pitched field,
        As ancient custom is of martialists,
        To dub thee with the type of chivalry,
        In solemn manner we will give thee arms: –
        Come, therefore, herals, orderly bring forth
        A strong attirement for the prince my son. –

                    Enter four Heralds, bringing in a coat-
                    armour, a helmet, a lance, and a shield.

        Edward Plantagenet, in the name of God,
        As with this armour I impall thy breast,
        So be thy noble unrelenting heart
        Wall'd in with flint of matchless fortitude
        That never base affections enter there;
        Fight and be valiant, conquer where thou com'st! –
        Now follow, lords, and do him honour too.

        DER.   [*Receiving the helmet*]
        Edward Plantagenet, Prince of Wales,
        As I do set this helmet on thy head,
        Wherewith the chamber of thy brain is fenc'd,
        So may thy temples, with Bellona's hand,
        Be still adorn'd with laurel victory;
        Fight and be valiant, conquer where thou com'st!

        AUD.   [*Receiving the lance*]
        Edward Plantagenet, Prince of Wales,
        Receive this lance into thy manly hand;
        Use it in fashion of a brazen pen
        To draw forth bloody stratagems in France
        And print thy valiant deeds in honour's books;
        Fight and be valiant, conquer where thou com'st!

        ART.   [*Receiving the shield*]
        Edward Plantagenet, Prince of Wales,
        Hold, take this target, wear it on thy arm;
        And may the view thereof, like Perseus' shield,

(III, iii)   Astonish and transform thy gazing foes
To senseless images of meagre death;
Fight and be valiant, conquer where thou com'st!

K. ED.   Now wants there nought but knighthood; which deferr'd
We leave till thou hast won it in the field.

[PR. ED.]   My gracious father, and ye forward peers,
This honour, you have done me, animates
And cheers my green yet-scarce-appearing strength
With comfortable good-presaging signs,
No otherwise than did old Jacob's words
When as he breath'd his blessings on his sons.
These hallow'd gifts of yours when I profane,
Or use them not to glory of my God,
To patronage the fatherless and poor,
Or for the benefit of England's peace,
Be numb my joints! wax feeble both mine arms!
Wither my heart! that, like a sapless tree,
I may remain the map of infamy.

K. ED.   Then thus our steeled battles shall be rang'd; —
The leading of the vaward, Ned, is thine;
To dignify whose lusty spirit the more,
We temper it with Audley's gravity;
That, courage and experience join'd in one,
Your manage may be second unto none:
For the main battles, I will guide myself;
And, Derby, in the rearward march behind.
That orderly dispos'd and set in 'ray,
Let us to horse; and God grant us the day!

Exeunt

SCENE IV

The Same

*Alarum. Enter a many Frenchmen fleeing. After them Prince Edward,
running. Then enter King John and Duke of Lorraine.*

K. JOHN.   O Lorraine, say, what mean our men to fly?
Our number is far greater than our foes.

LOR.   The garrison of Genoese, my lord,
That came from Paris, weary with their march,
Grudging to be suddenly employ'd,
No sooner in the fore-front took their place,
But, straight retiring, so dismay'd the rest
As likewise they betook themselves to flight;

(III, iv)   In which, for haste to make a safe escape,
               More in the clust'ring throng are press'd to death,
               Than by the enemy, a thousand-fold.

K. JOHN.   O hapless fortune! Let us yet assay
               If we can counsel some of them to stay.

[Exeunt]

Enter King Edward and Audley

K. ED.   Lord Audley, whiles our son is in the chase,
               Withdraw your powers unto this little hill,
               And here a season let us breathe ourselves.

AUD.   I will, my lord.   *Exit. Sound Retreat*

K. ED.   Just-dooming Heaven, whose secret providence
               To our gross judgment is inscrutable,
               How are we bound to praise thy wondrous works,
               That hast this day giv'n way unto the right
               And made the wicked stumble at themselves!

Enter Artois

[ART.]   Rescue, King Edward! rescue for thy son!

K. ED.   Rescue, Artois? what, is he prisoner?
               Or by violence fell beside his horse?

ART.   Neither, my lord; but narrowly beset
               With turning Frenchmen whom he did pursue,
                As 'tis impossible that he should scape
               Except your highness presently descend.

K. ED.   Tut, let him fight; we gave him arms to-day,
               And he is labouring for a knighthood, man.

Enter Derby

DER.   The prince, my lord, the prince! O, succour him;
               He's close encompass'd with a world of odds!

K. ED.   Then will he win a world of honour too
               If he by valour can redeem him thence:
               If not, what remedy? we have more sons
               Than one, to comfort our declining age.

Enter Audley

AUD.   Renowned Edward, give me leave, I pray,
               To lead my soldiers where I may relieve
               Your grace's son, in danger to be slain.
               The snares of French, like emmets on a bank,
               Muster about him; whilst he, lion-like,
               Entangled in the net of their assaults,
               Frantic'ly rends and bites the woven toil:

(III, iv)   But all in vain, he cannot free himself.

K. ED.   Audley, content: I will not have a man,
On pain of death, sent forth to succour him:
This is the day ordain'd by destiny
To season his courage with those grievous thoughts,
That, if he break out, Nestor's years on earth,
Will make him savour still of this exploit.

DER.   Ah, but he shall not live to see those days.

K. ED.   Why, then his epitaph is lasting praise.

AUD.   Yet, good my lord, 'tis too much wilfulness,
To let his blood be spilt that may be sav'd.

K. ED.   Exclaim no more; for none of you can tell
Whether a borrow'd aid will serve or no.
Perhaps, he is already slain or ta'en:
And dare a falcon when she's in her flight,
And ever after she'll be haggard-like:
Let Edward be deliver'd by our hands,
And still in danger he'll expect the like;
But if himself himself redeem from thence,
He will have vanquish'd, cheerful, death and fear,
And ever after dread their force no more
Than if they were but babes or captive slaves.

AUD.   O cruel father! – Farewell, Edward, then!

DER.   Farewell, sweet prince, the hope of chivalry!

ART.   O, would my life might ransom him from death!

K. ED.   But, soft, methinks I hear   [*Retreat sounded*]
The dismal charge of trumpets' loud retreat:
All are not slain, I hope, that went with him;
Some will return with tidings, good or bad.

*Enter Prince Edward in triumph, bearing in his hand his shivered
lance, and the King of Bohemia, borne before wrapped in the colours.
They run and embrace him.*

AUD.   O joyful sight! victorious Edward lives!

DER.   Welcome, brave prince!

K. ED.   Welcome, Plantagenet!

PR. ED.   First having done my duty, as beseem'd,
                 Kneels, and kisses his father's hand
Lords, I regreet you all with hearty thanks.
And now, behold, – after my winter's toil,
My painful voyage on the boist'rous sea
Of war's devouring gulfs and steely rocks, –
I bring my fraught unto the wished port,
My summer's hope, my travel's sweet reward:

(III, iv) And here with humble duty I present
     This sacrifice, this first fruit of my sword,
     Cropp'd and cut down even at the gate of death,
     The King of Boheme, father, whom I slew;
     Whose thousands had intrench'd me round about,
     And lay as thick upon my batter'd crest
     As on an anvil with their pond'rous glaives:
     Yet marble courage still did underprop;
     And when my weary arms with often blows,
     Like the continual-lab'ring woodman's axe
     That is enjoin'd to fell a load of oaks,
     Began to falter, straight I would remember
     My gifts you gave me and my zealous vow,
     And then new courage made me fresh again;
     That, in despite, I carv'd my passage forth
     And put the multitude to speedy flight.
     Lo, thus hath Edward's hand fill'd your request,
     And done, I hope, the duty of a knight.

K. ED. Ay, well thou hast deserv'd a knighthood, Ned!
     And, therefore, with thy sword, yet reeking warm
        His sword borne by a soldier
     With blood of those that fought to be thy bane,
     Arise, Prince Edward, trusty knight at arms:
     This day thou hast confounded me with joy
     And proved thyself fit heir unto a king.

PR. ED. Here is a note, my gracious lord, of those
     That in this conflict of our foes were slain:
     Eleven princes of esteem; fourscore
     Barons; a hundred and twenty knights;
     And thirty thousand common soldiers;
     And, of our men, a thousand.

[K. ED.] Our God be praised! Now, John of France, I hope,
     Thou know'st King Edward for no wantonness,
     No love-sick cockney; nor his soldiers, jades. —
     But which way is the fearful king escap'd?

PR. ED. Towards Poitiers, noble father, and his sons.

K. ED. Ned, thou and Audley shall pursue them still;
     Myself and Derby will to Calice straight,
     And there begirt that haven-town with siege:
     Now lies it on an upshot; therefore strike,
     And wistly follow while the game's on foot.
     What picture's this?   *[Pointing to the colours]*

PR. ED.   A pelican, my lord,

(III, iv)   Wounding her bosom with her crooked beak
              That so her nest of young ones may be fed
              With drops of blood that issue from her heart;
              The motto, '*Sic et vos*,' 'And so should you.'

                                                            Exeunt

                              ACT IV
                              SCENE I

                    Brittany. Camp of the English
              Enter Lord Mountford with a coronet in his hand;
                      with him the Earl of Salisbury.

MOUNT.   My Lord of Salisbury, since by your aid
          Mine enemy Sir Charles of Blois is slain,
          And I again am quietly possess'd
          In Britain's dukedom, know that I resolve,
          For this kind furth'rance of your king and you,
          To swear allegiance to his majesty:
          In sign wherof, receive this coronet.
          Bear it unto him, and withal mine oath,
          Never to be but Edward's faithful friend.
SAL.   I take it, Mountford: thus, I hope, ere long
          The whole dominions of the realm of France
          Will be surrender'd to his conquering hand.

                                                      Exit Mountford

          Now, if I knew but safely how to pass,
          I would at Calice gladly meet his grace,
          Whither I am by letters certified
          That he intends to have his host remov'd.
          It shall be so; this policy will serve: —
          Ho, who's within? Bring Villiers to me. —

                          Enter Villiers

          Villiers, thou know'st, thou art my prisoner,
          And that I might for ransom, if I would,
          Require of thee a hundred thousand franks,
          Or else retain and keep thee captive still:
          But so it is, that for a smaller charge
          Thou may'st be quit, an if thou wilt thyself;
          And this it is, procure me but a passport
          Of Charles the Duke of Normandy, that I
          Without restraint may have recourse to Calice
          Through all the countries where he hath to do,
          (Which thou may'st easily obtain, I think,

                                425

(IV, i)   By reason I have often heard thee say,
He and thou were students once together)
And then thou shalt be set at liberty.
How say'st thou? wilt thou undertake to do it?

VIL.   I will, my lord; but I must speak with him.

SAL.   Why, so thou shalt; take horse, and post from hence:
Only, before thou go'st, swear by thy faith
That, if thou canst not compass my desire,
Thou wilt return my prisoner back again;
And that shall be sufficient warrant for me.

VIL.   To that condition I agree, my lord,
And will unfeignedly perform the same.

Exit

SAL.   Farewell, Villiers. –
This once I mean to try a Frenchman's faith.

Exit

SCENE II

Picardy. The English Camp before Calais.
Enter King Edward and Derby, with Soldiers.

K. ED.   Since they refuse our proffer'd league, my lord,
And will not ope their gates and let us in,
We will intrench ourselves on every side,
That neither victuals nor supply of men
May come to succour this accursed town;
Famine shall combat where our swords are stopp'd.

DER.   The promis'd aid that made them stand aloof
Is now retir'd and gone another way;
It will repent them of their stubborn will.

Enter six poor Frenchmen

But what are these poor ragged slaves, my lord?

K. ED.   Ask what they are; it seems, they come from Calice.

DER.   You wretched patterns of despair and woe,
What are you? living men, or gliding ghosts,
Crept from your graves to walk upon the earth?

FIRST FR.   No ghosts, my lord, but men that breathe a life
Far worse than is the quiet sleep of death:
We are distressed poor inhabitants
That long have been diseased, sick and lame;
And now, because we are not fit to serve,
The captain of the town hath thrust us forth

(IV, ii)   That so expense of victuals may be sav'd.

K. ED.   A charitable deed, no doubt, and worthy praise. –
But how do you imagine then to speed?
We are your enemies; in such a case
We can no less but put you to the sword,
Since, when we proffer'd truce, it was refus'd.

FIRST FR.   An if your grace no otherwise vouchsafe,
As welcome death is unto us as life.

K. ED.   Poor silly men, much wrong'd and more distress'd! –
Go, Derby, go, and see they be reliev'd;
Command that victuals be appointed them
And give to every one five crowns a-piece:–

                   [*Exeunt Derby and Frenchmen*]

The lion scorns to touch the yielding prey,
And Edward's sword must flesh itself in such
As wilful stubbornness hath made perverse. –

Enter Lord Percy

Lord Percy! welcome: what's the news in England?

PER.   The queen, my lord, comes here to your grace;
And from her highness and the lord vicegerent
I bring this happy tidings of success:
David of Scotland, lately up in arms,
(Thinking, belike, he soonest should prevail,
Your highness being absent from the realm)
Is, by the fruitful service of your peers
And painful travel of the queen herself
That, big with child, was every day in arms,
Vanquish'd, subdu'd and taken prisoner.

K. ED.   Thanks, Percy, for thy news, with all my heart!
What was he, took him prisoner in the field?

PER.   A squire, my lord; John Copland is his name:
Who since, entreated by her majesty,
Denies to make surrender of his prize
To any but unto your grace alone;
Whereat the queen is grievously displeas'd.

K. ED.   Well, then we'll have a pursuivant despatch'd
To summon Copland hither out of hand,
And with him he shall bring his prisoner king.

PER.   The queen's, my lord, herself by this at sea,
And purposeth, as soon as wind will serve,
To land at Calice and to visit you.

K. ED.   She shall be welcome; and, to wait her coming
I'll pitch my tent near to the sandy shore.

(IV, ii)

Enter a [French] Captain

CAP.   The burgesses of Calice, mighty king,
Have, by a council, willingly decreed
To yield the town and castle to your hands,
Upon condition it will please your grace
To grant them benefit of life and goods.

K. ED.   They will so! then, belike, they may command,
Dispose, elect, and govern as they list.
No, sirrah, tell them, since they did refuse
Our princely clemency at first proclaim'd,
They shall not have it now, although they would;
[I] will accept nought but fire and sword,
Except, within these two days, six of them,
That are the wealthiest merchants in the town,
Come naked, all but for their linen shirts,
With each a halter hang'd about his neck,
And prostrate yield themselves, upon their knees,
To be afflicted, hang'd, or what I please;
And so you may inform their masterships.

Exeunt

CAP.   Why, this it is to trust a broken staff.
Had we not been persuaded, John our king
Would with his army have reliev'd the town,
We had not stood upon defiance so.
But now 'tis past that no man can recall,
And better some do go to work, than all.

Exit

SCENE III

Poitou. Fields near Poitiers. The French Camp.
Enter Charles of Normandy and Villiers.

CHAR.   I wonder, Villiers, thou shouldst importune me
For one that is our deadly enemy.

VIL.   Not for his sake, my gracious lord, so much
Am I become an earnest advocate
As that thereby my ransom will be quit.

CHAR.   Thy ransom, man! why need'st thou talk of that?
Art thou not free? and are not all occasions,
That happen for advantage of our foes,
To be accepted of and stood upon?

VIL.   No, good, my lord, except the same be just;
For profit must with honour be comix'd

(IV, iii) Or else our actions are but scandalous:
     But, letting pass these intricate objections,
     Will't please your highness to subscribe, or no?

CHAR. Villiers, I will not nor I cannot do it;
     Salisbury shall not have his will so much,
     To claim a passport how it please himself.

VIL. Why, then I know the extremity, my lord:
     I must return to prison whence I came.

CHAR. Return! I hope, thou wilt not.
     What bird that hath escap'd the fowler's gin
     Will not beware how she's ensnar'd again?
     Or what is he so senseless and secure,
     That, having hardly pass'd a dangerous gulf,
     Will put himself in peril there again?

VIL. Ah, but it is mine oath, my gracious lord,
     Which I in conscience may not violate,
     Or else a kingdom should not draw me hence.

CHAR. Thine oath! why, that doth bind thee to abide:
     Hast thou not sworn obedience to thy prince?

VIL. In all things that uprightly he commands.
     But either to persuade or threaten me
     Not to perform the covenant of my word
     Is lawless and I need not to obey.

CHAR. Why, is it lawful for a man to kill
     And not to break a promise with his foe?

VIL. To kill, my lord, when war is once proclaim'd,
     So that our quarrel be for wrongs receiv'd,
     No doubt, is lawfully permitted us:
     But, in an oath, we must be well advis'd
     How we do swear, and, when we once have sworn,
     Not to infringe it, though we die therefore.
     Therefore, my lord, as willing I return
     As if I were to fly to paradise.

CHAR. Stay, my Villiers; thine honourable mind
     Deserves to be eternally admir'd.
     Thy suit shall be no longer thus deferr'd;
     Give me the paper, I'll subscribe to it:
     And, wheretofore I lov'd thee as Villiers,
     Hereafter I'll embrace thee as myself;
     Stay, and be still in favour with thy lord.

VIL. I humbly thank your grace, I must despatch
     And send this passport first unto the earl,
     And then I will attend your highness' pleasure.

(IV, iii) CHAR.   Do so, Villiers; – and Charles, when he hath need,
Be such his soldiers, howsoe'er he speed!

Exit Villiers

Enter King John

K. JOHN.   Come, Charles, and arm thee; Edward is entrapp'd,
The Prince of Wales is fall'n into our hands,
And we have compass'd him, he cannot scape.

CHAR.   But will your highness fight to-day?

K. JOHN.   What else, my son? he's scarce eight thousand strong,
And we are threescore thousand at the least.

CHAR.   I have a prophecy, my gracious lord,
Wherein is written what success is like
To happen us in this outrageous war;
It was deliver'd me at Cressy's field
By one that is an aged hermit there.

[*Reads*]

'When feather'd fowl shall make thine army tremble,
And flint-stones rise, and break the battle 'ray,
Then think on him that doth not now dissemble,
For that shall be the hapless dreadful day:
Yet in the end thy foot thou shalt advance
As far in England as thy foe in France.'

K. JOHN.   By this it seems we shall be fortunate:
For as it is impossible that stones
Should ever rise and break the battle 'ray,
Or airy fowl make men in arms to quake,
So it is like, we shall not be subdu'd:
Or, say this might be true, yet, in the end,
Since he doth promise we shall drive him hence
And forage their country as they have done ours,
By this revenge that loss will seem the less.
But all are frivolous fancies, toys and dreams:
Once we are sure we have ensnar'd the son,
Catch we the father after how we can.

Exeunt

SCENE IV

The Same. The English Camp.
Enter Prince Edward, Audley, and others.

PR. ED. Audley, the arms of death embrace us round,
And comfort have we none, save that to die
We pay sour earnest for a sweeter life.
At Cressy field our clouds of warlike smoke
Chok'd up those French mouths and dissever'd them:
But now their multitudes of millions hide,
Masking as 'twere, the beauteous-burning sun;
Leaving no hope to us but sullen dark
And eyeless terror of all-ending night.

AUD. This sudden, mighty and expedient head,
That they have made, fair prince, is wonderful.
Before us in the valley lies the king,
Vantag'd with all that heaven and earth can yield;
His party stronger battled than our whole:
His son, the braving Duke of Normandy,
Hath trimm'd the mountain on our right hand up
In shining plate, that now the aspiring hill
Shows like a silver quarry or an orb;
Aloft the which, the banners, bannerets,
And new-replenish'd pendants cuff the air,
And beat the winds, that for their gaudiness
Struggles to kiss them: on our left hand lies
Philip, the younger issue of the king,
Coting the other hill in such array
That all his gilded upright pikes do seem
Straight trees of gold, the pendant[s] leaves,
And their device of antique heraldry,
Quarter'd in colours seeming sundry fruits,
Makes it the orchard of the Hesperides:
Behind us too the hill doth bear his height,
For, like a half-moon, op'ning but one way,
It rounds us in; there at our backs are lodg'd
The fatal cross-bows, and the battle there
Is governed by the rough Chatillion.
Then thus it stands, – the valley for our flight
The king binds in; the hills on either hand
Are proudly royalized by his sons;
And on the hill behind stands certain death,
In pay and service with Chatillion.

(IV, iv)   PR. ED.   Death's name is much more mighty than his deeds; –
Thy parcelling this power hath made it more.
As many sands as these my hands can hold
Are but my handful of so many sands;
Then, all the world, – and call it but a power, –
Easily ta'en up and quickly thrown away:
But, if I stand to count them sand by sand,
The number would confound my memory
And make a thousand millions of a task
Which, briefly, is no more, indeed, than one.
These quarters, squadrons, and these regiments,
Before, behind us, and on either hand,
Are but a power: when we name a man,
His hand, his foot, his head, hath several strengths;
And being all but one self instant strength,
Why, all this many, Audley, is but one,
And we can call it all but one man's strength.
He, that hath far to go, tells it by miles;
If he should tell the steps, it kills his heart:
The drops are infinite that make a flood,
And yet, thou know'st, we call it but a rain.
There is but one France, one King of France,
That France hath no more kings; and that same king
Hath but the puissant legion of one king;
And we have one: then apprehend no odds,
For one to one is fair equality. –

Enter a Herald from King John

What tidings, messenger? be plain, and brief.

HER.   The King of France, my soveriegn lord and master,
Greets by me his foe the Prince of Wales.
If thou call forth a hundred men of name,
Of lords, knights, squires, and English gentlemen,
And with thyself and those kneel at his feet,
He straight will fold his bloody colours up
And ransom shall redeem lives forfeited:
If not, this day shall drink more English blood
Than e'er was buried in [y]our British earth.
What is the answer to his proffer'd mercy?

PR. ED.   This heaven that covers France contains the mercy
That draws from me submissive orisons;
That such base breath should vanish from my lips,
To urge the plea of mercy to a man,
The Lord forbid! Return, and tell the king,

(IV, iv) My tongue is made of steel and it shall beg
  My mercy on his coward burgonet;
  Tell him, my colours are as red as his,
  My men as bold, our English arms as strong,
  Return him my defiance in his face.

HER. I go.   *[Exit]*

Enter another

PR. ED. What news with thee?

HER. The Duke of Normandy, my lord and master,
  Pitying thy youth is so engirt with peril,
  By me hath sent a nimble-jointed jennet,
  As swift as ever yet thou didst bestride,
  And therewithal he counsels thee to fly;
  Else, death himself has sworn that thou shalt die.

PR. ED. Back with the beast unto the beast that sent him;
  Tell him, I cannot sit a coward's horse.
  Bid him to-day bestride the jade himself;
  For I will stain my horse quite o'er with blood
  And double-gild my spurs, but I will catch him.
  So tell the carping boy, and get thee gone.

            [Exit Herald]

Enter another

HER. Edward of Wales, Philip, the second son
  To the most mighty Christian King of France,
  Seeing thy body's living date expir'd,
  All full of charity and Christian love,
  Commends this book, full fraught with prayers,
  To thy fair hand, and, for thy hour of life,
  Entreats thee that thou meditate therein
  And arm thy soul for her long journey towards.
  Thus have I done his bidding, and return.

PR. ED. Herald of Philip, greet thy lord from me;
  All good, that he can send, I can receive:
  But think'st thou not the unadvised boy
  Hath wrong'd himself in thus far tend'ring me?
  Haply, he cannot pray without the book;
  I think him no divine extemporal:
  Then render back this commonplace of prayer,
  To do himself good in adversity.
  Besides, he knows not my sin's quality
  And therefore knows no prayers for my avail;
  Ere night his prayer may be, to pray to God
  To put it in my heart to hear his prayer;

(IV, iv)   So tell the courtly wanton, and be gone.

    HER.   I go.

                                              [Exit]

    PR. ED.   How confident their strength and number makes them! –
        Now, Audley, sound those silver wings of thine,
        And let those milk-white messengers of time
        Show thy time's learning in this dangerous time;
        Thyself art bruis'd and bit with many broils,
        And strategems forepast with iron pens
        Are texted in thine honourable face;
        Thou art a married man in this distress,
        But danger woos me as a blushing maid:
        Teach me an answer to this perilous time.

    AUD.   To die is all as common as to live;
        The one in choice, the other holds in chase:
        For from the instant we begin to live
        We do pursue and hunt the time to die:
        First bud we, then we blow, and after seed;
        Then, presently, we fall; and, as a shade
        Follows the body, so we follow death.
        If then we hunt for death, why do we fear it?
        If we fear it, why do we follow it?
        If we do fear, how can we shun it?
        If we do fear, with fear we do but aid
        The thing we fear to seize on us the sooner:
        If we fear not, then no resolved proffer
        Can overthrow the limit of our fate:
        For, whether ripe or rotten, drop we shall,
        As we do draw the lottery of our doom.

    PR. ED.   Ah, good old man, a thousand thousand armours
        These words of thine have buckled on my back.
        Ah, what an idiot hast thou made of life,
        To seek the thing if fears! and how disgrac'd
        The imperial victory of murd'ring death!
        Since all the lives, his conquering arrows strike,
        Seek him, and he not them, to shame his glory.
        I will not give a penny for a life,
        Nor half a halfpenny to shun grim death,
        Since for to live is but to seek to die,
        And dying but beginning of new life.
        Let come the hour when he that rules it will!
        To live, or die, I hold indifferent.

                                         Exeunt

SCENE V

The Same. The French Camp.
Enter King John and Charles.

K. JOHN.   A sudden darkness hath defac'd the sky,
The winds are crept into their caves for fear,
The leaves move not, the world is hush'd and still,
The birds cease singing, and the wand'ring brooks
Murmur no wonted greeting to their shores;
Silence attends some wonder and expecteth
That heaven should pronounce some prophecy:
Where or from whom proceeds this silence, Charles?

CHAR.   Our men with open mouths and staring eyes
Look on each other, as they did attend
Each other's words, and yet no creature speaks;
A tongue-tied fear hath made a midnight hour
And speeches sleep through all the waking regions.

K. JOHN.   But now the pompous sun, in all his pride,
Look'd through his golden coach upon the world,
And on a sudden, hath he hid himself;
That now the under earth is as a grave,
Dark, deadly, silent, and uncomfortable.

A clamour of ravens

Hark! what a deadly outcry do I hear!

CHAR.   Here comes my brother Philip.

K. JOHN.   All dismayed: —

Enter Philip

What fearful words are those thy looks presage?

PHIL.   A flight, a flight!

K. JOHN.   Coward, what flight? thou liest, there needs no flight.

PHIL.   A flight!

K. JOHN.   Awake thy craven powers, and tell on
The substance of that very fear indeed,
Which is so ghastly printed on thy face:
What is the matter?

PHIL.   A flight of ugly ravens
Do croak and hover o'er our soldiers' heads,
And keep in triangles and corner'd squares
Right as our forces are embattled;
With their approach there came this sudden fog
Which now hath hid the airy floor of heaven
And made at noon a night unnatural

(IV, v)   Upon the quaking and dismayed world:
In brief, our soldiers have let fall their arms
And stand like metamorphos'd images,
Bloodless and pale, one gazing on another.

K. JOHN.   Ay, now I call to mind the prophecy;
But I must give no entrance to a fear. –
Return, and hearten up these yielding souls;
Tell them, the ravens seeing them in arms –
So many fair against a famished few –
Come but to dine upon their handiwork
And prey upon the carrion that they kill:
For when we see a horse laid down to die,
Although not dead, the ravenous birds
Sit watching the departure of his life;
Even so these ravens, for the carcases
Of those poor English that are mark'd to die,
Hover about, and, if they cry to us,
'Tis but for meat that we must kill for them.
Away, and comfort up my soldiers,
And sound the trumpets; and at once despatch
This little business of a silly fraud.

Exit Philip

Another noise. Salisbury brought in by a French Captain

CAP.   Behold, my liege, this knight, and forty more, –
Of whom the better part are slain and fled, –
With all endeavour sought to break our ranks,
And make their way to the encompass'd prince;
Dispose of him as please your majesty.

K. JOHN.   Go, and the next bough, soldier, that thou seest,
Disgrace it with his body presently:
For I do hold a tree in France too good
To be the gallows of an English thief.

SAL.   My Lord of Normandy, I have your pass
And warrant for my safety through this land.

CHAR.   Villiers procur'd it for thee, did he not?

SAL.   He did.

CHAR.   And it is current, thou shalt freely pass.

K. JOHN.   Ay, freely to the gallows to be hang'd,
Without denial or impediment: –
Away with him.

CHAR.   I hope, your highness will not so disgrace me
And dash the virtue of my seal-at-arms:
He hath my never-broken name to show,

(IV, v)   Character'd with this princely hand of mind;
And rather let me leave to be a prince
Than break the stable verdict of a prince:
I do beseech you, let him pass in quiet.

K. JOHN.   Thou and thy word lie both in my command;
What canst thou promise, that I cannot break?
Which of these twain is greater infamy,
To disobey thy father, or thyself?
Thy word, nor no man's, may exceed his power;
Nor that same man doth never break his word
That keeps it to the utmost of his power:
The breach of faith dwells in the soul's consent:
Which if thyself without consent do break,
Thou art not charged with the breach of faith. —
Go, hang him; for thy licence lies in me:
And my constraint stands the excuse for thee.

CHAR.   What, am I not a soldier in my word?
Then, arms adieu, and let them fight that list:
Shall I not give my girdle from my waist
But with a guardian I shall be controll'd,
To say, I may not give my things away?
Upon my soul, had Edward Prince of Wales
Engag'd his word, writ down his noble hand,
For all your knights to pass his father's land,
The royal king, to grace his warlike son,
Would not alone safe-conduct give to them,
But with all bounty feasted them and theirs.

K. JOHN.   Dwell'st thou on precedents? Then be it so. —
Say, Englishman, of what degree thou art.

SAL.   An earl in England though a prisoner here;
And those that know me call me Salisbury.

K. JOHN.   Then, Salisbury, say whither thou art bound.

SAL.   To Calice, where my liege, King Edward, is.

K. JOHN.   To Calice, Salisbury? then to Calice pack;
And bid the king prepare a noble grave
To put his princely son, black Edward, in.
And as thou travell'st westward from this place,
Some two leagues hence there is a lofty hill,
Whose top seems topless, for the embracing sky
Doth hide his high head in her azure bosom;
Upon whose tall top when thy foot attains,
Look back upon the humble vale beneath,
(Humble of late, but now made proud with arms)
And thence behold the wretched Prince of Wales,

437

(IV, v)   Hoop'd with a band of iron round about.
           After which sight to Calice spur amain,
           And say, the prince was smother'd and not slain:
           And tell the king, this is not all his ill,
           For I will greet him ere he thinks I will.
           Away, begone; the smoke but of our shot
           Will choke our foes, though bullets hit them not.

                                                    [*Exeunt*]

                              SCENE VI

                The Same. A Part of the Field of Battle.
                Alarum. Enter Prince Edward and Artois.

ART.   How fares your grace? are you not shot, my lord?
PR. ED.   No, dear Artois; but chok'd with dust and smoke
        And stepp'd aside for breath and fresher air.
ART.   Breathe then, and to't again: the amazed French
        Are quite distract with gazing on the crows;
        And, were our quivers full of shafts again,
        Your grace should see a glorious day of this: —
        O, for more arrows! Lord! that's our want.
PR. ED.   Courage, Artois! a fig for feathered shafts
        When feathered fowls do bandy on our side!
        What need we fight and sweat and keep a coil
        When railing crows out-scold our adversaries?
        Up, up, Artois! the ground itself is arm'd
        [With] fire-containing flint; command our bows
        To hurl away their pretty-colour'd yew,
        And to't with stones: away, Artois, away;
        My soul doth prophesy we win the day.

                                                    Exeunt

                    Alarum. Enter King John

K. JOHN.   Our multitudes are in themselves confounded,
        Dismayed and distraught; swift-starting fear
        Hath buzz'd a cold dismay through all our army,
        And every petty disadvantage prompts
        The fear-possessed abject soul to fly:
        Myself, whose spirit is steel to their dull lead
        (What with recalling of the prophecy
        And that our native stones from English arms
        Rebel against us) find myself attainted
        With strong surprise of weak and yielding fear.

(IV, vi)

Enter Charles

CHAR.   Fly, father, fly! the French do kill the French;
Some that would stand let drive at some that fly:
Our drums strike nothing but discouragement,
Our trumpets sound dishonour and retire;
The spirit of fear, that feareth nought but death,
Cowardly works confusion on itself.

Enter Philip

PHIL.   Pluck out your eyes and see not this day's shame!
An arm hath beat an army; one poor David
Hath with a stone foil'd twenty stout Goliaths:
Some twenty naked starvelings with small flints
Have driven back a puissant host of men,
Array'd and fenc'd in all accomplements.

K. JOHN.   Mordieu, they quoit at us and kill us up;
No less than forty thousand wicked elders
Have forty lean slaves this day ston'd to death.

CHAR.   O, that I were some other countryman!
This day hath set derision on the French,
And all the world will blurt and scorn at us.

K. JOHN.   What, is there no hope left?

PHIL.   No hope, but death, to bury up our shame.

K. JOHN.   Make up once more with me; the twentieth part
Of those that live are men enough to quail
The feeble handful on the adverse part.

CHAR.   Then charge again: if Heaven be not oppos'd,
We cannot lose the day.

K. JOHN.   On, away.

[*Exeunt*]

Enter Audley, wounded, and rescued by two squires

FIRST ESQ.   How fares my lord?

AUD.   Even as a man may do,
That dines at such a bloody feast as this.

SECOND ESQ.   I hope, my lord, that is no mortal scar.

AUD.   No matter, if it be; the count is cast,
And, in the worst, ends but a mortal man.
Good friends, convey me to the princely Edward,
That, in the crimson bravery of my blood,
I may become him with saluting him;
I'll smile and tell him that this open scar
Doth end the harvest of his Audley's war.

Exeunt

SCENE VII

The Same. The English Camp.
Enter Prince Edward, King John, Charles,
and all, with ensigns spread.

PR. ED.   Now, John in France, and lately John of France,
Thy bloody ensigns are my captive colours;
And you, high-vaunting Charles of Normandy,
That once to-day sent me a horse to fly,
Are now the subjects of my clemency.
Fie, lords! is't not a shame that English boys,
Whose early days are yet not worth a beard,
Should in the bosom of your kingdom thus,
One against twenty, beat you up together?

K. JOHN.   Thy fortune, not thy force, hath conquer'd us.

PR. ED.   An argument that Heaven aids the right. –

[Enter Artois, with Philip]

See, see, Artois doth bring with him along
The late good-counsel-giver to my soul! –
Welcome, Artois, and welcome, Philip, too:
Who now, of you or I, have need to pray!
Now is the proverb verified in you,
Too bright a morning breeds a louring day, –

Sound trumpets. Enter Audley

But, say, what grim discouragement comes here!
Alas, what thousand armed men of France
Have writ that note of death in Audley's face? –
Speak, thou that woo'st death with thy careless smile
And look'st so merrily upon thy grave
As if thou wert enamour'd on thine end,
What hungry sword hath so bereav'd thy face
And lopp'd a true friend from my loving soul?

AUD.   O prince, thy sweet bemoaning speech to me
Is as a mournful knell to one dead-sick.

PR. ED.   Dear Audley, if my tongue ring out thy end.
My arms shall be thy grave: what may I do,
To win thy life, or to revenge thy death?
If thou wilt drink the blood of captive kings
Or that it were restorative, command
A health of king's blood, and I'll drink to thee:
If honour may dispense for thee with death,
The never-dying honour of this day

(IV, vii)   Share wholly, Audley, to thyself, and live.

AUD.   Victorious prince, – that thou art so, behold
A Cæsar's fame in king's captivity, –
If I could hold dim death but at a bay,
Till I did see my liege thy royal father,
My soul should yield this castle of my flesh,
This mangled tribute, with all willingness
To darkness, consummation, dust and worms.

PR. ED.   Cheerly, bold man! thy soul is all too proud
To yield her city for one little breach
Should be divorced from her earthly spouse
By the soft temper of a Frenchman's sword.
Lo, to repair thy life, I give to thee
Three thousand marks a year in English land.

AUD.   I take thy gift, to pay the debts I owe.
These two poor squires redeem'd me from the French,
With lusty and dear hazard of their lives;
What thou hast given me, I give to them;
And, as thou lov'st me, prince, lay thy consent
To this bequeath in my last testament.

PR. ED.   Renowned Audley, live, and have from me
This gift twice doubled, to these squires and thee:
But, live or die, what thou hast given away,
To these and theirs shall lasting freedom stay. –
Come, gentlemen, I'll see my friend bestow'd
Within an easy litter; then we'll march
Proudly toward Calice with triumphant pace
Unto my royal father, and there bring
The tribute of my wars, fair France's king.

Exeunt

ACT V

SCENE I

Picardy. The English Camp before Calais.
Enter King Edward, Queen Philippa, Derby, soldiers.

K. ED.   No more, Queen Philippe, pacify yourself;
Copland, except he can excuse his fault,
Shall find displeasure written in our looks. –
And now unto this proud resisting town:
Soldiers, assault; I will no longer stay,
To be deluded by their false delays;
Put all to sword, and make the spoil your own.

Enter six citizens in their shirts, bare foot, with halters
about their necks.

CIT.   Mercy, King Edward! mercy, gracious lord!

K. ED.   Contemptuous villains! call ye now for truce?
Mine ears are stopp'd against your bootless cries: —
Sound, drums' alarum; draw, threat'ning swords!

1 CIT.   Ah, noble prince, take pity on this town,
And hear us, mighty king!
We claim the promise that your highness made;
The two days' respite is not yet expir'd,
And we are come with willingness to bear
What torturing death or punishment you please,
So that the trembling multitude be sav'd.

K. ED.   My promise? well, I do confess as much:
But I require the chiefest citizens,
And men of most account, that should submit.
You peradventure are but servile grooms
Or some felonious robber on the sea,
Whom, apprehended, law would execute,
Albeit severity lay dead in us:
No, no, ye cannot overreach us thus.

2 CIT.   The sun, dread lord, that in the western fall
Beholds us now low brought through misery,
Did in the orient purple of the morn
Salute our coming forth, when we were known;
Or may our portion be with damned fiends.

K. ED.   If it be so, then let our covenant stand,
We take possession of the town in peace:
But, for yourselves, look you for no remorse;
But, as imperial justice hath decreed,
Your bodies shall be dragg'd about these walls
And after feel the stroke of quartering steel:
This is your doom; — go, soldiers, see it done.

QUEEN.   Ah, be more mild unto these yielding men!
It is a glorious thing, to stablish peace;
And kings approach the nearest unto God,
By giving life and safety unto men.
As thou intendest to be King of France,
So let her people live to call thee king;
For what the sword cuts down or fire hath spoil'd
Is held in reputation none of ours.

K. ED.   Although experience teach us this is true,
That peaceful quietness brings most delight
When most of all abuses are controll'd,

(V, i)   Yet, insomuch it shall be known that we
               As well can master our affections
               As conquer other by the dint of sword,
               Philip, prevail; we yield to thy request;
               These men shall live to boast of clemency, –
               And, tyranny, strike terror to thyself.

CIT.   Long live your highness! happy be your reign!

K. ED.   Go, get you hence, return unto the town;
               And if this kindness hath deserv'd your love,
               Learn then to reverence Edward as your king. –

Exeunt

               Now, might we hear of our affairs abroad,
               We would, till gloomy winter were o'er-spent,
               Dispose our men in garrison a while.
               But who comes here?

Enter Copland and King David

DER.   Copland, my lord, and David King of Scots.

K. ED.   Is this the proud presumptious squire o' the north
               That would not yield his prisoner to my queen?

COP.   I am, my liege, a northern squire, indeed,
               But neither proud not insolent, I trust.

K. ED.   What moved thee then to be so obstinate
               To contradict our royal queen's desire?

COP.   No wilful disobedience, mighty lord,
               But my desert and public law of arms:
               I took the king myself in single fight;
               And, like a soldier, would be loath to lose
               The least pre-eminence that I had won:
               And Copland straight upon your highness' charge
               Is come to France and with a lowly mind
               Doth vail the bonnet of his victory.
               Receive, dread lord, the custom of my fraught,
               The wealthy tribute of my labouring hands;
               Which should long since have been surrender'd up,
               Had but your gracious self been there in place.

QUEEN.   But, Copland, thou didst scorn the king's command,
               Neglecting our commission in his name.

COP.   His name I reverence, but his person more;
               His name shall keep me in allegiance still,
               But to his person I will bend my knee.

K. ED.   I pray thee, Philip, let displeasure pass;
               This man doth please me and I like his words:
               For what is he that will attempt great deeds

(V, i)   And lose the glory that ensues the same?
            All rivers have recourse unto the sea;
            And Copland's faith, relation to his king. –
            Kneel therefore down; now rise, King Edward's knight:
            And, to maintain thy state, I freely give
            Five hundred marks a year to thee and thine. –

                    Enter Salisbury
            Welcome, Lord Salisbury: what news from Britain?
SAL.   This, mighty king: the country we have won;
            And John de Mountford, regent of that place,
            Presents your highness with this coronet,
            Protesting true allegiance to your grace.
K. ED.   We thank thee for thy service, valiant earl;
            Challenge our favour, for we owe it thee.
SAL.   But now, my lord, as this is joyful news,
            So must my voice be tragical again
            And I must sing of doleful accidents.
K. ED.   What, have our men the overthrow at Poitiers?
            Or is our son beset with too much odds?
SAL.   He was, my lord: and as my worthless self,
            With forty other serviceable knights,
            Under safe-conduct of the Dauphin's seal
            Did travel that way, finding him distress'd,
            A troop of lances met us on the way,
            Surpris'd, and brought us prisoners to the king;
            Who, proud of this and eager of revenge,
            Commanded straight to cut off all our heads:
            And surely we had died, but that the duke,
            More full of honour than his angry sire,
            Procur'd our quick deliverance from thence;
            But, ere we went, 'Salute your king,' quoth he,
            Bid him provide a funeral for his son,
            To-day our sword shall cut his thread of life;
            And, sooner than he thinks, we'll be with him,
            To quittance those displeasures he hath done':
            This said, we pased, not daring to reply;
            Our hearts were dead, our looks diffus'd and wan.
            Wand'ring, at last we climb'd unto a hill;
            From whence, although our grief were much before,
            Yet now to see the occasion with our eyes
            Did thrice so much increase our heaviness:
            For there, my lord, O, there we did descry
            Down in a valley how both armies lay.

                        444

(V, i)   The French had cast their trenches like a ring;
      And every barricado's open front
      Was thick emboss'd with brazen ordinance.
      Here stood a battle of ten thousand horse;
      There twice as many pikes, in quadrant-wise:
      Here cross-bows and deadly-wounding darts:
      And in the midst, like to a slender point
      Within the compass of the horizon, –
      As't were a rising bubble in the sea,
      A hazel-wand amidst a wood of pines,
      Or as a bear fast chain'd unto a stake, –
      Stood famous Edward, still expecting when
      Those dogs of France would fasten on his flesh.
      Anon, the death-procuring knell begins:
      Off go the cannons, that, with trembling noise,
      Did shake the very mountain where they stood;
      Then sound the trumpets' clangour in the air,
      The battles join: and, when we could no more
      Discern the difference 'twixt the friend and foe,
      (So intricate the dark confusion was)
      Away we turn'd our wat'ry eyes, with sighs
      As black as powder fuming into smoke.
      And thus, I fear, unhappy have I told
      The most untimely tale of Edward's fall.

QUEEN.   Ah me! is this my welcome into France?
      Is this the comfort that I look'd to have
      When I should meet with my beloved son?
      Sweet Ned, I would thy mother in the sea
      Had been prevented of this mortal grief!

K. ED.   Content thee, Philippe: 'tis not tears will serve
      To call him back if he be taken hence:
      Comfort thyself, as I do, gentle queen,
      With hope of sharp, unheard-of, dire revenge. –
      He bids me to provide his funeral;
      And so I will: but all the peers in France
      Shall mourners be and weep out bloody tears
      Until their empty veins be dry and sere:
      The pillars of his hearse shall be their bones;
      The mould that covers him, their cities' ashes;
      His knell, the groaning cries of dying men;
      And, in the stead of tapers on his tomb,
      An hundred fifty towers shall burning blaze,
      While we bewail our valiant son's decease.

(V, i)   *After a flourish, sounded within, enter a Herald*

HER.   Rejoice, my lord; ascend the imperial throne!
The mighty and redoubted Prince of Wales,
Great servitor to bloody Mars in arms,
The Frenchman's terror and his country's fame,
Triumphant rideth like a Roman peer:
And, lowly at his stirrup, comes afoot
King John of France together with his son
In captive bonds; whose diadem he brings
To crown thee with and to proclaim thee king.

K. ED.   Away with mourning, Philip, wipe thine eyes; —
Sound, trumpets, welcome in Plantagenet!

Enter Prince Edward, King John, Philip, Audley, Artois

As things, long lost, when they are found again,
So doth my son rejoice his father's heart,
For whom, even now, my soul was much perplex'd!

QUEEN.   Be this a token to express my joy,

Kiss

For inward passions will not let me speak.

PR. ED.   My gracious father, here receive the gift,

[*Presenting him with King John's crown*]

This wreath of conquest and reward of war,
Got with as mickle peril of our lives
As e'er was thing of price before this day;
Install your highness in your proper right:
And, herewithal, I render to your hands
These prisoners, chief occasion of our strife.

K. ED.   So, John of France, I see you keep your word.
You promis'd to be sooner with ourself
Than we did think for, and 'tis so indeed:
But, had you done at first as now you do,
How many civil towns had stood untouch'd
That now are turn'd to ragged heaps of stones?
How many people's lives might'st thou have sav'd
That are untimely sunk into their graves?

K. JOHN.   Edward, recount not things irrevocable;
Tell me what ransom thou requir'st to have.

K. ED.   Thy ransom, John, hereafter shall be known.
But first to England thou must cross the seas
To see what entertainment it affords;
Howe'er it falls, it cannot be so bad
As ours hath been since we arriv'd in France.

K. JOHN.   Accursed man! of this I was foretold,

(V, i)   But did misconster what the prophet told.

PR. ED.   Now, father, this petition Edward makes, –
To thee, [*kneels*] whose grace hath been his strongest shield,
That, as thy pleasure chose me for the man
To be the instrument to show thy power,
So thou wilt grant, that many princes more,
Bred and brought up within that little isle,
May still be famous for like victories! –
And, for my part, the bloody scars I bear,
The weary nights that I have watch'd in field,
The dangerous conflicts I have often had,
The fearful menaces were proffer'd me,
The heat and cold and what else might displease,
I wish were now redoubled twenty-fold;
So that hereafter ages, when they read
The painful traffic of my tender youth,
Might thereby be inflamed with such resolve
As not the territories of France alone,
But likewise Spain, Turkey, and what countries else
That justly would provoke fair England's ire,
Might, at their presence, tremble and retire!

K. ED.   Here, English lords, we do proclaim a rest,
An intercession of our painful arms:
Sheathe up your swords, refresh your weary limbs,
Peruse your spoils; and, after we have breath'd
A day or two within this haven-town,
God willing, then for England we'll be shipp'd;
Where, in a happy hour, I trust, we shall
Arrive, three kings, two princes, and a queen.

[*Exeunt*]

Index

Works by Shakespeare appear directly under title; works by others under author's name